I0126884

Sung Tales from the Papua New Guinea Highlands

Studies in Form, Meaning, and Sociocultural Context

Edited by Alan Rumsey & Don Niles

Sung Tales from the
Papua New Guinea Highlands

Studies in Form, Meaning, and Sociocultural Context

Edited by Alan Rumsey & Don Niles

ANU

THE AUSTRALIAN NATIONAL UNIVERSITY

E PRESS

ANU
E PRESS

Published by ANU E Press
The Australian National University
Canberra ACT 0200, Australia
Email: anuepress@anu.edu.au
This title is also available online at: http://epress.anu.edu.au

National Library of Australiam Cataloguing-in-Publication entry

Title: Sung tales from the Papua New Guinea highlands : studies
                                in form, meaning, and sociocultural
                                context / edited by Alan Rumsey & Don
                                Niles.

ISBN: 9781921862205 (pbk.) 9781921862212 (ebook)

Notes: Includes index.

Subjects: Epic poetry.
                                Ethnomusicology--Papua New Guinea.
                                Folk music--Papua New Guinea.
                                Papua New Guinea--Songs and music.

Other Authors/Contributors: Rumsey, Alan.
                                Niles, Don.

Dewey Number: 781.629912

All rights reserved. No part of this publication may be reproduced, stored in a retrieval system
or transmitted in any form or by any means, electronic, mechanical, photocopying or otherwise,
without the prior permission of the publisher.

Cover design and layout by ANU E Press

Cover image: Peter Kerua (centre) performs a *tom yaya kange* sung tale for Thomas Noma (left)
and John Onga (right) at Kailge, Western Highlands Province, Papua New Guinea, March 1997.
From a Hi8 video recorded by Alan Rumsey. A segment of the video is included among the
online items accompanying this volume. The *tom yaya kange* genre and a particularly beautiful
passage of it from a performance by Kerua are discussed by Rumsey in chapter 11; aspects of
Kerua's performance style are discussed by Don Niles in chapter 12.

Printed by Griffin Press

This edition © 2011 ANU E Press

Contents

Dedication

This volume is dedicated to the memory of
master bard Paul Pepa (c. 1959–2005) and
master exegete Richard Alo (1967–2007),
both of whom made enormous contributions to the project
before passing away at the height of their powers.

Contributors

Terrance Borchard went to Papua New Guinea after he received a Master of Divinity degree from Concordia Seminary in St. Louis, Missouri, in 1969. He became a fluent speaker of the Ipili language while working among the Ipili people in Paiela until 1974. Since that time, working with Ipili men to translate the Bible into their language has continued to provide opportunities to gain a deeper understanding of the unique features of their language. Terrance has a master of linguistics degree from the University of Texas in Arlington. The title of the dissertation he wrote for his PhD degree from Fuller Theological Seminary in Pasadena, California, is "Discourse Level Functional Equivalence Translation." [email: t.borchard@sil.org.pg]

Philip Gibbs, from New Zealand, first came to Papua New Guinea as a Divine Word missionary in 1973. He started out among the Ipili speakers of Porgera and Paiela, and presented a thesis on Ipili religion for a post-graduate diploma in anthropology at Sydney University. He studied linguistics with the Summer Institute of Linguistics in North Dakota and Oklahoma. Later he served as a parish priest in Central Enga and published on various aspects of life in the Enga Province. Philip has a doctorate in theology from the Gregorian University, Rome. In recent times he has been a researcher with the Melanesian Institute, Goroka, and research advisor on sexual health programmes in Papua New Guinea for Caritas Australia. Presently he is establishing an Institute for Social Concern based in Mount Hagen. [email: gibbs199@gmail.com]

Kirsty Gillespie received her PhD from the Australian National University in 2008 for her research into the music and culture of the Duna people of the Southern Highlands Province of Papua New Guinea. She is the author of *Steep Slopes: Music and Change in the Highlands of Papua New Guinea* (2010), and several book chapters and articles. In 2009 she released the compact disc *Ae Tinil Wen Lir / Music of Lihir* which featured songs from Lihir, New Ireland, Papua New Guinea. Kirsty is currently a research fellow at the University of Queensland, working with the people of Lihir on a cultural heritage programme for the islands. [email: kirsty.gillespie@anu.edu.au]

Frances Ingemann (PhD, Indiana University) is a retired professor of linguistics at the University of Kansas. She first came to the Ipili area during a year-long sabbatical in 1964. At that time she was sponsored by the Lutheran Church Missouri Synod, which had just begun mission work there and wanted information about the language. During that time, she was primarily located at the mission station in Yuyane in the Porgera valley, but made several trips to the Paiyala area to collect data on dialect differences. It was during these trips that performers of chanted folktales first came to where she was recording language samples. She returned for numerous shorter visits over a period of more than forty years. [email: fing@ku.edu]

Kenny Yuwi Kendoli is a Duna man, originally from the Aluni area, Southern Highlands Province, Papua New Guinea. He lived for many years at Rewapi in the Kopiago region, where he hosted and worked with visiting researchers in the disciplines of anthropology, ethnomusicology, and linguistics. Kenny attended the 2004 and 2006 Chanted Tales Workshops, and visited the Australian National University several times during the period 2003–7, where he contributed to classes, seminars, and workshops at the Research School of Pacific and Asian Studies. He has a particular interest in the sung story form of *pikono*, and has collaborated extensively on the translation and interpretation of *pikono* works with students and scholars.

Gabe C. J. Lomas began work in Héla Húli in 1968, after several years in ministry in the United Kingdom. He served in Burani, Goloba, Gubari (near Tari), and Gumu (Komo) for a period of over fourteen years, being parish priest in the last three places. He was part of a strong drive to incorporate Húli customs—especially various language genres—into Catholic liturgies, and has published many materials in Húli, a number of them in conjunction with Húli men and women. Gabe holds an MA in theology, an MA in linguistics from the University of Sydney, and a PhD in linguistics from Macquarie University. He has lectured in linguistics and worked in the Australian Adult Migrant Education Program. He is now retired and lives in Sydney. [email: gcjlomas@GabeLomas.org]

Don Niles is senior ethnomusicologist and acting director of the Institute of Papua New Guinea Studies, where he has worked since 1979. His Highlands research has focused on Hagen music and dance traditions, and he has been particularly interested in how sung tales relate to them. The author/editor of numerous books, articles, and audiovisual publications on various aspects of Papua New Guinea music and dance, Don also edits the Institute's music monograph series (*Apwitihire*) and journal (*Kulele*). He is an Executive Board member of the International Council for Traditional Music and the editor of their journal, *Yearbook for Traditional Music*. [email: dniles.ipngs@gmail.com]

Jacqueline Pugh-Kitingan researched Huli music for both her BA Honours degree (Monash, 1976) and PhD (Queensland, 1982). After years studying indigenous cultures in Sabah, she is currently an associate professor, holding the Kadazandusun Chair at Universiti Malaysia Sabah. Her many publications include the record album *The Huli of Papua Niugini* (Bärenreiter-Musicaphon, 1986) and the book *Selected Papers on Music in Sabah* (Universiti Malaysia Sabah, 2004). She is Borneo Research Council Regional Vice President for Sabah, a member of the International Council for Traditional Music's Study Group on

Performing Arts of Southeast Asia, and adjunct research fellow in anthropology in the School of Political and Social Inquiry, Monash University (2009–10). [email: jacquie@ums.edu.my, jacquiemusic@yahoo.com.au]

Hans Reithofer, from Austria, is currently working as lecturer and study programme coordinator at the Institute for Social and Cultural Anthropology at the University of Göttingen, Germany. He first came to Papua New Guinea in 1989, working with the Society of the Divine Word among the Ipili for several years. After graduate studies in anthropology at the University of Basel, Switzerland, he returned for two years of fieldwork among the Karinj in the Southern Highlands, whose creative engagement with Christianity is the subject of his PhD thesis, revised for publication as *The Python Spirit and the Cross*. Narrative traditions featured prominently in this engagement and set Hans on the track of the Sung Tales Project. [email: hreitho@gwdg.de]

Alan Rumsey is professor and head of the Department of Anthropology, College of Asia and the Pacific, Australian National University, and a fellow of the Australian Academy of Humanities. His research fields are Highland New Guinea and Aboriginal Australia, with particular focus on language and its relation to other aspects of culture and social life. For details see http://asiapacific.anu.edu.au/people/personal/rumsa_ant.php. Alan's recent publications include "Ethics, Language and Human Sociality," in *Ordinary Ethics: Anthropology, Language, and Action*, edited by Michael Lambek (2010); and "Lingual and Cultural Wholes and Fields," in *Experiments in Holism: Theory and Practice in Anthropology*, edited by Ton Otto and Nils Bubant (2010). [email: alan.rumsey@anu.edu.au]

Lila San Roque is a linguist. She received her doctorate from the Australian National University for a description of the grammar of simple sentences in Duna. Her research interests include Papuan languages, descriptive linguistics, evidentiality, and the linguistic expression of perception and knowledge assessments. Lila's previous publications include *I'saka: A Sketch Grammar of a Language of North-Central New Guinea*, co-authored with Mark Donohue (2004). She co-administers the Papua New Guinea Vernacular Education Network (VEN) mailing list, which aims to share information between people working with, researching, or developing the use of local languages in the formal and non-formal education sectors in Papua New Guinea. Those interested are invited to join at http://mailman.anu.edu.au/mailman/listinfo/ven.

Michael Sollis is a composer, artistic director, and researcher based in Canberra, Australia. In 2007 he received the University Medal for ethnomusicological research concerning Duna *pikono* sung stories in Southern Highlands Province, Papua New Guinea, after studying composition and anthropology at the Australian National University. Michael is a regularly performed composer, artistic director of the Griffyn Ensemble, and teaches composition at the Australian National

University School of Music. He is currently chair of the Australian Youth Music Council. His publications include "Tune-tone Relationships in Sung Duna *Pikono*" in *Australian Journal of Linguistics*. [email: sollis@tpg.com.au]

Andrew Strathern and **Pamela J. Stewart (Strathern)** are a husband-and-wife research team, based at the University of Pittsburgh. They have published over forty books and hundreds of scholarly articles on their research (see http://www.pitt.edu/~strather). Their publications on *pikono*, *kang rom*, and other Papuan New Guinean expressive genres include their joint books *Expressive Genres and Historical Change* (2005); *Gender, Song, and Sensibility: Folktales and Folksongs in the Highlands of New Guinea* (2002); and *Remaking the World: Myth, Mining and Ritual Change among the Duna of Papua New Guinea* (2002). Their research interests include religious and ritual practices (see their 2009 book *Religious and Ritual Change: Cosmologies and Histories*). Their recent published book chapters include: Strathern and Stewart, "The Appearing and Disappearing World of the Bogaiya: A Corner of Papua New Guinea Cultural History," in *A Mosaic of Languages and Cultures*, edited by Kenneth McElhanon and Ger Reesink (2010, available online); Strathern and Stewart, "Shifting Centres, Tense Peripheries: Indigenous Cosmopolitanism," in *United in Discontent*, edited by Dimitrios Theodossopoulos and Elisabeth Kirtsoglou (2010); and Strathern and Stewart, "Placing and Dis-placing the Dead," in *Religion and Retributive Logic*, edited by Carole M. Cusack and Christopher Hartney (2010). The Stewart and Strathern (University of Pittsburgh web-based, Language, History, and Culture) Archive is being launched in 2011. [joint email: pamjan@pitt.edu]

Acknowledgements

As editors of this volume, we wish to thank the following organizations for their assistance with various aspects of the work that has led to it: the Australian Research Council for funding the "Chanted Tales from Highland New Guinea" project during 2003–6; CulturaSenzaFrontiere for sponsorship of the 2004 Chanted Tales Workshop and the University of Goroka for providing an excellent venue for it; the staff of the Kefamo Conference Centre in Goroka for the outstanding service they provided for the 2006 Chanted Tales Workshop; and the Asia-Pacific Futures Network for providing funding for three honours students from Australia and New Zealand to attend that workshop as research trainees.

We appreciate the support of the National Broadcasting Corporation of Papua New Guinea for allowing excerpts from one of their recordings to be made available for this publication.

Thanks also to the many people who participated in one or both of the Goroka workshops and/or in other aspects of the project, but are not among the contributors to this volume, including Richard Alo, Alois Along, Aletta Biersack, Darren Boyd, Fred Errington, Karl Franklin, Deborah Gewertz, Laurence Goldman, Josep Haip, Nicole Haley, Ben Hall, Howard Halu, Chris Haskett, Paul Heineman, Kurita Hiroyuki, Teya Hiyawi, Jerry Jacka, Lisette Josephides, Linda Harvey Kelley, Jessica Kemp, Philip Kereme, Peter Kerua, Joseph Ketan, Regina Knapp, Paulus Konts, Ru Kundil, John LeRoy, Anna Lockwood, Mary MacDonald, Theodore Mawe, Anna Mel, Michael Mel, Gomb Minimbi, Wan Minimbi, Nick Modjeska, Andrew Noma, Thomas Noma, John Onga, Wapi Onga, Paul Palam, Paul Pepa, Anna Pundia, Joe Rex, Snow Ru, Tim Scott, Alice Street, Pita Tapuli, Ruth Tipton, Akii Tumu, Willie Wandaki, Polly Wiessner, and Oliver Wilson.

We would also like to thank Nicolas Peterson and Karen Westmacott of the Humanities and Creative Arts Editorial Board for their support, and Duncan Beard at ANU E Press for his constant advice and guidance through the process of preparing this manuscript for publication.

Finally, we would like to thank all the contributors for their ongoing interest in sung tales, their desire to write and publish about them in this volume, and their patience while waiting for its completion.

Alan Rumsey
Canberra

Don Niles
Port Moresby
April 2011

List of online items

The following downloadable files relating to this work are available from: http://epress.anu.edu.au/

Chapter Two (Kendoli)

1. PDF file of full interview with Kenny Kendoli by Lila San Roque

Chapter Three (Gillespie & San Roque)

2. Audio file of phrase of Duna *pikono* performance by Kiale Yokona, recorded by Kirsty Gillespie, 2005 (text 1)
3. Audio file of phrase of Duna *pikono* performance by Kiale Yokona, describing the full moon's bright light, recorded by Kirsty Gillespie, 2005 (text 2)

Chapter Four (Sollis)

4. Audio file of excerpt of Duna *pikono* performance by Kiale Yokona, recorded by Kirsty Gillespie, 2005 (text 1)
5. Audio file of excerpt of Duna *pikono* performance by Kiale Yokona, showing parallelism of musical elements, recorded by Kirsty Gillespie, 2005 (figure 1)
6. Audio file of excerpt of Duna *pikono* performance by Kiale Yokona, spoken text by Kenny Kendoli and Richard Alo (figure 2)
7. Audio file of excerpt of Duna *pikono* performance by Kiale Yokona, recorded by Kirsty Gillespie, 2005 (figure 2)

Chapter Five (Lomas)

8. Audio file of the Huli *bì té, Àe ndē* 'ah yes' (texts 2 and 3)

Chapter Six (Pugh-Kitingan)

9. Audio file of Huli *bì té* performed by Wandome, recorded by Jacqueline Pugh-Kitingan and Bronwyn Peters, 1975 (figure 7)
10. Audio file of Huli *bì té* performed by Bebalu, recorded by Jacqueline Pugh-Kitingan and Bronwyn Peters, 1975 (figure 11)

Chapter Seven (Gibbs)

11. Audio file of excerpt of Enga *tindi pii* performance, recorded by Philip Gibbs, 2002

Chapter Nine (Ingemann)

12. Audio file of lines 22–32 of Ipili *tindi* performance by Alua, recorded by Frances Ingemann, 1965

13. Audio file of lines 827–28 of Ipili *tindi* performance by Kaneanda, recorded by Frances Ingemann, 1965 (figures 3–4)

14. Audio file of line 24 of Ipili *tindi* performance by Yandapake, recorded by Frances Ingemann, 1964 (figure 5)

15. Audio file of line 68 of Ipili *tindi* performance by Kaneanda, recorded by Frances Ingemann, 1965 (figure 6)

Chapter Ten (Reithofer)

16. Audio file of excerpt of Karinj *enj* performance by Josep Haip, recorded by Don Niles, 2006

Chapter Eleven (Rumsey)

17. Audio file of opening lines from the story of Rosa and Koka in Ku Waru *tom yaya kange* performance by Paulus Konts, recorded by Alan Rumsey, 1997 (text 1)

18. Video file of excerpt of Ku Waru *tom yaya kange* performance by Peter Kerua, recorded by Alan Rumsey, 1997

Chapter Twelve (Niles)

19. Audio file of opening *amb kenan* in Melpa *kang rom* performance by Paul Pepa, recorded by Radio Western Highlands, 1980 (figure 2). Used with the permission of the National Broadcasting Corporation of Papua New Guinea

20. Audio file of opening of Melpa *kang rom* section in performance by Paul Pepa, recorded by Radio Western Highlands, 1980 (figure 3). Used with the permission of the National Broadcasting Corporation of Papua New Guinea

21. Audio file of excerpt of Melpa *kang rom* performance by Paul Pepa at 05:47.1, recorded by Radio Western Highlands, 1980. Used with the permission of the National Broadcasting Corporation of Papua New Guinea

22. Audio file of excerpt of Melpa *kang rom* performance by Paul Pepa at 06:37.5, recorded by Radio Western Highlands, 1980. Used with the permission of the National Broadcasting Corporation of Papua New Guinea

23. Audio file of excerpt of Melpa *kang rom* performance by Paul Pepa at 13:12.3, recorded by Radio Western Highlands, 1980. Used with the permission of the National Broadcasting Corporation of Papua New Guinea

24. Audio file of excerpt of Ku Waru *tom yaya kange* performance by Peter Kerua, recorded by Chris Haskett, 2006 (figure 6)

1. Introducing Highlands Sung Tales

Don Niles and Alan Rumsey

The genres of sung tales that are the subject of this volume are one of the most striking aspects of the cultural scene in the Papua New Guinea Highlands. Composed and performed by specialist bards, they are a highly valued art form. From a comparative viewpoint they are remarkable both for their scale and complexity, and for the range of variation that is found among regional genres and individual styles. Though their existence has previously been noted by researchers working in the Highlands, and some recordings made of them, most of these genres have not been studied in detail until quite recently, mainly because of the challenging range of disciplinary expertise that is required—in sociocultural anthropology, linguistics, ethnomusicology, and ethnohistory. To meet that challenge, with funding from the Australian Research Council an interdisciplinary research project on these genres was initiated at Australian National University in 2003. By 2006, when a week-long workshop on the tales was held in Goroka, Papua New Guinea, the project had grown to include fourteen researchers, from seven different universities and research institutes around the world (figure 1). These scholars come from all the disciplines referred to above, with field research experience in six different language regions within the overall project area.

This volume presents a set of interrelated studies by most of those researchers and by a Papua New Guinea Highlander who has assisted with the research based on his lifelong familiarity with one of the regional genres. As already suggested by the uptake of some of the related publications detailed in the penultimate section below, the studies presented here (all of them previously unpublished and written especially for this volume) are of ground-breaking significance not only for specialists in Melanesia or the Pacific, but also for readers with a more general interest in comparative poetics, mythology, musicology, or verbal art. Before introducing those studies and the genres themselves, we will provide a brief introduction to the overall region where they are found.

Figure 1. Participants at the conclusion of the 2006 Sung Tales Workshop, Kefamo, Eastern Highlands Province (near Goroka), 24 June 2006. *Sitting/kneeling (left to right):* **Paulus Konts, Andrew Noma, Howard Halu, Alois Along, Joe Rex, Alan Rumsey, Richard Alo, Pita Tapuli, and Wapi Onga.** *Standing (left to right):* **Lewa Onga (baby), John Onga, Ru Kundil, Chris Haskett, Lila San Roque, Gomb Minimbi, Kirsty Gillespie, Snow Ru, Gabe C. J. Lomas, Philip Gibbs, Kenny Yuwi Kendoli, Hans Reithofer, Nick Modjeska, Nicole Haley, Josep Haip, Oliver Wilson, Ben Hall, Wan Minimbi, Don Niles, Peter Kerua, and Michael Sollis.**

The region

The area within which we know that sung tales are composed and performed is shown in figure 2.

As can be seen from the inset map in the upper right corner of figure 2, this entire region lies within the interior of Papua New Guinea. Almost all of it is within the Highlands, where the settled areas lie at elevations of between 1,200 and 2,800 metres. The tropical highland climate, with its regular rainfall and year-round growing season, make much of this area well-suited to horticulture, which archaeology shows to have been going on there for at least five thousand years (Denham 2006). In the precolonial era, the central highlands—including most of the area shown as having sung tales in figure 2 and extending eastward for approximately 150 km—was by far the most densely populated part of the island and remains so, apart from the coastal cities of Port Moresby and Lae (where many Highlanders now live also). Not unrelatedly, the central highlands is the part of Papua New Guinea where the languages have by far the largest numbers of speakers. For example, the Huli language has been estimated to have approximately 250,000 speakers (Lewis 2007), the Hagen-Nebilyer-Kaugel dialect continuum over 200,000 (Rumsey 2006a:52), and Enga about 300,000

(Gibbs, this volume)—the most for any language/dialect group in Papua New Guinea. While none of these figures is very large by world standards, all are extraordinarily large in local terms, Papua New Guinea being a country with approximately 850 languages spoken by a total of about five million people.

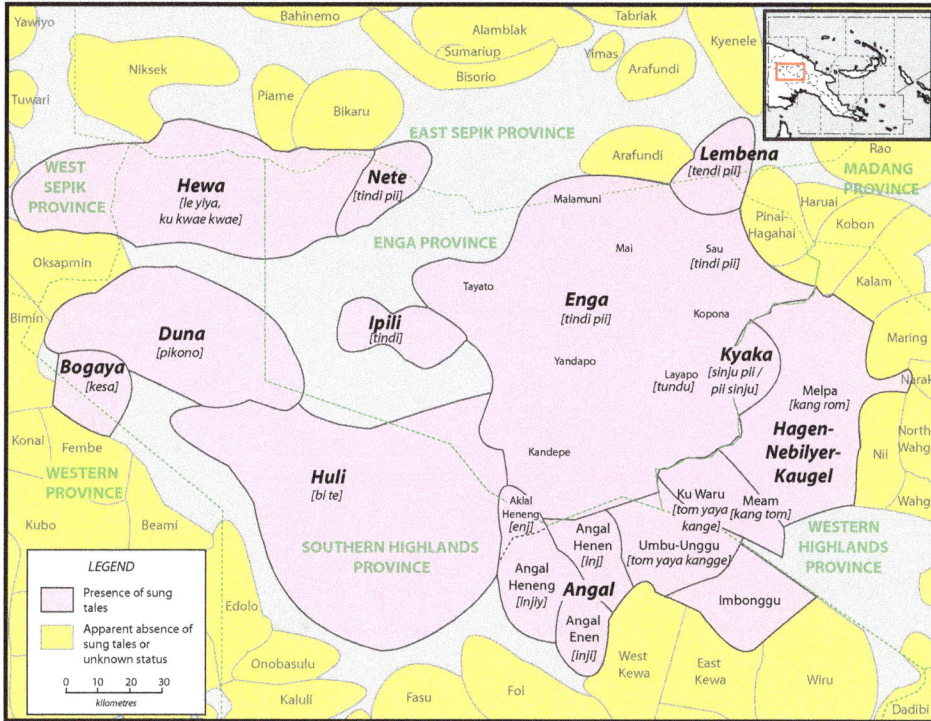

Figure 2. Sung tales in the Papua New Guinea Highlands. Language borders and names are based on maps found at the website of the Summer Institute of Linguistics, Papua New Guinea Language Resources (http://www.pnglanguages. org), with some modifications by Alan Rumsey and Hans Reithofer based on their own research.

While it has long been the most densely settled part of New Guinea, the central highlands was one of the last to come into contact with Europeans, which did not begin to happen until the 1930s. This means that, for much of the time during which many of the contributors to this volume have been doing research in region, there were still many people alive who could remember the period before the first Europeans arrived. This fact, along with the long isolation from the outside world, gives the genres treated here a special importance for comparative poetics, as they allow us to compare these genres with others found elsewhere in the world (for example, Scottish ballads as per Strathern and Stewart 1997, Homeric epics as per Rumsey 2001, or Chinese classical opera as per Rumsey 2007) with a high degree of confidence that any parallels that may be found are the result of independent developments rather than of direct historical influence.

Approximately a million people live within the entire region shown on figure 2; the vast majority of them are rural-dwelling subsistence farmers.[1] Sweet potato remains the staple crop across the region, supplemented by other long-established cultivars, including taro, bananas, sugar cane, and nut pandanus, and more recently introduced ones, such as cabbage, pineapple, avocado, and pawpaw. Across some of the region, especially in the eastern part, coffee is widely grown and is the main source of cash income. In the Ipili region, the Porgera gold mine, which has been in operation since 1989, has had a major effect on the local economy, as described by Borchard and Gibbs in chapter 8.

In the colonial era (which ended in 1975), public schools were established across most of the region, with schooling up to grade 6 being made available at local community schools and the higher grades at regional centres, where the best students could go and study as boarders. Partly because many families cannot afford the school fees that are now charged at all levels, and partly because the pay for teachers is not enough to attract them to the rural community schools, the overall standard of education and knowledge of English within the rural areas is seemingly lower in 2010 than it was in the 1980s. Across the region, local languages are still spoken as the first languages of nearly everyone, although nowadays nearly everyone can also speak Tok Pisin, the English-based creole that has become the country's main lingua franca. Politically, most people's strongest loyalties are to their local "lines" (tribe, clan, subclan, etc.), rather than to party, province, or nation, and the (usually short-lived) ruling alliances within the latter are built up out of the former.

Further ethnographic and historical background regarding particular areas within the overall sung-tales region is provided within the chapters pertaining to each. To conclude here regarding the region in general, we would like to point out that, taken together, the studies in this volume amply bear out a point made by Aletta Biersack in her introduction to a collection of studies concerning other aspects of the culture of a subset of the peoples treated here (Huli, Duna, and Ipili), namely that these peoples

> have always been *cosmopolitan*, initially on a regional scale and today increasingly nationally and globally. A study of these Papuan borderlands exposes what earlier approaches concealed from view: the extensiveness of traditional intercultural exchanges, the importance of indigenous local/global (that is, valley/regional) relations, and the centrality of questions of genesis and transformation to our empirical and theoretical work. (Biersack 1995:6; italics in original)

---

1 According to the 2000 census, only two of the handful of towns in the area had more than five thousand inhabitants: Mount Hagen (the capital of Western Highlands Province), with 33,623, and Mendi (capital of Southern Highlands Province), with 17,119.

In line with this salutary observation, although the people whose sung-tale traditions are considered in this volume long remained relatively isolated from the world outside the Highlands, as the reader will see from the following sections and the rest of the volume, those traditions show a pattern of multiple, cross-cutting similarities and differences that can only have been produced by a long history of social interaction and intercultural exchange within the overall region.

What are sung tales in the Papua New Guinea Highlands?

Notwithstanding the differences among the sung-tale genres found across the region delimited in figure 2, there are certain features that are common to all of them. Some of these are shared with other performance genres (e.g., ordinary storytelling, oratory, song), but others are distinctive to sung tales. Yet others are found only in sung tales, but not in all of the various regional genres of them. Here we will describe the main distinctive features of Highlands sung tales, noting the restrictions on their regional distribution where relevant.

Everywhere Highlands sung tales are vocal compositions performed solo and, to a large extent, composed during the performance. All across the region, the ability to do this is regarded as a specialized skill and is highly valued.[2] The performer is usually male, although female performers are found in at least some areas. No instruments or dance accompanies the performance, but the performer may sometimes gesture or sway. The performer is usually seated, although at least in the case of male performers, they may lie down when performing in some areas, especially among the Enga and Karinj.

The main aim of the performance is usually said to be entertainment, although sometimes with an element of instructional value as well. The audience may be all male, all female, or a mixture, and may be seated or lying down, according to the region concerned. Another variable is the audience's verbal response. This ranges from silence in the Hagen area, to regularly required one syllable interjections, such as in Huli, to more lengthy questions or comments in Duna. Where interjections occur, they do not interrupt the flow of the story, but may be used by the performer to shape expressions or events in a certain way. In many cases, small payment is made to the performer after the performance.

---

2   As exemplified for the Hagen area by the discussion of Paul Pepa and Paulus Konts in chapters 11 and 12 (cf. Rumsey 2006b), and as corroborated for other areas by discussion with sung-tale performers at the 2006 Goroka workshop, this skill seems generally to be developed by imitation rather than by explicit instruction or institutionalized apprenticeship.

In all performances, the language used is somewhat different from normal speech, involving special vocabularies, expressions, word substitutions, and vocables or extended vowels at the end of a line or section. The frequency of vocables and the different registers of esoteric speech vary across regions.

The story is presented as a narrative. It is not secret and is not considered "true," but the characters are placed in a real landscape of known places within the area where it is performed (although sometimes distant places, known only by repute, are also mentioned). The story often involves recognizably good versus bad characters, a journey to a distant land, and a romance. In some traditions, new people and places are inserted into more traditional stories. Sometimes encounters with spirits feature in the plot. Some groups find such stories inspirational before fighting or use stories involving a number of stock characters or featuring battles.

The melodic presentation of sung tales varies considerably throughout the region with respect to the melody itself, its range, and its contour. Usually the text is set syllabically (one pitch per syllable), but exceptions are frequent in some areas. The melodies of some sung tales bear an obvious relation to other genres more readily recognized as song. For most of the areas, however, our knowledge of musical expression is not advanced enough to allow any conclusions to be drawn on this question.

Other variables in presentation concern the presence or absence of a recurrent beat or pulse, or of a repeating metre. Tempo is also highly variable across the region, as is the length of sung phrases, of silences/breaths, and of the entire performance itself. Pugh-Kitingan (1981:332) reports that Huli *bì té* can "last for a few seconds, several minutes or hours." Enga *tindi pii* can be over an hour (Wiessner and Tumu 1998:27), while Duna *pikono* can last many hours. Performances in other areas lie between these extremes.

Finally, although in English we have given a special name to the genre under consideration here, in most areas the same word or expression is commonly used for sung tales and stories presented in normal speech, with only an acknowledgement that the former are considered especially aesthetically appealing. In the Hagen area, sung tales are specially named, but as a subtype of a narrative genre that also includes spoken stories. While in the Aluni area of the Duna-speaking region, the term *pikono* appears to only be used for sung tales (Strathern and Stewart, pers. comm., July 2010), in other parts of the same language area, *pikono* can apply to spoken stories as well (Gillespie and San Roque, this volume, chapter 3).

In the next three sections, more detailed consideration will be given to three particularly important aspects of the performance of sung tales: plots and characters, poetry, and music.

Sung-tale plots and characters

Throughout the Highlands of Papua New Guinea, there is often a fundamental division made between two types of narratives: one which relates events known or witnessed by the teller, the other which tends to contain more fantastic elements. So, for example, there are the contrasts between Enga *atome pii* and *tindi pii*, Kyaka *arome pii* and *sinju pii*, Melpa *teman* and *kang*, Ku Waru *temani* and *kange*, Karinj *arman* and *enj*, Erave *ramani* or *ora piei* and *lidi*, respectively. For such genres, a fact versus fiction dichotomy is too simplistic (see, for example, Merlan 1995; Rumsey 2001:200; Reithofer 2006:17–19), but wherever sung tales are found in the Highlands, they belong to the latter category. In most cases the stories rendered in sung form are ones that are sometimes also told in spoken form. But to a greater or lesser extent across the region, the plots and characters of the stories that are performed in sung versions tend to be drawn from particular subsets of the wider range that are told in ordinary spoken form. In what follows we will present a brief summary of some of the main tendencies in that respect, beginning with the Duna region at the western end of the project area and working our way east to the Hagen region.

The main plots and characters of Duna sung *pikono* are very informatively discussed and exemplified in chapter 2 by Kenny Yuwi Kendoli, a Duna (Yuna)[3] man with long insider experience of *pikono*. Consistent with earlier accounts of the genre by Haley (2002) and Stewart and Strathern (2002a, 2005), Kendoli highlights as leading dramatis personae the 'cannibal giants' (*auwape*), the '*pikono* boys', and 'beautiful women'. The cannibal giants were the first human-like beings to inhabit the earth, but were not fully human. The story-world of *pikono* is located in the ancestral past at a time when the cannibal giants and full-fledged humans of the present form were both alive, albeit in different zones. Mediating in some ways between these two kinds of beings is the figure of the *payame ima*, the 'Female Spirit' who typically takes the form of a beautiful young woman and acts as a guardian to the *pikono* boy, helping him defeat the cannibal ogre and grow into mature manhood. Most *pikono* tales centrally involve a journey undertaken by one or more of the *pikono* boys, who encounter obstacles and struggle to overcome them. Often, as pointed out by Kendoli, there are fights between the *pikono* boys themselves, which, as discussed and exemplified by Stewart and Strathern (2002a, 2005), may pit a pair of brothers against each other, one of them being a good one, who is nurtured by the Female Spirit, and the other a bad one, who teams up with the cannibal giants.

---

3   The term "Duna" (derived from a Huli designation) is conventionally accepted as standard reference in English and Tok Pisin (see also Haley 2002:14). The indigenous self-designating term which is used by Kendoli in his chapter is Yuna. This word may itself be interpreted as a gradable rather than absolute term (Strathern and Stewart 2004:11).

As Kendoli observes, in past times *pikono* had a close connection with the Duna bachelor cult, a ritual complex in which boys were held in seclusion and initiated into the mysteries of growth and attraction under the tutelage of ritual specialists who were said to be the 'husbands' of the Female Spirit (cf. Stewart and Strathern 2000b:15–16; 2002b:102–40). Although Kendoli is too young to have gone through the bachelor cult himself, according to what older men have told him (as reported in his chapter), it seems that the connection with *pikono* consisted both in the fact that the cult was one of the main settings in which they were performed, and in the fact that the main characters in them, the '*pikono* boys', were cast as initiands in the cult, who were aided by the Female Spirit in the course of their travels, just as were the actual initiands by her 'husbands' in the cult houses (cf. Stewart and Strathern 1999).

Among the Huli immediately to the southeast of the Duna, sung *bì té* tales have much in common with Duna *pikono*. The Huli too had a 'bachelor cult' (*hāroli*), with which the central male characters in *bì té* are often associated—although as pointed out by Lomas in chapter 5, "their status as *hāroli* is usually implied rather than stated." Lomas further explains that *bì té* bards

> have a wealth of traditional tales to draw upon, with generally two or more human characters in each tale. Sometimes a tale may carry a romantic interest, and there is nearly always some sort of supernatural element involved, such as a non-human spirit or a paranormal event … Frequently, one of the human characters goes off on a journey, often into a high mountainous rain-forest where *dāma* "spirits" dwell. These spirits may be ogre-type beings that eat human flesh, cannibals that devour each other, or slippery tricksters likened to the *íba tīri* 'eels' that inhabit the waterways. (Lomas, this volume; cf. Pugh-Kitingan, this volume)

Further to east among the Angal Heneng, there are many similarities between the typical plots of *enj* sung tales and the Huli and Duna ones summarized above. The cannibal ogre figure (locally known as Wan Heyo) appears in many tales as the central antagonist of the young male, and a Female Spirit figure as his guardian. Among the Angal Heneng as among the Enga to the north of them, the Female Spirit is identified with a "sky world" from which she comes down to help the boy, usually taking him back there with him (Reithofer, this volume). Other *enj* stories do not involve a sky woman or a cannibal at all, and are thought of as being more for entertainment than moral edification (ibid.).

The theme of the "sky world" and its interaction with the terrestrial one is perhaps most central among the Enga and Ipili, as described in the chapters by Gibbs and by Borchard and Gibbs. In these areas too, the stories often include cannibalistic ogres—both male and female—as central figures, and links to the male initiation rites are common. Gibbs (this volume) says of Enga *tindi pi* that the "underlying themes include the seeking of adulthood, a quest for beauty, and the search for a better world."

Further to the southeast and east, the sky world figures far less centrally, if at all, in sung tales in the Ku Waru and Melpa regions,[4] where they are known as *tom yaya kange* and *kang rom,* respectively. Nor was there any association with initiation rituals, which, as far as we know, were not practised within this region at any time within the reconstructable past. The kind of relationship between young male and female figures that appears most centrally in this area is not one of tutelage, but one of courtship. As discussed in the chapter by Rumsey, ten of the twenty-five sung tales from the Ku Waru region he has recorded display variants of a standard plot in which a young man sets out from his home to court a young woman he has heard about in a far-away place, wins her hand, but then encounters various obstacles in his attempt to bring her back to his home and marry her. Among the neighbouring Melpa—who are at the far eastern end of the sung tales region—*all* of the eight or nine *kang rom* that have been recorded display variants of this plot. While this gives them a distinctive cast quite different from the plots from further to the west that we have reviewed above, there is an intermediate link in that, as pointed out by Strathern and Stewart (2005:15–16), the plot and figure of the courted maiden in one of the sung tales recorded by Rumsey in the Ku Waru region (presented and discussed in chapter 11) share key elements with tales of the bachelor boy and the Female Spirit from the other regions as discussed above (although in this tale the relevant female protagonist is not explicitly identified as a sky being).

In short, as anticipated by the discussion above, across the entire region of the Highlands where sung tales are found, the range of traditional plots and characters in them is a continuous one, with differences of emphasis, and with some elements limited to particular subregions, but with some elements common to most of them. Among the latter are the centrality of a journey that is undertaken by the main character or characters—often a young man and woman who have come together of their own accord.

Especially in the eastern reaches of the sung-tales region, among the Melpa and Ku Waru areas, new variants of these longstanding plots and characters have been developed to deal with current themes. In the Ku Waru area discussed by Rumsey in chapter 11, one performer, Paulus Konts, has cast himself as the suitor in a tale with a standard plot of courtship that is, however, located in the here and now, with the journey taking place along the Highlands Highway and through the town of Mount Hagen. In another *tom yaya kange,* also featuring himself in the leading role, Konts sang of an imaginary journey to the coast to buy betelnuts and bring them back across the Highlands to the Porgera gold mine

---

4   None of the thirty or so sung tales recorded from this region involves sky people as dramatis personae. As discussed in chapter 11, there is some evidence that one such story was formerly performed as a sung tale, but no longer is.

in Enga Province to sell them at a great profit.[5] At the 2006 Goroka workshop, another Ku Waru bard, Peter Kerua, performed a *tom yaya kange* about a tribal war that his group was involved in at that time.[6]

In the neighbouring Melpa region, the last two *kang rom* by the renowned performer Paul Pepa were composed on commission from candidates in national-level elections in aid of their campaigns. At least one of them featured a journey of courtship (in a wide-bodied Toyota Land Cruiser, rather than on foot), used in an allegorical way to laud the candidate's ability to build coalitions and court the vote. In all of these cases, we see pre-existing plots and character types in the sung-tale genre being adopted, both to bring the genre into the contemporary world and to invite its audience to imagine that world in terms of the earlier one which is otherwise portrayed within such tales (as discussed in Rumsey 2006a).

In other cases the distinctive poetic and musical features of sung-tale genres have been used to present narratives that do not necessarily have any close connection with the longstanding plots and characters used for these genres. For example, sung-tale musical and poetic conventions have in several cases been drawn upon for presenting the Christian gospel[7] and for settings of Christian liturgy.[8]

Finally, another interesting case of the adaptation of features of the sung-tale genre has been reported by Goldman (1998) from his work on Huli children's "fantasy play." He found that during the course of their play routines, in a practice resembling some uses of "sportscaster talk" among Western children, Huli children would self-narrate the imaginary scenes they were acting out, playing the parts of, for example, Australian patrol officers, Papua New Guinea riot police, and urban criminals. Remarkably, when doing so even children as young as four to five years old would use the intonational style of *bì té* sung tales. While the characters and scenarios they were enacting bore no direct relation to those of *bì té*, by drawing on its performance conventions, at a more general level they placed the story-world of *bì té* in a two-way analogical relation with the contemporary one (cf. Rumsey 2005:71–74), attesting to the continuing salience of *bì té* as what Goldman (1998:145) calls "a way of making narrative sense of the world."

---

5   For plot summaries and discussion of these two stories by Konts, see Rumsey (2005:60–66).

6   For the first eight lines of this performance, see chapter 12.

7   For a Ku Waru case in which a Lutheran man from the Upper Kaugel Valley composed and performed a *tom yaya kange* about the life of Jesus, see Rumsey (2001:201).

8   Examples from his missionary work among the Enga were discussed by Philip Gibbs at the 2004 and 2006 Goroka workshops, as were examples from Huli by Gabe Lomas. As discussed and referenced in the section on published sources below, Lomas was the co-compiler of a Huli-language setting of the Roman Catholic mass that drew, inter alia, on the genre conventions of *bì té* sung tales.

Special forms of language used in sung tales

Sung tales often employ special vocabulary, different from that used in normal speech. In some cases this vocabulary is considered to be "archaic" or to have been borrowed from other languages. For example, in their transcription of part of a Duna *pikono,* Stewart and Strathern (2005:89–91) put asterisks next to words identified by Duna speakers as "archaic/poetic ('special,' not the ordinary usage in Duna day-to-day speech)" (ibid.:89). In discussing this vocabulary, they note that the usual word for 'cassowary' is *ukura,* but in *pikono* the term *yari* is used, a word found in neighbouring languages (ibid.:93). In chapter 2 of this volume, Kenny Kendoli comments extensively on the use of these special alternative vocabulary items or 'praise names', and how essential they are to good *pikono* performance. For many everyday Duna words there is more than one alternative *kẽiyaka* 'praise name' replacement form. In chapter 3, Gillespie and San Roque discuss the way in which alternative *kẽiyaka* expressions are used at particular positions with successive lines of *pikono*, especially in reference to places or features of the landscape (see also Stewart and Strathern 2000a; Strathern and Stewart, chapter 13, this volume; Gillespie 2010, chapter 2). Haley (2002) shows that some of the alternative *kẽiyaka* forms are associated with particular zones or regions within Duna country, so that, for example, a tree species for which there is a single word in everyday Duna will be called by different praise names depending on whether the characters in the story are encountering it in a montane forest or in a settled area at lower altitude.

Various kinds of substitute vocabulary are also common in Enga songs (Brennan 1970:28–30, 46–47) and other vocal traditions throughout the area.

With respect to the Melpa area, Strathern and Stewart (2005b:217) refer to the difficulties in transcribing and translating Melpa *kang rom* texts because of the "rich and archaic vocabulary that permeates the text," but also because of the possible variable interpretations resulting from slightly different hearings of the text, for example, whether the performer sings *pili* or *pilin, köni* or *könin.* Considering the speed of Melpa *kang rom* performances, such possibilities challenge all listeners.

Within the Ku Waru region to the southwest, Rumsey finds that words used in *tom yaya* sung tales are generally everyday ones, but that they are sometimes used in ways that are unique to *tom yaya kange.* This occurs especially with a set of oft-repeated formulaic lines that performers use to frame their narratives in relation to the performance event: "And who's ever heard such a thing? / And who's ever seen such a thing," "In my mind's eye the story unfolds," etc. There is also a standard expression that is often used to open a *tom yaya kange* performance—*ama na na na* (literally "Oh mother, I, I, I")—and other expressions that are used to close them: *konta mong rltup rltap* "Now the ball stops rolling," *dalu mong kerikar* "The banana-leaf curtains draw shut," etc. Certain other words are used only in *tom yaya kange* and are said to be part of what makes it "sound like *tom yaya kange*," as exemplified in chapter 11.

Another aspect of the poetic form of sung tales is the ordered interplay of repetition and variation, or what students of comparative poetics call "parallelism." A feature common to all the sung-tales genres treated in this volume is that the main level at which parallelism abounds is the *line*. From line to line, each instance of partial repetition establishes a framework within which there is significant contrast at equivalent positions. A Duna example, involving *yari,* the special word for 'cassowary' discussed above, is:

> *yusi yese yari no neya neyana nia*
>
> *isuku asaka yari neya neyana niao*
>
> *wale walu awuale yari neya neyana niao-o*

> the cassowary of Yusi Yese, I do not eat it,
>
> the cassowary of Isuku Asaka, I do not eat it
>
> the cassowary of Wale Walu Awuale, I do not eat it (Stewart and Strathern 2005:90–92, line nos. 65–67)

Similarly, a fragment of a *tindi pii* quoted by Lacey (1975:68–69) begins:

> *kaimini paina mende pea*
>
> *paina paina mende pea*
>
> *lyange tale kukupa paina mende pea*

The words *paina mende pea* conclude the first eight lines of the text. The ninth line is:

> *lyange tale kuku paina mende peaki lalo ongo pilyamoo*

Here a variation on *paina mende pea* is followed by *lalo ongo pilyamoo,* a phrase that marks the completion of a structural element that Lacey calls a "stanza," after which the performer pauses. During this pause "a member or members of the audience may utter brief comments or words of praise or encouragement to the performer" (ibid.:69).

Similar examples of parallelism are found in Huli *bì té:*

> *biruwa bai balu mondo biya*
>
> *bayali balu mondo biya*
>
> *limbiya balu mondo biya*
>
> *limbai balu mondo biya*
>
> *duliya balu mondo biya*

when he sat down, he killed a *bai* frog and fed it to them

he killed a *bayali* lizard and fed them

he killed a *limbiya* lizard and fed them

he killed a *limbai* rat and fed them

he killed a *duliya* lizard and fed them (Pugh-Kitingan 1981:735)

Finally, as an example of parallelism in a Karinj *enj*:

Kulwap nak hal amu homolangel pisa la

Ipilpap nak hal amu homolangel pisa la

Ipil holal nak hal amu homolangel pisa la

the boys/men from Kulwap came to compete for her

the Ipilpap boys/men came to compete for her

the Sangai boys from Ipili came to compete for her (Reithofer 2005:It. 7)

Further examples of parallelism are presented and discussed in chapter 10 from Karinj *enj* sung tales, in chapter 4 from Duna *pikono*, chapter 6 from Huli *bì té*, chapters 8 and 9 from Ipili *tindi*, and chapter 11 from Ku Waru *tom yaya kange*.[9]

Another special feature of the language of sung tales is the use of vocables, particularly in line- or section-final position. In the absence of a vocable, the final vowel of a word may be sustained. Stewart and Strathern (2005:88) note that each "notional line or segment of song" in Duna *pikono* "ends with the vocables o-o-o, dying off at the end of the segment and often answered by a noise of appreciation from the audience." The importance of vocables in defining a line of text has been described by Rumsey (2005:53) for Ku Waru *tom yaya kange* and Strathern and Stewart (2005b:216) for Melpa *kang rom*. Line-final vocables are also heard on recordings of Ipili *tindi* and Karinj *enj*. Aside from sung tales, sustained final vocables are a distinctive feature of Hagen oratory, that is, Melpa *el ik* (Strathern 1971:120, 182, n.1) and Ku Waru *el ung* (Merlan and Rumsey 1991:98–99). Many Ku Waru *tom yaya kange* have vocables appearing both at the end and in the middle portion of each line (Niles 2007:112–13; this volume). From the materials that have been examined so far, this combination of vocables appears to be unique to that region.

---

9 Parallelism is an example of a feature that, although common to sung tales, is by no means confined to them. It is a common feature of song texts, both within the region of sung tales: e.g., Ipili (Ingemann 1968), Duna (Stewart and Strathern 2005:88), Melpa (Strathern and Stewart 2005b:208–9; Niles, this volume); Karinj (Reithofer 2005), Enga (Talyaga 1973); and beyond: e.g., Wiru (Paia and Strathern 1977:6, 118–21), Central Buang in Morobe Province (Hooley 1987:74–75), Manambu in East Sepik Province (Harrison 1982:18–21), Kiwai in Western Province (Landtman 1913:290–303, 309–11), and Asmat in Papua province of Indonesia (Voorhoeve 1977:22). Indeed, parallelism is one of the most commonly occurring features in poetic genres around the world (Jakobson 1960; Fox 1977).

Vocables do not seem to be as prevalent in Huli *bì té,* but the regular interjections by the audience of *è* 'yes' at the end of lines or sections have a similar structural function. The importance of these interjections is apparent in the warning occasionally given by performers before they begin: "You say *è* or my parents will die!," thereby ensuring that children pay attention (Pugh-Kitingan 1981:332).

The music of sung tales

All types of Highlands sung tales are presented using pitch patterns that are different from those of normal speech. In all areas, text is generally set syllabically to the melody, that is, with one syllable per pitch. Exceptions tend to occur at the end of phrases and are noted below. Only in the Hagen area is an isometric, binary melody repeated over and over until the story is completed (e.g., Rumsey 2001:212; Niles, this volume). Lembena *tendi pii* melodies are also sung to a definite pulse, but melodies do not appear to be repeated. As little work has been done on *tendi pii,* not much more can be said about this aspect of their structure.

Pugh-Kitingan is one of the few researchers to have focused on music in the region. In many forms of Huli music, the three tones of the language (high-falling, mid-level, low-rising) are fundamental in determining melodic shape; similarly the rhythm of the performance is related to speech:

> There is no underlying pulse in Huli music; rhythm and form are determined by the structures of the word, sentences, and verses articulated. The pace of articulation in Huli music is as rapid as that of Huli speech. (Pugh-Kitingan 1984:96)

> Melody is generally dominated by speech-tone. This domination is so great that Huli melodic movement appears to derive its essential motivation from the tonal patterns of the words and lines articulated. Language is thus as important in influencing melodic structure as it is in determining rhythm and form in Huli music. (ibid.:118)

Huli *bì té* are no exception. Pugh-Kitingan concludes that

> speech-tone is the primary determinant of the melody with sentence terminating intonation producing the movement to the middle pitch at the end of lines. As in other genres of Huli music, rapid articulation sometimes causes adjacent words of the same speech-tone to share a tonally significant melodic shape. Where passages are based on a single pitch, slight fluctuations sounding about a quartertone from this pitch may indicate speech-tone. Lines also feature the purely melodic figure of a falling interval between outside pitches, which often contradicts the speech-tones of the words with which it coincides. (Pugh-Kitingan 1981:349)

Microtonal variations in pitch are also reflected in the melodies of Ku Waru sung tales, a language that also has a tone system, albeit rather simpler than the Huli one (Rumsey 2007). And, as noted above, *tom yaya kange* are sung to binary melodies, rather than having a melodic shape largely dictated by speech-tone.

In an initial analysis of examples of Ipili *tindi* by Niles, only three different pitches are used, having the intervallic relationship of D, C, and B. Sung phrases, that is, the sung portion between breaths, use any of these pitches, but consistently alternate in ending on a C, followed by a phrase ending on B.[10] (Note that such an alternation does not appear to have any relation to the binary melodies characteristic of Hagen sung tales: aside from these phrase-final notes, no other pitch transposition is involved.) The use of three pitches and the non-repeating nature of each phrase preceding the final pitch strongly suggest a similarity to Pugh-Kitingan's description of Huli *bì té*. Furthermore, Ipili also has a word-tone system, like Huli and other members of the Engan group of languages described below. But whether this melodic movement is dictated by speech-tone or is independent of it is not known.

Written descriptions of musical characteristics are usually much more general, if included at all. Lacey (1975:59) notes that performers in the Lagaip and Maramuni (Malamuni) regions of the Enga language area have a reputation for producing some of the most renowned performers of *tindi pii*. The "greatest and most beautiful creations of these forms have the qualities called *tipalya kondenge* or *toma lenge*. Such phrases refer to these performances as being a blend of beautiful rhythmic cadences and beautiful language." Elsewhere, he notes that these terms are used by Yandapo and Taiato (Tayato) speakers to describe performances that are "flowing like water and sounding like music and song" (ibid.:xxi). Yet, how is this realized? Until further work is done on the musical aspects of both *tindi pii* and songs, the answer is not apparent.

Initial analyses by Niles suggest that Enga *tindi pii* employ variable rhythmic values, a descending melodic shape for phrases, and a general lack of a prominent pulse. Phrases appear to end on either of two tones, a step apart, but not with the regularity in alternation described for Ipili above. Additionally, final syllables may end on a two-note melismatic descent, rather than just a sustained tone. Lastly, although the rhythm generally seems to mimic spoken speech, there are sung phrases in which the rhythms appear to be more "regular" and the melodic movement follows more discrete steps. These phrases are followed by longer breaths (e.g., about eight seconds, instead of breaths lasting less than a second) and appear to recur in a performance. Perhaps these are the ends of "stanzas" noted by Lacey and described above.

---

10 Successive phrases, alternately ending on one or another pitch spaced a step apart, are also a feature of some performances of Karinj *enj* (see chapter 10).

Karinj musical phrases also tend to initially undulate and then descend to the lowest pitch, which will then be sustained to conclude the phrase. Each phrase follows this pattern, ending on the same lowest pitch. The total range of pitches used is primarily a perfect fourth, with some higher pitches used occasionally. There does not appear to be a prominent pulse; rather, rhythmic values are highly variable, perhaps imitating spoken language. However, phrases ending alternately on tones a second apart were also heard in a performance of a Karinj *enj* by Josep Haip, during the Kefamo conference in 2006, thus demonstrating some linkages with Ipili and Enga genres (see chapter 10).

After noting that Duna *pikono* structure is in "clumps of phrases rhythmically juxtaposed, in which lines can be discerned but in practice run into each other," Stewart and Strathern (2005:89) note that a "downward trend of the voice of the performer indicates either a line ending or the ending of a clump of the kind we have just noted, or both." Consistent with the latter description, though expanding considerably upon it, Gillespie and San Roque in chapter 3 present an elegant analysis of the *pikono* musical-cum-textual line as bipartite in structure, consisting of a "descent" section followed by a "ground" section. In chapter 4, Sollis further explicates the structure of the *pikono* line and the relation between successive lines, showing that it often displays a kind of musical parallelism, and that there is an interplay between that and the parallelism across the associated lines of text. Further discussion of the musical aspects of Duna *pikono* is given by Chenoweth (1969), discussed below in the literature overview.

Preliminary analysis by Niles of examples of Bogaya *kesa* (recorded in 2003 by Anna Lockwood) shows a range of pitches extending over an octave. Phrase length is highly variable. While phrases tend to descend, sustained notes at various pitch levels, often involving short melismas to a lower pitch, are common. Similar comments can be made about examples heard of Hewa sung tales (recorded by Jessica Kemp in 2003), with the addition of phrasal sections of even beats, interspersed between those of rhythms seemingly reflecting spoken language.

As these general comments indicate, much more needs to be explored about the music of sung tales.

Related genres not considered sung tales

If sung tales share most of the features listed above, it is also important to consider genres that might also appear to share some of them, but differ in others and are therefore excluded from our focus. Note that some of the elements mentioned below that exclude certain performances from our definition of sung tales in the Highlands may be quite common in sung-narrative genres in other parts of the world.

For the Kamano of Eastern Highlands, Berndt (1992:111–15) describes a type of story called *kinihera,* told by male or female performers in formal storytelling sessions in a special house at the start of the rainy season. These tales are told around an oven of edible leaves to encourage the growth of garden crops. In addition, Kamano also perform dramatic enactments (*krina*) of various kinds, some based on *kinihera.* Yet, in spite of various contextual similarities, there is no indication that *kinihera* are performed in a special way other than a normal speaking voice. The same is true of many other areas with highly developed storytelling traditions.

There are numerous examples of long textual performances that *are* "sung," but which also must be excluded from our category of sung tales. For example, Iatmul *sagi* performances in the Middle Sepik may last over sixteen hours, and formal ceremonies centring on clan members require such performances (Spearritt and Wassmann 1996; Wassmann 1991). Various sections of *sagi* involve solo or group singing, always accompanied by a drum and split-bamboo beater, and occasionally the playing of flutes and voice modifiers. If such instruments are used, they are played in an area screened off from the other performers. The long sung texts relate the migration of ancestors of a particular clan. Long series of paired names must be remembered—a very considerable task—and words considered archaic are common. The often esoteric meaning of the texts is known to only a few elders. Lines of text end in vocables and much parallelism is involved. While other men, women, and children listen to the singing, no one tries to enter the screened area; access is restricted to a very few men. Women may dance in the outside area. From this short description, one can see that there are many features shared with sung tales as discussed in this volume. However, the use of instruments, dance, and unison singing differs from Highlands sung tales.[11] Furthermore the migration of clan ancestors related in *sagi* performances and the esoteric nature of such texts make them thematically very different from Highlands sung tales, taking them out of the realm of "entertainment."

Landtman (1913:289–301) reports Kiwai "serial songs," some of which comprise over fifty "verses." The texts often describe a "wandering" from Adiri, the land of the dead far to the west, moving gradually eastwards along the coast, "through the whole of the world known to the Kiwai people" (ibid.:295). Performances are associated with a variety of ceremonies conducted indoors. The singing is accompanied by dancing. A leader heads the procession and he introduces a text that is repeated by others until he feels it necessary to start a new text. Very long performances may be interrupted and continued on subsequent days. Hence, features such as the repetition of a line of text before introducing a new line, choral singing, dance, and the role of such serial songs in ceremonies, exclude them from the sung tales considered here.

---

11   Instruments do accompany epic song performances in other parts of the world (Reichl 2000:19ff.).

The long Trobriand Islands historical poems, transcribed and translated by Kasaipwalova and Beier (Kasaipwalova 1978; Kasaipwalova and Beier 1978a, 1978b, 1979), have been considered by Strathern and Stewart (2005a:12–13) as genres quite similar to those under examination in this volume. While this is certainly true in relation to aspects of their poetic construction, judging from recordings of such poems in the Institute of Papua New Guinea Studies, it appears that some, if not all, of such historical poems are sung in unison by a group—something which precludes the kind of semi-improvised composition-in-performance that is a key feature of Highlands sung tales.

Returning to the Highlands region that is the focus of this volume, Enga *sangai titi pingi nemongo* share many features in common with sung tales. Used in *sangai* bachelor cults,[12] *titi pingi* are described by Wiessner and Tumu (1998:39) as

> sacred poetry that describes the series of transactions by which a cult's sacred objects were purchased from another clan of high repute, brought secretly to the cult house after perilous journeys by night, and passed on through the generations. At each step of purchase or transmission, new lines or verses are added. Recitations can last up to thirty minutes, albeit with much repetition. Only ambitious and capable young men learn the poetry in its entirety; most remember only the fragments that contain essential historical information.

Wiessner and Tumu (ibid.:404–10) also provide a transcription, translation, and interpretation of seven verses of a thirteen-verse *titi pingi*. We exclude *titi pingi* from our category of sung tales because of their focus on the transmission of sacred objects. While this may be considered a journey of sorts, it is not a narrative told for entertainment, but to recall the history of sacred objects and their power to transform young men, with each clan or subclan having its own story (ibid.:230–32; also see Gibbs 1990).

The following description of Fasu (Southern Highlands) *mano ho-ra*, however, sounds very much like a sung tale, through the interaction with the audience (as found in sung-tale traditions to the west of Hagen), the special mode of delivery, the addition of the vocable *-o,* repetition, etc.:

> A legendary narrative known as *mano ho-ra* 'man speak customary' is characterized by two final verb suffixes … All stories involve interaction between 'good' and 'bad' characters.

---

12   Apparently originating in the central Enga, *sangai* diffused eastwards and is called *sandalu* in the Layapo area. Although similar to *sangai,* there were some important differences in *sandalu,* notably, for our discussion, "the recitation of poems for the sacred objects was either omitted or greatly abbreviated" in the latter (Wiessner and Tumu 1998:238).

The storyteller did not want to tell these stories into a tape recorder. He had to bring his children along and tell them the story. The reason became evident. Every now and then the story teller interjected a question to the audience: 'Now what do you think of that'. This occurred at climactic points when something was grandiose beyond explaining. Sometimes at the beginning of the story there was a rhetorical question asked of the audience.

These stories are told in speech-song 'Sprechstimme' 'speaking voice'. The story is not sung, and is not spoken, but has the character of both being delivered in a manner half way between. Each character in the story has his own voice quality. Hence quotes are not marked in formulaic fashion. The main characters which appear in nearly all the stories are an old man, an old woman, a young man and a young woman. Sometimes there are children and sometimes animals. The characters are known by the voice quality and by story teller.

To the verbal suffixes of dependent clauses -o is added. In the speech-song style this vowel can be drawn out and adds to the rhythm of the speech-song style. This style also makes for much repetition, that is, the same thing is said again and again.

The stories are hard for the naive listener to comprehend. There is much implied information. Each story has a moral at the end. This is not explicitly stated, but is definitely implied. Because these stories are stated in code-like terms, an example will not be given. These stories hinge between speech and song. (Loeweke and May 1980:95–97)

In May and Loeweke's subsequent Fasu dictionary, the only reference we have been able to find to something similar is *mano hosie* 'tell the mano legend' (May and Loeweke 1981:73–74), listed under the verb *horakā* 'speak, sing', however, we are not given further information here as to what the "mano legend" is.[13] Subsequent correspondence with anthropologist Kurita Hiroyuki (emails to Niles, 10 October 2006, 23 October 2006), who was very familiar with the linguistic work of May and Loeweke for his own research with the Fasu, has clarified questions relating to this genre: the teller of *mano ho-ra* adopts different voice qualities to represent different characters, but otherwise the presentation resembles normal speech.

---

13   According to May and Loeweke's Fasu dictionary, *Māno* is the name of a village, while, as a noun, *máno* is a 'title given to a boy child' or, as an adjective, has meanings such as 'small, young, new' (May and Loeweke 1981:145).

Terminology

Researchers often have to face difficult decisions in deciding how to translate terms from one language to another, particularly if features relevant to the sense of a term in one language do not neatly correspond to those in another. As a result, some authors may translate the name for a certain type of narrative tradition as "myth," others as "legend," "folktale," or simply "story." Such issues become even more of a concern in comparative studies involving many languages. Here, researchers must use certain terms that may quite adequately describe a genre in one region, but not be quite as appropriate in a different one. When the genre being considered does not have a convenient name in the language of writing (English, in this case), the difficulty is further compounded.[14]

The genre we are calling "sung tales" has been given a variety of names by different authors—for example, "ballads," "epics," etc. Indeed, the name of the ARC project concerning them used "chanted tales." While some researchers were attracted to this name, particularly because of the implication that such performances are also enchanting compositions (which they certainly are), ethnomusicologists have raised concerns over the use of the word "chant" (also see the discussion by Pugh-Kitingan in chapter 6).[15]

But is "sung narrative," "sung story," or "sung tale" any better? Certainly all genres considered here are narratives or stories, but are they sung? We argue that one of the features that distinguishes this genre from spoken narratives or tales is the special mode of delivery used by the performer. But if this delivery cannot be called "chanted" or "spoken," is it "sung"? For the genre of sung tales, there *is* greater variation in the pitches used than in normal speech, and there often does seem to be a melodic framework in which sung tales are presented. However, if

---

14 Some of these issues of terminology have been considered by Reichl (2000:12–13) and Strathern and Stewart (2005a:16–18).
15 For example, in the volume of the *Garland Encyclopedia of World Music* devoted to Australia and the Pacific, the glossary defines "chant" as "recitational singing, often on one or two tones, with rhythms deriving from those of the words" (Kaeppler and Love 1998:1027). While some of the sung tales considered here might be considered "recitational" in nature, with a limited use of pitches and with rhythms derived from spoken language, there are many examples where this is much less true, unclear, or totally inaccurate. But objections to the word "chant" go beyond just an inadequate characterization of musical features. "Chant" often has pejorative associations: "As a handy label for Oceanic song, the word *chant* appears in all forms of literature, in all periods, usually meaning that the described music did not have the tonal variety of European music" (Love 1998:36). Furthermore, "outside observers often distinguish less melodically varied and more rhythmically word-dependent renditions by a term like *chant*, which, for the more melodically varied and less word-dependent rendition, they contrast with a term like *song* ... Since the introduction of the words *chant* and *song*, many [Pacific] cultures have used these terms to categorize the old and the new" (Love and Kaeppler 1998:321). None of the contributors to this volume believe that the traditions considered in it are inferior to any other traditions in the world. And, as illustrated in some of the articles here, there can be many parallels between the melodies used for sung tales and those used for other genres more readily recognized as song. In Papua New Guinea at least, "chant" and "song" are *not* used to differentiate old and new traditions, and we do not wish to encourage such a usage. For all these reasons, there are difficulties in using "chant" as either a noun or a verb for these traditions, despite their undeniable ability to enchant.

we look for evidence in the verbs used to indicate the performance of sung tales in the different languages concerned—in the expectation, for example, that they might be different from those used for the normal telling of stories or even the same as those used for singing—we often find that it is unhelpful in resolving such a query. In many traditions, there is no special word for 'to sing', rather 'to say' is used. And there appears to be no special verb used anywhere to describe the performance of sung tales as opposed to the telling of any other story or the "saying" of a song. For example, in the Hagen area, the verb used to describe the telling of all stories, including sung tales, is one that when used by itself means 'to hit'. While this may seem particularly appropriate for Hagen sung tales considering their fast, metric presentation, a *kange* story told in a normal speaking voice is also 'hit'.

The word "ballad" might appear to be more apt in emphasizing aspects of narrative, popular themes, and the importance as entertainment, but the term seems to be usually applied to performances using strophic texts, that is, a changing text set to a repeating melody (Bronson 1980). While this might be an appropriate description for some areas in the Highlands, in others, such a repeating melody is absent.

There are also certain similarities between the sung tales considered here and the long epics often associated with traditions more distant geographically and/ or chronologically. Reichl (2000:14) notes that epic poetry is narrative, metric, often of great length, and archaic. Some of these features are also typical of sung tales. Yet, the heroic, often martial, nature usually associated with epics (ibid.) is not appropriate for all the Papua New Guinea traditions. Even here the boundaries between the terms for such genres are quite fluid, since "certain types of ballad might also be classified as epic song" (Anon. 1980).

Although preferring to use "ballads" in reference to the Melpa *kang rom* and Duna *pikono* they have studied, Stewart and Strathern (2002a) also refer to them as being "sung" (p. 122) or "chanted" (ibid.) and as "chanted epics" (p. 135). Such variation indicates some of the difficulties in finding appropriate English terminology.

Hence, while no one term seems totally adequate, and all could be argued to have some sort of validity, "sung narrative," "sung story," or "sung tale" could be considered preferable in emphasizing the importance of a narrative and its presentation in something other than normal speech, possibly more akin to singing. Nevertheless, we have not imposed conformity of usage in the contributions here. Rather, authors use whatever terms they feel most appropriate and comfortable with.

In the introduction to the volume he has edited called *The Oral Epic: Performance and Music*, Karl Reichl discusses some features of sung stories, particularly in Europe and Asia. He notes a common contrast between melodies that are stichic (the same melody for every line of poetry) and strophic (melodies that require more than one line of poetry) (Reichl 2000:4). While some of the melodies considered here could probably be called strophic, stichic is certainly an inappropriate description for the remainder where there may be considerable melodic variation between lines. Reichl also points out that "the musical aspect is of importance, at least when it comes to properly understanding the metrical structure of an orally performed poem" (ibid.:10). Although he is here referring specifically to the ambiguous nature of the metre of the verse in Russian epic called *bylina,* the same could be said even more strongly for Melpa *kang rom* and Ku Waru *tom yaya kange.* In these Hagen cases, the melody absolutely determines the metric structure of the poetry. Yet, in other examples of sung tales considered here, this is not so. Generalizing further, Reichl observes that

> as narratives, epics tell a story, i.e., the emphasis is on words and their meaning and not (primarily) on music. If in the light of our discussion of (poetic) metre, music fulfils a quasi-metrical function, i.e., that of helping to group the words into rhythmical, repetitive units, then music plays primarily a structural role. And it follows from these assumptions that this type of melody will be fairly simple, modelled on the inflections of speech rather than developing into full-fledged song. (Reichl 2000:15)

But what are the boundaries between a melody "modelled on the inflections of speech" and "full-fledged song"? Rather than tackle such a thorny issue, it seems better to conclude that "the performance of epic adapts itself to the musical styles current in a particular region" (Reichl 2000:20) and that, aside from structural issues, singing enables the performer to make his or her voice carry further and increase the audibility of the tale (ibid.:21).

Distribution of sung-tales genres and languages

Figure 2 shows the areas in Southern Highlands, Enga, and Western Highlands provinces where sung tales are found. Vernacular names for sung tales are given in brackets beneath language names in bold italics. Adjacent areas where sung tales are absent or for which data are inconclusive are also shown. In such a mapping, the absence of a feature is just as important as its presence. Distributional mapping is particularly difficult in this case, however, in that one cannot always assume that no mention of sung tales in the literature means absence. For example, the extensive early ethnographic materials written by missionaries on the Hagen area make no mention of *kang rom.* Nevertheless, consultation of the existing ethnographic literature on the area, coupled with queries to individual researchers and, more generally, on Internet email lists suggest that most of the absences on the map are valid.

In spite of this, the map should only be considered a conservative indication of the distribution of sung tales. For example, such a genre might be present in some of the other languages in Angal-Kewa subgroup—that is, particularly in areas where closely related languages are associated with such a genre.[16] To date, however, our knowledge remains incomplete. One of the purposes of this volume is to stimulate research in such areas of uncertainty.

Is there any relationship between the genetic grouping of languages here and the presence or absence of sung tales? According to the most recent classification of languages in this region of Papua New Guinea (Ross 2005; Pawley 2005), many of these languages belong to the Trans New Guinea family—a large group of over three hundred languages spread across the whole island (see Ross 2005:34, map 5). Throughout much of this area, no sung tales are found. Hence, our focus here is primarily on the consideration of lower order groups and subgroups.[17]

Within the Trans New Guinea family, Ross (2005:35, table 7) has identified a number of major groups of languages, some of which are represented on figure 2. The list in figure 3, which should be examined in relation to figure 2, illustrates the distribution of sung tales arranged according to language classification. The name of the genre, where known, is included. Absences for entire groups or subgroups are noted. Languages belonging to the groupings that appear on the map are specified.

The only first-order group of the Trans New Guinea family in which all language members have sung tales is Duna-Pogaia, consisting of only two languages, with Duna speakers far outnumbering those of Bogaya. In the much larger Engan group, the Huli language (a subgroup itself) and most languages of the Enga subgroup also have sung tales, with fewer representatives in the Angal-Kewa subgroup. Finally, the only subgrouping of the Chimbu-Wahgi group known

---

16 A work of fiction concerning the Imbonggu area by Linda Harvey Kelley (1984:43–44) contains a scene where a woman tries to comfort her daughter, so the mother begins to "sing a story." While the story is made-up (Linda Harvey Kelley, pers. comm. to Niles, 9 March 2011), the opening fragment is certainly reminiscent of sung tales in the Hagen area, and most lines of the English text end in vocables. However, the vocable most often used (-*iyo*) has not previously been heard in Melpa *kang rom* or Ku Waru *tom yaya kange*. Furthermore, -*iyo -iyo -iyo -iyo -iyo* is also used as a replacement for a line of text. While we have not previously encountered this in sung tales, it is a common feature of songs in the Hagen area, as Kelley herself illustrates (ibid.:35–36). Perhaps these features are a bit of poetic licence or misremembering on her part, or perhaps they are distinctive elements of performance practice in the Imbonggu area. Certainly further research is needed to clarify the situation. Aside from this representation in fiction, Imbonggu speakers confirm that sung tales are performed in the region; as such, their presence is shown in figure 2.

17 For the sake of simplicity, throughout this discussion first-order groupings of languages within a family are called "groups"; lower level groupings within these groups are called "subgroups."

to have sung tales is the Hagen subgroup, in which all languages have them. Significantly, all other first-order groups of the Trans New Guinea family lack sung tales, at least according to present knowledge.

TRANS NEW GUINEA FAMILY
Duna-Pogaia group
     Duna   *pikono*
     Bogaya   *kesa*
Engan group
  Angal-Kewa subgroup*
     Angal Enen   *inji*
     Angal Henen   *inj*
     Angal Heneng   *injiy*
     Aklal Heneng dialect *enj*
     Erave   .   —
     Kewa, East   —
     Kewa, West   —
     Samberigi   —
  Enga subgroup
     Bisorio   —
     Enga   *tindi pii, tundu*
     Ipili   *tindi*
     Kyaka   *sinju pii, pii sinju*
     Lembena   *tendi pii*
     Nete   *tindi pii*
  Huli subgroup
     Huli   *bi té*
Chimbu-Wahgi group
  Chimbu subgroup   — [subgroup not shown on map]
  Hagen subgroup†
     Imbonggu   [present]
     Ku Waru   *tom yaya kange*
     Meam   *kang tom*
     Melpa   *kang rom*
     Umbu-Unggu   *tom yaya kangge*
  Jimi subgroup   — [Maring shown on map]
  Wahgi subgroup   — [Nii shown on map]
Oksapmin group   — [Oksapmin shown on map]
Ok group   — [Bimin shown on map]
East Strickland group   — [Fembe, Gobasi, Konai, Kubo, Samo shown on map]
Bosavi group   — [Beami, Edolo, Kaluli, Onobasulu shown on map]
West Kutubu group   — [absent; Fasu shown on map]
East Kutubu group   — [absent; Foi shown on map]
Wiru group   — [absent; Wiru shown on map]
Madang group   — [absent; Kalam, Kobon shown on map]

SEPIK FAMILY
Sepik Hill group   — [only present in Hewa; Alamblak, Bahinemo, Bikaru, Hewa,
                      Niksek, Piame, Sumariup, Tuwari, Yawiyo shown on map]
     Hewa   *le yiya, ku kwae kwae*

PIAWI FAMILY   — [Haruai, Pinai-Hagahai shown on map]

RAMU-LOWER SEPIK FAMILY   — [Arafundi, Rao, Yimas shown on map]

YUAT FAMILY   — [Kyenele shown on map]

Figure 3. The distribution of sung tales arranged according to language classification. (* The names of Angal languages are based on information supplied by Hans Reithofer; † The names of Hagen languages are based on information supplied by Rumsey.)

The only non–Trans New Guinea family language in which sung tales are known to be performed is Hewa, a member of the Sepik Family, Sepik Hill group. Other languages belonging to this group are mostly located to the north of Hewa.

Hence, considering only first-order groups of the Trans New Guinea family, we find that sung tales are particularly associated with Duna-Pogaia and Engan languages. Within the latter at lower divisions, sung tales are found in Huli, most of the Enga subgroup languages, and in all of the Angal languages of the Angal-Kewa subgroup. Within the Chimbu-Wahgi group, sung tales are only found in the westernmost subgroup, Hagen. These relations and mappings might be taken to suggest an origin somewhere in parts of Southern Highlands or Enga and diffusion from there, although the evidence from language groupings is by itself not particularly compelling, since language difference apparently presents no obstacle to the spread of such a genre in this region.[18]

Within the languages associated with sung tales, there are some obvious cognates of vernacular names for the genre. Enga *tindi pii,* Kyaka *sinju pii* or *pii sinju,* and Lembena *tendi pii* clearly cluster together. The *pii* part of these forms means 'talk/speech, language, word' (Lang 1973:85)[19] and is also cognate with the first word in Huli *bì té* 'talk/words story' (Pugh-Kitingan 1981:332). Enga/Ipili *tindi,* Angal Enen *inji,* Angal Henen *inj,* Angal Heneng *injiy/enj,* Kyaka *sinju,* and Lembena *tendi* may also be cognate with East Kewa *lidi/lindi* and West Kewa *iti.* The Kewa terms refer to a type of story, generally believed to be fictional (LeRoy 1985). Anthropologists who have worked in the Kewa area have not reported sung tales there, although Summer Institute of Linguistics worker Karl Franklin, believes that such stories can be "chanted, often in a falsetto voice" (email to Rumsey, December 2002). However, in the absence of recordings or further information, it remains unclear whether these are examples of sung tales or not. Nor would the mere presence of a cognate term for any of the ones listed above for the Duna-Pogaia or Engan groups necessarily attest to the presence of sung tales, since none of those terms refers only to sung versions. Such evidence would be more telling within the Chimbu-Waghi group, since the known terms from there refer specifically to sung versions of *kange* tales.

---

18 A relevant factor is that there is generally extensive bi- and multilingualism in border areas between the languages. For discussion of a typical example in the Southern Highlands and reference to literature on others within the region, see chapter 10.

19 Frances Ingemann (email to Alan Rumsey, 26 February 2008) reports that among the Ipili, *tindi* is used to refer to stories and *tindi pii* refers to the special vocabulary used in them. From this it would seem that Ipili *pii* at least in this context has a more restricted sense than Enga *pii* or Huli *bi,* referring specifically to word(s).

Although the Duna language is genetically only very distantly related to Huli,[20] Duna *pikono* are similar in some ways to Huli *bì té*, thus showing that language similarities or differences do not necessarily reflect comparable degrees of relatedness in other cultural features. As another example, Lembena *tendi pii* appear to be similar to the Hagen style of sung tales in the use of melodies involving a very definite, regular pulse; however, the melodies do not appear to be repeating, binary ones. The Lembena language is part of the Engan group, whereas Hagen languages are part of the Chimbu-Wahgi group.

Overview of main publications on sung tales

The first published reference to a genre of sung tales appears to be Glasse's mention of Huli '*pi te*', which he describes as 'folk stories' in contrast to *mana* 'myths' (Glasse 1965:33).[21] However, he gives no indication of any special manner of presentation, so he may not have heard them performed as sung tales; it is only from the subsequent work of other researchers that we know them as such.

Using materials collected by Summer Institute of Linguistics translators Dennis and Nancy Cochrane, ethnomusicologist Vida Chenoweth differentiates three Duna singing styles: that used for dance songs, the sprechstimme of "chant," and that for "the intimate narrative or 'ballad'" (Chenoweth 1969:219).[22] Although the Duna term for them is not specified, the identification of the latter style as sung *pikono* is obvious from her description (pp. 224–27). Focussing on melodic and rhythmic aspects of performance, Chenoweth also notes that: the melodic form of such ballads is dependent on the text (p. 224); ballads vary considerably in length, a 74-line one being described as one of as the longest she has found in New Guinea (p. 225);[23] textual parallelism is common, with word substitutions occurring at the beginning of lines, rather than the end (pp. 225–26). Chenoweth

---

20   "Genetic" distance is measured in terms of the incidence of shared features presumably resulting from retention from a common proto-language, as per the standard comparative method used within historical linguistics. Not considered in such an account are similarities resulting from "borrowing"—the diffusion of words and other features from one language to another resulting from interaction between people who speak both of them. There has evidently been a considerable amount of such diffusion from Huli to Duna, resulting in extensive shared vocabulary (Voorhoeve 1975:395). This is consistent with the fact that there has apparently been considerable cultural diffusion of other sorts between Huli and Duna, presumably including that which has resulted in the similarities between Duna *pikono* and Huli *bì té*.

21   See chapter 6 where Pugh-Kitingan discusses Glasse's incorrect gloss of *mana* as 'myths'.

22   In a later summary of the findings in this article, Chenoweth (2000) states that her analysis was done in 1968 and refers to materials collected in 1964 by the Cochranes. Chenoweth further notes that "ballads follow speech rhythm whereas *sing-sings* ... follow the rhythm of the dance" (p. 179).

23   Actually a footnote from Nancy Cochrane reveals that Duna people commented that this was one of the shorter versions since it was recorded when it was cold (Chenoweth 1969:225, n. 11). By way of comparison, of the three Duna sung *pikono* performances that have been transcribed and translated in full by Lila San Roque, all by different performers, one runs to 424 lines, another to approximately 1,200, and another to approximately 2,500.

(1969:226–27) then outlines some plots of *pikono* and concludes by highlighting musical contrasts in the three styles of singing surveyed. This appears to be the first attested recognition of a genre of sung narratives as something distinct from song and storytelling, but related to both.

Following a brief mention of *pikono* by Modjeska (1977:107, 322), knowledge of this genre has been much expanded through the research and publications of Andrew Strathern (who first recorded *pikono* in 1991) and Pamela Stewart (e.g., Stewart and Strathern 2002a; 2005; Strathern and Stewart, this volume), Haley (2002), Gillespie (2010), and San Roque (Gillespie and San Roque, this volume). Some recorded excerpts of *pikono* accompany Strathern and Stewart (2000). Sollis (2006, 2010) considers modifications of word tone in Huli and Duna sung tales, and their relation to the melodies in which the tales are performed.

Writings on various regional sung-tale genres by a number of authors started to appear in 1975. Pugh-Kitingan began her examination of Huli *bì té* in an Honours thesis (Pugh 1975:10–30) and, after later research, further considered the genre in her work on Huli vocal and instrumental genres (Pugh-Kitingan 1981:332–50, 710–87; 1984:115–16; 1998). This was followed by Goldman's anthropological work (Goldman 1983, 1998) and the linguistic research of Lomas (1988). Lomas was also a co-compiler of *Ngodehondo bi lamiya* (Alexishafen: SVD Press, 1977), which includes "Misa iba gana," a setting of the Catholic mass based on traditional Huli expressive genres, including *bì té.*

Also in 1975, Lacey wrote extensively about Enga oral traditions, devoting considerable discussion to *tindi pii* (Lacey 1975:59–60, 68–73, 264–67, and elsewhere); he also notes that the Laiapo (Layapo) name for sung tales is *tundu* (p. xx). Lacey includes a listing of "Collections of Enga Oral Sources in a Written Form," which contains references to at least eight manuscripts concerning *tindi pii* (pp. 313–14). In a subsequent article, Lacey (1979:194–96) presents the legend of Pandakusa. Although it is not specifically identified as *tindi pii,* his comments on the context, audience interaction, and evaluation of it "like running water, [which] flowed as a creation rich in music and wisdom" (ibid.:194) suggest that it is. Wiessner and Tumu (1998:26) consider *tindi pii* as myth, characterizing it as "free text, preferably told in rhythmic chant." They further explain that "when narrated by experts, [*tindi pii*] are recited in a poetic chant with repetitive rhythmic patterns and rhyme. Complex and colourful images are used to challenge listeners and hold their attention. A single myth can go on for over an hour, requiring extraordinary verbal skill on the part of the narrator" (ibid.:26–27).

To the west, Gibbs (1975, 1978) wrote on Ipili *tindi,* providing translations of stories and interpretations in two theses. He notes that "chanting stories is an achieved art mastered by few" (Gibbs 1975:102). Recordings of this genre were made by linguist Frances Ingemann beginning in the 1960s. In addition to one conference paper on Ipili courting songs (Ingemann 1968), she has compiled recorded examples of various genres for archival purposes (Ingemann 1987), from which one fragment of a *tindi* has been published (Niles and Webb 1987:Enga-11). Research on Ipili *tindi* has also continued with the work of Biersack (1999).

Beginning his fieldwork in 1964 in the Hagen area, Andrew Strathern first recorded a Melpa *kang rom* in 1965. Although his first published reference to this genre appears to be in a radio script including musical examples prepared for the National Broadcasting Commission (1983:4), since that time he and Pamela Stewart have written in considerable detail about this genre, particularly since 1997 (e.g., Strathern 1995, 1998; Strathern and Stewart 1997a, 2000), leading to a book with a chapter devoted to the subject of ballads (Stewart and Strathern 2002a:121–45) and an edited volume on expressive genres in which they examine *kang rom* in their introduction (Strathern and Stewart 2005a:11–18) and in a separate chapter (Strathern and Stewart 2005b). Their work has considered such aspects of *kang rom* as poetic translation, plots, textual parallelism, and interpretation. A short extract of one *kang rom,* recorded by Niles and Strathern in 1982, has been published (Niles and Webb 1987:Western Highlands-5). Other excerpts of *kang rom* performances accompany Strathern and Stewart (2000).

To the southwest among the Ku Waru people, Alan Rumsey and Francesca Merlan began their fieldwork in 1981. Although they recorded some *tom yaya kange* in the early 1980s (Rumsey 1995), it became a main focus of Rumsey's work from 1997. Beginning with his 2001 article in which a full *tom yaya kange* text is transcribed and translated, Rumsey has written about this and other texts with respect to their metric, melodic, and poetic features in increasing detail (e.g., Rumsey 2002, 2005, 2006a, 2006b, 2007, 2010). His interest in the work of other researchers on sung tales prompted the preparation of an ARC grant proposal, which was accepted and has led to the project from which this volume has arisen (for details of which, see http://chl.anu.edu.au/anthropology/chantedtales/). Although first exposed to and interested in *kang rom* and Melpa songs through fruitful collaborative research with Andrew Strathern beginning in 1982, Niles's involvement in the ARC project encouraged him to write about Hagen sung tales, particularly in comparison with other melodic forms in the area (Niles 2007, 2009). Michael Mel (2005) argues that Hagen sung tales are important vehicles for building a sense of community and of belonging in such a community.

In a collection of stories from the Kaugel (Umbu-Unggu) area, Lepi and Bowers (1983:5) observe that *kange* are "normally told in a quick, sing-song voice," but neither of them appears to have published more on this subject.

Although a number of researchers have worked in the Mendi area, Reithofer appears to be the first to have written about sung tales from the region, based on his 1998–2000 research among the Karinj. The Karinj speak the Aklal Heneng dialect of Angal Heneng. Here *enj* are described as "origin myths, folk tales," in contrast to *arman* "remembered history, genealogies" (Reithofer 2006:19, fig. 1). *Arman* appears to be cognate with Melpa *teman,* Ku Waru *temani,* Ipili *temane,* and Erave *ramani,* and may also relate to Enga *atome* and Kyaka *arome.* All of these terms emphasize the more historical nature of the stories concerned, in contrast to the less historical nature of *enj.*

Information on sung tales in other regions is minimal. Missionary linguists Draper and Draper (2002:393) note Kyaka *sinju pii* or *pii sinju* as a "tale, story, legend, myth, folklore," distinct from *arome pii* "which is believed to be true" (ibid.). Obviously *sinju pii* and *arome pii* are cognate with Enga *tindi pii* and *atome pii,* respectively, but given that the latter can refer to spoken tales as well as sung ones, in the absence of sound recordings it remains unclear whether *sinju pii* are ever sung.

Summer Institute of Linguistics worker Paul Heineman has shared recorded examples of Lembena *tendi pii* with us, but has not done detailed work on them yet. Jerry Jacka has recorded sung tales in the Nete area (email to Rumsey, April 2003). Two ANU anthropology students recorded, transcribed, and translated sung tales during their fieldwork in the Southern Highlands Province in 2004: Jessica Kemp recorded Hewa *le yiya* 'clan narrative' and *ku kwae kwae* 'before story' at Wanakipa; Anna Lockwood recorded Bogaya *kesa* at Ekali.

Plan of the volume

As in the discussion of plots and characters above, the order of exposition within the rest of this volume runs generally from west to east, beginning with Duna *pikono* (chapters 2–4), then moving to Huli *bì té* (chapters 5–6), Enga *tindi pii* (chapter 7), Ipili *tindi* (chapters 8–9), West Mendi *enj* (chapter 10), Ku Waru *tom yaya kange* (chapters 11–12), and Melpa *kang rom* (chapter 12). The final chapter (13) closes the circle by considering aspects of Melpa *kang rom* in relation to Duna *pikono* (and, for good measure, works from classical antiquity by Hesiod and Virgil). For most of these regional genres there are treatments from two or three different disciplinary perspectives from among the trio of sociocultural anthropology, linguistics, and ethnomusicology. In each case where those multiple perspectives are brought to bear, they are deployed not in isolation from each other, but in combination, providing insights that would not otherwise be possible.

Furthermore the opening chapter to the Duna section, following up on this one, comes from a fourth perspective that very usefully complements all the others—that of an insider from the Duna area with long experience as a research assistant and interpreter of the local lifeways to interested outsiders such as we expect will be the main readers of this volume. Since many of the points discussed by Kendoli with respect to *pikono* pertain in a general way to most or all of the other regional genres of sung tales discussed in this volume, his chapter can serve as a Highlander's-eye introduction to the whole volume, complementing the present one in that respect.

Acknowledgments

For their valuable comments on an earlier version of this chapter, we wish to thank Jacqueline Pugh-Kitingan, Hans Reithofer, Lila San Roque, Pamela Stewart, Andrew Strathern, and two anonymous referees.

References

Anonymous. 1980. "Epic Song." In *The New Grove Dictionary of Music and Musicians*, edited by Stanley Sadie, vol. 6, 22. 20 vols. London: Macmillan.

Berndt, Catherine H. 1992. "Journey along Mythic Pathways." In *Ethnographic Presents: Pioneering Anthropologists in the Papua New Guinea Highlands*, edited by Terence E. Hays, 98–136. Studies in Melanesian Anthropology, 12. Berkeley: University of California Press.

Biersack, Aletta. 1995. "Introduction: The Huli, Duna, and Ipili Peoples Yesterday and Today." In *Papuan Borderlands: Huli, Duna, and Ipili Perspectives on the Papua New Guinea Highlands*, edited by Aletta Biersack, 1–54. Ann Arbor: University of Michigan Press.

———. 1999. "The Mount Kare Python and His Gold: Totemism and Ecology in the Papua New Guinea Highlands." *American Anthropologist* 101: 68–87.

Brennan, Paul W. 1970. "Enga Referential Symbolism: Verbal and Visual." In *Exploring Enga Culture: Studies in Missionary Anthropology*, edited by Paul W. Brennan, 17–50. Second Anthropological Conference of the New Guinea Lutheran Mission. Wapenamanda: New Guinea Lutheran Mission.

Bronson, Bertrand H. 1980. "Ballad §I: Folk and Popular Balladry." In *The New Grove Dictionary of Music and Musicians*, edited by Stanley Sadie, vol. 2, 70–75. 20 vols. London: Macmillan.

Chenoweth, Vida. 1969. "An Investigation of the Singing Styles of the Dunas." *Oceania* 39 (3): 218–30.

———. 2000. *Sing-sing: Communal Singing and Dancing in Papua New Guinea.* Christchurch: Macmillan Brown Centre for Pacific Studies.

Denham, T. P. 2006. "The Origins of Agriculture in New Guinea: Evidence, Interpretation and Reflection." In Blackwell Guide to Archaeology in Oceania: Australia and the Pacific islands, edited by I. Lilley, 160–88. Oxford: Blackwell.

Draper, Norm, and Sheila Draper. 2002. *Dictionary of Kyaka Enga, Papua New Guinea.* Pacific Linguistics, 532. Canberra: Australian National University.

Fox, James J. 1977. "Roman Jakobson and the Comparative Study of Parallelism." In *Roman Jakobson: Echoes of His Scholarship*, edited by Cornelis H. van Schooneveld and Daniel Armstrong, 59–90. Lisse: Peter de Ridder Press.

Gibbs, Philip. 1975. "Ipili Religion Past and Present." Diploma in Anthropology thesis, University of Sydney.

———. 1978. *"Kaunala Tape*: Towards a Theological Reflection on a New Guinea Initiation Myth." MA thesis, Catholic Theological Union (Chicago).

———. 1990. *"Titi Pingi:* Theology of an Engan Praise Poem." *Catalyst* 20 (2): 117–36.

Gillespie, Kirsty. 2010. *Steep Slopes: Music and Change in the Highlands of Papua New Guinea.* Canberra: ANU E Press. http://epress.anu.edu.au/steepslopes_citation.html.

Glasse, Robert M. 1965. "The Huli of the Southern Highlands." In *Gods Ghosts and Men in Melanesia*, edited by Peter Lawrence and Mervyn J. Meggitt, 27–49. Melbourne: Oxford University Press.

Goldman, Laurence R. 1983. *Talk Never Dies: The Language of Huli Disputes.* London: Tavistock Publications.

———. 1998. *Child's Play: Myth, Mimesis and Make-believe.* Oxford: Berg.

Haley, Nicole. 2002. *"Ipakana Yakaiya*: Mapping Landscapes, Mapping Lives; Contemporary Land Politics among the Duna." PhD dissertation, Australian National University.

Harrison, Simon. 1982. *Laments for Foiled Marriages: Love-songs from a Sepik River Village.* Boroko: Institute of Papua New Guinea Studies.

Hooley, Bruce A. 1987. "Central Buang Poetry." In *Perspectives on Language and Text: Essays and Poems in Honour of Francis I. Andersen's Sixtieth Birthday*, edited by Edgar W. Conrad and Edward G. Newing, 71–88. Winona Lake, Indiana: Eisenbrauns.

Ingemann, Frances. 1968. "The Linguistic Structure of an Ipili-Paiyala Song Type." 6 pp. Paper presented at the 8th International Congress of Anthropological and Ethnological Sciences, Tokyo.

———. 1987. [Cassette of Ipili music with notes]. IPNGS x87-096. Music Archive, Institute of Papua New Guinea Studies.

Jakobson, Roman. 1960. "Closing Statement: Linguistics and Poetics." In *Style in Language*, edited by Thomas A. Sebeok, 350–77. Cambridge, MA: Massachusetts Institute of Technology Press.

Kaeppler, Adrienne L., and J. W. Love, eds. 1998. *Australia and the Pacific Islands*. The Garland Encyclopedia of World Music, 9. New York: Garland Publishing.

Kasaipwalova, John. 1978. *Yaulabuta, Kolupa, deli Lekolekwa (Pilatolu Kilivila Wosimwaya)*. Port Moresby: Institute of Papua New Guinea Studies.

Kasaipwalova, John, and Ulli Beier. 1978a. *Lekolekwa: An Historical Song from the Trobriand Islands*. Port Moresby: Institute of Papua New Guinea Studies.

———. 1978b. *Yaulabuta: The Passion of Chief Kailaga; An Historical Poem from the Trobriand Islands*. Port Moresby: Institute of Papua New Guinea Studies.

———. 1979. "Exile: An Historical Poem from the Trobriand Islands." *Gigibori* 4 (2) (August): 47–48.

Kelley, Linda Harvey. 1984. "Totopo—Tenth Wife." *Bikmaus* 5 (4) (December): 21–87 (revised as: *Toropo: Tenth Wife*. Port Melbourne: Rigby Heinemann, 1995).

Lacey, Roderic. 1975. "Oral Traditions as History: An Exploration of Oral Sources among the Enga of the New Guinea Highlands." PhD dissertation, University of Wisconsin.

———. 1979. "Heroes, Journeys and Change: Themes in Precolonial Religious Life in Papua New Guinea." In *Powers, Plumes and Piglets: Phenomena of Melanesian Religion*, edited by Norman C. Habel, 194–209, 220–21. Bedford Park: Australian Association for the Study of Religions.

Landtman, Gunnar. 1913. "The Poetry of the Kiwai Papuans." *Folklore* 24: 284–313.

Lang, Adrianne. 1973. *Enga Dictionary with English Index*. Pacific Linguistics, C 20. Canberra: Australian National University.

Lepi, Pundia, and Nancy Bowers. 1983. "Kaugel Stories: *Temane* and *Kangi*." *Oral History* 11 (4): 1–145.

LeRoy, John. 1985. *Kewa Tales*. Vancouver: University of British Columbia Press.

Lewis, Neryl. 2007. "Conflict Vulnerability Assessment of the Southern Highlands Province." In *Conflict and Resource Development in the Southern Highlands of Papua New Guinea*, edited by Nicole Haley, 149–64. Canberra: ANU E Press.

Loeweke, Eunice, and Jean May. 1980. "General Grammar of Fasu (Namo Me)." *Workpapers in Papua New Guinea Languages* 27: 5–106.

Lomas, Gabe C. J. 1988. "The Huli Language of Papua New Guinea." PhD dissertation, Macquarie University. http://hdl.handle.net/1959.14/22313.

Love, J. W. 1998. "Views from the Continent." In *Australia and the Pacific Islands*, edited by Adrienne L. Kaeppler and J. W. Love, 34–42. The Garland Encyclopedia of World Music, 9. New York: Garland Publishing.

Love, J. W., and Adrienne L. Kaeppler. 1998. "The Analysis of Speech in Musical Contexts." In *Australia and the Pacific Islands*, edited by Adrienne L. Kaeppler and J. W. Love, 321–22. The Garland Encyclopedia of World Music, 9. New York: Garland Publishing.

May, Jean, and Eunice Loeweke. 1981. *Fasu (Námo Mē)–English dictionary*. Ukarumpa: Summer Institute of Linguistics.

Mel, Michael A. 2005. "The Need for Strong and Balanced Communities through Education: *Kang Rom* (Story-telling) as a Way of Building Communities in PNG." 11 pp. Paper presented at the 2005 National Curriculum Reform Conference, 13–15 July 2005.

Merlan, Francesca. 1995. "Indigenous Narrative Genres in the Western Highlands of Papua New Guinea." In *Proceedings of the Second Annual Symposium about Language and Society, Austin*, edited by Pamela Silberman and Jonathan Loftin, 87–98. Texas Linguistic Forum, 34. Austin: University of Texas.

Merlan, Francesca, and Alan Rumsey. 1991. *Ku Waru: Language and Segmentary Politics in the Western Nebilyer Valley, Papua New Guinea*. Studies in the Social and Cultural Foundations of Language, 10. Cambridge: Cambridge University Press.

Modjeska, Charles J. Nicholas. 1977. "Production among the Duna: Aspects of Horticultural Intensification in Central New Guinea." PhD dissertation, Australian National University.

Niles, Don. 2007. "Sonic Structure in *Tom Yaya Kange*: Ku Waru Sung narratives from Papua New Guinea." In *Oceanic Music Encounters—the Print Resource and the Human Resource: Essays in Honour of Mervyn McLean*, edited by Richard Moyle, 109–22. Research in Anthropology and Linguistics Monograph, 7. Auckland: University of Auckland.

———. 2009. "Encapsulations of Indigenous Knowledge: Chanted Tales from the Papua New Guinea Highlands." In *Reframing Indigenous Knowledge: Cultural Knowledge and Practices in Papua New Guinea*, edited by Steven Edmund Winduo, 122–29. Waigani: Melanesian and Pacific Studies.

Niles, Don, and Michael Webb. 1987. *Papua New Guinea Music Collection*. Eleven cassettes and book. Boroko: Institute of Papua New Guinea Studies. IPNGS 008.

Paia, Robert, and Andrew Strathern. 1977. *Beneath the Andaiya Tree: Wiru Songs*. Boroko: Institute of Papua New Guinea Studies.

Pawley, Andrew. 2005. "The Chequered Career of the Trans New Guinea Hypothesis: Recent Research and Its Implications." In *Papuan Pasts: Cultural, Linguistic and Biological Histories of Papuan-Speaking Peoples*, ed. Andrew Pawley, Robert Attenborough, Jack Golson, and Robin Hide, 67–107. Pacific Linguistics, 572. Canberra: Australian National University.

Pugh, Jacqueline. 1975. "Communication, Language and Huli Music: A Preliminary Survey." Honours thesis, BA with Honours, Monash University, Melbourne.

Pugh-Kitingan, Jacqueline. 1981. "An Ethnomusicological Study of the Huli of the Southern Highlands, Papua New Guinea." PhD dissertation, University of Queensland.

———. 1984. "Speech-tone Realisation in Huli Music." In *Problems and Solutions: Occasional Essays in Musicology Presented to Alice M. Moyle*, edited by Jamie Kassler and Jill Stubington, 94–120. Sydney: Hale and Iremonger.

————. 1998. "Highland Region of Papua New Guinea: Southern Highlands Province: Huli." In *Australia and the Pacific Islands*, edited by Adrienne L. Kaeppler and J. W. Love, 536–43. The Garland World Encyclopedia of Music, 9. Washington: Garland Publishing.

Reichl, Karl. 2000. "Introduction: The Music and Performance of Oral Epics." In *The Oral Epic: Performance and Music*, edited by Karl Reichl, 1–40. Wilhelmshaven: Verlag für Wissenschaft und Bildung. Intercultural Music Studies, 12.

Reithofer, Hans. 2005. [Recordings and documentation of Karinj music and stories]. 2 compact discs. Music Archive, Institute of Papua New Guinea Studies. IPNGS x05-005.

————. 2006. *The Python Spirit and the Cross: Becoming Christian in a Highland Community of Papua New Guinea*. Göttinger Studien zur Ethnologie, 16. Münster: LIT Verlag.

Ross, Malcolm. 2005. "Pronouns as a Preliminary Diagnostic for Grouping Papuan Languages." In *Papuan Pasts: Cultural, Linguistic and Biological Histories of Papuan-Speaking Peoples*, ed. Andrew Pawley, Robert Attenborough, Jack Golson, and Robin Hide, 15–65. Pacific Linguistics, 572. Canberra: Australian National University.

Rumsey, Alan. 1995. "Pairing and Parallelism in the New Guinea Highlands." In *SALSA II: Proceedings of the Second Annual Symposium about Language and Society, Austin*, edited by Pamela Silberman and Jonathan Loftin, 108–18. Texas Linguistic Forum, 34. Austin: University of Texas.

————. 2001. "*Tom Yaya Kange*: A Metrical Narrative Genre from the New Guinea Highlands." *Journal of Linguistic Anthropology* 11 (2): 193–239.

————. 2002. "Aspects of Ku Waru Ethnosyntax and Social Life." In *Ethnosyntax: Explorations in Grammar and Culture*, edited by Nicolas J. Enfield, 259–86. Oxford: Oxford University Press.

————. 2005. "Chanted Tales in the New Guinea Highlands of Today: A Comparative Study." In *Expressive Genres and Historical Change: Indonesia, Papua New Guinea, and Taiwan*, edited by Pamela J. Stewart and Andrew Strathern, 41–81. Anthropology and Cultural History in Asia and the Indo-Pacific. Hants: Ashgate Publishing.

————. 2006a. "The Articulation of Indigenous and Exogenous Orders in Highland New Guinea and Beyond." *The Australian Journal of Anthropology* 17 (1): 47–69.

————. 2006b. "Verbal Art, Politics, and Personal Style in Highland New Guinea and Beyond." In *Language, Culture and the Individual: A Tribute to Paul Friedrich*, edited by Catherine O'Neil, Mary Scoggin, and Kevin Tuite, 319–46. Munich: Lincom.

————. 2007. "Musical, Poetic and Linguistic Form in *Tom Yaya* Sung Narratives from Papua New Guinea." *Anthropological Linguistics* 49: 237–82.

———— 2010. "A Metrical System that Defies Description by Ordinary Means." In *A Journey through Austronesian and Papuan Linguistic and Cultural Space: Papers in Honour of Andrew K. Pawley*, edited by John Bowden and Nikolaus Himmelmann, 39–56. Pacific Linguistics, 615. Canberra: Pacific Linguistics.

Sollis, Michael. 2006. "Tonal Variation amongst Chanted Tales of Papua New Guinea." Undergraduate research paper, Department of Anthropology and Archaeology, and Research School of Pacific and Asian Studies, Australian National University. 53 pp.

————2010. "Tune-tone Relationships in Sung Duna *Pikono*." *Australian Journal of Linguistics* 30: 67–80.

Spearritt, Gordon, and Jürg Wassmann. 1996. "Myth and Music in a Middle Sepik village." *Kulele: Occasional Papers on Pacific Music and Dance* 2: 59–84.

Stewart, Pamela J., and Andrew Strathern. 1999. "Female Spirit Cults as a Window on Gender Relations in the Highlands of Papua New Guinea." *Journal of the Royal Anthropological Institute* 5: 345–60.

————. 2000a. "Naming Places: Duna Evocations of Landscape in Papua New Guinea." *People and Culture in Oceania* 16: 87–107.

————. 2000b. *Speaking for Life and Death: Warfare and Compensation among the Duna of Papua New Guinea*. Senri Ethnological Reports, 13. Osaka: National Museum of Ethnology.

————. 2002a. *Gender, Song and Sensibility: Folksongs and Folktales in the Highlands of New Guinea*. Westport, CT: Praeger.

————. 2002b. *Remaking the World: Myth, Mining and Ritual Change among the Duna of Papua New Guinea*. Smithsonian Series in Ethnographic Inquiry. Washington, DC: Smithsonian Institution Press.

————. 2005. "Duna *Pikono*: A Popular Contemporary Genre in the Papua New Guinea Highlands." In *Expressive Genres and Historical Change: Indonesia,*

Papua New Guinea and Taiwan, edited by Pamela J. Stewart and Andrew Strathern, 83–107. Anthropology and Cultural History in Asia and the Indo-Pacific Series. Hants: Ashgate.

Strathern, Andrew. 1971. *The Rope of Moka: Big-men and Ceremonial Exchange in Mount Hagen, New Guinea*. Cambridge Studies in Social Anthropology, 4. Cambridge: Cambridge University Press. (re-issued with corrections and new preface, 2007.)

———. 1983. "The Melpa." Radio programme script prepared for the National Broadcasting Commission. 4 pp.

———. 1995. "Chant and Spell: Sonemic Contrasts in a Melpa Ritual Sequence." *Ethnomusicology* 39 (2) (Spring/Summer): 219–27.

———. 1998. "Highland Region of Papua New Guinea: Western Highlands Province: Melpa." In *Australia and the Pacific Islands*, edited by Adrienne L. Kaeppler and J. W. Love, 516–22. The Garland Encyclopedia of World Music, 9. New York: Garland Publishing.

Strathern Andrew, and Pamela J. Stewart. 1997. *Ballads as Popular Performance Art in Papua New Guinea and Scotland.* Centre for Pacific Studies Discussion Papers Series, 2. Townsville: James Cook University of North Queensland.

———. 2000. "Melpa Ballads as Popular Performance Art." In *Papers from Ivilikou: Papua New Guinea Music Conference and Festival (1997)*, edited by Don Niles and Denis Crowdy, 76–84. With one cassette. Boroko: Institute of Papua New Guinea Studies and University of Papua New Guinea.

———. 2004. *Empowering the Past, Confronting the Future: The Duna People of Papua New Guinea*. Contemporary Anthropology of Religion Series. New York: Palgrave Macmillan.

———. 2005a. "Introduction." In *Expressive Genres and Historical Change: Indonesia, Papua New Guinea and Taiwan*, edited by Pamela J. Stewart and Andrew Strathern, 1–39. Anthropology and Cultural History in Asia and the Indo-Pacific. Hants: Ashgate Publishing.

———. 2005b. "Melpa Songs and Ballads: Junctures of Sympathy and Desire in Mount Hagen, Papua New Guinea." In *Expressive Genres and Historical Change: Indonesia, Papua New Guinea and Taiwan*, edited by Pamela J. Stewart and Andrew Strathern, 201–33. Anthropology and Cultural History in Asia and the Indo-Pacific. Hants: Ashgate Publishing.

Talyaga, Kundapen. 1973. *Enga Eda Nemago: Meri Singsing Poetry of the Yandapo Engas*. Papua Pocket Poets, 40. Port Moresby: [n.p.].

Voorhoeve, C. L. 1975. "Central and Western Trans-New Guinea Phylum Languages." In *New Guinea Area Languages and Language Study, Vol. 1:Papuan Languages and the New Guinea Linguistic Scene*, edited by Stephen A. Wurm, 345–459. Pacific Linguistics, C 38. Canberra: Australian National University.

———. 1977. "Ta-poman: Metaphorical Use of Words and Poetic Vocabulary in Asmat Songs." In *New Guinea Area Languages and Language Study, Vol. 3: Language, Culture, Society and the Modern World*, edited by Stephen A. Wurm, 19–38. Pacific Linguistics, C 40. Canberra: Australian National University.

Wassmann, Jürg. 1991. *The Song to the Flying Fox: The Public and Esoteric Knowledge of the Important Men of Kandingei about Totemic Songs, Names and Knotted Cords (Middle Sepik, Papua New Guinea)*. Translated by Dennis Q. Stephenson. Apwitihire: Studies in Papua New Guinea Musics, 2. Boroko: National Research Institute.

Wiessner, Polly, and Akii Tumu. 1998. *Historical Vines: Enga Networks of Exchange, Ritual, and Warfare in Papua New Guinea*. Smithsonian Series in Ethnographic Inquiry. Bathurst: Crawford House Publishing.

2. Yuna *Pikono*

Kenny Yuwi Kendoli

Preface

Kenny Yuwi Kendoli is a Yuna[1] man, born at Hayuwi in the Aluni area, Southern Highlands Province. His primary place of residence at the time this chapter was written was Hirane in the Kopiago area. Kenny has more than a decade of experience working with researchers in the disciplines of anthropology, ethnomusicology, and linguistics. He has worked closely on the recording, transcription, and translation of several *pikono* performances and, along with the late Richard Alo, has contributed extensively to ongoing examination and discussion of *pikono* as a genre. He has also attended numerous *pikono* performances as an audience member.

In this chapter, Kenny outlines the place of *pikono* within Yuna culture, and describes some distinctive content and performance characteristics of the genre. He comments on the experience of being an audience member and suggests some criteria for evaluating the skills of a *pikono* performer. He reflects on change and continuity in *pikono* practice, and outlines views concerning the future of the genre.[2]

This chapter is based on Kenny's spoken words from an interview with Lila San Roque, conducted mostly in Tok Pisin. Kenny then assisted with the translation into English, provided additional clarification concerning some issues discussed in the interview, and approved the editing and arrangement of the text. The original interview is reproduced in full in the online supplementary material to this volume (online item 1).

Introduction: *Pikono* was really at the source of things

In the past, *pikono* was really at the source of things. The older men would sit at the men's house and perform *pikono*. As the *pikono* was going on, they would

---

1   Kenny indicated that he preferred that the indigenous term "Yuna," rather than the term "Duna" (as is conventional in written English material), be used throughout this chapter.
2   Questions asked in this interview were based on a list compiled by Kirsty Gillespie, Nicole Haley, and Lila San Roque, drawing upon their individual research; various discussions concerning *pikono* with Richard Alo, Kenny Kendoli, and Petros Kilapa; and topics raised during the 2006 Chanted Tales Workshop (Goroka).

think about killing pigs, looking after pigs, making gardens, and going to war. These things are the real source of the older men sitting in the men's house and performing *pikono*.

Previously, women, girls, and younger boys didn't listen to *pikono*. It belonged to men and the bachelor-cult boys. Sometimes, a few of the ones who lived in the bachelor cult, preparing the food, and transmitting the practices, knew *pikono* and the way it is performed. They would gather the young bachelor boys to sit down together and listen. I haven't done this myself, but that's what people say they used to do.

There are two kinds of stories. One is *pikono*, another is what is called *hapia po* 'before story' [events of previous times]. Children and women tell these stories. They are *hapia po*. *Pikono* stories are really of earlier times and practices; they describe battles, pig-killing, and so on. When *pikono* stories are performed, these *pikono* boys are described building houses or making gardens. The next morning the audience members will remember this and think about it—right, I'll do it, I'll do the same things. So when they go to make a garden or kill a pig, the work will go well.

They will follow the *pikono* boy's example. They remember the story they have heard—oh, this young man, he made a garden, he was eager to work—so they will finish the garden in two or three days. And it's the same for tending pigs, killing pigs, and for going to war as well. The day before a battle, they tell traditional stories and, going to war the next day, they'll feel reckless and brave, and they will fight. He has taken courage the previous night, so he will fight. If he has been tending pigs, looking after pigs until he has a great many, and if he has many gardens, now he will think about taking two or three or four wives, too.

Content: Stories begin in the lowlands

In the stories it's not usual to describe things happening in mid-altitude areas [i.e., areas of current domestic settlement]. Sometimes people describe lowland places, they start there and come up to mid-altitude areas. All the stories begin in the lowlands. Then they come up to the mountains, to the colder high-altitude zone, and this is how the story will continue. It can't start in the mountains and travel downwards; this would be wrong. At the end of all the stories as well, they will travel around this place and that place, and then return to the lowlands again for the final place at the end of the story.

The way a *pikono* story goes is that a young man, for example Yeripi Pake or Sayanda Sayape, will make a garden, live within the bachelor-cult precinct, travel and fight, go up to the mountains where nut pandanus grows, travel back, kill pigs and tend pigs, marry, and finish up in the lowlands.

Sometimes the places in the *pikono* story are not real places, but the *pikono* teller will describe *pikono* places in the story. Sometimes real places, for example up in the mountains, will be put in the story too. Sometimes, when they are counting the mountains and the waterways, the high mountain areas will be named in the story, and sometimes lowland areas will be named.

There are particular special birds, trees, and nut pandanus [that can be referenced in *pikono*]. Fruit pandanus cannot be included in the story. If the performer includes fruit pandanus in the story, you will know this is not genuine *pikono*. But nut pandanus will be included. There are special kinds of nut pandanus, trees, and birds too. Rushes and grasses will be included, as will casuarina trees, particular special trees. Waterways too will be included, but not all waterways will be named. The large waterways of the lands of the cannibals will be included, for example *ipa rouya* [Rouya River].

The borders—the waterways and mountains—between the *pikono* people and the cannibal giants will be included because they mark the boundary of the two groups. The *pikono* people and the cannibal giants are enemies so they don't live together. However the *pikono* boys fight amongst each other as well. But later when they want to fight the cannibal giants, they will join together. They have their own enemies. They fight between themselves, but when they want to fight with the cannibal giants they become allies.

[Meeting beautiful women, fighting cannibals, and so on] are all things from *pikono* stories. In *hapia po* stories, things get cut short; for example, when older women or mothers are trying to get their children to sleep, they'll tell a story but not a very long one, maybe just five or ten minutes. This isn't *pikono*, this is just *hapia po*. A detailed description of a beautiful woman or a battle and suchlike only occurs in *pikono*.

In *hapia po* stories as well, these things are included: oh, there was a lovely young woman, she saw smoke rising in the distance and followed it. This kind of thing will happen in *hapia po*, but it will be brief, lasting maybe four or five minutes, until the children have gone to sleep.

Pikono stories are not for describing real events. They are an inspiration to make gardens, kill pigs, go to war. If you just told them in ordinary speech, it would just go for an hour or so and be over. If you didn't include counting the mountains and waterways and so on, it would only last about an hour. However, when you keep going, counting all the waterways and so on, it will last a long time.

Skill and delivery: Their own way of performing

During a *pikono* performance, people don't speak as in ordinary conversation. The performer will change [his style of delivery], it is like singing, but the melody and voice are different. For singing songs, [the voice or melody] is high. The Adam's apple [vibrates] (hums some notes). This is how it goes. Now it is like this, the way that women mourn. Mourning is another kind of musical performance. It [*pikono*] is similar to mourning songs, but mourning songs are only short. In *pikono* the performer will keep counting waterways and mountains, going on and on, then have a rest to smoke and eat. Then they start again, and after one or two hours, counting the names throughout this time, they will rest again to drink or smoke. But their performance is different and something special, because we others are not able to follow it easily ourselves or sing along.

It's a difficult thing. We others will forget things, mountain places, waterways, counting all the names is too hard for us. They have their own special way of performing, whereas our speech is ordinary. It is hard for us to count [the landscape features] and this sort of thing. With an experienced *pikono* performer, some of the older men who were alive in the old days would also find it hard to follow the counting of the waterways and mountains and so on.

[A performer's knowledge and skill] is something out of the ordinary. We say, hey, what kind of a mind does he have? How many boxes of things does he have inside there? We say, what, does he have a little machine inside his head to play cassette tapes or something? We really say that.

[For describing landscape features] the performers will use praise names. For example, if they are talking about Horaile [a place], they won't say "a Horaile man once lived" or "the sun's going down over Horaile." They won't say the name Horaile. You'll hear something like *heka ayuka* and you will realize, ah, he's going to Horaile now. For Karuka too, it's the same; Aluni too, it's the same; Hirane too, it's the same. They won't say Hirane and so on. They will say things like *awi yungu wanetia, yopo, yeke, akura, pakura*, and you'll realize, oh, he's arrived at Hirane, hasn't he?

They [the performers] use praise names for things like wild pig and cassowary. They won't use the real names in the *pikono*. They won't say *ukura* [cassowary], "there was one *ukura*," or this sort of thing. They won't say, "I want to kill a *khawua* [wild pig]," no. It's not possible to use these words. These are heavy on the tongue, and the performers are reluctant to use them because people will think this is not a genuine story. They will only use praise names. The rule is that you can't use real names. In the past our ancestors said this and so people follow this practice.

The sound of them [praise names] is enjoyable. If you use a word like *khawua* [wild pig], well there is only a single word to be said, if you use *ukura* [cassowary], it's just a single word. This is flavourless. So they don't use these in the story. They use praise names, for example, *rakali antia, rekeya antia* [praise names for wild game] and these will be more flavoursome. So the audience will be pleased.

This is real *pikono*. If it's a *hapia po* story, then you'll just sit down normally and talk in the normal way. Then you'll know it's a *hapia po* story or just some kind of narrative, for example, something that happened last year or whatever.

Response and evaluation: They told this story and I listened

[I first heard *pikono*] when I finished grade 6 in 1980. This was in Aluni. They were doing this at the men's house. They were having a men's pig-killing, a *reke ita*, and I went there with my father. They told this story and I listened. I thought it was just some story or whatever, and I fell fast asleep. Everyone kept on calling out, sitting there for ages, and I thought, what kind of story is this that they're telling? Now I realize that this was *pikono*.

I was a child, I had just finished grade 6 and I didn't enjoy the story because it was hard for me to understand. How did it begin and how did it end, they were counting the mountains and waterways, and I thought, they're up to something, all the men keep calling out! This was in 1980, around December.

I heard *pikono* at other times and became more interested. After I became a married man, I would hear that *pikono* performers were coming. They would stay at my house and say that they wanted to perform *pikono*. From these times I understood more and more, and now it's all clear to me. Now I am keen for *pikono* performers to come to my house, and I am interested to listen.

It's like watching a film or something like that. If you've seen John Commander and Chuck Norris films, when you hear a *pikono* story you'll think about them again. Hearing about the battles, you'll think, ah Yeripi Pake [a *pikono* hero] must be like Chuck Norris or Mel Gibson, able to defeat so many enemies although he is only one.

With some *pikono* performers, the stories themselves are the same, but some performers don't count the mountains and rivers and locations step by step in sequence. They jump over to here, then over to there, come back, go this way, come back again, and this is not so good to listen to. If the start goes this way, the finish comes this way. Okay so starting from here again, counting the mountains and waterways, here in Hirane, naming the places of Hirane itself, then naming the places of Hagini [area contiguous to Hirane], if it's like this, this will be so flavoursome and you'll be riveted, you won't feel sleepy. If you skip Hagini and come back to Hirane and go to Suwaka [non-contiguous area] then go back to Hirane again, this is confusing and makes it hard to stay interested. Also, if their voices go very low, it can be hard to understand, or if their pronunciation is strange or unclear, the story is hard to understand.

[Some currently renowned performers are] Kiale, Kiliya, Alipulu, Teya, and Teya's brother Samson. Teya's brother Samson speaks Bogaia, Yuna, English, Tok Pisin, and Hewa. He can perform in all of these. He has only schooled to grade 10, but he can perform *pikono* in five languages.

I have three *pikono* favourites. One is a *pikono* man named Urungawe Pukani, in a performance by Kiliya; another is Amina Kelo, in a performance by Luke Ranga from Yokona. Amina Kela is a dog looked after by Yeripi Pake that transforms into a water spirit at night and goes hunting. In the morning Yeripi Pake can't understand where the game has come from. I only heard this story recently, and it is an extremely interesting story.

They're favourites of mine. I really like them and these two are the ones that I particularly enjoy. Another one is Yeripi Pake. There are a lot of stories about Yeripi Pake, but one story is that a woman took him to the cannibal areas to fight. This was a story told by Teya. The woman had the power to turn light to darkness and make herself and Yeripi Pake invisible. The cannibals could hear the twang of Yeripi Pake's bowstring as he shot them, but they couldn't see him anywhere. And she fought as well, stabbing the cannibals with her long fingernails. In this story the two of them climb up into the top of a pine tree and go to the land of the cannibals. The cannibals had killed Yeripi Pake's brother and carried him off. So they went to fight them there. The woman Ula Rendeyame went with Yeripi Pake to battle there. These three stories are my favourites.

I really like to hear about the dance celebrations and ceremonies in *pikono*, and living at the bachelor cult and killing pigs. I am extremely interested to hear about when the *pikono* boys go and fight with the cannibals. I'm always really excited to hear about this because the cannibals get the *pikono* boys and then I get quite furious sitting there. [When we hear about the cannibals killing a *pikono* boy] everyone gets really angry. Everyone [in the audience] will call out, for example, when they hear about a young woman, *heee!* Everyone will call out because they're excited to hear the woman's voice. The *pikono* tellers change their voices to pretend that it is actually the woman talking. At this point everyone will call out.

[Listening to *pikono*] we think, oh, this place that he is in now is the lowland plains. At this time, when they are in the lowlands, I will remember the Strickland

Gorge and areas like this [where KK himself has travelled extensively], ah, now they are there. When they go up to the mountains, we will think, aah, now they must be in a place like that, a different place, and remember [mountain places we have been to ourselves].

Suppose you have four or three brothers and one of them has died in a fight, or suppose a baby sibling was lost, left hanging alone in its netbag cradle when the parents were taken. When this sort of thing happens in a story—for example, if a pair of brothers goes to fight and one dies—I will remember my own brother who died in a fight. Or if the *pikono* boy is orphaned and alone in the forest, I will remember my brother who was lost as an infant. Or if my mother has died, when the mother [in the story] is killed and carried off, I will think about how my own mother died or something like that, I will think about it again. All these sorts of things arise. Or if [someone in the *pikono*] dies by the coast or far away, he will think again about his own brother who died in Port Moresby or Mt. Hagen or Lae, he will be reminded again. It comes out of one's memory.

Continuity and change: *Pikono* must stay with us

Some others and I have the opinion that *pikono* must stay with us. It is the practice of our ancestors. We can't lose it. I think that if we hang onto it, that is better.

For example, a *pikono* now inspires garden-making. It does not inspire trouble. If we are working the gardens, looking after pigs, and settled at home, if trouble comes our way, well, we know that the *pikono* boys went to fight when it was called for. So we will fight. If we're just living quietly, okay we'll live quietly. If people speak of attending the bachelor cult, and if it existed, we could go there to learn about life, it would teach the younger children how to behave and grow up well. Now we realize that the bachelor cult is a little bit like church. All children, mothers, men, and women must attend church. The missionaries can look after them there. If we could hang onto both the bachelor cult and church together, things would be peaceful and without trouble. But this is difficult now, because the men who knew about the bachelor cult are all passing away.

[The early missionaries] said that exchange practices, the bachelor cult, and the practice of killing pigs, cooking them, and making offerings to the *ipa ane* water spirits, they said these things are of Satan, leave them. Everyone thought this was true and they abandoned these practices. People like me, living now, we think that *pikono* and the bachelor-cult practices were good things, but they are lost.

The first missionaries forbade *pikono*. Earlier on, they forbade it. A few men who didn't join the mission would do these things secretly. Now everyone, including Christians, is interested to listen to *pikono*.

In my area, Aluni, people still talk about [earlier *pikono* performers, such as,] Kiliya's father Hipuya, Welia from Nawua, and Mbakali Raka. People still remember them now. They say, these families were the ones to do really excellent *pikono*. People say now that Kiliya is taking the place of his father, Hipuya. People say that Teya and Samson's father before them used to do traditional stories, but not so well. Now, people say that the *pikono* that the two [brothers] do is excellent. Kiale's father used to do the traditional stories, and people say that Kiale is taking the place of his father.

Pikono has not changed significantly from earlier times. One small change is that performers now include places like Port Moresby, Rabaul, and Buka when they are counting places and so on. Before, our ancestors did not count these places. Then people started going to Port Moresby and returning, or going to Buka or Rabaul and other coastal places and coming home. At this time people started to include them in the counting, they heard the travellers' descriptions and included these places.

A few changes and replacements have arisen, but we can hear now that things are correct, it is done rightly. They don't skip places or make mistakes in counting the mountains or waterways of the coastal areas. They include all of the places from this place at the origin, travelling all the way to the end. [The way the stories go] is true to the past. Talking about bombs [in the battle scenes] and so on are just trivial changes.

I think that [we will keep doing *pikono*]. Now, people like me and others are really interested in hearing *pikono*, so I think we won't lose it. We will keep it going, keep beginning.

[Having research done] is quite good. We can describe it now and later, when my children are grown, they will see the books if we have a copy. The kids can follow it and say, oh, so this is someone who did *pikono* is it? We should look for this. The knowledge and memories we have or the tapes and so on that we have made can be kept, they can follow this. I think it's good that this is done.

Something else that we have been thinking about is to make a film acting out the *pikono*. We could do the action of the *pikono* first and later the *pikono* tellers could sit down and tell the story. We've already thought about this. Act the *pikono* first and then explain to the storyteller, okay, this happens like this and like this, and finishes like this. Or, for example, you're sitting there, and then if you go to shoot a pig or fight with a man, the *pikono* teller will go to this location too. They can tell the story as a voiceover [while the others are doing the filmed action]. Many of the *pikono* tellers and other men want to do this. They are really interested in making a *pikono* film.

We're very interested in *pikono*, and I'm pleased to be doing this description now. It's good to produce the book as we didn't have this previously. Now if children or other Yuna people see this book, they will know what has been done and who did it.

3. Music and Language in Duna *Pikono*

Kirsty Gillespie and Lila San Roque

Introduction

The relationship between music and language has been a topic of scholarship for many years, across the academic world. In the Duna "sung story" genre of *pikono*, systems of music and language are interdependent and it is this relationship that our chapter explores.

In keeping with the topic of this volume, our discussion only relates to *pikono* that is sung. Sung *pikono* is considered by the Duna to be the height of the craft, and this is the mode of delivery for male performances. Women also create *pikono*, however the performance context and their delivery of *pikono* is much different. Men typically sing *pikono* to groups of men in men's houses at night (see Kendoli, this volume). Women, on the other hand, tell (rather than sing) *pikono* to other women or to children, often in their homes, as reported by Modjeska (1977:332). We have found that often the *pikono* told by women feature sections of sung text that most commonly illustrate a musical event of some kind, such as a courting song or a lament, which occurs within the story. Predominantly, however, women's *pikono* are in spoken form, and as such will not be discussed here.[1]

We focus on men's sung performance of *pikono*, but in particular we examine a performance of *pikono* by one man, Kiale Yokona, whom we met in March 2005 at Hirane parish[2] in the Kopiago area, where we were both conducting our doctoral research. Kiale arrived from the neighbouring parish of Mbara, and word quickly spread that he would be telling a *pikono* at the Hirane men's house that night. We dropped by the men's house briefly and, conforming to the gender rules governing the space, arranged for him to perform for us the next evening in another location. The result was a recording of a *pikono* of just under three

---

1 Another issue for further exploration concerns how the predominantly sung genre of *pikono* overlaps with the spoken genre of *hapia po*, and how these categories are defined and mobilized by different Duna individuals and communities.

2 The term "parish" was introduced to Melanesian anthropology by Hogbin and Wedgwood, who define it as "the largest local group forming a political unit," elaborating that "each parish, then, is composed of persons associated with a certain tract of land, bearing a distinctive name" (1953:243, 253). In using the term parish we follow other scholars of Duna culture, who in turn followed terminology used by Modjeska (Haley 2002:15). Parish divisions were present in pre-contact times, and are known in Duna as *rindi* ('land(s)'). See Modjeska (1977), Stürzenhofecker (1998), Haley (2002), and Strathern and Stewart (2004) for further information concerning Duna parish divisions and membership rights and responsibilities.

hours in length[3] made by Gillespie, which has been transcribed and translated in its entirety by San Roque and Kenny Kendoli, with assistance from Richard Alo. The portrait of Kiale shown in figure 1 was taken the day after this performance.

This *pikono* performance is used as a point of departure to discuss the structure of *pikono*, both musical and linguistic, and how it relates to other Duna genres. In particular, we point out the presence of repetition which comes about through the use of "praise name" sequences, the process of which is known in the Duna language as *ipakana yakaya* (see Haley 2002:6–10, 117–25; Stewart and Strathern 2005:87–88, 93; Gillespie 2010a, 2010b). We also explore the functions of identifiable parts of the Duna *pikono* structure, and discuss the audience responses that performances elicit.

Structural units within *pikono*

We begin with a description of what a typical *pikono* sounds like. The musical element under discussion here is melodic contour. The term "melody" will not be used, as *pikono* does not have a defined sequence of pitches that can be identified as constituting a melody, but rather, a defined sense of pitch shape and direction. As *pikono* is essentially a solo tradition, there is no form of harmony to be analysed. In addition, as is typical of most Duna ancestral genres, the genre is non-metred, and so neither will rhythm be discussed. The focus then is on pitch and its relationship to text.

Pikono can be broken down into units that we, for the purposes of this discussion, have called phrases, which generally consist of several lines.[4] Phrases and the lines therein are demarcated in terms of melodic contour, pauses, and textual structure. The final word in a phrase normally has a sustained final vowel, or has a vowel added to it (e.g., *o* or *e*). In Kiale's performance, this sung vowel often leads into a hum as Kiale closes his lips and maintains a voiced airflow for a few moments before taking a breath and beginning the next phrase. In his performance, a single phrase is typically ten to twenty seconds long, and rarely more than thirty seconds. Textually, it is not unusual for one *pikono* phrase to comprise what is basically a single sentence, with additional exclamations, repetitions, and narrative expressions.

---

3   There were three short breaks in this performance, the first two instigated by the performer and audience, the third to replace the battery in the recording device. The performance was thus recorded in four parts of varying lengths: (*a*) c. 30 min; (*b*) c. 1 hr 18 min; (*c*) c. 21 min; and (*d*) c. 39 min.

4   Unlike the general understanding of what constitutes a "phrase" in vocal studies, the unit here is not defined by breath.

Figure 1. Kiale Yokona at Hirane parish, March 2005 (photo by Kirsty Gillespie).

Each *pikono* phrase can be subdivided into two sections, the first we call the "descent," and the second we call the "ground." We have not encountered any indigenous terms that conventionally identify and label these sections.[5] Figure 2 shows the pitch trace of the *pikono* phrase that we discuss in detail in the following section, with line numbers corresponding to the text lines shown in text 1. The overlaid arrows schematically represent the characteristic pitch movement of the descent and ground sections of a typical phrase.

---

5   In her initial musical analyses of *pikono*, Gillespie gave these two sections the working labels "body" and "coda" respectively. However, these terms appear hierarchical, suggesting that the second section is not as significant as the first—almost peripheral to it—which is not the case. For that reason, these labels are no longer used.

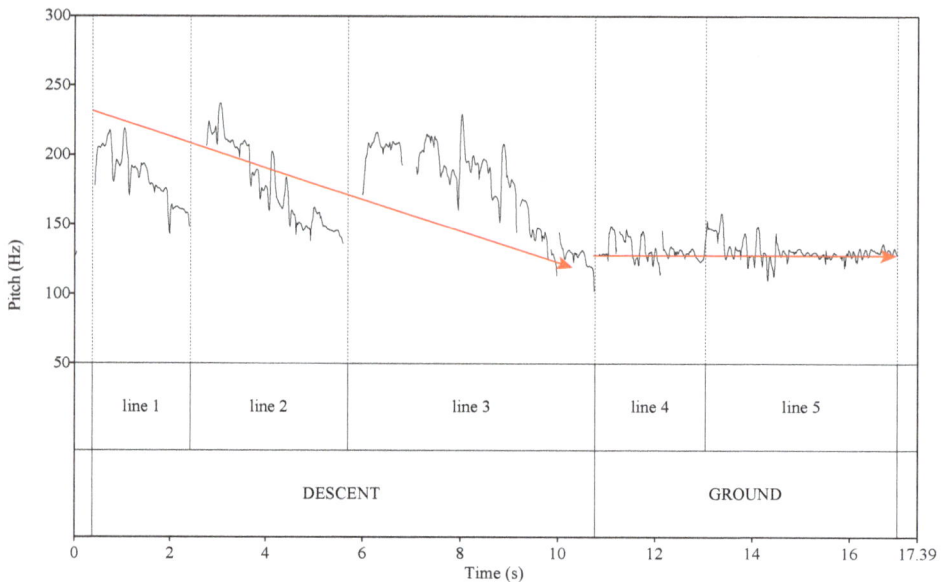

Figure 2. Pitch trace of the *pikono* phrase shown in text 1, showing the descent and ground sections (drawn using the program Praat).

The descent marks the beginning of the *pikono* phrase. It is named such for its melodic contour: generally it begins around a fifth or sixth above the tonal centre (sometimes more, as the *pikono* performance progresses) and gradually descends to that tonal centre, with some melodic diversions along the way. There is often a brief dip down to a tone just below this tonal centre and back again to mark the arrival of the ground section, as can be seen in figure 2. This descent is one of the most distinctive characteristics of the genre—as most Duna song genres exhibit a range of around two whole tones, *pikono* is the genre with the widest melodic range.[6]

The second section of the *pikono* phrase we have called "ground." This label is intended to reflect both the predominance of the tonal centre (the "foundation" of the melodic contour) and the focus on landscape features within the text that often occurs at this point. Beginning on the tonal centre (where the previous section concluded), this section is marked by repetition that focuses on the tonal centre, briefly visiting the tones on either side of it. In cipher notation, this pattern can be generally represented as 1 2 1 −2 1, where 1 is the tonal centre, 2 a step above it, and −2 a step below. Often tone 3 is also employed, and tone 2 is more often used than tone −2. Cipher notation, also used by Jacqueline Pugh-Kitingan in her description of song of the neighbouring Huli people (Pugh-Kitingan 1981),

---

6   This statement excludes genres that incorporate dance, such as *mali*, in which song text is punctuated by falsetto calls an octave above.

is helpful to describe the pitches employed in Duna *pikono*, as they are not based on a pre-existing scale or form of tuning, but rather on their relationship to each other (Chenoweth 1969).

While the melodic direction of the descent section can be generally anticipated, the descent of each *pikono* phrase is different. The ground section, however, presents a repeated and predictable melodic formula that occurs in other Duna genres, most notably in women's laments. Working in tandem with this, textual lines within the descent section are normally quite different from each other, with little repetition occurring from line to line. However the ground section is built around a repetitive textual frame (commonly modelled on the final line of the descent section), containing parallel iterations of specialized *kẽiyaka* vocabulary terms.

Duna *kẽiyaka* vocabulary is identified and discussed by Haley as "a special esoteric vocabulary of praise names and honorific forms" (Haley 2002:132). *Kẽiyaka* terms for a single item are often phonologically very similar to each other, differing with respect to a single phoneme or syllable. In *pikono* text, *kẽiyaka* terms can be used in a variety of ways, for example, replacing common vocabulary items in the descent section of a phrase or enriching the identity and history of characters in the narrative (see Kendoli, this volume). In the ground section of a *pikono* phrase, *kẽiyaka* occur as part of a sequence, in which several *kẽiyaka* terms for a single item (typically a landscape feature) are used in a conventional order (see also Strathern and Stewart, this volume). A *kẽiyaka* normally occurs within a framing phrase, and at each iteration of the frame a new *kẽiyaka* is substituted for the one preceding. This distinctive textual and melodic pattern is termed *ipakana yakaya*,[7] which has been described by Duna speakers as "counting rivers and mountains" (see Kendoli, this volume).

A *pikono* phrase close-up

Text 1 shows the text and English translation of a single *pikono* phrase from Kiale's performance. At this point in the story, one of the main female characters, Kundaleme, is trying to persuade one of the heroes, Kaloma Koli, to go on a journey with her to meet the spirit of his close companion, Sayanda Sayape (who has recently been killed by man-eating giants). She explains that Sayanda Sayape is going to appear to him, accompanied by a group of female spirits, and deliver an important message. We have divided the text into lines according to a combination of features, including breath breaks, grammatical units, and melodic contour. *Kẽiyaka* terms are underlined in the Duna text and appear in

---

7   An alternative earlier spelling of this is *ipakana yakaiya* (as used in Haley 2002).

italics in the English translation, as do exclamations and narrative markers.[8] Text in curly brackets shows spoken audience responses, a topic that will be returned to later in this chapter.

Text 1. Text and translation of a single phrase from Kiale's performance. An audio file of this example can be found in online item 2.

hiwakuya kata yaritia	they are all coming out *it was heard*
ake yaritia sopa aipe ruwanania	*what then it was heard* who is below, he will speak
mm yaritia sayanda sayape yaritia etona	*mm it was heard* Sayanda Sayape *it was heard* across
<u>*pei popo*</u> *ndu sutia kena*	there you will see the *pei* Hewa *popo* feathers shake
<u>*palu pelei popo*</u> *ndu sutia kenania*	you will see the *palu pelei* Hewa *popo* feathers shake
<u>*yana ayano popo*</u> *ndu sutia kenania*	you will see the *yana ayano* Hewa *popo* feathers shake
{keno nganda!}	{we two will go!}
	(from recording by Kirsty Gillespie 2005:vol. 3.2, track 3, 0.27–0.44)

As can be seen in text 1, *kẽiyaka* vocabulary is introduced towards the end of the third line. The "framing" text here (<u>*popo*</u> *ndu sutia kena(nia)*) itself includes a *kẽiyaka* word, *popo*, which is a poetic term for a fluffy kind of cassowary feather. The cassowary feathers are further identified as coming from the (low altitude) Hewa area, one of the Duna's neighbouring language groups, and this is the place that is consecutively named in the ground section of this phrase. The *kẽiyaka* terms create some assonance with repetitions of certain sounds and sound sequences, for example *p*, *p–l–*, and *yan–*. Note also that the textual frame is not exactly replicated, as the morpheme *-nia*[9] is added to the verb *kena* ('will see') in the fourth and fifth lines, but not present in the third. It is in fact common practice for the framing text to differ slightly from line to line.

Figure 3 represents an approximation of the pitch contour of this phrase.

In figure 3, the descent section comprises the first two lines, whilst the ground section comprises the final line. The tonal centre is C; the descent begins approximately a sixth above this centre, descending by the end of the second line to the tonal centre, touching, as is typical, on the (semi)tone below this centre. The ground section then begins, reinforcing the tonal centre and the tone above it, D (these pitches can be represented in cipher notation as 1 and 2, respectively). This same pattern of low tones in a restricted range characterizes the melodic patterning of the *ipakana yakaya* process, and is particularly reminiscent of the Duna lament song genre *khene ipakana* (see Stürzenhofecker 1998:43–46; Stewart and Strathern 2000:92–94; Gillespie 2010a; 2010b:85–121; Kendoli, this volume).

---

8   As in the sung story genres of other language groups of the region, there are certain formulaic markers that recur in sung *pikono* texts and frame it as a narrative. Different performers use slightly different markers (or combinations of markers), although they all normally highlight the fact that this is a story that is being told now, about long-ago things that have been described before. In the performance under discussion, the marker Kiale uses most commonly is *yaritia*, which means roughly 'it was heard'.

9   This morpheme occurs after verbal inflection and emphasizes the speaker's conviction in the truth of their utterance.

Figure 3. Pitch contour of the phrase in text 1.

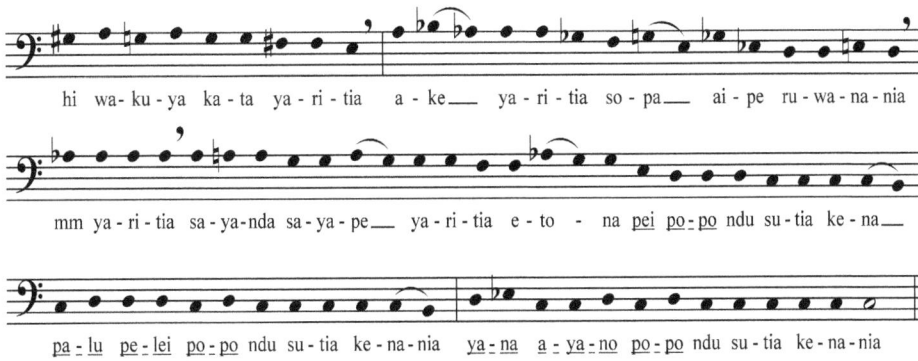

hi wa- ku - ya ka - ta ya - ri - tia   a - ke____ ya - ri - tia so - pa____   ai - pe ru - wa - na - nia

mm ya - ri - tia sa - ya - nda sa - ya - pe____ ya - ri - tia e - to - na pei po - po ndu su - tia ke - na____

pa - lu pe - lei po - po ndu su - tia ke - na - nia   ya - na   a - ya - no po - po ndu su - tia ke - na - nia

This example can be considered as a typical *pikono* phrase. In particular, note that the first *kẽiyaka* of the sequence appears at the end of the descent section as the singer approaches the tonal centre (and the ground section). The repetitions of alternative *kẽiyaka*, each set in a recurring textual phrase introduced with the first *kẽiyaka*, and featuring the melodic repetition of tones 1 and 2, are the formula of the ground section (see also Sollis, this volume, concerning melodic parallelism across the ground sections of adjacent *pikono* phrases).

Engaging with the narrative

We turn now to a consideration of *pikono* as narrative performance designed to create and maintain audience engagement, and provoke appreciative and heartfelt response (see also Strathern and Stewart, this volume, concerning pedagogic attributes of *pikono*). We reflect upon possible contrastive functions of the descent and ground sections of the *pikono* phrase in regard to this and argue here that they can be viewed as functionally distinct for much of the performance. The focus of the descent section is generally on narrative content, advancing the action of the story and maintaining a dynamic thread of events. The ground section encourages an expanded appreciation of imagery that attaches to these events, an increased absorption in the perceptual world of the characters, and perhaps cues an experience of the performance as something that is personally moving, evoking one's own memories and experiences.

It is generally true to say that each phrase in a *pikono* introduces a new item or activity, and advances a notch in the narrative. Throughout most of Kiale's *pikono* text, it is within the second and/or third lines of the descent that the plot or action of the story progresses. Since the ground section of the *pikono* is built around a repetitive sequence it cannot normally introduce new narrative content.

Looking at text 1, the first line is a recapitulation of the activity described in the preceding phrase; the first word *hiwaku-* ('all come out') repeats the verb that concluded the previous ground section.[10] Thus, the first line of the descent links the coming activity to what has just occurred. The second line of this phrase starts with a semantically fairly empty refrain *ake yaritia* (translated here as 'what then, it was heard') that Kiale uses many times in his performance, most frequently at the beginning of the second line of the descent, as seen here. The following question, *sopa aipe* 'who (is) below?', is also a stock phrase, signifying to the audience that we are about to hear the name of a character in the story and find out what he or she is up to. This motif only occurs in the descent section of *pikono* phrases, as this is where new characters are brought into the story or where a known character reappears in the narrative. In this case we hear (through the words of Kundaleme) that the spirit of Sayanda Sayape is going to communicate with Kaloma Koli, coming out dancing to meet him.

It can be seen from text 1 that "what happens next" is not necessarily transparently articulated, but may be implied or interpreted through a combination of conventional and/or story-specific associations, as well as a knowledge of *kẽiyaka* vocabulary. At the basic level of lexical recognition, a hearer needs to know (or deduce) the *kẽiyaka* for Hewa and for cassowary feathers. These terms are mutually re-enforcing and informative, as cassowaries are held to be numerous in the lowland Hewa area, and this collocation of "[Hewa *kẽiyaka*] *popo*" is additionally a recognizable trope in Kiale's performance. A listener further needs to make the association that Sayanda Sayape is adorned with cassowary feathers, which is suggested by cues earlier in the story and other recurring metaphors, as well as knowledge of the practice of body decoration generally (see also Sollis, this volume).

The image introduced in the descent and reiterated in the lines of the ground section is also potentially complex. The description of the feathers' movement evokes the dancing movement of Sayanda Sayape, but can also allude to the idea that he travels from the land of the dead on a swaying and shaking cane bridge. The *kẽiyaka* for feathers used here (*popo*) also references a more standard vocabulary item for gathering mist or cloud. The repetition of this line in the ground section perhaps allows time for a fuller comprehension and envisioning of both the narrative activity and rich poetic image that is described. Kaloma Koli's beloved friend will come back to him at last, suspended in a mist of trembling feathers.

It can be noted that the lines here specifically describe a *visual* image, presenting the movement of the feathers as a complement clause of the verb *kena* '(you)

---

10 This "tail-head linkage" (de Vries 2005)—i.e., the repetition of the preceding final verb to begin a new sentence—is a very common pattern in Duna narrative generally (see also Giles 1972).

will see'. These words are spoken in the story by Kundaleme to Kaloma Koli, but as there is no frame for this reported speech (e.g., '… she said') included in these lines,[11] it is possible to identify the "seer" as not only Kaloma Koli but also the audience members of the *pikono* performance, being spoken to by Kiale (see also Borchard and Gibbs, this volume).

This turning towards the personal witnessing of the image described may also be reflected in the semantics of grammatical markers that occur on final verbs. It is generally in the ground section, or the final transitional line of the descent, that we reach the final verb of the major sentence of the phrase. In ordinary spoken Duna, final verbs are commonly marked for the grammatical category of "evidentiality"; that is, they can encode the information source that the speaker has for their utterance (see, e.g., Chafe and Nicholls 1986, Aikhenvald 2004). The verbal marker *-tia*, for example, normally indicates that the speaker or hearer saw the event that is being described. In Duna narrative, the viewpoint of a main character can be conventionally adopted as the information source that is indicated. For example, in conversation a speaker typically uses *-tia* to mark a statement describing something that they have personally witnessed, but in telling a story they can use it to mark events that the main character witnesses in the course of the narrative (see San Roque 2008:309–18, 333, 377, 388, 430–35 for further discussion and examples).

The verbal markers used in *pikono*, particularly as they occur in the ground section, thus encourage the hearers to place themselves as direct perceivers of the events, absorbed in the world that is being sung. In contrast to this, the more explicitly narrative marker *yaritia* ('it was heard') as deployed by Kiale in this performance occurs frequently in the descent section, but is relatively rare in the ground section. At the commencement of a phrase and in presenting new narrative content, Kiale reminds the audience that it is a story they are listening to, but in the recurring imagery of the ground section, Kiale invites the audience to identify themselves as perceptual experiencers of the narrated phenomena rather than of a narrative performance.

The close resemblance in melodic and textual structure of the ground section of *pikono* with the Duna lament genre of *khene ipakana* highlights a potential for further emotional and personal engagement. Such engagement may include the identification of death and loss in the story with one's own experiences of bereavement (see Kendoli, this volume).

---

11 In conversational Duna and in most Duna narrative speech, it would be usual to express words spoken by another as complement clauses within bracketing forms of the (irregular) verb *ruwa-* ('say').

Sex and the moon

We have focused so far on phrases in which the descent section introduces new information to the story, and these make up the majority of Kiale's *pikono*. There are several occasions, however, in which a new phrase does not advance the plot, but in which the descent section closely mirrors that of the previous phrase as a particular image or theme is expanded and reiterated in new ways. This is most clearly the case in chains of phrases that describe the movement of light as day turns to night and/or night to day.

There are two such sequences in Kiale's performance, the first detailing the travelling of the setting sun (lasting approximately 3.5 minutes), the second describing the shifting light of the moon (lasting approximately 4.5 minutes) and then the spreading light of dawn the following day (lasting approximately 2.5 minutes). Both of these sequences begin immediately after a male and female heroine have been dancing together at a public event and are either about to start or have already started on an overnight journey.

In the phrases of these sections, descent sections are comparatively brief, while ground sections are typically extended. The introductory text of the descent is similar from phrase to phrase, providing some reference to the movement of the light or the astral body itself, while the ground section details the names of the places where the light falls, and commonly details an activity that becomes visible there.[12] The text of a phrase within one of these sequences in Kiale's performance is shown in text 2. At this point Kiale is describing the bright light of a full moon, falling upon unsuspecting young women in its path.

Text 2. Kiale's description of the full moon's bright light falling upon young women. An audio file of this example can be found in online item 3.

keya hoyaki iwakurane yaritia	looking to this side it sinks down closer *it was heard*
e yaritia <u>awi</u> hutia kia hini papa hani	*ah it was heard* these *awi* Hirane ones right here try to cover themselves with fern fronds
no yão reinia riya <u>etopi</u> hutia kia hini papa hanirane	I'm sitting with nothing on they cry, these *etopi* Hirane ones tried to cover themselves with fern fronds
{continuing comments}	
<u>kura</u> <u>akura</u> <u>pakura</u> <u>rilipi</u> <u>ramapu</u> *hutia kia hini papa hanirane koa*	these *kura* Hirane *akura* Hirane *pakura* Hirane *rilipa* Hirane *ramapu* Hirane ones tried to cover themselves with fern fronds
{indecipherable comment} *{ndu narayani}*	{there's not one [woman] here!}
	(from recording by Kirsty Gillespie 2005:vol. 3.2, track 3, 3.51–4.02)

---

12   This can be seen as a form of higher-level parallelism, in which the descent section provides framing text that is repeated in the descent of the following phrases, and the theme of the ground section remains fairly constant, with only the identity of the places changing significantly.

It can be noted that, rather than changing one *kẽiyaka* term within each line (as was seen in text 1), the final line of this phrase contains five *kẽiyaka* terms for Hirane parish listed one after the other. This is a common feature of phrases within the moon/sun sequences, in which up to seven separate *kẽiyaka* may be condensed into a single iteration of the framing text. This example also clearly shows cumulative sound repetition features, especially in the three adjacent terms *kura, akura, pakura*; this can also be described as a form of parallelism at the level of individual sounds, as *kura* remains constant while the first syllable of the word changes. Figure 4 represents an approximation of the pitch contour of the last two lines of this phrase.

Figure 4. Pitch contour of the last two lines of the phrase in text 2.

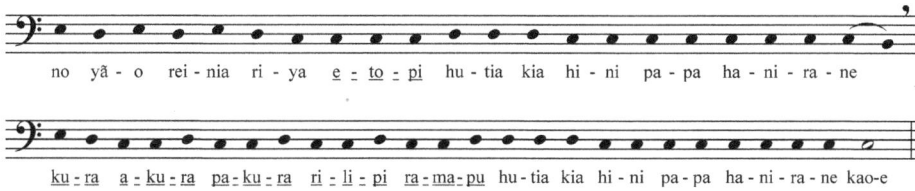

This example clearly shows melodic repetition which is typical of musical settings of *kẽiyaka.* Four of the five *kẽiyaka* in the sequence of the last line feature the exact same patterning. Whilst the first *kẽiyaka* of this sequence, *kura*, descends to the tonal centre over the tones 3 and 2, the next four *kẽiyaka*—each three syllables in length—are set to the pattern 1 1 2 (that is, two syllables on the tonal centre and then one a step above). It is also apparent that the textual setting for this *kẽiyaka* sequence and the line above it—*hutia kia hini papa hanirane*—are identical, with the first three syllables on the second tone (2) and the remainder on the tonal centre (1). Figure 5 shows figure 4 represented in cipher notation with the distinctive 1 1 2 pattern shown in bold type and underlined.

Figure 5. Pitch contour of figure 4, shown in cipher notation.

no yã-o rei-nia ri-ya e-to-pi hu-tia kia hi-ni pa-pa ha-ni ra-ne
3 2 32 3 21 111 2 22 111 11 111

ku-ra a-ku-ra pa-ku-ra ri-li-pa ra-ma-pu hu-tia kia hi-ni pa-pa ha-ni ra-ne koa
3 2 **1 1 2 1 1 2 1 1 2 1 1 2** 2 2 2 1 1 1 1 1 1 1 1

In the phrase exemplified, the light of the full moon reveals the nakedness of the Hirane women and in the following phrases goes on to shine upon female inhabitants of other areas along its path. Further, a suitable prelude to sexual intimacy was described in the narrative preceding this sequence as Kaloma Koli and Kundaleme danced together and set off planning to spend the night in each other's company. Thus, this extended moon/sun sequence can be interpreted as alluding to a potential for courting and sexual activity. Given this context, it is striking to observe the predominance of the tones 3 and 2 in an alternating pattern in this example: this exact pitch pattern, followed by a prolonged 1 with adjacent pitch 2, is the identifying melodic feature of the Duna courting genre *yekia*, also known as *laingwa* (see Stewart and Strathern 2002:77–87).[13] Kiale's use of melodic (and textual) structures that are characteristic of a performance genre specifically concerned with attracting a sexual partner perhaps strengthens the textual and thematic allusion to courting and sex, topics which are likely to engage the imaginative and personal interest of the listeners during these interludes (as well as spark ribald banter).

Audience response

As we have seen in the previous examples, the text of the ground section in particular tends to be imaginatively evocative, building on the information provided in the descent section, and provoking the hearers to engage with the story as something to construct for themselves. Such active engagement can be prompted by the necessity of interpreting oblique imagery and esoteric vocabulary, and through the encouragement to "envision" the narrated activity from within the narrated world. The melodic contour of the ground section, in conjunction with the use of *kẽiyaka* vocabulary may also be evocative in another sense, as it can reference other recognizable Duna performance genres that are appropriate to occasions of intense personal feeling, such as deep sorrow or sexual excitement. We return here to a closer consideration of this audience response to and identification with the *pikono*, particularly as it is externalized through utterances that accompany the performance.

Vocalized responses of a *pikono* audience typically occur either during or following the ground section of a phrase. They can take a variety of forms, for example, wordless exclamations, conventionalized sound patterns (e.g., representing birdcalls), conventional phrases (*home kone*, meaning roughly 'exactly so'), prompts to the performer, or free-form comments on the narrative. These interjections are generally called or spoken (e.g., as opposed to being sung) and are usually independent of the pitches articulated by the performer. Duna *pikono* audience responses thus contrast to those of the Huli genre *bì té*, where regular audience interjections are typically highly constrained in terms of their form and placement (see Lomas, this volume), and are usually pitched at the tonal centre established by the singer (Pugh-Kitingan 1981:332–33).

---

13 A thematic parallel can also be proposed in that it is in these passages that the performer most clearly exhibits his virtuosity in rapidly listing a great number of *kẽiyaka* terms. This can be compared to a function of *yekia* in which the singing men try to impress a potential partner, for example, through persuasive reference to their land's richness and ripeness.

Audience responses can assert a close involvement with the narrative. For example, the audience member's call, *keno nganda!* ('we two will go!'), in text 1 expresses a complete identification of the speaker with a character in the narrative—that is, he speaks for Kaloma Koli in reply to the persuasive argument of Kundaleme to travel with her. Alternatively, audience comments may bring the narrative into the performance setting. In the sun/moon sequences, the audience waits expectantly for the light of the sun or the moon to pass over familiar lands, or even over the place where they now sit listening to a *pikono* performance. This is the case in text 2, where as the light of the moon reaches Hirane (where Kiale's performance is taking place) and shines upon the naked women, an audience member calls out, *ndu narayani!* ('there's not one here!').

As is strongly evident in text 2, it is within the *ipakana yakaya* sequences of the ground section of a phrase that reference to real-world places is most strongly and consistently made. Identifiable places can be a major touchstone for a personal response to the performance.[14] The "action" of the narrative may be new, mirrored in the unpredictability of the melodic variations of the descent section, but locations referenced by *kẽiyaka* are often intimately known, coinciding with predictable melodic and textual structures. Audience members' responses can reinforce their strong personal connection with places, for example, when they themselves contribute *kẽiyaka* terms to the performance, prompting Kiale and declaring their knowledge of and relationship to the location that is being named.

Conclusion

Close analysis of the music and language of sung *pikono* contributes to an understanding of the performance at several levels. Pitch and text delineate essential structural units of *pikono*, identified here as a higher-level unit, the phrase, which is composed of two further units, the descent and ground. The descent tends to introduce new information, whereas the ground repeats what is already familiar.

Distinctive musical and linguistic features of the ground section (in contrast to the descent) include: a narrow and predictable melodic range; sonic repetition (of both pitches and phones); increased use of grammatical "viewpoint" markers;

14 Kendoli (this volume) comments on the function of places as linking a *pikono* story to one's own memories, as hearing them named reminds the hearer of times they have spent in these (or similar) areas. Kendoli also mentions that the places named in *pikono* commonly include currently uninhabited areas, and he elaborated on this (pers. comm., 7 March 2007) as typically including areas of previous settlement. He pointed out that hearing about these areas provokes a sense of nostalgic longing, as one remembers that recent ancestors once lived here but have since passed away, leaving unpeopled tracts of land resonant with family history. This theme is re-enforced in the *pikono* narrative, as it is common for a hero to come upon abandoned settlements during his travels. The desolate house and garden is in fact a recurring motif in several Duna narrative genres as a site of mystery, regeneration, and reunion.

pointed reference to real-world locations; and allusion to other Duna performance genres through the use of *kẽiyaka* vocabulary in combination with recognizable melodic formulae. These features may encourage a listener to experience the ground section as a place to absorb and become absorbed in the narrative content and imagery introduced in the descent, and build a close involvement in the *pikono*. This imaginative and emotional engagement can inspire a *pikono* audience to actively contribute to the performance as a soundscape, a story, and an expressive and personally moving event.

References

Aikhenvald, Alexandra. 2004. *Evidentiality*. Oxford: Oxford University Press.

Chafe, Wallace, and Johanna Nichols. 1986. *Evidentiality: The Linguistic Coding of Epistemology.* Norwood, NJ: Ablex Publishing Corporation.

Chenoweth, Vida. 1969. "An Investigation of the Singing Styles of the Dunas." *Oceania* 39 (3): 218–30.

de Vries, Lourens. 2005. "Towards a Typology of Tail-head Linkage in Papuan Languages." *Studies of Language* 29: 363–84.

Giles, Glenda. 1972. "Duna is Not Greek, But How Far Can One Go?" *The Bible Translator* 23 (4): 406–12.

Gillespie, Kirsty. 2010a. "Giving Women a Voice: Christian Songs and Female Expression at Kopiago, Papua New Guinea." *Perfect Beat* 11 (1): 7–24.

———. 2010b. *Steep Slopes: Music and Change in the Highlands of Papua New Guinea.* Canberra: ANU E Press. http://epress.anu.edu.au/steepslopes_ citation.html.

Haley, Nicole. 2002. "*Ipakana Yakaiya*: Mapping Landscapes, Mapping Lives; Contemporary Land Politics among the Duna." PhD dissertation, Australian National University.

Hogbin, H. Ian, and Camilla H. Wedgwood. 1953. "Local Grouping in Melanesia." *Oceania* 23 (4): 241–76.

Modjeska, Charles J. Nicholas. 1977. "Production among the Duna: Aspects of Horticultural Intensification in Central New Guinea." PhD dissertation, Australian National University.

Pugh-Kitingan, Jacqueline. 1981. "An Ethnomusicological Study of the Huli of the Southern Highlands, Papua New Guinea." PhD dissertation, University of Queensland.

San Roque, Lila. 2008. "An Introduction to Duna Grammar." PhD dissertation, Australian National University, Canberra.

Stewart, Pamela J., and Andrew Strathern. 2000. "Naming Places: Duna Evocations of Landscape in Papua New Guinea." *People and Culture in Oceania* 16: 87–107.

———. 2002. *Gender, Song and Sensibility: Folksongs and Folktales in the Highlands of New Guinea.* Westport, CT: Praeger.

———, eds. 2005. *Expressive Genres and Historical Change: Indonesia, Papua New Guinea and Taiwan.* Anthropology and Cultural History in Asia and the Indo-Pacific Series. Hants: Ashgate.

Strathern, Andrew, and Pamela J. Stewart. 2004. *Empowering the Past, Confronting the Future: The Duna People of Papua New Guinea.* Contemporary Anthropology of Religion Series. New York: Palgrave Macmillan.

Stürzenhofecker, Gabriele. 1998. *Times Enmeshed: Gender, Space and History among the Duna of Papua New Guinea.* Stanford, CA: Stanford University Press.

4. Parallelism in Duna *Pikono*

Michael Sollis

Introduction

This chapter builds upon the previous two by examining how parallelism occurs between musical elements and linguistic elements in a performance of Duna *pikono*. In chapter 2, Kenny Kendoli describes the significance of *pikono* in Duna culture. Kirsty Gillespie and Lila San Roque provide a detailed analysis of the musical and linguistic form of *pikono* in chapter 3. In this chapter I focus on parallelism in a particular performance of *pikono* by Kiale Yokona in 2005 which was recorded by Gillespie and linguistically transcribed by Lila San Roque.

Firstly, I will introduce Roman Jakobson's concept of parallelism as a way of understanding the interaction between musical and lingual elements in a sung performance. Secondly, I will show how parallelism operates with respect to either lingual elements or musical elements in Kiale's *pikono*. Thirdly, I will show two different ways in which parallelism operates *between* lingual elements and musical elements in Kiale's *pikono*. It is hoped that such a study will exemplify how parallelism operates with respect to musical elements and lingual elements in sung performances generally.[1]

The concept of parallelism as an analytical tool

Roman Jakobson's formulation of the poetic function and description of parallelism in linguistics (1960) provides a powerful tool for bridging the gap between musical and linguistic aspects of song.[2] Jakobson describes the poetic function as being directed towards the message of a speech act (ibid.:356) and says that it "*projects the principle of equivalence from the axis of selection into the axis of combination*" (ibid.:358, italics in original). The poetic function allows a speaker to select a paradigmatic unit such as a word (the linguistic principle of selection) and place it into combination with other linguistic elements (the linguistic principle of combination) which are drawn from the same paradigmatic set, thus displaying their paradigmatic relatedness (or in Jakobson's terms, their "equivalence") along the syntagmatic axis. For example, Jakobson considers Caesar's victory message "Veni, vidi, vici" (I came, I saw, I conquered). Words are selected which are paradigmatically related in that all are verb

---

1   This paper comes out of a broader investigation into the relationship between music and language in Duna *pikono* (Sollis 2007).
2   Ruwet (1987) also invokes Jakobson in a musical analysis, but only in regards to semiotics. Feld (1988:75) lists Jakobson in a summary of perspectives on style which can be applied to music.

forms of the same grammatical class: first person singular past indicative. Furthermore, the three words are phonetically very similar, all starting with *v*, having two syllables, and ending with the vowel *i*. The concept of poetic function explains the process of creating Caesar's victory message (through the projection of paradigmatic units) and explains the realization of Caesar's victory message as a poetic form. Jakobson broadens the concept and suggests:

> Rhyme is only a particular, condensed case of a much more general, we may even say the fundamental problem of poetry, namely *parallelism* … equivalence in sound, projected into the sequence as its constitutive principle, inevitably involves semantic equivalence, and on any linguistic level any constituent of such a sequence prompts one of the two correlative experiences which Hopkins neatly defines as "comparison for likeness' sake" and "comparison for unlikeness' sake." (ibid.:368, italics in original)

In the case of song, the way musical elements are projected into recurring combination may create "likeness" or "unlikeness" among linguistic elements and vice versa. This is an extension of Jakobson's thesis that parallelism makes sense of the interaction between metre and meaning in poetry (ibid.:369), but in this case applied to song.

The elements of poetic form that intuitively manifest parallelism in a fundamental way are also present in music. The musicologist Leonard Meyer remarks that *"style is a replication of patterning, whether in human behaviour or in the artefacts produced by human behaviour, that results from a series of choices made within some constraints"* (Meyer 1989:3, italics in original). Meyer's insight evokes Jakobson's thesis regarding selection and combination, suggesting that parallelism is a fundamental part of musical composition and perception.

Parallelism with respect to a musical element or lingual element

Throughout Kiale's *pikono* there are numerous instances of parallelism with respect to either a lingual element or a musical element. With respect to a lingual element, consider the passage shown in text 1,[3] in which Kiale lists different praise names referring to bridges. Praise names are series of special words used to describe landscape, animals, feathers, hair, and other significant features. These praise names are not used in everyday speech, may be secret, and are recited in series within Kiale's *pikono*.[4]

---

3 San Roque's linguistic transcript and recording is in four volumes. Here and below, the passages I have excerpted are identified by volume number in parentheses, followed by a time code in minutes and seconds, which indicates the time of the extract within that volume as shown in the transcript.
4 Praise names in Duna have been extensively studied by Nicole Haley (2002). Haley's definition of praise names is generally restricted to landscape, flora, and fauna. Other important words are defined by Haley as "honorific" (2002:149). The indigenous term for praise and honorific names is *keiyaka*.

Text 1. Excerpt from linguistic transcription and translation of Kiale's *pikono*—(vol. 4) 0:13. An audio file of this example can be found in online item 4.

Mm ima ima rayane kititaom	Mm the woman the pair of them went down
Anene ru aya sokota riya so	The pair returned on the *ru ayu* bridge
Rundu aya sokota riya so	The pair returned on the *rundu ayu* bridge
Papi aya sokota riya so	The pair returned on the *papi ayu* bridge

In text 1, Kiale recites several praise names for bridge—*ru aya* in line 2, *rundu aya* in line 3, and *papi aya* in line 4. These praise names are framed by the repeated phrase *sokota riya so*. In this instance, three words form a paradigmatic set referring to bridge—the words *ru aya*, *rundu aya*, and *papi aya*, are placed into relation with one another. The repeating framing phrase *aya sokota riya so* creates "equivalence" between these praise names, which is projected over time in the syntagmatic axis. This instance of parallelism is an important poetic device in the telling of *pikono*, particularly with respect to the listing of praise names.

An example of parallelism with respect to musical elements can be found in the repeated types of melodies that occur throughout Kiale's *pikono*. Gillespie and San Roque (chapter 3) identify what they call the "phrase" as the basic unit in *pikono*. A phrase usually begins a descending melody (or series of descending melodies) of a musical fifth or sixth towards a tonic note, which Gillespie and San Roque describe as a "descent" and which provides most of the narrative content of the phrase. This is usually followed by a series of melodies based around the tonic note; Gillespie and San Roque describe this as a "ground," which elaborates on the narrative, often by listing praise names.

Figure 1 consists of a consecutive series of six grounds using Gillespie and San Roque's classification.[5] In this instance, parallelism can be found through the first three grounds corresponding with the last three grounds—the first and fourth grounds both begin on an E and end on a C; the second and fifth grounds both begin on an E and end on a C; and the third and sixth grounds both begin on a D and end on a C. More generally, each ground, through repetition and variation of various musical elements (such as different starting pitches in the above example), is placed in parallel relationships with all the others. In this case, the narrow melodic descents that constitute the grounds comprise a set of paradigmatic musical units. This creates a structural equivalence between the first three grounds and final three grounds (corresponding to the text that refers to a different set of praise names in the first three grounds and the final three grounds, discussed below). The principle of equivalence, through which these descents form a paradigmatic set, is projected onto the axis of combination through their occurrence in the same syntagmatic position within the *pikono*.

---

5   The middle staff in figure 1 notates the beat derived from accented syllables. The top staff provides imaginary beats that are more constant for analytical purposes only, as a more regular pulse. The boxed sections refer to the descriptions below of the parallelism of one element causing equivalence in another element (type B).

Figure 1. Examples of parallelism of musical elements in Kiale's *pikono*—(vol. 2) 1:50. An audio file of this example can be found in online item 5.

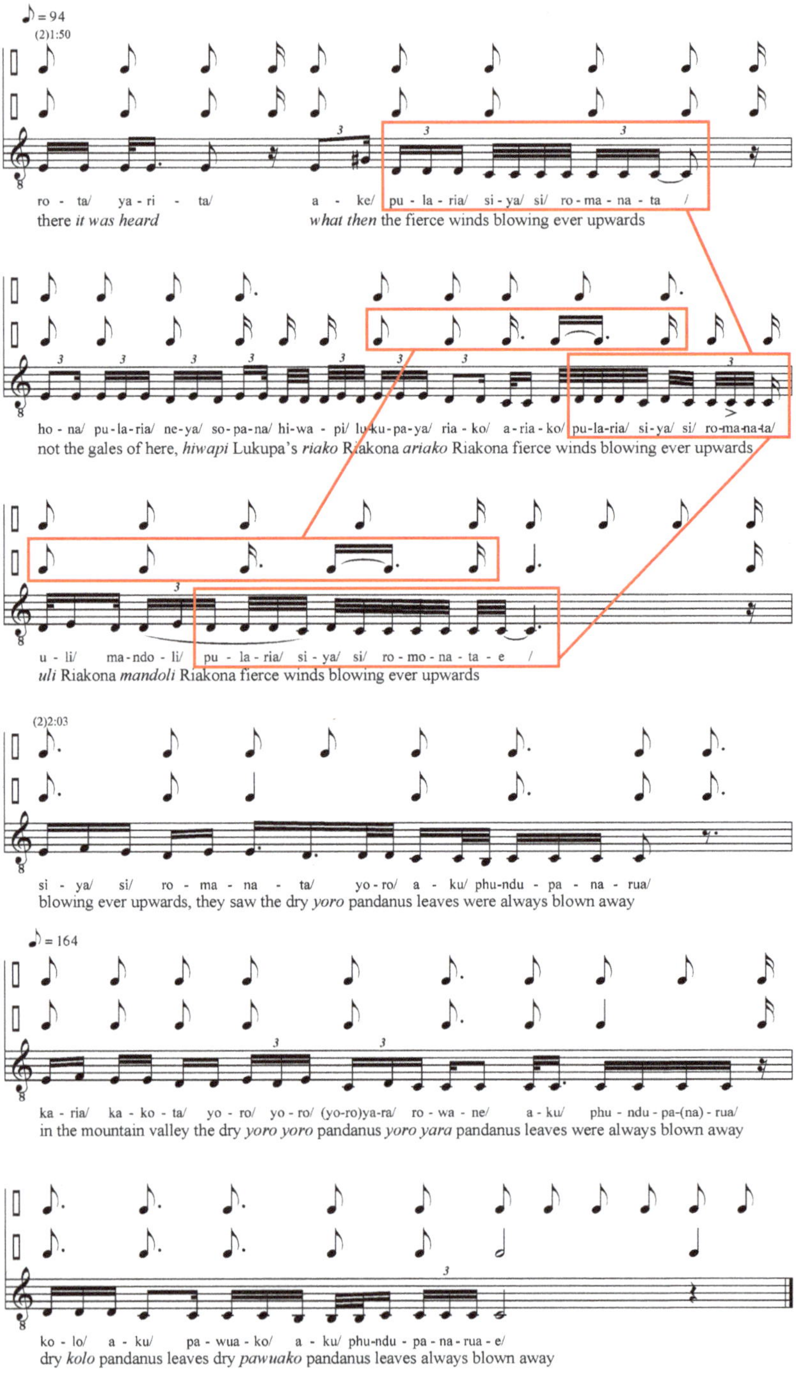

The above examples illustrate how parallelism can operate with respect to either a lingual element or a musical element. However, the performance of song is essentially both lingual and musical, and it can be seen how parallelism operates *between* musical elements and lingual elements. This happens in two different ways, which will be discussed in the following section.

Parallelism between musical elements and lingual elements

Type A: A single stretch of sound as both a musical element and lingual element

Parallelism between a musical element and a lingual element can be seen in two different ways. Firstly, consider the case where a single stretch of sound realizes both a musical element and lingual element. Duna is a tonal language, in which some words are spoken with particular pitch contours that are used to distinguish among semantic meanings, creating "tone-melody." The lingual text that Kiale sings, therefore, implies a particular tone-melody. This tone-melody may not correspond with the pitch contour that is sung—the "tune-melody." The degree of correspondence between the two can be measured as a tune-tone correspondence.[6] In this instance, a single stretch of sound that Kiale sings implicates both a musical element (the pitches that he is actually singing) and a lingual element (the pitches that correspond to the semantic meaning of the lingual text). Semantically distinctive values of pitch are thus mapped out when Kiale sings them.

In September 2006 I worked with two Duna speakers, Kenny Kendoli and Richard Alo, who recited certain lines from Kiale's *pikono* in a normal speaking voice.[7] The pitch contours of their phrases were studied using broadband audio spectrographs of the words both in isolation and in sentences,[8] which were compared to Kiale's sung melodic contour in his *pikono*. This experiment thus provided scope to analyse the tune-tone correspondence for single words as well as for general intonation over a spoken phrase to see the effects of tone sandhi.[9]

---

6   The terms "tone-melody," "tune-melody," and "tune-tone correspondence" have been adapted from Leben (1985).
7   These lines were chosen in collaboration with Lila San Roque.
8   For this I made use of the Praat software, which can be obtained from http://www.fon.hum.uva.nl/praat/.
9   Tone sandhi includes the ways in which the tone of a given syllable is affected by its position within a larger utterance due to vocal intonation over the course of the utterance. For example, due to the gradual drop in pitch that tends to occur over the course of an utterance between one breath and the next ("declination"), a word with a rising tone melody may be realized with a level pitch, whereas in the same position within the utterance a word with a level tone-melody would be realized with a falling pitch.

Figure 2 shows an example of the comparisons between the spoken (in cipher notation above) and sung (in musical notation below) texts.[10]

Figure 2. Comparison between spoken (above, in cipher notation) and sung versions (in musical notation) of the same text—(vol. 1) 18:23. Audio files of this example can be found in online items 6–7. Online item 6 is the spoken text from Kenny Kendoli and Richard Alo; online item 7 is Kiale Yokona singing the same text in performance of *pikono*.

In the example in figure 2, a tune-tone correspondence occurs on the first occurrence of the word *nane*. The following two words *wapia* and *nane* were not included in the spoken version of this line by Kenny and Richard as they make no linguistic sense. The word *sopayane* is spoken with a rising tone-melody and sung with a rising tune-melody (although the final syllable /ne/ falls to an E, it is relatively short in duration and seems to lead on to the following word *ayu*). A tune-tone correspondence continues over the words *ayu ke*, but a deviation occurs on the word *rurinda*, where there is a spoken falling tone-melody but a sung rising tune-melody.

A summary of the overall findings is presented in figure 3. Each entry indicates the number of occurrences where a certain tone-melody (on the vertical axis), including tone-sandhi effects, was performed as a certain tune-melody (on the horizontal axis). The number of tune-tone correspondences for each tone-melody is notated in bold along the diagonal axis, with a percentage of total occurrences for each tune-melody indicated below.

Generally, a low tune-tone correspondence was found for falling tone-melodies, and a high correspondence was found for both rising and level tone-melodies. This may be due to the descending melodies commonly sung in *pikono*. Since there is a general descent across consecutive words in many *pikono* phrases, maintaining a tune-tone correspondence for falling tone-melodies may cause the sung melody to "descend-too-far." This in part explains the tune-tone deviation

---

10 The staff notation represents the notes Kiale sings during his *pikono*. The two series of numbers above the staff represent in cipher notation the relative pitches spoken by Kenny and Richard, respectively, in their spoken version of Kiale's sung text. A ">" represents a strong declination in the spoken version. The words spoken by Kenny and Richard differ slightly from Kiale's sung version to preserve the meaning and linguistic sense of the phrase in a spoken context outside of *pikono* performance. Kenny and Richard speak the words *ayu ipa kuruku ngotine nane sopayane ayu ke rurinda pina*. Each speaker says the line slowly word-by-word and repeats the whole line in normal speech; the other speaker then follows the same sequence. The words *ayu ipa kuruku ngotine* are lacking from the sung version; the latter begins with *wapia nane*. The sung version also concludes with words not found in the spoken version (*hii ru konae*).

that occurred upon the word *rurinda* in figure 2—in this instance, Kiale was towards the end of his melodic descent, and to descend any further would disrupt the musical form. Here, the musical structure of descending words in a phrase transforms a falling spoken tone-melody into a rising sung tune-melody.[11]

Occurences of tune-melody

	rising	falling	level	concave
rising	30	1	6	0
falling	2	4	7	2
level	3	1	8	0
concave	2	0	1	0

Percentages that a tune-melody occurs for a given tone-melody

	rising	falling	level	concave
rising	**81%**	3%	16%	0%
falling	13%	**27%**	47%	13%
level	25%	8%	**67%**	0%
concave	67%	0%	33%	0%

(left vertical axis label: Occurences of tone-melody)

Figure 3. Distribution of tune-tone correspondence.

Here we thus see a single stretch of sound realizing a lingual element (tone-melody) and musical element (tune-melody). Words spoken with a falling toneme tend to transform into a level tone-melody when sung, which becomes a characteristic feature of Kiale's *pikono*. In this instance, a single composite paradigmatic unit (the sung word), simultaneously figures as both a musical element and a lingual element, which both share a phonetic dimension of pitch. A paradigmatic unit in this way figures in relations of parallelism with respect to both a musical element and lingual element. In this instance parallelism *between* both musical elements *and* lingual elements may cause an interaction between musical and lingual elements, exemplified by the tune-tone deviations that often occurred over falling tone-melodies. In figure 2, for example, Kiale transforms the word *rurinda* from a falling spoken tone-melody to a rising sung tune-melody. This deviation represents the combination of a falling tone-melody (linguistic element) and rising tune-melody (musical element) as constituting a paradigmatic unit. This paradigmatic unit is then projected in the same position on the syntagmatic axis in relation to the descent structure of the *pikono*—the deviation repeats in order for the melody not to "descend-too-far."

---

11 The analysis of tune-tone correspondence in Duna *pikono* and the phenomenon of tune-tone correspondence generally can be found in Sollis (2010).

Type B: Parallelism of one element causing equivalence in another element

In type B, the parallelism of a musical element can lead to equivalence between lingual elements and vice versa. This occurred many times throughout Kiale's *pikono*. For instance, in figure 1, the words *pularia siya si romanata* appear at the end of the first descent describing the fierce winds. There is parallelism between two combined paradigmatic units—the musical sequences of pitches and the linguistic words—which are projected into the axis of combination by framing praise names associated with fierce winds *ariako* and *mandoli* in lines two and three. The pitches and words are thus repeated together (with the exception of a raised *ya* in *siya* on the second line). This corresponding parallelism between one musical element (pitch) and a lingual element (words) exemplifies a *simple level* of interplay, where both musical and lingual elements are associated with each other in a constant manner.

By contrast, a *complex interplay* can be seen to occur in grounds 2 and 3 of figure 1, between two musical elements (the melody and the rhythm/beat pattern) and a lingual element. This occurs through the repetition of a different paradigmatic unit, in this instance the pattern of musical beats ♪ ♪ ♪.♫. ♪ that occurs in both the second and third lines. This is associated with the parallelism of the words/melody. However, the two instances of parallelism are disjunct—they do not directly correspond with each other. The beat pattern—and resulting rhythmic text-setting—is out of phase with the word/melody parallelism that also occurs over these lines. This suggests a degree of independence between various musical and lingual dimensions, and a complex interplay between them, resulting in the disjunct parallelism that is found.

Over the course of Kiale's *pikono*, there are several instances of a higher-order parallelism, where the semantic equivalence of lingual-elements was projected through the repetition and variation of musical-elements. In one two-minute extract, parallel occurrences of musical elements occurred between sections of the *pikono* listing praise names of feathers, names of boys, cassowaries, and hair. Interestingly, this corresponds to what we know of Duna cosmology, where there are cultural associations linking feathers, boys, and hair (Stewart and Strathern 2002:149, Haley 2002:149). In this instance, semantic equivalence between praise names for feathers, boys, and hair is projected through parallel occurrences of musical structure.

Such instances of parallelism establish a relationship between musical elements and lingual elements in the performance, such as the simple and complex alignment of different musical elements and linguistic elements shown in figure 1. Parallelism of a musical element can thus project equivalence of a linguistic element and vice versa. In this way, parallelism between musical elements and lingual elements figures as part of broader cultural and social processes by establishing and reproducing cultural relationships—such as that between hair and feathers in Kiale's *pikono*—and creating a Jakobsonian "equivalence" between them.

The brief analysis above demonstrates several ways in which parallelism operates between lingual elements and musical elements within Kiale's *pikono*. Through understanding how parallelism works with respect to both language and music, a broader understanding of the interaction between music and language within song can be reached.

References

Feld, Steven. 1988. "Aesthetics as Iconicity of Style, or 'Lift-up-over Sounding': Getting into the Kaluli Groove." *Yearbook for Traditional Music* 20: 74–113.

Haley, Nicole. 2002. "*Ipakana Yakaiya*: Mapping Landscapes, Mapping Lives; Contemporary Land Politics among the Duna." PhD dissertation, Australian National University.

Jakobson, Roman. 1960. "Closing Statement: Linguistics and Poetics." In *Style in Language*, edited by Thomas A. Sebeok, 350–77. Cambridge, MA: Massachusetts Institute of Technology Press.

Leben, William R. 1985. "On the Correspondence between Linguistic Tone and Musical Melody." In *African Linguistics: Essays in Memory of M. W. K. Semikenke*, edited by Didier L. Goyvaerts, 335–43. Studies in the Sciences of Language, 6. Amsterdam: Benjamins.

Meyer, Leonard B. 1989. *Style and Music: Theory, History, and Ideology.* Philadelphia: University of Pennsylvania Press.

Ruwet, Nicolas. 1987. "Methods of Analysis in Musicology." *Music Analysis* 6 (1–2): 11–36.

Sollis, Michael. 2007. "Musical-lingual Interplay in a Papua New Guinea Sung Story." Honours thesis, Australian National University.

———. 2010. "Tune-tone Relationships in Sung Duna *Pikono*." *Australian Journal of Linguistics* 30: 67–80.

Stewart, Pamela J., and Andrew Strathern. 2002. *Gender, Song and Sensibility: Folksongs and Folktales in the Highlands of New Guinea*. Westport, CT: Praeger.

5. Sung Tales in Héla Húli

Gabe C. J. Lomas

Sociocultural context

The Húli people live in the central mountains of the Papua New Guinea mainland, and number some 250,000 (Haley 2007:155). Across the language community there are minor dialectal variations associated with areas of migration (Lomas 1988:27–30), but these do not significantly affect communication. However, as regards the neighbouring Duna, Dugaba, and Obena peoples, language does affect communication—despite a Húli claim that they share a common ancestor called Héla—since each group speaks a language largely unknown to the others.

In Héla Húli, the tradition of chanting tales around the fire at night is found everywhere and has been a feature of Húli society from time out of mind. These tales, lasting for anything from a few minutes to several hours,[1] are called *bì té*,[2] or 'talk clump/cluster/stand'.[3] Women chant *bì té* sitting with groups of women, men with groups of men, and while the primary purpose of these tales is to provide diversions, they treat social relationships and experiential knowledge that reflect many of the sociocultural values of the Húli community. Thus, they also teach ideational and behavioural norms, and, indeed, women have traditionally used *bì té* as a form of "infotainment" for their daughters and other girls, while boys and young men are always among those who listen to and are influenced by the tales sung by men.

Nowadays, although Húli society is changing, and schools, politics, money, local businesses, and the creeping spread of AIDS are causing ever increasing concerns and taking up more and more community attention, *bì té* performances continue to be esteemed and respected.

---

1   Pugh-Kitingan (1981:332, and also this volume) says "a few seconds to several minutes or hours." I have not heard any very short *bì té*, nor any very lengthy ones. The longest I remember lasted about twenty minutes.
2   In this chapter, the usual linguistic conventions are followed as far as possible in transcribing Húli. However, the programs used to produce the present publication in its various e-book forms have trouble in displaying letters with both a tilde (˜)—indicating nasalization—and an accent. Because of this, it has been decided to represent nasalization with an underlining (_),which then allows the nasalized item to display an accent, too, if necessary. The other diacritics used are: a grave accent (ˋ) to indicate words uttered on a falling tone; an acute accent (ˊ) to show words with rising tones; and a macron (¯) for level tones. Since tone is perturbed in the singing of *bì té*, Húli transcriptions of *bì té* texts and any quotations taken from them do not carry diacritics. Note that post-consonantal *w* signals consonantal labialization, and dots within Húli words indicate morpheme boundaries.
3   The word *té* occurs in the collocation *īra té* 'stand/cluster/clump of trees', where *īra* means 'tree(s)'. It is also possible that the *té* in *bì té* could be a derivative of *téne* 'root'.

Bards have a wealth of traditional tales to draw upon, with generally two or more human characters in each tale. Sometimes a tale may carry a romantic interest, and there is nearly always some sort of supernatural element involved, such as a non-human spirit or a paranormal event. Very often, members of the *hāroli* 'bachelor cult' figure in the tales, although their status as *hāroli* is usually implied rather than stated.[4] Frequently, one of the human characters goes off on a journey, often into a high mountainous rain-forest where *dāma* 'spirits' dwell. These spirits may be ogre-type beings that eat human flesh, cannibals that devour each other, or slippery tricksters likened to the *íba tīri* 'eels' that inhabit the waterways.

The setting for each tale comprises the general and specific features of the Húli countryside: swamps, rivers, high ominous mountains with their deep forests and dark caves, cultivated garden plots and their produce, coloured clays, and the artefacts and adornments associated with them, along with the flora and fauna of the landscape and traditional Húli rituals. Such are the referents in *bì té*.

Each story occurs within the constructs of Húli cosmology and is held to embody "truth," although there is a general reluctance for people to claim that the events of any particular *bì té* actually occurred, and bards may use modulation to distance themselves from asserting the reality or otherwise of the tales they sing.[5]

There is no special term in Húli for 'bard', such a person being called simply a *bì té lāga* 'story-utterer/teller'. In the same way, people who perform on musical instruments that enable the articulation of words, such the *gàwa* 'mouth bow' and *hìri júle* 'jaw's harp', are simply *lāgaru* 'utterers'—occasionally *bāgaru* 'strikers/strummers'—of these instruments. Such skills are acquired mainly by watching and imitating others. From childhood onwards, Húli are exposed to *bì té*, and snatches of the genre sometimes surface in everyday activities.[6]

Bards become proficient[7] by paying attention to storytellers, remembering their stories and any special language used, imitating and practising chanting techniques, and making the stories their own. An individual bard will usually know a few tales well, although accomplished performers will have larger repertoires.

---

4   There might be a nexus here between *bì té* and their Duna equivalent, *bi gono* 'true talk', which are mostly tales woven round the activities of Duna *nane* 'bachelors' (see Kendoli; Gillespie and San Roque; and Sollis, all this volume.)

5   Modulation is typically expressed in English as "ought," "would," "should," etc. The grammatical form used to express such meanings is a modal suffix (see Lomas 1988:157–63). I am grateful to Lila San Roque, whose questions (pers. comms.) about Húli "evidentials" prompted me to investigate this *bì té* characteristic.

6   Goldman (1998:111) records a couple of well-known *bì té* lines being recycled by children at play.

7   It would be a mistake to think of a Húli bard as a Homeric figure, a sort of wandering entertainer. A better comparison is that of the self-taught mouth-organ player in Western society, who acquires the ability to play a variety of tunes by listening to them, observing other players, and then trying things out.

Tales are sung unaccompanied by musical instruments, and each performance is a new creation in that it is tailored by the bard to suit the audience present. Indeed, there is a sense in which *bì té* are joint constructions, shaped by the interaction of singer and listeners, the latter being expected to signal their involvement by interjecting *è* 'yes' periodically throughout the narrative. This participatory feedback also helps to keep the listeners awake, since bards often maintain rhythm by swaying or shifting slightly from side to side as they chant, and listeners tend to sway in unison with them in the smoke and drowsy warmth of the fire.[8]

The sound-wave printout in figure 1 is a fragment from a film soundtrack in which a *bì té* is performed around a fire at night.[9] *È* 'yes' is interjected initially to encourage the bard when he first pauses for breath and is then repeated intermittently, often triggered by formulaic markers that end in the vocable, *-o* [o:]. Notice how the audience sometimes intrudes on the bard's performance and can obscure it. The printout also displays the turn-taking conventions of the *bì té* genre,[10] illustrated in a transcription of the rest of the opening segment of *Húli īgiri mbīra* (text 1):[11]

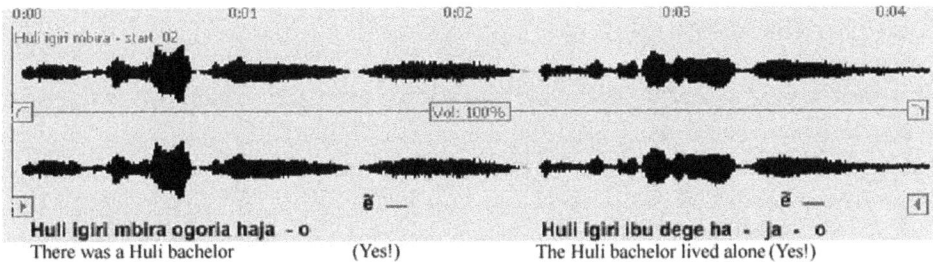

Huli igiri mbira ogoria haja - o   (Yes!)   Huli igiri ibu dege ha - ja - o
There was a Huli bachelor   (Yes!)   The Huli bachelor lived alone (Yes!)

Figure 1. Beginning of *Húli īgiri mbīra*.

The sociocultural situations in which *bì té* are sung are reflected in their storylines and in the characters involved. Bards attempt to convey this through the texture of the language they use, and I propose here to examine that language in an attempt to display the linguistic functions that cause the audience to be moved by and to identify with the characters and events in the tales. But first, it is necessary to say something about the functional model of language that will be used in this discussion and about the Húli language itself, bearing in mind that "the basis of Huli music is language" (Pugh-Kitingan, this volume): a useful insight in regard to the Húli descendants of Héla.

---

8   Listeners are often warned at the outset to pay attention and to keep saying *è* 'yes', lest the bard's mother or their own mothers should die.

9   To be found in *Amongst the Huli*, an Australian Broadcasting Corporation television film from 1976.

10   Other Húli dialogic genres have their own turn-taking rules—cf. Lomas (1988:347–63).

11   There are more examples of *bì té* audience participation in Pugh-Kitingan (1981:739–52). The English glosses of *bì té* transcriptions are arranged to line up with the corresponding Húli as far as possible. This makes them a little uneven at times.

Text 1. Further transcription of *Húli Īgiri mbīra* (the column between the Húli text and its translation shows the audience response).

		aud.	
	Húli	*resp.*	*gloss*
2.	Ogoria-o.		Right here.
3.	Bi mbira-o.		There's something to be said.
4.	Ega mbira homole barija,		It seems you killed a bird,
5.	larama abijani-o.	ẽ	we say it was like that.
6.	O ega hole, laja-o.	ẽ	Oh, there'll be a bird, he said.
7.	Bi hole, laja-o		There'll be talk, he said.
8.	Hega wai dege laja-o.	ẽ	Only a fighting axe, he said.
9.	Biabe bia laja-o.		Do some work, he said.
10.	Tisa wali dege, laja-o.	ẽ	Only a woman teacher! he said.
11.	Geraila.		Run!
12.	Goti-o.		There's a dispute.
13.	Agali-o.		Man.
14.	Agama bia wi …		Put a cape down …
15.	dai bia-o ….	ẽ	go back …

Functional linguistic perspective

Húli encodes experiential happenings—actions, events, and existential states—as semantic configurations called PROCESSES.[12] Grammatical subjects and objects that figure in these processes are called PARTICIPANTS, either signalled explicitly or implied by devices such as verbal suffixes. Other elements involved are CIRCUMSTANCES, which generally indicate manner and location in time and space. All these items, taken together, comprise semantic categories that explain in a general way how Húli linguistic structures encode the phenomena of the natural world. Typically, processes are realized by verbal groups,[13] participants by nominal groups, and circumstances by adverbial groups and suffixes.

Underlying all this is a system embedded in the language that covertly classifies the Húli cultural perception of these phenomena, the dual pivots of this system being existential verbs (EV) and adjunct and pro-verb (APV) constructions.[14] Existential verbs (EVs) categorize the participants to which they refer according to the postures that these referents habitually assume, while adjunct and pro-verb constructions (APVs) covertly classify different processes, grouping them roughly into the categories AFFECTIVE, EFFECTIVE, ARTIFACTIVE, and LOCATIONAL. This classificatory system plays a role in tracking and predicting the referents in *bì té*, and the conventions it invokes assist those following the story (figure 2).

---

12   The labels PROCESS, PARTICIPANT, and CIRCUMSTANCE are taken from Halliday (1994:308–39).

13   The term "group" here refers to grammatical units intermediate between a word and a clause.

14   All abbreviations used are listed in a table at the end of this chapter.

EV	REFERENTS
ká	rising from the ground, rooted in it or free moving; independent; strong or potentially harmful (e.g., men)
béda	low or squat on the ground; arboreal; dependent; non-threatening; weak or timid (e.g., birds)
ngā	placed on or living flat on the ground (e.g., snakes)
páda	subterranean; cave dwelling; within other things or areas (e.g., clans)
dá	protruding or emanating from another thing; hanging or growing on or adhering to another thing (e.g., fruit)

Figure 2. Existential verbs and their referents.

In figure 2, the existential verbs are shown in their lexicon forms, each having the basic gloss 'is/exists'. These forms are grammatically third-person (3), simple present tense (SmpPres)—that is, 3 SmpPres—although all persons and numbers occur in the SmpPres paradigm of EVs. If the referent's normal posture is altered, the EV can also change—for example, *īra ká* 'there's a tree/wood' is used of an upright tree, *īra ngā* 'there's a tree/wood' of a tree that has been chopped up; *wāli béda* 'there's a woman' refers to a woman being present, but *wāli ká* 'there's a woman' draws attention to her posture or her position.

The 3 SmpPres forms in which the EVs appear do not differentiate for number. Thus, *ká* is a portmanteau morpheme for all third persons, singular, dual, and plural. As we shall see, when the *dāma* 'spirit' in the story *Àe ndē* 'ah yes' goes outside the cave and howls across the hills, the EV *ka* could refer to a single entity, or to two entities, or to three or more.

126.	Ambwa **ka** ai be, laja,	"Who's there on Ambwa?" it yelled,
128.	Ne **ka** ai be, laja,	"Who's there on Ne?" it shouted,
130.	Geloba **ka** ai be, laja,	"Who's there on Geloba?" it called,

We can predict that *ka* has as referent(s) an entity or entities that is/are powerful and potentially harmful and, given the setting, that these expected referent(s) is/are thus probably other *dāma*. But it is only when the reply comes back, that we can predict that *ka* in lines 127, 129, and 131 more than likely refers to a single entity on each occasion, and that three other *dāma* have probably now entered the story.

135.	O biarume la dai bija.	Those (spirits) shouted back.
136.	I̱ na hende, i̱ na hende, laja,	"I saw nothing!" "I saw nothing!" (each) said,

That the referents are indeed *dāma* becomes apparent as the *bì té* unfolds.

Another feature of existential verbs is that although they have only SmpPres forms, each EV is semantically linked to a verb that can be affixed for tense and aspect, and can thus function as an EV in situations outside the SmpPres.[15] Thus *ká* is associated with *hé* 'be, stand, have'; *béda* with *bíru* 'sit, squat'; *ngā* with *wí* 'place, put, lay'; *páda* with *pálu* 'lie down/sleep'; and *dá* with *dē* 'extrude, emanate, radiate'. It needs to be noted that the stem-final vowels shown here change according to the suffixes they receive (see Lomas 1988:98–101). An example of this feature of the existential verbs (EV) function is found in the second line of *Àe ndē* 'ah yes':

2. Agali mbira ogoria ha.ja.   *   There was a man living there.

In this example, *haja* (*he.ja*) is the third-person simple past (3 SmpPst) of *hé* 'be/ stand/have' (with the *-ja* affixed to the Event *he-*), functioning in this context as the past of *ká* 'is/exists'. Like all third-person affixes, *-ja* does not discriminate for number, so that in *āgali hàlirali* 'eight men' (cited later in this chapter) we get:

1. Agali halirali ogoria ha.ja.   There were eight men living here.

The second pivotal form of the Húli classificatory system impacting on *bì té*, and indeed on all Húli utterances, is the adjunct and pro-verb (APV) construction. This consists of an adjunct—a nominal item, such as *bì* 'talk, speech'—used with a dummy verb, such as *lē* 'utter'. Each dummy verb can be used by itself, but its co-occurrence with an adjunct restricts it to a specific semantic signal, determined by the meaning of the adjunct. Thus, while the nominal *bì* means 'cry, talk, speech', and the dummy verb *lē* means 'utter', *bì lē* means 'to talk' or 'to speak'; the nominal *manda* 'head' in collocation with *bī* 'make, do' means 'head do/think'. Similarly, *gāmu* 'spell, sorcery' in conjunction with *bī* 'make, do' means 'to make sorcery, cast a spell', while *ábi* 'compensation, wergild' and *bī* 'make, do' yield 'pay indemnities'.

In this way, APVs covertly group processes into three classes. Class 1 processes are focussed for the most part on affective, auto-benefactive processes that have their origins with or within the participant that is the grammatical actor; they have dummy verbs that carry the final stem-vowel "e." Class 2 processes have dummy verbs whose final stem vowels are "i," their semantic domain being happenings external to but generated by the main participant. Class 3 processes, ending in stem-final "u," are mainly used of the participant's movements and posture. While these classes are largely ordered by the morphophonemics of the language, they reflect also the boundaries of the semantic domains outlined above, with the overlapping indicated in figure 3. For the (verb) stems in figure 3, *C* stands for consonant; *X* is an unspecified number of syllables; *V* stands for verb; *( )* means "optional"; *ʷ* indicates labialization; and, *e, i,* and *u* are the stem-final vowels.

---

15   See the discussion of EVs in Lomas (1988:282–85).

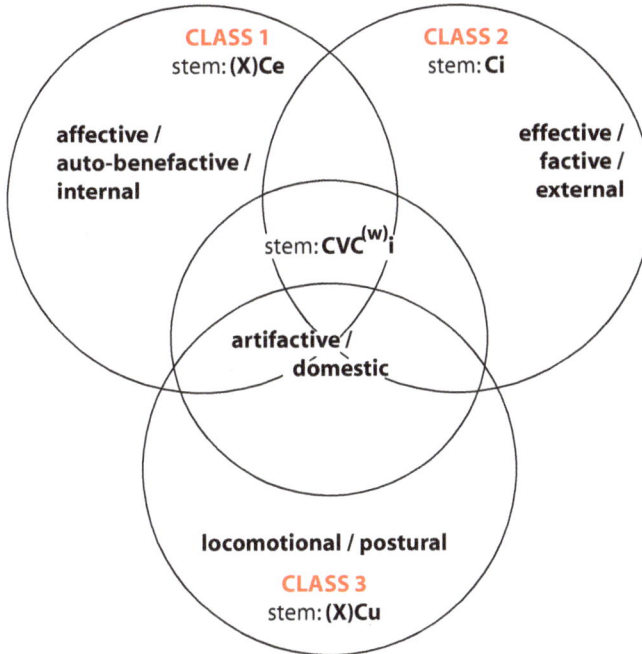

Figure 3. Húli processes.

The stem of a verb is the core of the process and has the functional label Event (EVN). This core, the Event, can attract suffixes and affixes. The primary affix has the function of relating the process to the location of the speaker in time or in space, and is called the Finite (FIN). Finites can signal time, aspect, modulation, or modality, or they can conflate these operations.[16] Subsequent affixes function as Auxiliaries (AUX), lending further modality, modulation, or locational specification to the process.

Húli is a verb-final language, and it might be useful to note that the unmarked pattern of grammatical constituents in an utterance or sentence is (X)(S)(O)V. In this formula, brackets again denote "optional," X is an unspecified number of occurrences of the sequence SOv; S is the grammatical subject, O the grammatical object, v a medial verb (form), and V a non-medial verb (form). In careful (citation) speech aimed at achieving clear communication, a medial verb form always signals that an utterance is incomplete. But *bì té* is not citation speech, and does not hold consistently to this canonical word order, as we shall see. Nevertheless, the APV system generally confines the bard to the use of certain predictable language functions when describing happenings, and this can help in following *bì té* storylines—as is illustrated in the use of processes in *Àe ndē* 'ah yes'.[17]

---

16   My analysis of these points of Húli grammar is considerably influenced by the insights of Foley and Van Valin (1984).
17   See the section "Further Points" at the end of the *bì té*.

Textual features of *bì té*

The textuality of *bì té* is made up of structural components and cohesive components. These bind and link the text together to keep it unified and at the same time contribute to its unfolding and development.

Among the structural components is the Topic-Comment (TC) sequence, which operates within clauses but can also be active across clause complexes. The Topic is the participant about which something is being said, while the Comment is what is being said about it. At clause level, the Topic can be indicated by an ergative (ERG) affix or a definitive (DEF) affix, marking the participant to be talked about. Thus, for example, line 24 of *Àe ndē* 'ah yes' has the following in which the DEF affix *-ni* clarifies that it is the bright red pandanus that is being talked about here as being carried in the stringbag.

> 23. biago.ni hana manda bija-o.   he prepared to carry that in his stringbag.

A further structural component creating textuality is information giving, which in many cases shadows the TC pattern by following information that is already known (Given) with fresh (New) data. In sung discourse, the Given-New (GN) structure tends to operate mainly with the internal constituents of a clause, but can also be at work across clause complexes.

Cohesive components that contribute to textuality are reference, ellipsis-substitution, conjunction, and lexical cohesion.[18] Of these, *reference* is a relationship between participant or circumstantial elements functioning as a semantic link within or beyond the text. Such relationships are signalled by Deitics (DCs)—linguistic pointing devices, typically pronouns, determiners, and possessives. Examples of referential items are *a*, *that*, and *he* in "There was *a* man living here. Well, one day *that* man, *he* …" (lines 2–4 of *Àe ndē* 'ah yes' below).

Ellipsis-substitution sets up lexico-grammatical relationships, rather than semantic ones, and can occur in environments such as polar or "yes/no" exchanges, for example,

> *íbu mīni Maga bè* 'is his name Maga?'
>
> *ndò* 'no' ("his name isn't Maga" is in ellipsis, substituted for *Maga, ndò*).

Not infrequently, the adjunct of an APV constructions is omitted during exchanges, as in:

> *ibugwa bì lāja bè* 'did he talk-utter' (i.e., 'did he speak')
>
> *nāle* 'not utter' (*nāle* substitutes for "he didn't speak," which is in ellipsis).

---

18   Here the analysis relies on Halliday (1994:308–39), where an explanation of these terms occurs.

Conjunction typically involves semantic relationships between contiguous elements of the same rank, such as between clauses or between nominal items. One of these relationships is elaboration (shown in analysis by =), which is the expansion of one element by another through exposition, exemplification or clarification.

Another relationship is extension (shown by +), in which one element attenuates the semantic content of the other by adding to it, or by stating exceptions or alternatives. A third relationship is enhancement (×), in which one element qualifies the other as regards location, cause, or manner.

A fourth is locution ("), which is the projection of a process encoding speech, thoughts, or emotions.

Lexical cohesion concerns the relationship between lexical elements, often involving them in two or more cohesive ties. It is typically realized by repetition, the use of semantically linked words such as synonyms and collocations, and by lexical scatter—in particular the scattering throughout a text of key words. The function of this device is to hold the text together as it unfolds, and it does so with cumulative effect.

As we explore *bì té* texts later in this chapter, instances of some of these types of cohesion will be illustrated.

Bì té and spoken discourse

While every *bì té* follows to a large extent a subject-object-verb (SOV) sequence in clauses, medial verb forms sometimes occur in utterance-final position, while in the case of locutions (see Lomas 1988:258–60), the final projecting verb is sometimes deleted. These are characteristics that *bì té* share with spoken discourse, in which utterances are frequently left unfinished, and new topics are launched whose connection with the one that is being abandoned might only be apparent to those who share the assumptions and expectations of whoever is constructing the text.

Other spoken discourse features in *bì té* are lexical elisions, irregular grammatical forms, self-correcting tags, and grammatically intricate clause complexes. Nominal groups can involve embedded verbal groups (for details, see Lomas 1988:381 (sect. 12.8.2.7)), which is another indication that *bì té* are spoken texts being sung. Indeed, although *bì té* necessarily lack many of the prosodic features of spoken discourse, Pugh-Kitingan (1981:332, 335–36, and also this volume) has shown that the tonal system of spoken Húli impacts on its melodic structure.

In careful or citation speech, switch-reference—which involves a change in the grammatical subject being referred to—is signalled on verbs in utterance-medial position, but, because *bì té* are freshly created oral texts—akin to spoken discourse and containing hesitations and re-wordings, and omitting medial verb forms—this referential system does not always work. Thus it is that we can get in *bì té* such as *Àe ndē* 'ah yes':

5.	Hela Obena pole, **lo.wa**,	having declared, I'll go off to Hela Obena,
6.	manda **manda bi.ja**-o.	(he) got everything ready.

Here, *lo.wa* 'having said' is a medial verb form and leads to the expectation that the main verb will retain the same grammatical subject—and it does, 3 simple past tense. But further along we find this convention ignored: the affix *-alu* of the medial verb form *anda pi.alu* 'going inside' predicts that the same grammatical subject will continue in the next part of the clause—but it does not. At this point, it appears that the referential system has broken down.

50.	**anda pi.alu, alendo ha.ja,**	(he) going inside, it was afternoon,

This *bì té* is set within the landscape of the high mountains, and it predictably draws upon appropriate vocabulary. The three registers—or specialized vocabulary sets—that figure most prominently in *bì té* are *kài* 'poetry', *mána* 'lore', and *tājanda* 'high bush' (Lomas 1988:291–301), all of which include sets of mnemonic, culture-specific, nominal items.[19] These items sometimes manipulate the vowel harmony system of the language (Lomas 1988:86–97) and, together with other phonological variations introduced by a bard, can give the impression that assonance is a marked feature of *bì té* performances. However, the incidence of sound correspondence between syllables does not constitute a marked feature of the genre, while, similarly, alliteration—the occurrence of words in close proximity that begin with the same or a similar sound—occurs in many Húli genres and is not an identifying characteristic of *bì té*.[20]

---

19 Nominal groups or elements that make them up.

20 It can be seen from a cursory examination of lines 1–11 of *Àe ndē* 'ah yes', that sound correspondences occur initially, medially, and finally in words, thus:

1	ae	ae	...le	la...	
2	Aga...	ogo...	...ria	...ria	
3–6	aga...	...ago...	...la	...le	lo...
	manda	manda			
7–11	aga...	...ago...	...wa	...we	...wa
	...we	...le	...le	...le	...le	lo...

If we look at a text of *té bāme* 'desultory speech' that is similar in size, we get similar results. The sound correspondences are shown in bold, thus:

Ani bialu, o ìni andaga piru. Ani puwa, o ìni hangu andaga biralu, o wali andaga piru. O Paga berearia, o Paga berearia piru. Jawi biabe bule. Jawi magadi pole. E jawi magadi pole bedo.

Both texts show evidence of sounds being echoed across groups two or three times. In the *bì té* there are at least six groups in which a sound is echoed once and four in which a sound is echoed twice. In the *té bāme*, the corresponding numbers are something like nine groups with one echo and three groups with two echoes. While not conclusive, this random comparison suggests that assonance is not a marked feature of *bì té*.

It must be noted that some bards follow the conventions of phatic discourse genres[21] (Lomas 1988:334–63) and use simple past (SmpPst) tense affixes, rather than formulaic markers, to elicit the required audience participation, *è* 'yes'. This is one of the consequences of *bì té* being on a continuum between melodic chanting and recitative declamation.

Àe ndē 'ah yes'

Each *bì té* is an episodic speech event, comprised of utterance units that are typically realized as nominal and verbal groups. Bards naturally facilitate the physical delivery of their *bì té* through pauses for breath, which in turn divide the utterance units into clusters. These clusters may or may not be logically grouped, the function of thus ordering them being performed by formulaic markers that usually append the *-o* vocable.

The texts presented in this section of the chapter are arranged to display utterance units, usually one per line, and are grouped in logical clusters that I shall call meaning units. This has sometimes meant overriding the groups dictated by the formulaic markers. I shall focus on one tale, *Àe ndē* 'ah yes',[22] in which the marker most frequently used is *lārima, ábijani-o* 'we said, that's how it was'. However, examples from other tales will also be discussed.[23]

Àe ndē 'ah yes' uses the traditional theme of a man deciding to go off into the high northwestern mountains and participate in a *dàwe* ceremony—a dance and pig-kill (often for dead warriors), with the possibility of a courting session at night and the opportunity to acquire another wife. His destination is Héla Óbena, where he will be a stranger to the language and customs of the inhabitants, and where he will have to brave the unknown, relying on the dubious claim of once having shared a common ancestor with them.

The particular version of the tale sung here briefly outlines the man's preparation for the journey, his onerous climb to a place in the high bush where he is accosted by *dāma* 'malevolent spirit(s)', his dance with and attack on the *dāma*, and his

---

21 For example, small talk and other kinds of desultory social exchanges.

22 These tales seldom have names, but I have called this one *Àe ndē* 'ah yes' because the bard frequently uses this phrase as a filler to help him compose his next line. I shall also give names to the other *bì té* that are cited, such as *Húli īgiri mbīra* 'a Húli youth', used above.

23 Contamination of data is a constant problem when recording performances of sung tales. The Húli community's *è* 'yes' frequently intrudes on the recitation and blots it out—as can be seen from its second occurrence in figure 1—while other background clamour may render segments of a *bì té* recording unintelligible. There are no audience *è* 'yes' responses on the track *Àe ndē* 'ah yes'. Situations like this, even when the clear delivery of the text of the *bì té* is of central importance, contaminate the data. Indeed, any attempt to record a *bì té* performance, by film, audio-recorder, or simply note-taking, is an intrusion into the authentic situation and introduces variables that the fieldworker has to reckon with.

return. When the bard got to this last section of the tale, his rate of delivery had slowed a little, and he seemed to cut the narrative short, briefly recapitulating the story and then simply stating that the man went home.[24]

Introductory section: Lines 1–26

Figure 4 is a sound-wave printout of the first twenty-six lines of *Àe ndē* 'ah yes'. The bard received no positive feedback after his first or second breathing pauses. Lack of audience participation might have had an influence on the pattern of subsequent pauses, and was possibly a factor in the precipitous ending he gave to the tale (lines 209–20). That being said, there is still evidence of the bard endeavouring to construe the tale along with the audience by pausing from time to time, often after using the *-o* vocable that invites hearers to respond.

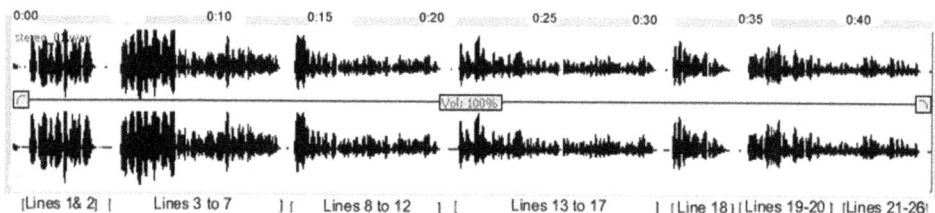

Figure 4. Sound-wave printout of lines 1 to 26 of *Àe ndē*.

Figure 4 shows the pace adopted by the bard, and the intervals between pauses. The story is framed between an introductory section (lines 1–26) and a brief summary at the end (lines 211–20). Lines 1–26 tell of the man's decision to travel, his preparation of artefacts and food, and then his departure. This introductory section, displayed in text 2, does two important things: it sets the scene for the rest of the tale, and it establishes some of the devices that will be used to carry it forward.

Introductory section: Analysis of structural components

Topic-Comment structure

The opening clause in line 1 is a formulaic filler that allows the bard to decide how to begin his recitation. The Topic of the next clause, line 2, is the participant *agali mbira* 'a man'. This Topic is then qualified by the Comment *ogoria haja*

---

24   Other variants of this tale omit or telescope some episodes—such as the hero's preparation—but expand other parts of it. Thus, one has the hero roasting a *dāma* and sprinkling it with salt before going back home. The other *dāma* slowly return and reveal that they have a cannibal streak when they taste the cooked meat, find it delicious, and set about killing each other to obtain more; see Lomas (1988:380–85).

'was living here' and becomes marked in line 4 by acquiring the ergative (ERG) affix *-me* at *agali biago.me* 'that man'; it is then similarly foregrounded in line 9. In this way, *agali mbira* 'a man' is set up as the main Topic of the *bì té*.

Text 2. Introductory section of *Àe ndē* 'ah yes' (* = pause for breath). An audio file of this example can be found in online item 8.

1. Ae … ae ale be, laja-o.		"Ah, what then?" he said.
2. Agali mbira ogoria haja-o.	*	There was a man living here.
3. Mbiru nde,		Well, one day,
4. agali biagome, ibu		that man, he
5. Hela Obena pole, lowa,		declared, I'll go off to Hela Obena,
6. manda manda bija-o.		and got everything ready.
7. Ani buwa,		Having done that,
8. ae nde,		ah yes,
9. agali biagome howa,		this man of himself,
10. dawe hole pole, lowa		deciding, "I'll go to a *dawe* celebration"
11. —Hela Obena—	*	—in Hela Obena—
12. dawe hagane jaribu manda bija.		he prepared some *dawe* accessories.
13. Hiri lajabi manda bija.		He got a prize drum ready.
14. Ege nubi manda bija.		He prepared a stout stringbag.
15. Ae nde, manda bu		Ah yes, all equipped,
16. Hela Obena pole haja-o.	*	he was set to leave for Hela Obena.
17. Ae nde,		Ah yes,
18. ibugwa alabubabi manda bija.		he readied some choice greens.
19. Hiwa degebi manda bija,		He prepared a portion of sago,
20. larima, abijani-o.		we said, that's how it was.
21. Goloba angamabi manda bija-o.		He got ready some bright red pandanus.
22. Ae nde,		Ah yes,
23. biagoni hana manda bija-o		he prepared to carry this in his stringbag.
24. Ani bijagola howa-o, ae nde,	*	Having done all this, ah yes,
25. Hela Obena pole, lowa,		he said, "I'm going to Hela Obena,"
26. pija, larima-o.	*	and off he went, we said.

Lines 5–6 are probably best regarded as a single Comment, with Topic-Comment (TC) structures embedded in each of the clauses. Lines 10–12 can be similarly analysed.

Lines 13 and 14 display Topic switches, *hiri lajabi* 'fine drum' and *ege nubi* 'stout stringbag'[25] being the new Topics, each followed by the Comment *manda bija* 'prepared'. Both clauses are equal, neither dependent on the other, a relationship which is labelled paratactic. They are elaborations of *agali biagome … dawe hagane manda bija* 'that man … prepared some *dawe* accessories' (lines 9–10),

---

25 Or: 'a stringbag for ceremonial stones'. However, there is no reference to the use of such stones in this *bì té*.

and this elaboration continues through lines 18, 19, and 21. The clauses in these lines display Topic switches and set up *manda bija* 'prepared' as the Comment in each case.

Line 23 makes a marked return to the main Topic of the *bì té*, affixing the definitive (DEF) *-ni* to the determiner (DET) *biago* 'that (man)', then adding the Comment *manda bija* 'prepared'. This is a prelude to rounding off the whole of the introduction by foregrounding *Hela Obena* as the Topic of the medial projecting clause in line 25 (*lowa* 'he said'), then adding the simple Comment *pija* 'he went'.

This segment contains an example of "non-canonical" grammar, since careful citation speech would demand that the medial form of *-le* 'utter' should have the affix *-lu* 'saying' when the concluding verb is a verb of motion; but here, *pija* 'he went' follows the medial form, *lowa* 'having said', which has the affix *-wa* (see Lomas 1988:126–28).

Given-New structure

The Given-New (GN) structure of line 2 delivers New information in the collocation *agali mbira* 'a man' and recycles this as Given in lines 4 and 9. New information conflates with the Comments *ogoria haja* 'was living here' (line 2), *Hela Obena pole, lowa* 'declaring, I'll go to *Hela Obena*' (line 5) and *manda manda bija-o* 'got ready' (line 6).

Line 10, *dawe hole* 'to hold a *dawe*', can be seen as New, although the semantic link between *Hela Obena* and *dawe* could mean that it is socioculturally a Given. Less marginal is *dawe hagane jaribu* '*dawe* accessories', which is a good candidate for being New information. And in this it sets the pattern for the clauses in lines 12, 18, 19, and 21, in which New conflates with Topic—each being an exemplification of the New information, *dawe hagane jaribu* '*dawe* accessories' of the clause in line 10.

The clause in lines 22–23 returns the participant *biagoni* 'that (man)' as Given and adds *hana manda bija-o* 'prepared to carry in his stringbag' as New. There is a similar GN:TC conflation in lines 24–26.

Structural components: Summary

The function of structural components in creating text is to set up elements within clauses and clause chains as items that must be noted and about which things can be said. Known data generally come towards the beginning of a clause, to be followed by data that have not already been presented. This is the anticipated and unmarked way in which a text is construed and makes for its communicability. However, occasional departures from these customary patterns can produce a salient texture, the unusualness of which can assist in information-giving.

These introductory lines of *Àe ndē* 'ah yes' indicate how the structural components TC and GN contribute to its textuality. They foreground the main participant, the man, and then hold up for consideration his decision to go on a journey and also the items he prepared for that purpose. Having first the journey, then the artefacts and foodstuffs, construed as Topical and New, foregrounds them and ensures they are communicated as being significant.

Referential cohesion

Mbira 'one/a' in line 2 is a numeral functioning as a non-specific Deitic, referring to the nominal item that immediately precedes it, *agali* 'man'. *Mbiru* 'one day/once/once upon a time' in line 3 is also a numeral functioning as Deitic, its reference being homophoric—that is, pointing inwards to itself, the particular time of the story. In line 4, *biagome* 'that' refers back to its immediate predecessor, *agali* 'man', while *agali biagome* 'that man' is a collocation that refers anaphorically—pointing back—to the collocation *agali mbira* 'a man' (line 2) and cataphorically—pointing ahead—to its own reoccurrence in line 9. The determiner *biagoni* 'that one' in line 23 is an anaphoric reference to the other determiners mentioned and possibly reaches back to *agali mbira* 'a man' in line 2, since the adessive affix *-ni* adds a greater spatio-temporal reach to the determiner *biago* 'that'.

Some of the cohesive ties are exophoric, referring to things outside the text of the *bì té*, such as *Hela Obena*, line 5, which demands sociocultural knowledge that is not given. Other such exophoric referents are the *dawe* and the associated artefacts and foodstuff that the man gets ready. This helps to link the tale to the realia of the Húli cosmos.

Thus, these links of semantic cohesion reach forward, beyond this introductory section and into the main body of the *bì té* itself.

Ellipsis-substitution cohesion

Line 1 is formulaic (see above), but can also be taken as a direct quotation:

Ae	*ae*	*ale*	*be,*	*laja.*
Ah	ah	what-like	?	(he) said.

The class 1 Affective-internal Process *lē* 'utter/say' with which it ends, follows the projected locution *ae ... ae ale be*,[26] in which the process is in ellipsis. The omitted process could be reconstructed as one of the existential verbs in figure 2.

There is a kind of continuous covert elliptical referencing in Húli: the portmanteau morphemes (which simultaneously indicate more than one person or grammatical category) that are the Finites (FIN) and Auxiliaries (AUX) of the affixing system also carry semantic signals for person and number. For example, throughout this *bì té*, the FIN is frequently *-ja*, the third-person simple past tense (3 SmpPst) affix that we have met previously and which plays a significant part in tracking the main referents. There are, however, some problems, since *-ja* and other 3 SmpPst affixes do not discriminate for number and this can cause ambiguities. Some other FINs, such as the purposive (PURP) modal affix *-le* 'in order to' in lines 5, 10, 16, and 25, go further and signal neither person nor number.

Ani 'thus' in line 7 is a substitution for the adjunct *manda manda* 'preparation' of the previous line, here in ellipsis. Lexico-grammatical cohesive ties are set up through ellipsis of the reiterative *manda* from the APV *manda manda bija-o* 'preparation make/do' ('prepare') in lines 12, 13, 14, 15, 18, 19, 21, and 23. *Mànda bī*—literally, 'head make/do'—carries the semantic signal 'thought/ knowledge make/do' ('think/know'), so listeners have to ignore this and retrieve the meaning 'prepare' from the APV after line 6.

Conjunctive cohesion: Nominal groups

The nominal group in line 2 comprises a nominal qualified by a number word that functions as a Deitic, thus:

Agali	*mbira*
NOM	DC
A man	

Here, the Deitic (DC) elaborates the nominal (NOM) *agali* 'man' and serves to narrow down its identity. This pattern is repeated in the next nominal group that we meet, which is *agali biagome* 'that man' in line 4, repeated in line 9.

Hela Obena is a nominal group complex, consisting of two separate nominals in sequence. It is a collocation, which supplies the listener with a familiar and widely understood concept.

Line 12 has the nominal group complex *dawe hagane jaribu* '*dawe*-making artefacts', which can be analysed as two nominals in elaborating—that is, restating or exemplifying—parataxis, the first of which is an embedded nominal group consisting of two further nominals in the same kind of relationship.

---

26   *Bè* is an interrogative marker, the equivalent of "eh?" in spoken English and of the sign "?" in written discourse.

dawe	hagane	jaribu
NOM 1	NOM +2	
NOM 1		NOM +2

The second of the embedded nominals, *hagane* 'making', is derived from the customary aspect of the verb *ha.ga* (see Lomas 1988:123), of the affective auto-benefactive process *hē* 'stay/have/be/act' nominalized by the definitive affix *-ne*, thus:

ha	-ga	-ne
STM.stay/have/be/act	CUST	DEF

This derived nominal functions in the embedded group as a Classifier (CL), signifying what kind or type of *jaribu* 'artefacts' are being referred to.

Then, in lines 13 and 14 the content of the concept *jaribu* is displayed by two non-contiguous nominal groups, each of which contains two items. The first comprises an Epithet (EP) that elaborates on the item that is head of the group, *laja.bi* 'drum'—which carries the functional label Thing (TH). The second group is made up of two nominals, the first functioning as Classifier of the second. These groups can be shown thus:

Hiri	laja. bi
fine/special	drum. like
EP	TH
A prize drum	

Ege	nu. bi
stout/strong	stringbag. like
CL	TH
A stout stringbag	

In these groups, it is the strength of the stringbag that is being referred to, likewise the perceived special quality of the drum, both Classifier (CL) and Epithet (EP) embodying the affective attitude of the bard. Similarly, the nominal groups in lines 19 and 21 have EPs that are attitudinal: *Hiwa dege* 'a (*whole*) portion of sago' and *Goloba angama* 'vermillion (not simply *red*) pandanus'.[27] The bard wished to tell his listeners what kind of artefacts and (in his opinion) splendid foodstuffs the man prepared.

Conjunctive cohesion: Verbs, verbal groups, and group complexes

Of the verbs used in lines 1–26, eight are class 1 (affect/auto-beneficial/internal), eleven are class 2 (effective/artifactive/external), and four are class 3 (locomotive/postural). Not surprisingly, the class 1 verbs chiefly appear when the bard sings of the man deciding to go away; class 2 verbs (in this case, every one is *bī* 'make/do') when he is getting ready; and class 3 verbs (here mostly *pù* 'go') when his departure is being sung about.

---

27 *Gòloba* is the Húli name for vermillion clay. The Húli for red pandanus is *ábare*.

The initial formulaic clause, line 1, functions to focus the bard's audience on the purpose of the gathering, as well as providing him with a lead-in to his performance.

The clause complex that occurs in lines 4–6 contains a locution, *Hela Obena pole* (shown by " in the analysis) nested within its projecting clause (CLS), *ibu ... lowa*, the whole being embedded within a clause that it enhances through a paratactic relationship (indicated by roman numerals in the analysis). This allows the bard to foreground *manda manda bija* (he can later dispense with one of its adjuncts and still maintain coherence), while continuing the account of the man's decision making.

agali biagome,	ibu,	Hela Obena pole		lowa	manda manda bija-o
man this	he	Hela Obena in-order-to-go		having said	head head did/made
			CLS "3		
			CLS ˣ2		
		CLS 1			
This man, having decided to go to Hela Obena, made ready.					

Then, lines 7–12 provide us with a complex of six or seven clauses, depending on how they are analysed.

Ani buwa	agali biagome howa	dawe hole	pole	lowa	dawe hagane jaribu manda bija
thus did	man this being	dawe to have	to go	said	dawe making artefacts head did
			CLS ˣβ	CLS α	
CLS 1	CLS ˣ2	CLS "4		CLS ⁺3	CLS ˣ5
Having done that, this man, being there, having said, I'll go to have a *dawe*, prepared artefacts for it.					

The relationship between the clauses embedded in the locution is one of hypotaxis, one clause subordinate to the other (indicated here by Greek letters), CLS β enhancing CLS α while the relationship between the non-embedded clauses is paratactic, CLS 2 enhancing CLS 1, and CLS 4 being the locution of CLS 3, which extends CLS 2 and is enhanced by CLS 5.

But *howa* is one of the *íba tīri* 'slippery eels' of the Húli language (Lomas 1988:170–71) and can often be glossed as 'from', which would conflate clauses (CLS) 2–3 and bring the projecting process *lowa* into CLS 2. This would produce a complex of just six clauses, with CLS 2 projecting and nesting CLS 3, thus:

Ani buwa	agali biagome howa	dawe hole	pole	lowa	dawe hagane jaribu manda bija
thus did	man this from	dawe to have	to go	said	dawe making artefacts head did
		CLS ˣβ	CLS α		
CLS 1	CLS ˣ2	CLS "3			CLS ˣ4
Having done that, this man, being there, having said, I'll go to have a *dawe*, prepared artefacts for it.					

Lines 13 and 14 are both single clauses, but they elaborate on the previous clause in line 15, exemplifying the *jaribu* 'artefacts' readied by the man. To do this, they use the repetitive elision *manda bija* 'readied' and fill the participant slot with a nominal group. This configuration is formulaic, recurring in lines 18, 19, and 21, and being picked up again later in the *bì té* (lines 154, 156, and 158) to create further cohesive ties.

The clause complex in lines 15 and 16 is unusual, in that *bu* is the stem form (i.e., Event (EVN)) of *bī* 'make/do', and in the form in which it appears here can receive a realis affix (the consecutive aspect *-wa* (Lomas 1988:142–43)) as its Finite (FIN) or any one of six irrealis affixes. Or it could be the first EVN in a serial two-verb chain, *po* 'go' with its modal FIN *-le* 'in order to' being the other. However, the EVN *bu* 'make/do' does not readily collocate with the EVN *po* 'go', and the chain would be interrupted by the paired nominal *Hela Obena*. These factors make serialization an unlikely option.

manda bu	Hela Obena po. le	ha. ja-o
A PV	EVN. FIN (mod.)	EVN. FIN (tense)
head done	Hela Obena in-order-to-go	(he) was/had
CLS 1	CLS +2	CLS +3
He was ready to go to Hela Obena.		

A further clue is the use of *hē* 'is/has' as the non-medial verb in final position, to give the sense of the man being in a state of readiness: recall that *hē* is an associate of the EV—existential verb—*ká* 'be/exist'. In that case, *pole* and *haja* enhance *bu*, and this complex is seen to be three clauses in paratactic enhancement.

However, the clause in line 23 does contain a serial verb string:

biagoni	hana	manda bi. ja-o
NOM	EVN	A EVN.FIN (tense)
this one	carry	head did
Participant		Process
(He) prepared to carry that in his string bag.		

The bard uses this type of configuration later on in the tale, notably in lines 29–32. Such verbal collocations can become quasi-idiomatic and are apparent in chunks of memorable formulaic text commonly found in *bì té*.

In the clause complex present in lines 24–26, the projecting clause *lowa* is an extension of CLS 1, with CLS 4 an extension of CLS 2, of which CLS 3 is a projection. The relationship between each of these clauses is one of parataxis:

Ani bijagola howa,	Hela Obena pole	lowa,	pija
thus did-when from there	Hela Obena in-order-to-go	(he) having said	(he) went
CLS 1	CLS "3	CLS +2	CLS +4
Having done that of his own accord, and having decided to go to Hela Obena, he set off.			

The Mood of the formulaic clause that begins the opening section of *Àe ndē* 'ah yes' is interrogative, and is used to focus attention on the audience and its intent. This Mood is then switched to declarative, which is maintained until the end of the section, with some modality used to signal the irrealis of activities not yet completed.

There is a total of twelve clauses in this first section, including four group complexes of three or more. Five of the single clauses are formulaic, elaborating previous clauses by participant substitution and adjunct elision, thus setting up cohesive anaphoric links. The clauses in groups are related mainly in parataxis, the relationships being largely enhancing and extending, with three of the four groups including locutions. These relational ties establish conjunctive cohesion within the verbal groups and verbal group complexes, assisting the logic of the text and thus lending to its coherence.

Conjunctive cohesion: Lexical cohesion

I shall consider chiefly repetition and lexical scatter, which are in overlap.

Repeated on a fairly regular basis throughout *Àe ndē* 'ah yes' is the formulaic vocable *-o* at the end of each meaning unit (recall that a meaning unit is a logical cluster of utterance units). When it occurs, it is appended to the final word in the unit, thus:

1.	*laja-o*	said
2.	*haja-o*	lived
6.	*manda manda bija-o*	prepared
16.	*haja-o*	was
20.	*larima, abijani-o*	we said, that's how it was
21.	*manda bija-o*	readied
23.	*hana manda bija-o*	prepared to carry
26.	*larima-o*	we said

Of the above, 20 and 26 are formulaic and not part of the narrative. Indeed *larima abijani-o* quickly becomes the dominant extra-narrative formulaic expression, occurring another forty-two times after this opening section. Variants, such as *larima* (and even *abijani*) without the appended *-o* also occur. Another extra-narrative formula, *ae nde* 'ah yes', occurs nine times, and its variants *ae* and *nde* are repeated randomly across the text. Devices such as the repetition and scattering of formulaic lexical items throughout the text function to maintain its cohesion.

Thus, the word *agali* 'man' occurs in line 2 and is anaphorically referenced in lines 4 and 9, and a further five times later in the tale. Such lexical referencing continues with *mbira* 'one/a' of line 2 being echoed by *mbiru* 'one day' in line 3. Then *biago(me)* 'that' of line 4 is repeated in line 9 and again, as *biago(ni)* 'that one', in line 23. There are a further nine such anaphoric links to this referent in the rest of the text.

The key collocation *Hela Obena* appears in line 5 and then reappears in lines 11, 16, and 25, forming a cohesive chain that is reactivated again right at the end of the tale in line 214. Its use at line 11 shows the bard consciously breaking the rhythm and sequence of the narration to foreground it as a key lexical item, although it is not clear whether this is done for affective purposes or whether he is using it as a filler to buy himself time.

The item *pole* 'in order to go' occurs in line 5, and is then repeated in lines 10, 16, and 25, and twice more later in the text.

The multiple occurrences of *mànda* 'head' have been noted. As a lexical item, it first appears in line 6 and is repeated nine times across the introductory twenty-six lines, and four more times later in the text. Indeed, the APV *(mànda) mànda bī* 'prepare' is akin to a redundant echo utterance that allows the participants in the process to become salient.

Similarly, *dawe*, introduced in line 10, is repeated in line 12, again near the middle of the tale (lines 162 and 166) and then four lines from the end (line 217).

The items the man prepared for the journey—artefacts in lines 13–14, foodstuffs in lines 18, 19, and 21—are all linked together by the conjunctive morpheme *-bi* 'and'. This device is repeated later in the text when the man eats (lines 73–77) and prepares to dance (lines 152–59).

Cohesive components: Summary

Cohesion is aided by anaphoric, cataphoric, and exophoric deixis that link up past and upcoming portions of the text and also tie the text itself into the Húli sociocultural cosmos, and the assumptions and expectations that go with it.

At the same time, conjunctive adjuncts, the omission of adjuncts in APV constructions and the nebulous nature of portmanteau verbal affixes aid cohesion by engaging the listener and forcing her/him to reconstruct the text as it is created by the bard, retrieving meanings from previous portions of it or simply applying acquired inherent knowledge of how the language works.

The bard marshals nominals into groups and group complexes, which adhere through the logical ordering of their linguistic constituents and the semantic ties that are generated. These ties are mostly paratactic, elaborating the qualities of the nominal items with which they are conjoined. Some nominals are derived from verbals and display complex structures, while some nominal groups contain further groups embedded in them. All these various forms are woven together to link up into the texture of the *bì té*.

Verbs of the three grammatico-semantic classes are used predictably and set up a pattern that discloses their underlying semantic fields. Thus, although class 2 verbs are well represented in those chunks of text that treat the man's activities prior to leaving, they occur only another fifteen times in the next 196 lines, which are focussed mainly on the affective activities of the *bì té* characters.

Verbal groups cohere through semantic ties of elaboration, extension, and enhancement, and are mostly in paratactic conjunction. In this way, they hold the tale together and carry its message forward. But these groups require prediction skills on the part of listeners, since the bard sometimes employs elements such as the nebulous *howa* 'from/having been there' or produces quasi-serial constructions. They assume attentive referential tracking in that they employ a number of portmanteau morphemes that carry no signal for number and sometimes none for person. In later portions of this *bì té*, there are instances of verbs and verbal groups generating confusion because of lack of concord or because of non-grammatical switching between Topics.

Introductory section: How it works

This introductory section of *Àe ndē* shows how the bard uses the language functions at his disposal. There is a cline of consciousness in the choice of these functions, from those over which he has little or no control, to those where control is more conscious and even deliberate. At one end of the cline are functions such as the covert classificatory system that dictates which process types are to be selected and also the portmanteau affixing system that obscures important information about who is involved in the situation or performing the action.[28] At the other end of the cline are functions more under the bard's conscious control, such as utterance-initial anaphoric bridges, deictic referencing, self-correcting tags, and the use of the formulaic *-o* vocable and repetitive echo utterances.

The bard invites his listeners to assent to the message he is delivering and indicates to them when that assent is appropriate. He adds New to previously Given information as he goes along, thus developing the tale as a unit, and chooses when to make Topic changes salient. He configures processes in such a way that they build the story cogently. He imparts his own reactions to the listeners by his choice of wording and through devices such as attitudinal Epithets. He uses a scatter of associated words throughout his text to help its cohesiveness and to maintain its coherence.

There are some functional devices pertaining to the *bì té* genre that are not displayed in these introductory lines of *Àe ndē*, and some that do not occur in the rest of this particular tale, either. The remainder of the story is given as text 3 and is accompanied by brief comments in the following section. In the course of these, I shall deal with *bì té* characteristics that do not appear in *Àe ndē*.

---

28 This is perhaps not so critical for native speakers of the language.

Text 3. *Àe ndē* 'ah yes', lines 27–220—*beginning*. **An audio file of this example can be found in online item 8.**

27. Pialu hearia nde,
28.   ali gaea mbaria bijagoria-o.

Well, while he was travelling,
the weather was very fine there.

29. O iba na doma,
30.   ghangulu iba na doma bija.
31. Iba liba na doma,
32.   hundu ale iba na doma bija-o.   *

Oh, he quaffed and forded water,
swallowed and crossed fresh water.
He quaffed and forded deep water,
swallowed and crossed shallow water.

33. Diribiwabe godabe,
34.   lajani.

Pluck some bamboo shoots,
he would have said.

35. Golomabu halimbu jajija,
36.   larima, abijani-o.   *

He would have had a staff of strong bamboo,
we said, that's how it was.

37. Ae nde,
38.   ibu pija,
39.   larima, abijani-o.

Ah yes,
he travelled along,
we said, that's how it was.

40. Ibu hajagola,
41.   lola winiru
42.   gili gele henge daja.
43. Ae, lola winiru
44.   ndibu ndabu langa daja,
45.   larima, abijani-o.   *

While he was going,
strewn across the way
were sparkling leaves, on which he trod.
Yes, there covering the path,
glinting leaves, through which he crunched,
we said, that's how it was.

46. Pu gimbu pu gimbu pija,
47.   larima, abijani-o.

He hurried along, on and on,
we said, that's how it was.

48. Ibu pialu hearia,
49.   anda haubaneni howa;
50.   anda pialu, alendo haja,
51.   larima, abijani-o.   *

As he was travelling,
he entered the deep, dark bush;
going inside, it was afternoon,
we said, that's how it was.

52. Alendo hajagola, ae nde,
53.   anda haubaneni ho bule,
54.   palija-o.

Since it was afternoon, ah yes,
he wanted to rest in the deep bush,
and he lay down.

55. Ani bijagola howa,
56.   anda ho bama leda,
57.   larima, abijani-o.   *

After he decided that,
going in, he keeps quiet,
we said, that's how it was.

58. Anda anda mbira naibi hearia handaja
59.   O biagoria howa
60.   aberu leberu
61.   mbira baiheru pupu dege wija,
62.   handaja-o.   *

He saw there wasn't a single house there.
There, where he was,
someone, yesterday or a couple of days ago
left bits of a spirit offering lying around,
that's what he saw.

63. O bagoria ubu handaja.
64.   Ubu anda handa hearia,
65.   (larima, abijane)
66.   abe lebe bairu bija—
67.   nde, damame uru nalu pijija,
68.   laja-o.   *

He looked around where he was.
While he peered into the bush,
(we said, that's how it was)
the remains were left one or two days ago—
"ah, spirits have eaten something and gone,"
he said.

69. Ani pijagola howa,
70. o biagoni na laja dagwa hondowa
71. ira de laja,
72. larima, abijani-o.   *

Since they had departed,
this man, seeing how they had feasted,
lit a fire,
we said, that's how it was.

73. Ani buwa,
74. alebubabi naja,
75. larima, abijani-o.

Having done that,
he ate some choice greens,
we said, that's how it was.

76. Hiwa degebi naja,
77. larima, abijani-o.

He ate the portion of sago,
we said, that's how it was.

78. No hajaria howa,
79. ogoria ira de lowa,
80. palija-o.   *

Having finished eating,
and having made a fire here,
he lay down.

81. Palearia,
82. mbiraga palene hearia,
83. larima, abijani-o.   *

While he was sleeping,
darkness fell over his sleeping form,
we said, that's how it was.

84. Dugu dama mbira ela nahe ibuwa
85. andaga bere laja.
86. Gogoraliru au nubi
87. larema abijani-o
88. —emenja-o.   *

A dreadful, sickening spirit approached,
crept inside, and squatted itself down.
It's matted hair was like a stringbag,
we said, that's how it was
—it would have been small.

89. Ede beni handade bere laja-o.

It sat itself down and stared across.

90. De lene manda bu hearia,   *
91. ani bijagola,
92. o biago ibugwa,
93. nde, manda bijagola,
94. o mbira pendole, lowa;
95. agali biago ema nabi palu wija
96. larima, abijani-o.   *

It readied a lighted brand when there,
and when it did that,
he himself,
well, when it readied it,
thought, "I feel there's a presence here";
but this man lay motionless,
we said, that's how it was.

97. Palearia, o biagome,
98. u pada hajagola howa—
99. ae nde, igiri howa—
100. dehabi handaja,
101. larima, abijani-o.

While he lay there, this spirit,
when the man lay asleep—
ah yes, the bachelor lying there—
it stared into his eyes,
we said, that's how it was.

102. Nguihabi handaja,
103. larima, abijani-o.

It scrutinised his nose,
we said, that's how it was.

104. Halehabi handaja,
105. larima abijani-o.   *

It examined his ears,
we said, that's how it was.

106. De irihabi ga haja,
107. larima, abijani-o.

It sniffed his eyebrows,
we said, that's how it was.

108. Ga halu hearia-o,
109. o bagoni mbira ema nabi wija

While it was sniffing,
this man didn't move at all,

111. Ani bijagola howa,	When it had done that,
112. dugu dama biagome nu padaja,	this dreadful spirit rattled the stringbag,
113. —emene biagome. *	—this little one.

114. Irani deago dugu mijagola,	Taking up a firebrand,
115. ge gibanibi hedaja,	it burnt the man's toenails and fingernails,
116. larima, abijani-o.	we said, that's how it was.

117. Agali biagome ema nabi wija,	This man lay motionless,
118. larima, abijani-o.	we said, that's how it was.

119. Ge gibanibi hedaja	It scorched his toenails and fingernails,
120. larima, abijani-o. *	we said, that's how it was.

121. Agali biagome ema nabi wija	The man lay without moving,
122. larima, abijani-o. *	we said, that's how it was.

123. Ani bijagola howa	After doing this,
124. ibu tagira pijagola	when it went outside,
125. (larima, abijani-o)	(we said, that's how it was)
126. Ambwa ka ai be, laja,	"Who's there on Ambwa?" it yelled,
127. larima, abijani-o. *	we said, that's how it was.

128. Ne ka ai be, laja,	"Who's there on Ne?" it shouted,
129. larima, abijani-o.	we said, that's how it was.

130. Geloba ka ai be, laja,	"Who's there on Geloba?" it called,
131. larima, abijani-o. *	we said, that's how it was.

132. Ogoria mbira wialu pijidago	"Someone's gone and left something here—
133. ainaga be, laja,	whose is it?" it yelled,
134. larima, abijani-o. *	we said, that's how it was.

135. O biarume la dai bija.	These spirits shouted back.
136. I na hende, i na hende, laja,	"I saw nothing!" "I saw nothing!" each said,
137. larima, abijani-o. *	we said, that's how it was.

138. Ndo, emene biagome howa,	But this little one itself,
139. Ibu ngwai handadaba!	"All of you come and look!
140. Ogoria mbira wialu pijidago	Someone's left something here;
141. handamija, laja	let's see what it is," it shouted,
142. larima, abijani-o. *	we said, that's how it was.

143. Ani lajagola howa,	After it had said that,
144. o biarume, dama biarume,	these, these spirits,
145. ngwai haja,	gathered together,
146. larima, abijani-o. *	we said, that's how it was.

147. Agali biagome berega da hinajagola,	The man started up and twisted round,
148. (larima, abijani-o)	(we said, that's how it was)
149. dama biago tagira puwa	the spirit, having gone outside,
150. uju biagoria o lalu hearia tambu	was calling out up there at the same time,
151. larima, abijani-o. *	we said, that's how it was.

152.	Ibugwa nde,	Yes, he himself,
153.	(larima, abijani-o)	(we said, that's how it was)
154.	ege nubi manda bija,	prepared a stout stringbag,
155.	larima, abijani-o.	we said, that's how it was.

156.	Baru w<u>ai</u>bi manda bija,		He set up a mirror,
157.	larima, abijani-o.	*	we said, that's how it was.

158.	Hurwa hulugumabi manda bija,	He prepared a ceremonial reed skirt,
159.	larima, abijani-o.	we said, that's how it was.

160.	Ani bijagola,		When he did that,
161.	(larima, abijani-o)	*	(we said, that's how it was)
162.	mali dawe uju biagoria		up towards the *dawe* dance
163.	tagira pijagola;		he then went outside;
164.	langulu laja,		he beat the *dawe* rhythm,
165.	larima, abijani-o.	*	we said, that's how it was.

166.	Mali dawe langulu lajagola,		When he beat the *dawe* dance rhythm,
167.	(larima, abijane)		(we said, that's how it was)
168.	dugu dama mo ngwai howa,		having gathered the dreadful spirits,
169.	gi ga, gi ga, laja,		he laughed and jeered,
170.	larima, abijani.	*	we said, that's how it was.

171.	Gi ga, lowa bija handala,		As he jeered,
172.	mbiru wiaria,		at that time lying there,
173.	(larima, abijane)		(we said, that's how it was)
174.	ira deagome maru laja,		the wood burnt through at its centre,
175.	larima, abijani.		we said, that's how it was.

176.	Do kangu lajagola howa.	*	When the fire had died down,
177.	o biagoria imu lu pila haja,		those around it fell into a deep sleep,
178.	larima, abijani-o.	*	we said, that's how it was.

179.	Imu lu paji paji bijagola howa,		When they lay around, sound asleep,
180.	agali biagome howa	*	the man himself—
181.	nama nai tiga wijago		a digging stick was left in the ground there
182.	ja mijagola howa,		—he, having grabbed it,
183.	(larima, abijani-o)	*	(we said, that's how it was)
184.	o biago nga, lajagola,		cried out, "Here it is!"
185.	dama biago damanego,		and, this spirit's kin,
186.	li ba, nai ba, uju ba,		he struck out at them left, right and centre,
187.	amu ba bija,		all over the place,
188.	larima, abijani-o.	*	we said, that's how it was.

189.	Baja handala		While he was hitting out,
190.	dugu dama emene biarume		those nasty little spirits
191.	(larima, abijani-o)		(we said, that's how it was)
192.	dindi h<u>au</u>habi anda pija.		jumped into piles of loose soil.
193.	Dandu wiaruhabi anda pija.		They fled into cracks around about.
194.	Ege kaba wiaru anda pija,		They rushed into nearby caves,
195.	larima.		we said.
196.	Dindi uli wiaruhabi anda pija,		They slipped into holes in the ground,
197.	larima abijani-o.	*	we said, that's how it was.

198.	O biago piai hajagola howa,	*	When they had completely scattered,
199.	ega bi laja,		a bird twittered,
200.	larima, abijani-o.	*	we said, that's how it was.

201.	Ega bi lajagola		With the coming of dawn,
202.	agali biagome, hondo habe,		this man, "Hold on!"
203.	lajagola howa-o,	*	having said,
204.	ibugwa nu wijaru		his stringbag and things lying about,
205.	dugu mu hanajagola;		he gathered them up,
206.	jari wiaru hanajagola;		put the decorations in his stringbag,
207.	baru wairubi hanajagola howa,	*	then, having put in his mirror,
208.	pole wijagoria, pija,		he went off, since it was time to leave,
209.	larima, abijani-o.	*	we said, that's how it was.

210.	Ibu pu gimbu pija.		Quickly he'd journeyed there and back.
211.	Pialu …		Going along …
212.	anda pialu howa-o;	*	when he got close to home:
213.	ae, ibu pole wijagoria bamba;		ah, he'd long decided to travel there;
214.	Hela Obena pialu howa,		having been to Hela Obena,
215.	anda pialu howa,		and now, close to home,
216.	oba ala halu—		he laughed aloud—
217.	mali daweru ngulu lalu;		"A *dawe* dance and beating the drum;
218.	o bagoria halu;		making it there;
219.	ani bialu,		and after that,
220.	nde, dai bini, laja.		ah, he'd made it back," he said.

Further points

The setting for a journey such as this is often a short period of drought (line 28), allowing the bard to use the widely known idiomatic expression found in lines 29–32, the selection of a staff (lines 33–36), jingles associated with crunching through a carpet of dry leaves (lines 40–45), and an idiom for travelling swiftly and tirelessly (line 46). The narrator has tapped into a source of familiar formulaic structures that occur in many *bì té*.

The covert classificatory system of the language can be seen in that class 3 processes figure largely in sections to do with movement (lines 27–46, 188–96, 209–13) and in sections to do with the deportment of the spirit and the man within the house (lines 84–89, 97–101). Class 1 predominates when the bard is singing of processes that centre on the actor, as in lines 28–36, 58–79, 98–108, 141–51, 166–87, and 198–208, while class 2 processes are scarcely represented after line 26, the focus after that point turning to how the characters are affected, rather what they effect.

Lines 33–35 show two instances of the bard modifying his claims about the sureness of his text. The AUX -ni affixed to *laja* 'said' functions as a modal[29] and modulates the force of the assertion to *laja.ni* 'would have said'. Similarly, the modal AUX -*ja* affixed to *jaja* to produce *jaji.ja* 'grasped/held/carried' modulates it to 'probably held/carried' or 'would have held/carried'. Besides softening on his own assertions, the bard also uses modulation when describing the man's assessment (line 67) of what had taken place: he affixes the AUX -*ja* to the verbal *pija* 'went/left' to come up with *nalu pijija* 'it seems spirits have eaten here and left'. This attenuates the strength of the man's claim and signals that, based on the external evidence of what had happened, the man conjectures that the spirit must have moved on. Lines 67–68 are analysed thus:

nde	*dama.me*	*uru*	*na. lu*	*pi. ji.*	*ja*	*la. ja-o*
conjunction	spirit. ERG	these	eat. SIM1	go.3 SmpPst. MOD		utter.3 SmpPst
Ah, the spirit ate these and probably left, he decided.						

The determiner (DET) *uru* is functioning as an anaphoric Deitic (DC), pointing back to the bits of spirit offering in lines 61 and 66.

Further modulation is used when recording the *dama*'s cry that someone must have intruded into its domain: *wialu pija.da.go* 'someone's gone and left something' (lines 132 and 140). In these instances, the modal Auxilliary (AUX) -*da* (plus the determiner AUX -*go* 'that one') is affixed to *pija* 'went/left', indicating that the *dama* is trying to account for what it currently sees, basing its conjectures on the present evidence before it.

Other *bì té* also contain examples of bards having recourse to modulation to signal the detachment of themselves or their story characters from the verity of the incidents they relate. Take, for example, these lines from the story *Wāndari kìrali* 'two girls' in text 4:[30]

Text 4. Extract from *Wāndari kìrali* 'two girls'.

5. Nogoru libuni hangu biago.ni.ja balu   They themselves were alone killing pigs
6. oali naga.ne.ja, laja-o.   they used to eat here, he said.

The Deitic *biago* 'that' is suffixed with the definitive AUX -*ni* to indicate that it refers to the proximate pronoun *libuni* 'the two themselves', while the modulating AUX -*ja* signals that there was indirect visible evidence for this at the time referred to. Similarly, the nominalized item *naga.ne* 'eating' in line 6, which is analysed in the same way as the nominal *haga.ne* 'having' in line 12 above, carries the same modulating affix, -*ja*.

---

29 An array of such affixes is available for a bard to modulate from the perspectives of story character and also of performer; see Lomas (1988:124 (sect. 5.2.6), 157, 158–60, 218).

30 This excerpt comes from a recording made in Burani, January 1969. The transcription is by Joseba Pungwa, Maga Magaja, and myself, 1969.

In the course of *Àe ndē* 'ah yes', the formulaic *ábijani-o* occurs frequently. This formula comprises the adverbial *ábi* 'how/like what' with the modal AUX *-ja* and the definitive AUX *-ne*.[31] The final vowel of the definitive AUX assimilates regressively to the [+high] feature of the appended vowel [o:], although in lines 170 and 175 the [o:] was not realized. These affixes together signal that the past indirect visible evidence on which the speaker relies is strong.[32] Such modulating and distancing of self from claiming actuality for the narrated events occurs in many *bì té*, and *ábijani-o* frequently functions to assist this.

The item *emenja-o* 'little' in line 88 is an instance of a self-correcting tag—as are *Hela Obena* in line 11 and *emene biagome* 'that little one' in line 113.[33] This is a point of affinity between *bì té* and spoken discourse, both sharing this device.

Lines 90–95 contain a piece of text that illustrates how difficult referential tracking can be. The grammatical actor in lines 90 and 91 is the *dāma* 'spirit'. Switch-referencing is signalled on the AUX *-gola* of line 91, and the Deictic *biago* 'this' refers anaphorically not to the spirit but to the man, elliptically encoded in the portmanteau verbal affixes of lines 80–82. Line 93, with *-gola* affixed to *bija* 'made/did', leads to the expectation of a switch back to *dāma* as actor of *lowa* 'having said'. But the man is clearly the referent in lines 94–95, which leaves line 93 to be read as a kind of correction or after thought, establishing that the man became aware of the *dāma* as it prepared the lighted brand. Such problems of referent tracking are not uncommon in *bì té*.

The resolution of another tracking problem, across lines 96–101, is assisted by the exophoric reference *igiri* 'unmarried man' (line 99) to *ibagija* 'bachelor initiate', in view of the items he prepared for the *dàwe*, his rapid and untiring trekking, and his unflinching toughness when tortuously examined—all consistent with the behaviour expected of a member of the *hāroli* 'bachelor cult'.[34]

Lines 126–30 name *Ámbwa, Nè,* and *Géloba*, well-known mountains to the north of Tari. This brings into focus a feature of *bì té* tales: almost every one of them proposes an identifiable landscape in which the tale was enacted. Here it is the high bush up around the Tari Gap, the bard inviting his listeners to enter a region known to be dangerous, with all the fears and tensions that this evokes.

But in other tales, it is lists of known domesticated *hāma* 'open areas' in the bush or clan grounds that function to establish the landscape. Thus the story *Wāndari tèbira* 'three girls'[35] includes a list of places close to the area in which it was performed (text 5):

---

31 See Lomas (1988:158). Another analysis would see *ábijani* spelt *ā bìjani* 'how/thus it would have been done'.
32 Compare, e.g., Pugh-Kitingan (1981:740–48 (*bì té* by Bebalu)).
33 *Emenjã* 'little' is probably an elision of *emene* 'little' and the modulating affix *-ja*, to indicate the degree of certainty with which this is stated—i.e., 'it would have been small'.
34 Indeed, David Handabe wanted the text "corrected" to *ibagija howa* 'the bachelor himself' (Dominic McGuinness, pers. comm.).
35 This excerpt comes from a recording made by Maga Magaja in Burani, January 1969; transcription by Joseba Pungwa, Maga Magaja, and myself, 1969.

Text 5. Extract from *Wāndari tèbira* 'three girls'.

Labumabu dagwa pijagola	They went to a place like Labumabu
Iba Togo dagwa pijagola	They went to a place like Iba Togo
Hambuali andaga dagwa pijagola	They went to a clan-ground like Hambuali
Labumabu andaga dagwa pijagola	They went to a clan-ground like Labumabu
Ibagija andaga dagwa pijagola	They went to a clan-ground like Ibagija

Set formulaic patterns and lists such as this are a feature of *bì té*, and we have already seen something of them in lines 13–14, 18–21, 152–59, 192–96, and 204–7 of *Āe ndē* 'ah, yes'. Nominal items can include lists of clan names, coloured clays, bird species, reptiles, types of pig, artefacts, bodily organs, clouds, and so forth. These are part of the affective content of the tale, functioning to evoke emotional states, adding to the tale's effect. More poetically performed parts of a *bì té* import lists of associated vocabulary from the *kài* 'poetry' register to do this, drawing on inventories such as:

clouds	bodily organs	clays
lúngi	*jāma*	*díndi*
hálungi	*jàmali*	*dígili*
jùgai	*hígili*	*ámbwari*
jàgame	*hágai*	*ámbwago*
bōgo	*lèmbo*	*méle*
bógale	*lèwale*	*mèjale*

These lexical associates are used extensively in other genres that draw on the *kài* register, notably *ō hé* 'keening chant', *gàwa* 'mouth bow', *ū* 'courting chant', and *íba gána* 'song' (Lomas 1988:292). The "clouds" listed above function to evoke the notion of wistful beauty; the "bodily organs" to signify affective states and emotions; and "clays" are used to symbolize coloured adornments or significant happenings.

Besides using these linguistic devices to engage the listeners and in a sense to transport them into the realm in which the *bì té* takes place, there is another device a bard can use. This involves switching from third-person affixes to second-person affixes, thus seeming to be engaging the story-characters directly as if they were present,[36] or perhaps addressing the listeners as if they had become part of the saga. Consider the text in text 6:[37]

---

36 Cheetham has claimed that third-person singular forms are used for dual and plural, while non-pronominal third-person subjects can attract second-person dual and plural forms in *bì té* (Cheetham 1978:16–27). Pugh-Kitingan (1981:348) called attention to this phenomenon of person-switching in *bì té*. She considered the possibility that the performer might be talking to the story-characters, but decided that it was "a stylistic device." I thank Laurence Goldman for reminding me of this possible interpretation (pers. comm.).

37 From a recording made by Joseba Pungwa in Burani, January 1969; transcription by Joseba Pungwa, Maga Magaja, and myself, 1969.

Text 6. Extract from *Āgali hàlirali* 'eight men'.

1. Agali halirali ogoria haja.   There were eight men.

2. Agali halirali ti Nduna jago ogoria haja.   The eight men were from Duna side.

3. Howa, ae   Then, ah,
4. hina hiri bo, lowa,   saying, let's dig up and bake kumara,
5. irabu timbuni, Ilu li nga ale,   a big forest, like Ilu up there,
6. ha pirimija-o.   into it you all seemingly went.

7. Ilu li nga ale puwa,   Having gone up to the place like Ilu,
8. hina hirialu   baking kumara,
9. harimija-o.   you seemingly remained.

10. Ae ore, mbiru hai harimi.   Ah, truly, you stayed a whole day.

The eight men—whose activities quickly reveal them to be *hāroli* 'bachelors'—are put in the setting of Mt. Ilu, which is near to where the story was performed. Initially, the text displays grammatical concord, with agreement between the third-person plural subject (the eight men) and the verb form *haja* 'was', the Finite (FIN) being the portmanteau morpheme *-ja*, the third-person simple past tense (3 SmpPst) affix. But in the next utterance cluster this becomes second-person plural SmpPst, modulated by the modal AUX *-ja* (line 7). This signal continues in line 9, but the modulation is dropped in line 10. The significant thing has been the switch from third to second person. This means that the bard could have been addressing the eight men as if they were there, or he could have been addressing the listeners themselves.

Similar Person-switching occurs in *Wāndari kìrali* 'two girls' (text 7):

Text 7. Extract from *Wāndari kìrali* 'two girls'.

1. Wandari kirali ogoria howi haja-o.   There were once two girls
2. Wandari kirali biago libu ogoria howa   These two girls, from here,
3. ae libu hangu biragonijago,   well, the two living all by themselves,
4. biru ore ogoria biru wiribi.   you two did well, here together.

At this point it appears that the bard switches to talking to the two girls directly, moving from third-person simple past tense in line 2, to second-person dual SmpPst in line 4, as shown in the analysis:

wi.	*ribi*
STM.	2 Dl SmpPst
you two placed/stayed	

The two girls go off on a journey and split up, and the narrator immediately returns to using 3 singular (Sg) verb forms.[38] However, one of the girls meets a young man (*hāroli*) in the bush, and the bard says:

39.	Igiri taga baba harimi	You (many) were embarrassed, with the boy

This is the first occurrence of the 2 Pl (plural) form, and the bard now seems to be addressing his listeners, perhaps inviting them to identify with the characters in the tale.

An explanation of some instances of third- to second-person switching might be that the second person could have a generic function in Húli—much as it has in modern English.[39] Number, no longer signalled grammatically in most varieties of English, is formally realized in Húli by the pronominal and suffixing systems. This would account for third-person dual becoming second-person dual, and third-person plural becoming second-person plural.

However, person-switching does not occur in every *bì té*, and it is just one of the devices available to bards for use in constructing linguistic texture. Other devices include the choice of appropriate processes and nominal items, the interrelating of groups and group complexes through a variety of semantic and structural ties, the maintenance of cohesive links throughout the narrative by intricate (and generally successful) referential systems, and exophoric links to the shared sociocultural cosmos to provide a setting for the tale. Other linguistic features have been noted in this chapter, but our knowledge will doubtless be further enhanced when trained Húli linguists begin to turn their attention to *bì té*. Hopefully, they will shed further light on how the Húli language functions to create such highly esteemed tales, and how it coaxes audiences into identifying with the human characters in them.

Acknowledgements

I wish to record my debt of gratitude to those who have worked with me on the text of *Àe ndē* 'ah yes', and who have facilitated the production of this chapter: Edward Ekari; Magdalene Kibili; Dominic McGuinness, OFMCap; David Handabe; Samuel Driscoll, OFMCap; Isaiah Dimba, OFMCap; and especially Howard Halu, whose expertise and insights have been invaluable.

---

38   Sydney Gould, who worked among the Húli for twenty years or more, and Laurence Goldman reckon that in spoken discourse people use second-person dual / second-person plural also as third-person dual / third-person plural to indicate "continuity" of action—that there is more information to come. If the action is final, then people would use a third-person form (Goldman, pers. comm.).

39   As in the song title, "*You've* Got to Have Heart!" A more extensive example is: "*The three men* travelled from Sydney to Alice Springs overland. *They* carried their camping equipment with them in a four-wheel drive vehicle. *You've* got to have a sturdy truck for a journey like that. And *you* can't afford to forget anything essential. Yet, incredibly, *they* ran short of fuel on the second day."

Abbreviations used

function symbol	*meaning*	*explanation*
=	Elaboration	a relationship between two elements in which one is explained in more detail by the other
x	Enhancement	a relationship between two elements whereby one displays further the value of the other
+	Extension	a relationship between two elements in which one indicates the scope of the other
"	Projection	a relationship between two clauses, one indicating that the other is spoken
2	2nd Person	pronoun or verbal affix
3	3rd Person	pronoun or verbal affix
A	Adjunct	nominal item
APV	Adjunct+Pro-Verb	nominal item + dummy verb form
AUX	Auxiliary	affix of verb affixing system
C	Consonant	grammatical item
CL	Classifier	nominal: type indicator
CLS	Clause	process
CUST	Customary	verbal aspect; habitual behaviour
DC	Deitic	indicator; "pointing" word
DEF	Definitive	nominal item or affix
DET	Determiner	nominal affix
Dl	Dual	pronoun/verb signifying number two
EP	Epithet	nominal item
ERG	Ergative	nominal affix
EV	Existential Verb	denotes simple existence
EVN	Event	core of a verb
FIN	Finite	a verbal affix
GN	Given-New	a cohesive textual system
MOD	Modal	verbal aspect/affix
NOM	Nominal	usually realised by nouns/adjectives
O	Object	grammatical item
Pl	Plural	three or more
PURP	Purposive	modal verbal affix
PV	Pro-Verb	verbal item
Sg	Singular	one; single person
S	Subject	grammatical item
SIM1	1st Simultaneous	verbal aspect
SmpPres	Simple Present	verbal tense
SmpPst	Simple Past	verbal tense
STM	Stem	unaffixed/undeclined item
TC	Topic-Comment	a cohesive textual system
TH	Thing	functional head of nominal group
V	Verb / Final Verb	complete forms in an utterance
v	Medial Verb	incomplete forms in an utterance
X	Unspecified number	constituents (of sentence/verb stem)

References

Australian Broadcasting Corporation. 1976. *Amongst the Huli.* Television documentary.

Cheetham, Brian. 1978. "Counting and Number in Huli." In "The Indigenous Mathematics Project," edited by David F. Lancy, special issue, *Papua New Guinea Journal of Education* 14: 18–30.

Foley, William A., and Robert D. Van Valin, Jr. 1984. *Functional Syntax and Universal Grammar.* Cambridge: Cambridge University Press.

Goldman, Laurence R. 1998. *Child's Play: Myth Mimesis and Make-Believe.* Oxford: Berg.

Haley, Nicole, ed. 2007. *Conflict and Resource Development in the Southern Highlands of Papua New Guinea.* Canberra: Australian National University.

Halliday, M. A. K. 1994. *An Introduction to Functional Grammar.* London: Edward Arnold.

Lomas, Gabe C. J. 1988. "The Huli Language of Papua New Guinea." PhD dissertation, Macquarie University. http://hdl.handle.net/1959.14/22313. (additional ethnographic section, plus illustrations, at *The Huli People of Papua New Guinea: A Study in Sociolinguistic Change*, 1998. http://www.GabeLomas.org.)

Pugh-Kitingan, Jacqueline. 1981. "An Ethnomusicological Study of the Huli of the Southern Highlands, Papua New Guinea." PhD dissertation, University of Queensland.

6. An Ethnomusicological Discussion of *Bì Té*, the Chanted Tales of the Huli

Jacqueline Pugh-Kitingan

Introduction

The Huli inhabit the Tagali River basin and surrounding areas, a region of about 6,180 square kilometres that lies mainly between the altitudes of 1,550 and 3,500 metres. There are no distinct seasons in this part of the world. Daily morning sunshine and afternoon rains encourage the cultivation of the staple sweet potato. The Huli also rear pigs as their most important exchange item, which is used for bridewealth and debt settlement.

An egalitarian society with a cognatic descent system and multilocal residence, the Huli do not live in villages, but in small hamlets dispersed amongst their sweet potato gardens on clan (*hāmeigini*) lands. Each hamlet basically contains two main houses—one for a man, his sons around seven years or older, and any visiting male kin, and the other for his wife, unmarried daughters, younger sons, and any visiting female kin. Huli society has strict gender segregation based on cultural beliefs about behavioural etiquette and bodily pollution, and men and women traditionally do not enter each others' dwellings. The houses are small, closed structures, each with a doorway covered by horizontal wooden slabs. They are built flat on the ground to retain heat during the cold night hours. A fire burns inside each house, and its smoke filters through and helps to preserve the grass roof (figure 1). At night, the house members lie around the fire on the ground or on low, sleeping ledges attached to the wall.[1]

1 These observations are based on fieldwork carried out from December 1974 to February 1975 as an undergraduate honours student at Monash University, and later during 1977 and 1978 as a doctoral candidate at the University of Queensland. The texts of the two *bì té* examples discussed in this chapter were checked and translated in 1976 with Mr. Tege Tandagua, a Huli teacher who was then staying in Brisbane and whose help is gratefully acknowledged. My doctoral candidature (1976–81) was funded under a Commonwealth Postgraduate Research Award, while the field trips in 1977 and 1978 were sponsored by the Amy R. Hughes Scholarship, awarded by the Australian Federation of University Women. Since those days, I have had periodic contacts with various Huli and expatriate friends from the Southern Highlands, but have not had the opportunity to return to Papua New Guinea. For reference, see Peters (1975), Pugh (1975), and Pugh-Kitingan (1977, 1979, 1980, 1981, 1982, 1984, 1986, 1992, 1998a, 1998b, 2005).

Figure 1. Haralu, a Huli man from Bebenete, in front of his house (photo by author).

Both Huli men and women are characteristically individualistic, verbose, and domineering, and gender relations may be described as ones of segregated equality. In former times, young unmarried men often joined the celibate *hāroli* group in the bush for a time, to develop their strength for adulthood. During this optional bachelor seclusion, initiates or *īgiri hāroli* ('boy' *hāroli*) were trained and disciplined by senior *hāroli* instructors, while growing their hair (a symbol of masculine strength) to be made into wigs. The *hāroli* were a cult devoted to the veneration of Tiame, a beautiful mythical woman, who according to Huli oral history was murdered in ancient times. Special magical plants called *íba gíya*— which were said to have sprouted from her blood and dismembered body parts— were kept by the *hāroli* and cuttings were given to initiates (who were then called *íba gíya*) as symbols of their chastity during seclusion. Once a young man had passed his initiation, he could continue on as a *hāroli* or return to society and prepare for marriage.[2]

Bì té (*bì* = words, talk, talking; *té* = story) are long fireside stories, told in the houses of both men and women to entertain children and other relatives during the night hours. The Huli distinguish between *bì té* and *bì hēnene* ('true words' or 'true stories'), which are the myths and oral history of the people. Glasse (1965:33) uses the term *mana* for myths, but this is not correct. The Huli describe *mána* as 'rules' or 'instructions', referring to customary and ritual norms based on supernatural sanction, correctly translated by Lomas (this volume, chapter 5) as 'lore'. *Mána* ranges from traditional moral values taught to children, to solemn instructions on appropriate behaviour given to *hāroli* novices by their instructors, as well as ritual specifications for certain ceremonies conducted by other kinds of ritual specialists. Both *bì hēnene* and *bì té* may contain simple elements of *mána*. Thus, *bì té* can sometimes be used to convey important cultural values to children while entertaining them.

Bì hēnene are usually recited in a speaking voice, while *bì té* are chanted on three main pitches. Unlike *bì hēnene, bì té* are usually composed extemporaneously and can last from a few minutes to several hours, depending on the skill and whim of the storyteller (Pugh 1975:10–30, Pugh-Kitingan 1981:332–50, 710–87).

As with other Huli non-ritual musical genres, aptitude, personal interest, and exposure to the genre while young determine the proficiency of a storyteller. If a child grows up in a household where one of the members is skilled in performing *bì té*, he or she may also develop talent as a storyteller. No instruction is given. Children hear *bì té* from an early age, and an interested young storyteller develops

---

2 Information about the *hāroli* and their practices was graciously given by former *hāroli* instructors from Bebenete, including the late Senior Land Mediator Madiabe Haroli (Dombe Mia Madiabe), Haraya, Diabe, Igilu, Wanabe, and Yule Tagobe. I am most grateful for help given by my research assistant Mr. Bogaya Newai, who interpreted during our interviews.

skill through listening to many stories and informally trying out the style. Over time, the talent of this individual becomes recognized by others, as that person is asked to entertain members of the house where they live.

The performance event

The storyteller usually begins by instructing the listeners "You say *è* [yes]" or even "You say *è*, or my parents will die."[3] This ensures a regular interjection of the word *è*, chanted on a level pitch by one of the listeners, which tells the performer that the story is not being wasted on a sleeping audience in the dark. It also serves as a prompting device to help the performer continue with the development of the story.

Bì té are chanted in prose form in which sentences or sections usually end with linking expressions such as *lāya* ('said') or *lārugo ábiyani-ō* ('which I said that-o'). Although they are chanted at the end of sections, these expressions are not actually parts of the story, but merely help to maintain the flow of articulation as the performer composes the next sentence. Occasionally the chanted prose might break into poetic verse in passages where one of the characters in the story cries a lament or plays a musical instrument through which poetry is articulated. These chanted poetic passages can also function as linkages between sections in the story or may lead up to a dramatic conclusion.

Bì té usually end simply with the spoken statement *ài ōgoni* ('that's all'). Within the boundaries of the opening announcement and this concluding expression, the performer is free to develop the narrative theme of the story in any way he or she desires.

Although *bì té* are normally composed on the spot, some performers develop their own stock of favourite stories, and some chant tales that they heard as children. The skill of the storyteller lies in his or her ability to develop the tale and maintain the flow of words without losing track of the events in the story or boring the listeners to sleep.

Bì té as Huli music

Bì té performance style resembles relaxed singing, punctuated by the periodic *è* interjection by one of the listeners. The Huli, however, do not regard *bì té* style as singing, but simply say it is *bì té*, emphasizing the storying function of the genre. Although they perform a wide variety of both vocal and instrumental

---

3   The underline (_) below a vowel, such as in *è* and the *a* in *gàwa*, indicates nasalization.

music that uses language, the Huli have distinct classifications for each genre. Singing or *íba gána* includes men's courting house songs (*dàwanda ṳ̄*), Christian songs (*Ngōdenaga íba gána*), and contemporary popular songs heard over the radio. Traditional Huli singing is a group performance, in which men sing in a loud falsetto, and songs have fixed poetic structures. *Bì té*, however, are rambling solo prose forms that sometimes include poetic episodes, and male storytellers do not perform falsetto. Perhaps *bì té* musical style can be loosely referred to as chanting. *Bì té* are not chants, however, and the verb 'chanting' is used here as an alternative to 'singing' to reflect Huli musical concepts and convey the idea of melodic recitation.

Bì té are chanted using a melodic cell of three basic pitches of which the middle one functions as a tonic or tonal centre. The upper pitch sounds a whole tone above this, while the lowest is a semitone or tone below the tonic. Sentences usually begin on the central pitch and feature the falling minor or major third between the outside pitches before resolving back onto the tonal centre. The *è* interjection by one of the listeners also falls on this central pitch at the end of each line (figure 2).[4]

Figure 2. Main pitches used in *bì té* by Akoari Tamabu, recorded at Hoiebia, 1 January 1975.

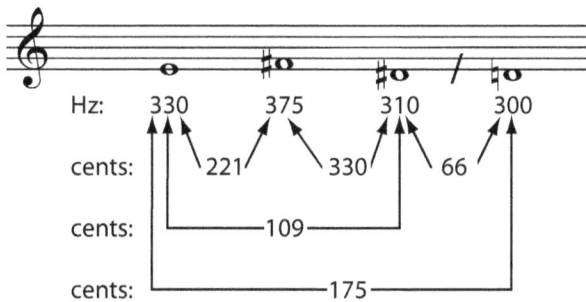

During long *bì té*, the storyteller very occasionally might include additional melodic material, particularly a descending stepwise movement from a pitch lying a major third above the tonal centre down to the lowest pitch (Pugh 1975:11–17). This then moves back to the original melodic cell, often via a short intervening motif (figure 3).[5] At other times, a performer may occasionally

---

4 Coincidentally, this pitch arrangement is also used for certain ritual chants, including *mànda gāmu* ('wig magic') for growing *hāroli* initiates' hair and *íba gíya gāmu* for preparing the initiates to receive their *íba gíya* plants, as well as some kinds of *dágia gāmu* or women's love charms. The use of this pitch arrangement facilitates the chanting process. Parallelism and alternate changing archaic terms are features of the poetic structures of these chants. In form and function, they are very different from *bì té*.

5 The performer Akoari Tamabu, who used the pitch arrangements in figures 2 and 3, was a young man of around thirty years at the time of recording, but was renowned as a storyteller among men in the Hoiebia area.

break into normal speech. This can occur towards the end of a long story as the storyteller grows tired, or at other times it may be a stylistic device to indicate a heightened exclamation by one of the characters in the story.

Figure 3. Additional melodic material used in *bì té* by Akoari Tamabu, recorded at Hoiebia, 1 January 1975.

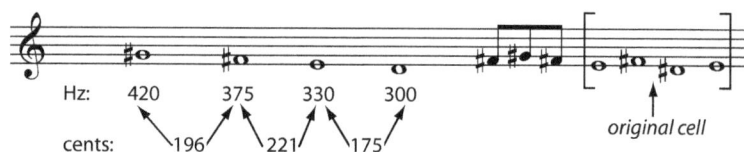

Sometimes when recounting poetry articulated through the orally-resonated double-stringed musical bow *gàwa,* said to be played by a character in a story, the storyteller may change the melodic material used for chanting the story to that which represents the tuning of this instrument (figure 4). Here the tonic pitch represents that of the outer string of the instrument, while the pitch roughly a major third above this corresponds to that of the inner string, and the highest pitch represents the inner strand when it is stopped by the *gàwa*-player's thumb (Pugh 1975:23–28).[6]

As I have shown elsewhere (Pugh-Kitingan 1981, 1984), the basis of Huli music is language. The Huli do not have a specific term equivalent to the English word "music." Except for drumming, which is denoted by permutations of the verb root *bá* 'to hit', all types of musical performance are described with expressions involving words based on *lā* 'to say'. Huli believe that thoughts form in a person's emotional heart (*bú*), located in the physical heart (*búbìri*) in the chest. Thoughts rise in breath from the lungs to the mouth and then roll off the tongue as words. The linguistic expression of poetry characterizes most of their music, including the performance of solo musical instruments, such as the *gàwa* bow, the bamboo

---

6   The *gàwa* is an orally-resonated, double-stringed musical bow that is strummed with a small thin stick. It is said to have been originally invented by a woman in olden days and is played solo by both skilled men and women (Pugh 1975:148–86; Pugh-Kitingan 1977:220–30; 1981:175–98, 397–447). During *gàwa* performance, the inner string sounds a major third above the outer string. As the performer rapidly strums the strings, he or she stops the inner string with the left thumb, thereby raising its pitch a semitone higher so that is sounds a fourth above the outer strand. The strings on a man's *gàwa* pass under the wood at the mouth end and over the wood at the longer opposite end, while on a woman's instrument a single strand is looped around the mouth end to form two strings that pass under the wood at the opposite end. A woman thus stops the inner string from above with the pad of her thumb, while a man stops it from below with the plane of his thumbnail. The performer reshapes the external sound energy of the *gàwa* with the oral cavity to articulate words (the vocal cords remain silent), which are heard in the instrumental timbre sound of the strings and their upper partials (Pugh-Kitingan1977). Stopping and unstopping the inner string gives melodic shape to the speech-tones of the words, with a fall to the outer strand pitch at the end of phrases indicating sentence-terminating intonation (Pugh-Kitingan 1984:89–99). In the example of figure 4, the storyteller, the woman Wandome from Walete, was also an expert *gàwa* player, who tended to tune her inner string somewhat flat, and this interval of a flattened major third was reflected in her performance.

jew's harp or jaw's harp *hìriyúla*—which are played by both men and women—and, to a lesser extent, two of the *gùlupóbe* panpipes blown by men (Pugh 1975, Pugh-Kitingan 1977, 1981, 1982, 1984).

Figure 4. Change in melodic material used in *bì té* by Wandome, recorded at Walete, 13 February 1975.

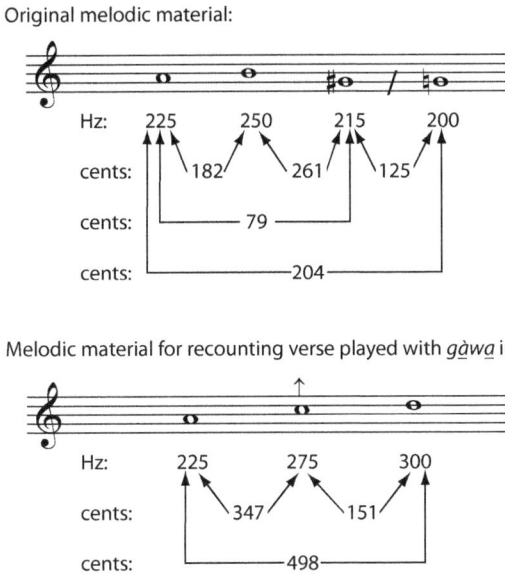

Original melodic material:

Melodic material for recounting verse played with *gàwa* in story:

Although they have various expressions for melody (*lō pódo, lō póda* 'break the speaking'; *lō pódo ìri dāli, lōpodopoda, lōpodalu* 'break the speaking up and down'; *gīlinine óre pōdolene* 'decoration very breaking'; or simply just *pōdolene* 'breaking') and ostinato (*lā āmuhá* or 'going along straight', lit. 'speak straight along a valley stand'), the Huli do not have concepts of metre and rhythm (Pugh-Kitingan 1981:150–58). Linguistic articulation produces pace and rhythmic structures in music, while speech-tone largely determines melodic shape within the characteristic pitch arrangement or melodic cell for a specific genre. Huli is a tone language that has three contrastive word-tones: low-rising, high-falling, and mid-level, here indicated with an acute accent ('), a grave accent (`), and a macron (¯), respectively, with sentence-terminating intonation producing a fall on verb affixes at the end of statements (Rule 1977:10; Rule and Rule 1970a:x–xi).[7]

---

7   In keeping with the practice of Rule and Rule (1970a, 1970b), these marks are shown on the first syllable of the word, although the pitch patterns marked by them pertain to the word as a whole. Somewhat counter-intuitively, the Rules used an acute accent (') for high-falling tone and a grave accent (`) for low-rising, as the tone marks were used to indicate the relative tone of the first syllable in each word. While I have followed their practice in that respect in my previous writings on Huli, here, for that sake of consistency with Lomas's chapter and at the editors' request, I follow the more standard practice of using the acute accent (') for low-rising tones and the grave (`) for high-falling tone.

In Huli music it is the speech-tones of words that produce the micro-melodic structures within a given pitch arrangement. As will be shown below, this is seen in *bì té* performance where speech-tone is largely outlined in the melodic patterns between the three pitches, with sentence-terminating intonation producing the resolution onto the central pitch at the ends of sentences. Sometimes the characteristic falling figure between the outside pitches may distort the speech-tone of some words somewhat just before the resolution onto the central pitch, as with the words *Kándime, lībuni, mbīruagi,* and *íbugua* in Wandome's *bì té* of figure 7 (figure 5).

Figure 5. Examples of speech-tone distortions by falling third figure, exemplified on the words *Kándime, lībuni, mbīruagi,* and *íbugua* in *bì té* by Wandome, recorded at Walete, 13 February 1975 (from figure 7).

As a storytelling genre, *bì té* thus exemplifies the fundamental importance of language in Huli music. In addition to the linking expressions and *è* interjections, the basic three-pitch cell and the characteristic recurring falling figure between its outer pitches provide melodic frameworks for telling the story which enable the performer to continue for as long as possible without tiring.

Bì té as Huli oral literature

Although they may sometimes refer to historical characters, *bì té* are essentially fiction. Some have happy endings, but most end tragically.

Each story has two or three main characters, among which there are usually a male and a female. Stories frequently tell of events that occur either during a journey or while one of the characters is absent elsewhere. This may reflect the Huli practice of multilocal residence, whereby individuals periodically go to reside with different cognatic kin to maintain influence amongst various ambilineal clans.

Supernatural elements—including spirits that are often represented by birds such as parrots and magical transformations in which children turn immediately into handsome adults—are common features, as are amazing feats such as a boy constructing a hanging bridge across a river within a few minutes. These stories often describe situations that would be unmentionable in everyday life, such as a young man and a young woman travelling together on a journey, or a celibate *hāroli* bachelor wooing and marrying a young woman. Although such behaviour is unacceptable in Huli society, it provides entertaining storytelling material.

Bì té composed by women often include descriptions of *hāroli* painted in bright colours and wearing their ochre-coloured or black crescent-shaped wigs, which are similar to the ceremonial costumes worn by married men during *māli* dancing, except that *hāroli* wear their string bags tied across their chests and do not carry drums or dance (figure 6). Women are generally curious about this exclusive male group, and in the past girls eagerly anticipated marrying handsome young men who had completed their terms as *hāroli*. *Bì té* composed by men frequently feature heroines who display the characteristics that Huli men most admire in women. Heroines are not only beautiful and outspoken, but capable of planting gardens, cutting firewood, rearing and slaughtering pigs, and can even prepare ground ovens—highly capable, in contrast to their incompetent male counterparts in the stories.

Two performances of *bì té*

The following examples illustrate two individual performance styles of *bì té*. The first tells a tragic tale, while the second has an outrageous, comic ending.

Performance by Wandome

Figure 7 (see appendix 1) shows a *bì té* by the woman Wandome (figure 8) from Walete in the Tani *hāmeigini* (Pugh-Kitingan 1981:333–36, 711–23).[8]

---

8   This was recorded on 30 January 1975 at Walete.

Figure 6. The ceremonial costume of a *máli* dancer with the crescent-shaped wig and yellow face paint is similar to that worn by *hāroli* bachelors when parading in public as a test, but *hāroli* do not dance with drums (photo by author).

Figure 8. Wandome at Walete in 1977 (photo by author).

Wandome's *bì té* tells the story of a mythical woman named Bebogo Wane Kandime ('Bebogo's daughter Kandime'). The following synopsis is summarized from the detailed translation after the transcription in figure 7:

> There were once two people, Bebogo's daughter Kandime and her brother, who just lived there all the time. One day, the young man said, "I'm going to the Hele Obena country [to the east of the Huli], but you stay here, Bebogo's daughter Kandime. If you get thirsty, drink from the Gugubia River which I'm damming here; if you hunger for pig meat, eat the wild ones which we caught down there in the bush. But don't go away down there, just stay here." So she stayed there.

Then one day, she went outside down there. She found some clay ground and, scooping it up, she painted her body. Next, she found a pandanus tree, the leaves of which could be woven into a rain-cape. As she tried to pull down the tree, she found a parrot's egg on top. "This is how I will eat it," she said, "I won't prepare it." So she swallowed it whole.

When she returned home, she sat down and gave birth to a baby boy named Clay Ground Gilara. So Gilara and his mother stayed there all the time and the boy grew up.

As he was getting older, his uncle who had gone to the Hele Obena returned calling out "I'm coming!" When Clay Ground Gilara saw him coming, he said "I'm going to put a bridge across the Gugubia River." His uncle was coming leading two Hele Obena pigs with cut ears, accompanied by two Hele Obena women carrying salt packets in their stringbags.

As they were coming, the boy was putting the bridge across the Gugubia River and his mother was watching. "If I shake when I stand over the middle of the Gugubia, call out 'Clay Ground Gilara my son, my unexpected son, don't fall!'" he said to his mother. But when he was standing, shaking on the bridge over the Gugubia, his mother didn't say anything, even though he kept his eyes on her as he shook.

When she didn't say anything, some parrots came screeching and carried the boy away. As they were going, the boy's arm bones turned into wings, and he said "Break off my wing and give it to Mother." That's all.

The tragic ending to this *bì té* shows that children and kin should not be treated with callous indifference. If the woman had truly cared for her special son, she would have cried out to calm his fear of falling as he balanced precariously above the raging river, while constructing the delicate vine suspension bridge. Since she showed no concern for him, the parrots, from whose egg he had originated, took him from her. She may have feared explaining her unexpected son to her brother, who had warned her not to wander off into the bush. The son's parting gift to his mother of his broken wing bone is a desperate plea for remembrance.

This story contains much magical and supernatural imagery. Bebogo Wane Kandime, the name of the main character, is also the name of a female *dāma* (demon) known throughout the Huli area. The poetic term *húliya*—which Wandome uses for this character, her brother, and the boy—was often employed in magic chants associated with the *hāroli* cult, and its use here also suggests a magical aspect to these characters. They are able to perform impossible superhuman feats. After discovering a parrot egg at the top of a pandanus palm, the woman swallows it whole, and then gives birth to a baby son on her return home. Later as his uncle returns from the east, the youth immediately constructs a suspension bridge across the Gugubia River. The arrival of screeching parrots, which are symbolic of spirits, and the metamorphosis of the boy into a parrot as he is carried off by the birds are also supernatural elements that provide an eerie end to the story.

Nevertheless, since the traditional Huli worldview often perceives the spiritual realm as a parallel to the physical world, the characters also engage in human activities. The main character paints herself in clay and makes a rain-cape of pandanus leaves (symbolic of hoping for a baby—a Huli mother usually carries her new baby wrapped in the pandanus rain-cape inside her stringbag that hangs from her head). Her brother goes on a trading expedition to the Wage or Wola people to the east and returns with pigs, wives, and salt, yodelling as he comes home.

Most of Wandome's *bì té* is chanted in a soft, melodious voice in prose form with *lāya* ('said') as the linking expression. She uses three main pitches, of which the highest is a whole tone above the main pitch, and the lowest sounds a minor third and sometimes a major third below the highest (figure 9).

Figure 9. Main pitches used in in *bì té* by Wandome (figure 7), recorded at Walete, 30 January 1975.

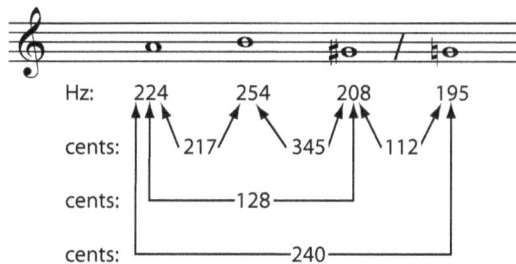

The words of the young man to his mother, however, fall briefly into poetry with the repeat of the expressions "Say 'Clay Ground Gilara my son don't fall!'" and "Say 'My unexpected son don't fall!,'" where *búri bóbi lālu mínini* and *bárina bóbi lālu mínini* are poetic alternatives for "unexpected son" (figure 10). The use of poetic parallelisms here helps to capture the attention of the listeners, leading them towards the dramatic conclusion of the story.

Figure 10. Clay Ground Gilara's poetic plea to his mother, in square brackets (from figure 7).

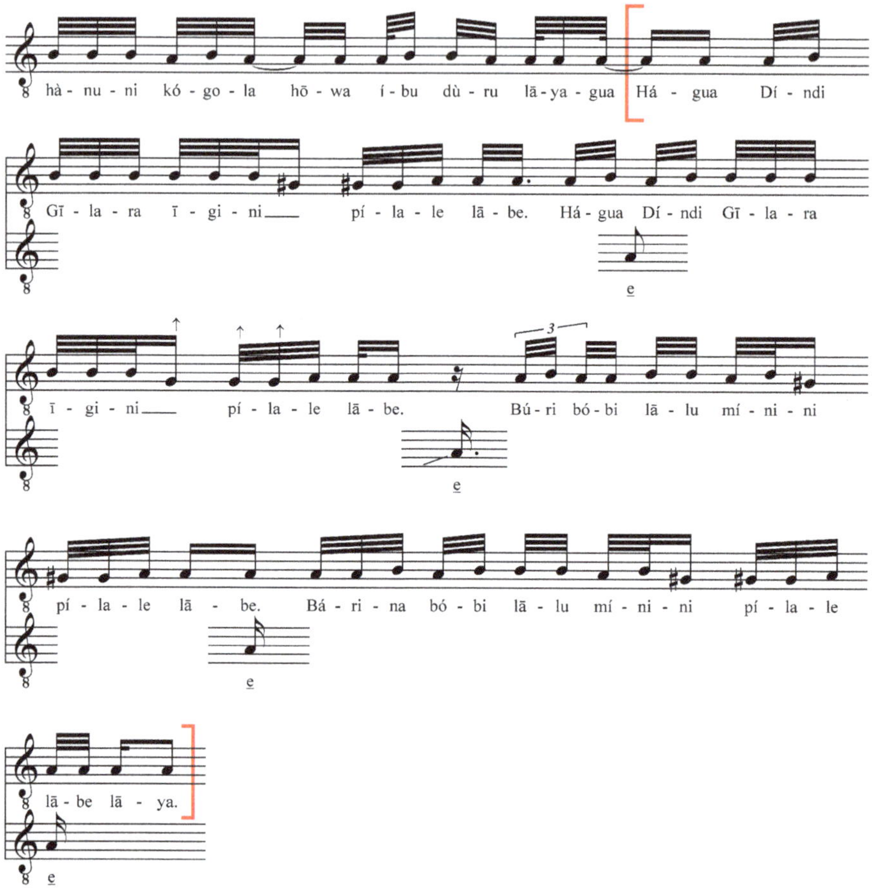

It can be seen from following figure 7 that melodic shapes within the recitation are mainly determined by the speech-tones of the words articulated. Low-rising tone produces rising patterns between the pitches, high-falling tone causes falling figures, while mid-level tone words can be chanted level on any of the three main pitches (but usually the higher two), and sentence-terminating intonation generally produces a level resolution onto the main central pitch at the end of statements. The falling interval of a third between the outside pitches usually corresponds with high-falling tone words, but as mentioned above this is also a stylistic device occurring before sentence-terminating resolution onto the main pitch that assists the storyteller in maintaining the chanted flow. This is a melodic feature of the last syllable of the level tone word *īgini* and also of the low-rising tone word *mínini* in figure 10; in this context of the short repetitive statements made by the character, it emphasizes the sense of poetic verse.

Performance by Bebalu

The *bì té* shown in figure 11 (see appendix 2) was performed by Bebalu (figure 12), who also comes from Walete in the Tani *hāmeigini* (Pugh-Kitingan 1981:339–42, 739–52).[9]

Figure 12. Bebalu at Walete in 1978 (photo by author).

---

9   This was recorded on 6 February 1975, during a rainstorm; rain can be heard on the zinc roof from the words *Ìra ibira háyagola.*

The story can be summarized briefly as follows (the literal translation follows the transcription in figure 11):

> Listen, I'm telling a story. Once there was a girl who went for a walk. When she had gone quite a distance, she stopped because night was falling. She found a man's house with bundles of sugarcane tied up, and sat down there.
>
> While she was sitting there, an old man came along carrying firewood and put it down. As he was chopping it up, a chip flew off and hit the girl. When the man went to fetch it, he discovered the girl and carried her to where she could lie down and put her there.
>
> After this, the five young men who had gone hunting returned, bringing a possum in their bags for their "father" to cook. He cut the possum into seven portions. When he did that, the five youths said, "Father there are six of us here. Whose is the seventh piece which you've cut?" So the man said "I will eat it myself," and he put it aside to feed the girl when the others were sleeping during the night.
>
> At midnight when he had fed the girl, he tied the long hair of the eldest boy to that of the others and tied their *dāmbale* aprons and *mindibu* waist strings all together. Then he sat playing his *gàwa̱* (double-stringed musical bow) through which he said:
>
> "Water flooded the house on the ground.
>
> Water flooded the girl on the ground.
>
> Water flooded the house at Daralu,
>
> I'm decorating in yellow.
>
> I'm decorating Igila.
>
> I'm decorating Debela.
>
> I'm decorating pigs.
>
> I'm decorating Gila and Gilambo."
>
> Because he said that, parrots flew away screeching. Since those five young men were all tied together, how could they stand up? They just sat in a row.
>
> Then those two became husband and wife and their descendants spread everywhere. We are descended from them as it is often said. That's all.

Bebalu's use of the term *bālamanda* or *bālama ānda* for the men's house implies that this was the abode of *hāroli* in the bush. This is also suggested by the description of the young men having long hair that could be tied together, since part of the training for *hāroli* initiates involved growing their hair to be made into ceremonial wigs. The reference to the young men having caught a possum or *tìa* (here elaborated as *tìage* and *tìabo*) may also be an oblique allusion to *hāroli*. The mythical woman Tiame, venerated in the *hāroli* cult, is named Tia in the *íba gíya gāmu* ritual verses chanted to prepare initiates to receive their *íba gíya* (Pugh-Kitingan 1981:326–27, 698–99). As a woman, the performer would not be familiar with the ritual practices and chants of the *hāroli*, although she would probably know something of the Tiame myth and associate it with the bachelor group. Actual *hāroli* reportedly did not eat possum or any food baked in ashes, but the mention of *tìa* in the story and its verbal association with Tia or Tiame may also inform the listeners that the men in the story are *hāroli*.[10]

Since the old man in the story was a senior *hāroli*, the five initiates addressed him as *ába* ('father'). His association with the young woman and his expression of love for her through the poetry articulated with his *gàwa*, ended his career as a *hāroli* forever. The reference to screeching parrots flying off at the sound of his instrument not only adds dramatic colour to the story, but symbolizes the loss of his spiritual powers developed through years of discipline away from women and normal society in the bush. This passage is obviously fictitious, since the *gàwa* is not usually played by *hāroli*, unlike the *gùlupóbe* panpipes that a bewigged man usually carries around and blows as a form of personal diversion to pass time. At the conclusion of their training, *hāroli* initiates have their wigs placed on their heads and each is presented with a set of *gùlupóbe*.

Bebalu accidentally uses the word *hūrala* from *hūra* ('woman's reed skirt') when describing the youths' clothing being tied together, and also uses *hìriyúla* ('jaw's harp' or 'jew's harp', a free aerophone or lamellophone) for the man's musical bow before correcting it to *gàwa*. The term *mándibula* is an alternative for *míndibu* (waist strings). Throughout her *bì té*, she uses *lāya* ('said') as a chanted, linking expression between sentences.

As shown in the transcription, Bebalu chants most of her story in a singing vocal timbre, before breaking into heightened speech in the last part where she refers to the five initiates sitting tied together in a row, unable to rise. For most of her *bì té*, until the middle of the *gàwa* verse of the old man, she uses three main pitches, of which the lowest sounds either a semitone or whole tone below the main pitch (figure 13). The *è* interjection by one of the listeners also rests on the main pitch.

---

10   Former *hāroli* claimed that the group ate mostly sweet potatoes, vegetables (edible ferns), and occasionally pig meat (but not fat) that had been steam-cooked in ground ovens. They did not eat food roasted in ashes. This was believed to encourage initiates to grow thick reddish hair that could be made into wigs.

Figure 13. Main pitches used in *bì té* by Bebalu (figure 11), recorded at Walete, 6 February 1975.

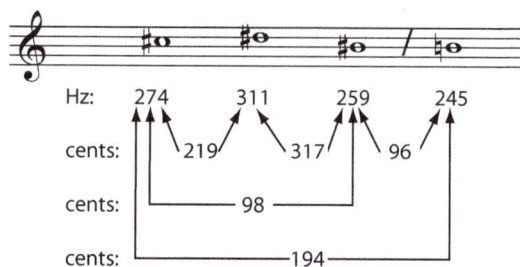

As in Wandome's example, Bebalu's performance features the falling third figure between the outer pitches that sometimes distorts speech-tone, as for the words *háyagola*, *īgini*, *lēaria*, and *bárume* in figure 14. But usually the speech-tones of words determine the actual melodic microstructures with sentence-terminating intonation producing resolutions onto the central tonic pitch at the end of sentences. The linking expression *lāya* at the end of sections is also chanted on this pitch, and in most cases this is followed by the *è* interjection.

Figure 14. Examples of speech-tone distortions by falling third figure, exemplified on the words *háyagola, īgini, lēaria,* and *bárume* in Bebalu's *bì té* (figure 11).

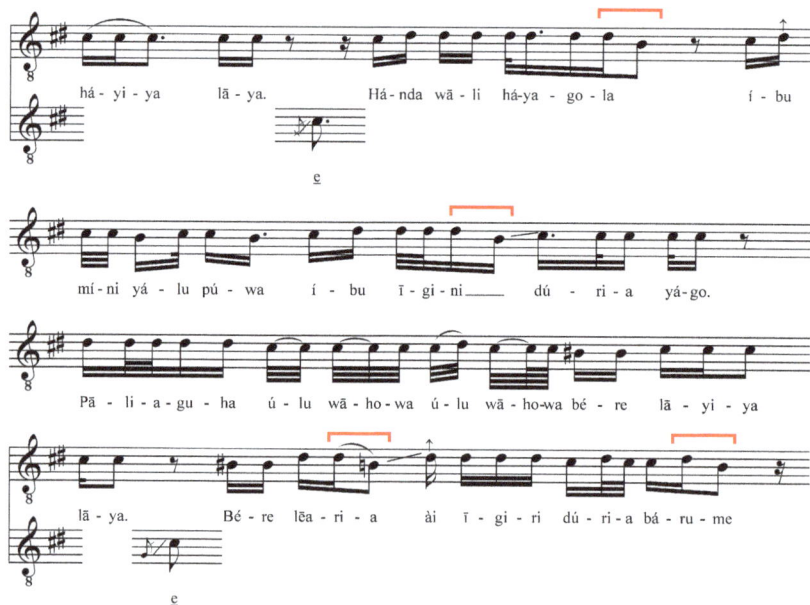

As mentioned earlier, there is no sense of metre or recurring rhythm as in Western music or in the sung tales of the Hagen region as described in chapters 11 and 12. Rather, the inherent linguistic tone patterns of the words determine micro-rhythmic structures.

A new pitch arrangement emerges during the section recounting the *gàwa* verse from the words *Ígila báli lāro*. Here, the lowest pitch is not used. Instead a new pitch sounding a major third above the central pitch is taken up (figure 15). Although this new pitch arrangement is not the same as that of an actual *gàwa*, it is Bebalu's way of distinguishing the sound of the instrument from the rest of the story. The tonic now becomes the lowest pitch, and this is reminiscent of *gàwa* music where the pitch of the outer string sounds as a tonic ostinato below the pitches of the inner strand, and also coincides with sentence terminating intonation as in *gàwa* poetry. Unlike Wandome, who is renowned for her skill as a *gàwa* performer and hence often chants the same pitch arrangement as that of the bow when recounting *gàwa* verses in her *bì té*, Bebalu is not skilled in this instrument. Thus her new pitch arrangement in this part of her story differs somewhat from the actual instrument.

Figure 15. Pitches used by Bebalu for recounting poetry articulated with *gàwa* (figure 11).

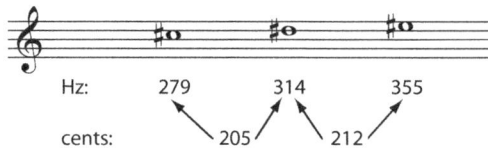

As explained above, when playing the *gàwa*, the performer reshapes the sound energy of the instrument with the oral cavity to articulate words (figure 16). These words fall into poetry that often alludes to love. Thus although *gàwa* performance requires great skill and is regarded by the Huli as their supreme artistic achievement, it is hardly an activity considered appropriate for a *hāroli* instructor like that in the story here.

The poetry said to have been expressed through the man's *gàwa* in Bebalu's story is typical of Huli love poetry, which consists of repetitions of short lines with a changing word (usually a place name or clan name that identifies an individual) in each line (such as are described and analysed under the rubric of "parallelism" in chapters 1, 4, 6, 8, 9, 10, and 11 of this volume). In this story, the flood symbolizes the main character's love for the girl, while the "house on ground" and *Dáralu* is where the *bālama ānda* is located. References to yellow ceremonial paint and pigs suggest the man's thoughts of marriage—when he will present a number of pigs as bridewealth to the girl's parents—and *Ígila*, *Débela*, *Gìla*, and *Gílambo* are the names of ambilineal clans to whom he is related cognatically.

Figure 16. Gagime, a woman from Bebenete, playing her *gàwa̱* (photo by author).

From the word *Ígila*, the speech-tones of words largely determine the melodic structures within this new pitch arrangement, with verse lines resolving onto the lowest pitch as sentence-terminating intonation. The rising-then-falling melodic patterns of *Ígila* and *Dábela*, both of which have low-rising word-tones are caused by this. In the case of the line *Gìla Gílambo báli lāro,* where *Gìla* has a high-falling word-tone and *Gílambo* is low-rising, both syllables of *Gìla* are chanted on the highest pitch, and the two names share a combined, tonally-significant shape (figure 17).

Figure 17. Poetry articulated by the old man with his *gàwa* in Bebalu's *bì té* (figure 11).

After this section that recounts the man's *gàwa* verse, Bebalu breaks into heightened speech as she describes the five *hāroli* initiates who, having been tied together while asleep, are suddenly awakened and unable to rise. Her loud narration captures their stunned surprise at the sound of the instrument's love verse, and her repetition *Hèya àu hèyuabe tōba hō bérearia. Hèya àu hèyoabe tōba hō bēreria* ("How could they rise up? They just sat in a line") presents a hilarious picture of the five youths tied together in a row. Instead of a sad ending, Bebalu's *bì té* ends on a happy note by referring to the marriage of the man and the girl.

Conclusions

The *bì té* fireside stories of the Huli constitute a musical genre in which the storyteller uses a characteristic melodic cell of three main pitches from which to chant his or her tale. Chanted linking expressions between sections in the story and regular melodic interjections of *è* ('yes') from one of the listeners, as well as a recurring falling figure between the outside pitches that resolves onto the central main pitch near the ends of statements, help the performer to maintain the flow of words and ideas.

As a musical genre, *bì té* exemplifies the importance of language in Huli music. Unlike many other cultures in the world, the Huli do not compose "music" and then fit words to the tunes. Rather each Huli genre has its own characteristic pitch arrangement or cell that is used as a vehicle for language articulation. In *bì té* as in other genres of Huli music, the pace and structure of articulation determines speed and micro-rhythmic patterns, while melody is nearly always shaped by the speech-tones of words with sentence-terminating intonation producing a resolution onto the main pitch at the end of statements. The skill of a musician is determined by his or her ability to articulate rapidly and develop a narrative theme, without losing the flow of ideas or "thoughts from the heart."

Although *bì té* is a prose form composed of sentences of various lengths, it can also include passages of poetry and heightened speech for dramatic effect in the story. Story themes are usually based around two or three characters, and can include supernatural elements and fantastic episodes. While these stories may provide instruction for children, for example by warning them of the dangers of wandering off into the bush, they are primarily told for entertainment. Hence they may describe activities and relationships that would be unacceptable or even unbelievable in everyday life, such as a senior celibate *hāroli* bachelor falling in love with a young woman. Nevertheless, *bì té* do reflect both the traditional worldview and life of the Huli, as characters encounter spirits, plant gardens, build houses, construct hanging bridges, undertake journeys, marry and give birth, and join *hāroli* in the bush.

Despite inroads made by outside media, such as radios and cassette or CD players, skilled *bì té* storytelling continues to be an important genre of nightly entertainment in the houses of both Huli men and women. This is not only because the stories reflect Huli life, but also undoubtedly because *bì té* as a musical genre springs from the basic need of the individual to express his or her thoughts in language. In expressing these thoughts in chanted story form, the skilled performer is able to engage the listeners and maintain their interest and attention.

References

Glasse, Robert M. 1965. "The Huli of the Southern Highlands." In *Gods Ghosts and Men in Melanesia*, edited by Peter Lawrence and Mervyn J. Meggitt, 27–49. Melbourne: Oxford University Press.

Peters, Bronwyn. 1975. "Huli Music: Its Cultural Context, Musical Instruments and *Gulupobe* Music." Honours thesis, BA with Honours, Monash University.

Pugh, Jacqueline. 1975. "Communication, Language and Huli Music: A Preliminary Survey." Honours thesis, BA with Honours, Monash University.

Pugh-Kitingan, Jacqueline. 1977. "Huli Language and Instrumental Performance." *Ethnomusicology* 21 (2): 205–32.

———. 1979. "The Huli and Their Music." *Hemisphere* 23: 84–89.

———. 1980. "Language Articulation Using Musical Instruments in the Southern Highlands of Papua New Guinea." Abstract in "Structured Session on Acoustical Aspects of Australasian Music," *Tenth International Congress on Acoustics*, vol. 1: 51.

———. 1981. "An Ethnomusicological Study of the Huli of the Southern Highlands, Papua New Guinea." PhD dissertation, University of Queensland.

———. 1982. "Language Communication and Instrumental Music in the Southern Highlands of Papua New Guinea—Comments on the Huli and Samberigi Cases." *Musicology* 7: 104–19.

———. 1984. "Speech-tone Realisation in Huli Music." In *Problems and Solutions: Occasional Essays in Musicology Presented to Alice M. Moyle,* edited by Jamie Kassler and Jill Stubington, 94–120. Sydney: Hale and Iremonger.

———. 1986. *The Huli of Papua Niugini.* Recordings by Jacqueline Pugh-Kitingan and Bronwyn Peters; commentary, photographs, and map by Jacqueline Pugh-Kitingan. Music of Oceania series, edited by Hans Oesch. Institute for Musicology, University of Basel. Bärenreiter-Musicaphon BM SL 2703. One 30 cm, 33 1/3 rpm disc.

———. 1992. "Huli Yodelling and Instrumental Performance." In *Sound and Reason: Music and Essays in Honour of Gordon D. Spearritt*, edited by Warren A. Bebbington and Royston Gustavson, 61–108. St. Lucia: Faculty of Music, University of Queensland.

————. 1998a. "Understanding Music: Timbre: Huli Yodeling." In *Australia and the Pacific Islands*, edited by Adrienne L. Kaeppler and J. W. Love, 298–99. The Garland World Encyclopedia of Music, 9. Washington: Garland Publishing.

————. 1998b. "Highland Region of Papua New Guinea: Southern Highlands Province: Huli." In *Australia and the Pacific Islands*, edited by Adrienne L. Kaeppler and J. W. Love, 536–43. The Garland World Encyclopedia of Music, 9. Washington: Garland Publishing.

————. 2005. "Dance and Drumming amongst the Huli of the Southern Highlands of Papua New Guinea—the Ethnosemantics, Structure and Change of Group Performance in a Culture of Individuals." In *Global and Local Dance in Performance*, edited by Mohd Anis Md Nor and Revathi Murugappan, 175–87. Kuala Lumpur: Cultural Centre, University of Malaya and Ministry of Culture, Arts and Heritage Malaysia.

Rule, W. Murray 1977. *A Comparative Study of the Foe, Huli and Pole Languages of Papua New Guinea.* Oceania Linguistic Monographs, 20. Sydney: University of Sydney.

Rule, W. Murray, and Joan E. Rule. 1970a. *Statement of the Phonology and Grammar of the Huli Language.* Tari: Asia Pacific Christian Mission.

————. 1970b. *Huli–English English–Huli Dictionary.* Tari: Asia Pacific Christian Mission.

Appendix 1

Figure 7. *Bì té* **by Wandome (duration: 2:17)**—*beginning.* **An audio file of this example can be found in online item 9.**

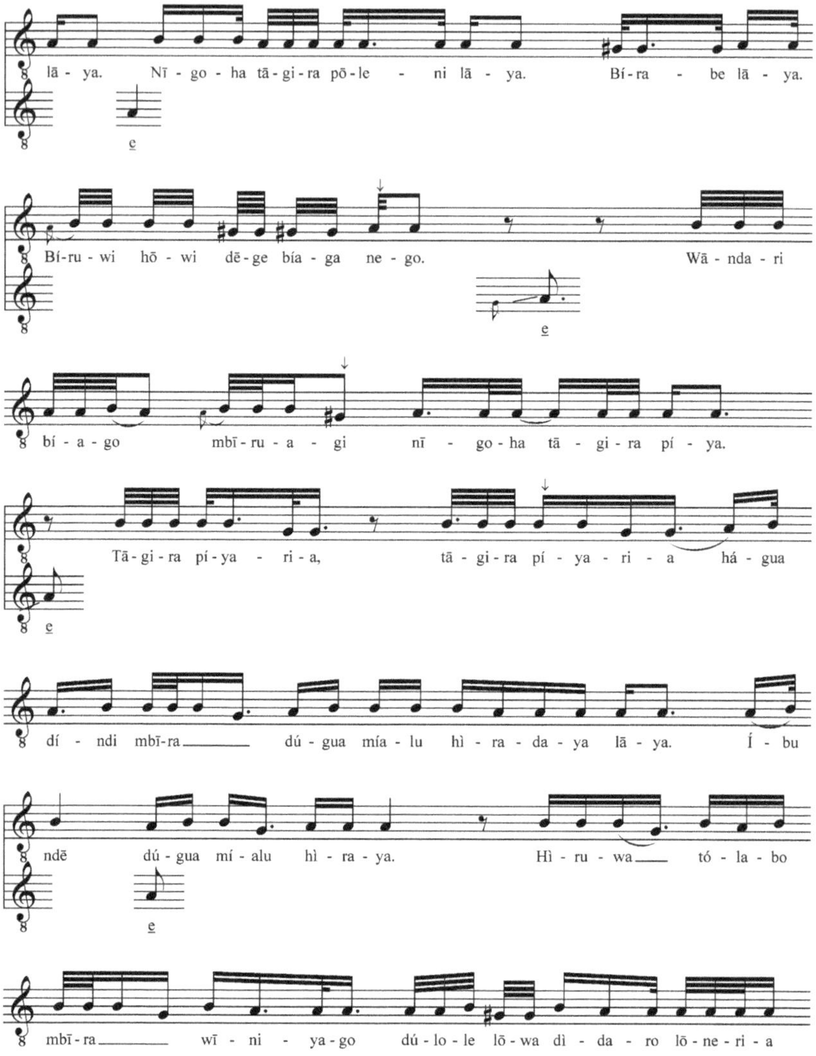
lā - ya. Nī - go - ha tā - gi - ra pō - le - ni lā - ya. Bí - ra - be lā - ya.
e
Bí - ru - wi hō - wi dē - ge bía - ga ne - go. Wā - nda - ri
e
bí - a - go mbī - ru - a - gi nī - go - ha tā - gi - ra pí - ya.
Tā - gi - ra pí - ya - ri - a, tā - gi - ra pí - ya - ri - a há - gua
e
dí - ndi mbī - ra dú - gua mía - lu hì - ra - da - ya lā - ya. Í - bu
ndē dú - gua mí - alu hì - ra - ya. Hì - ru - wa tó - la - bo
e
mbī - ra wī - ni - ya - go dú - lo - le lō - wa dì - da - ro lō - ne - ri - a

é- ga ú-ru-bu ngá-wa - e hà - ba - ne mbī - ra_____ tó - la - bo

e

pú - ni - ni wī - ni - ya lā - ya. Í - ni à-gua ó - re

e

nó - le lō - wa, nà - ma-nda bē - ro lō nēa-ri - a mbè - do-go bī - a

lā - ya. Í - bu dái bī - ya-go-la hō - wa bí - ru - wa hú - li - ya ī-gi - ri

e

Há - gua Dí-ndi Gī - la - ra hái mó-go-bia hā-na - ya.

e

Ài Gī - la - ra ái-ya Gī - la - ra-la bí-ru - wi hō - wi dē - ge

bía-ga-ne-go. Ài ī - gi - ri wā-he - ó - re____ wā-he - ó - re hē-a-go-la

lō - wa. Ī-gi - ri wā - he ká-ru - bi hā-ya-go-la hō - wa. I - bu

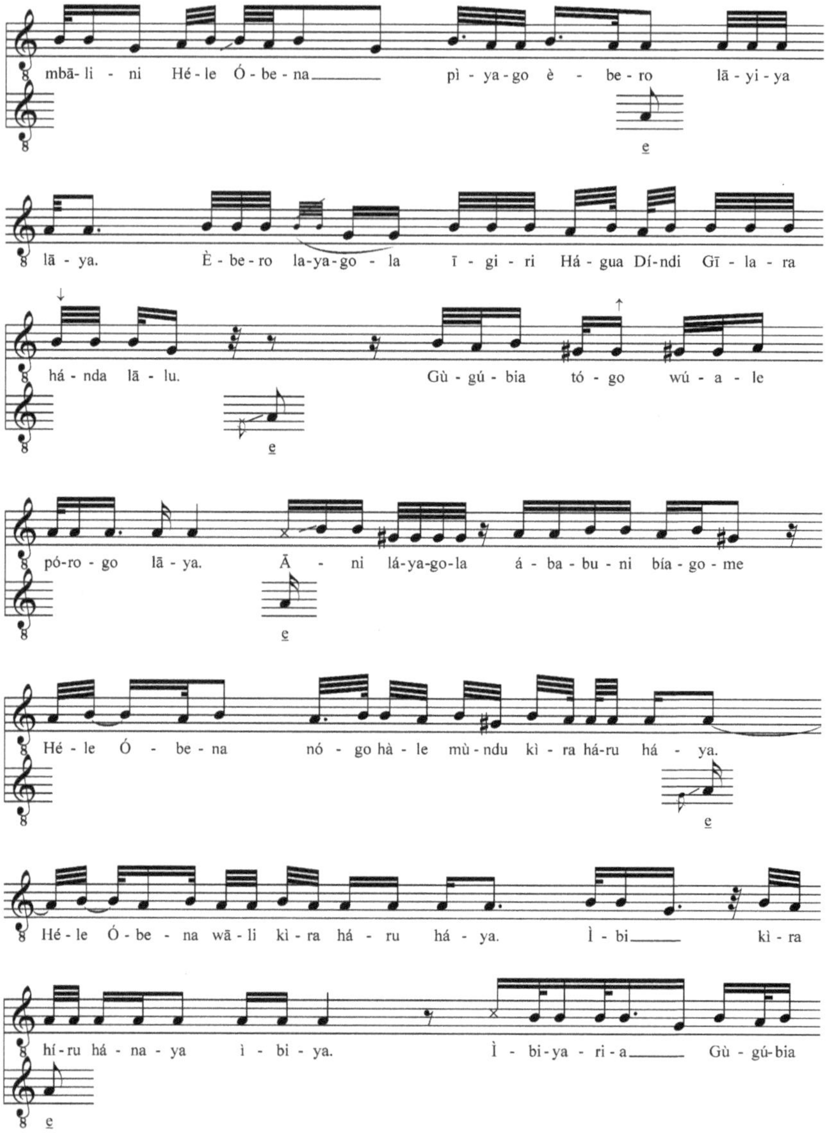
mbā- li - ni Hé - le Ó - be - na pì - ya - go è - be - ro lā - yi - ya
e
lā - ya. È - be - ro la - ya - go - la ī - gi - ri Há - gua Dí - ndi Gī - la - ra
há - nda lā - lu. Gù - gú - bia tó - go wú - a - le
e
pó - ro - go lā - ya. Ā - ni lá-ya-go-la á - ba - bu - ni bia - go - me
e
Hé - le Ó - be - na nó - go hà - le mù - ndu kì - ra há-ru há - ya.
e
Hé - le Ó - be - na wā - li kì - ra há - ru há - ya. Ì - bi kì - ra
hí - ru há - na - ya ì - bi - ya. Ì - bi - ya - ri - a Gù - gú-bia
e

tó - go wí - a - lu hē - ā - go - la ī - gi - ri
bí - a - go - me la - lu í - bu ái-ya hō - ndo lā - lu. Gù - gú - bi - a
e
hà - nu - ni kó - go - la hō - wa í - bu dù - ru lā - ya - gua Há - gua Dí - ndi
Gī - la - ra ī - gi - ni pí - la - le lā - be. Há - gua Dí - ndi Gī - la - ra
e
ī - gi - ni pí - la - le lā - be. Bú - ri bó - bi lā - lu mí - ni - ni
3
e
pí - la - le lā - be. Bá - ri - na bó - bi lā - lu mí - ni - ni pí - la - le
e
lā - be lā - ya. Ài â - ni lô - wa Gù - gú - bia - ni tó-go wí - a - lu
e

hē - a - go - la hō - wa í - bu ái-ya há-nda lā - be lā - ya dá - gua nà - la - lu,
e
nà - la - lu nà - la - lu bí - ya - go - la dè í - bu ái - ya - ni dè
í - bu ái - ya - ni bía - a - bo. Ī - gi - ri bía - go - me dú - ru wá - lu lā - a - bo.
e
Dè í - bu ái - ya - ni í - bu ái - ya há - nda lā - ya. Nà-la-ya-go-la
e
é - ga ú - ru - bu ngá - we gì - ya kì - ya lā - lu í - ba - lu, ī - gi - ri
bía - go yá - lu pú - do - go lā - ya. Pí - ya - go - la lō - wa
e
í - bu ái - ya - na - ga ī-gi-ri bí - a - go - me pá - ya - lu kū - ni gì
bā - re - ya - ne ō - go dē - ge í - bu ái - ya - hō - ndo pó - lo mí - a - lu
í - bu - ni yá - lu pú - do-go lē - ne lā - ya. Ài ōgo-ni hō-ndo
e
lā - ya.

È   Húliya mbīrala Bébogo   wāne   Kándime mēndela.   *È   lā   è   lābe.*
Yes. Boy   first&   Bebogo's daughter Kandime second&.   (Yes say yes say.)
Yes. There were once two persons, Bebogo's daughter Kandime and a "man." (Say yes now, say yes later.)

Bébogo   wāne   Kándime mēndela, lībuni bíruwi hōwi dēge bíaganego.   *Mbīruagi, húliya*
Bebogo's daughter Kandime second&, they sat stood only which usually do. One day, boy
Bebogo's daughter Kandime and the other, they just lived there all the time. One day, that "man"

bíago   íbugua Héla   Óbena pòrogo.   Bébogo   wāne   Kándime ína bírabe   lāya.
that one he   "Hela Obena I'm going. Bebogo's daughter Kandime you sit,"   said.
said, "I'm going to Hela Obena country.   Bebogo's daughter Kandime, you stay here.

Íba   nōa   bīyagua Gùgúbia dāda   bù yú ānda   wérogo   nábe, lāya.
"Water want to drink if you do, Gugubia stream drained/dammed in which I'm putting drink" he said.
If you want to drink water, drink the Gugubia River which I'm damming in.

Nógo nōa   bīyagua bāi gābua ní   hīnariba   nábe lāya.
"Pig want to eat if you do, wild pig down we (2) caught eat" he said.
If you want to eat pig, eat the wild ones we caught down there in the bush.

Nīgoha   tāgira pōleni   lāya.   Bírabe lāya.   Bíruwi hōwi   dēge bíaga nego.
"Down there outside don't go" he said. "Sit" he said.   Sat stayed only which usual do.
Don't go outside down there," he said. "Stay here," he said. She just lived there all the time.

Wāndari bíago   mbīruagi nīgoha   tāgira píya. Tāgira píyaria,   tāgira píyaria   hágua
Girl that one one day down there outside went. Outside when went, outside when went clay
But one day that girl went outside, down there. When she went outside, she found some clay

díndi mbīra dúgua míalu hìradaya   lāya. Íbu ndē dúgua míalu hìraya.
ground one pull out get painted on body said. She then pull out get painted on body.
ground and scooping it up she painted her body (said). She then scooped it up and painted her body.

Hìruwa   tólabo   mbīra wīniyago dúlole   lōwa   dìdaro   lōneria   éga úrubu ngáwae
Having painted pandanus one found to weave when said when tried to pull down bird parrot
After having painted herself, she found some pandanus leaves with which to weave a raincape, and when she tried

hàbane mbīra tólabo   púnini wīniya lāya.   *Íni   àgua óre nóle   lōwa,*
egg   one pandanus on top found said.   "I myself how very I'll eat" saying
to pull them down, she found a parrot egg on the top (said).   "This is how I will eat it," she said,

nàmanda bēro   lō   nēaria   mbèdogo bīa   lāya. Íbu dái   bīyagola
"I'm not preparing" saying when she ate swallow without chewing said. She when she returned
"I won't cook it," so saying she swallowed it whole (said).   Then when she returned

hōwa bíruwa húliya īgiri Hágua Díndi Gīlara hái   mógobia hānaya.   *Ài Gīlara   áiya*
stayed sat "boy" boy Clay Ground Gilara banana flower she gave birth to. So Gilara's mother
home, having sat down, she gave birth to a boy named Clay Ground Gilara.   So Gilara and his

Gīlarala bíruwi hōwi   dēge bíaganego.   *Ài   īgiri wāheóre wāheóre hēagola lōwa.*
Gilara& sit stay only which usually do.   Then boy old very old very became was saying.
mother just lived there all the time.   Then the boy grew very very big.

Īgiri wāhe kárubi hāyagola   hōwa. Ibu mbālini   Héle Óbena pìyago   èbero
Boy old mature when he was staying. His "sister" (uncle) Hele Obena which went "I'm coming"
The boy grew up to maturity.   His uncle who had gone to Hele Obena country came calling out,

lāyiya   lāya.   Èbero   layagola   īgiri Hágua Díndi   Gīlara hánda lālu.
he shouted said.   "I'm coming" when he said boy Clay   Ground Gilara look   saying.
"I'm coming" (said).   When he said "I'm coming," the boy Clay Ground Gilara was watching.

Gùgúbia tógo   wúale   pórogo   lāya.   Āni   láyagola   ábabuni bíagome
"Gugubia bridge I will put I'm going, see" he said.   Then when he said that uncle that one
"I'm going to build a bridge across the Gugubia River," he said. Then when he had said that, his uncle came

Héle Óbena nógo   hàle   mùndu kìra háru háya.   Héle Óbena wāli   kìra háru háya.
Hele Obena pig   ear   cut   two was looking after. Hele Obena women two were looking after.
bringing two pigs with cut ears from Hele Obena country. Two Hele Obena women were looking after the pigs.

Ìbi   kìra híru   hánaya   ibiya.   Ìbiyaria   Gùgúbia tógo wíalu
Salt two packet were carrying in string bag came.   While they were coming Gugubia bridge puttting
They came carrying two packets of salt in their string bags. While they were coming, that boy was building

hēāgola   īgiri bíagome lalu   ibu áiya   hōndo lālu.   Gùgúbia hànuni   kógola
when it was standing boy   that one saying his mother look · saying.   "Gugubia in the middle where I stand
the bridge across the Gugubia River and his mother was watching.   "If I shake when I'm standing over

hōwa   ibu dùru lāyagua Hágua Díndi   Gīlara ígini pílale   lābe. Hágua Díndi   Gīlara ígini
standing if I   shake 'Clay Ground Gilara son don't fall!' say. 'Clay Ground Gilara son
the middle of the Gugubia, say 'Clay Ground Gilaria, my son,   Clay Ground Gilara, my son,

pílale   lābe. Bùri bóbi lālu mínini pílale   lābe. Bárina bóbi lālu mínini pílale   lābe lāya.
don't fall' say. 'Unexpected son   don't fall!' say. 'Unexpected son   don't fall!' say" said.
don't fall,' say. 'My unexpected son, don't fall!' say. 'My unexpected son, don't fall!,' say," he said.

Ài   āni   lōwa Gùgúbiani tógo wíalu hēagola   hōwa   ibu áiya   hánda lābe lāya
Then having said, on Gugubia bridge putting when he was there standing his mother didn't say he said
Having said that, when he was standing on the bridge over the Gugubia, his mother wouldn't say what he

dágua nàlalu,   nàlalu nàlalu   bíyagola   dè ibu áiyani   dè ibu áiyani   bíaabo.
like didn't say, didn't say, didn't say; when he did that eye his mother on eye his mother on kept doing.
told her, she didn't say, didn't say, didn't say it; when he did that, he kept watching and watching his mother.

Īgiri bíagome dúru wálu lāabo. Dè ibu áiyani   ibu áiya   hánda lāya. Nàlayagola   éga
Boy that one kept shaking.   Eye his mother on his mother look said. When she didn't say bird
That boy kept shaking.   He kept watching his mother in anticipation.   When she didn't say that,

úrubu ngáwe gìya   kìya lālu ibalu, īgiri bíago yálu púdogo lāya. Píyagola   lōwa ibu
parrot   screeching noise said came boy that one carried away said. When they went saying, his
some parrots came screeching and carried that boy away (said).   When they went off, that

áiyanaga īgiri bíagome páyalu kūni gì bāreyane ōgo dēge ibu áiya-hōndo pólo míalu íbuni yálu
mother's son that one bones   arm wings   here only he "Mother to break give, to her take"
boy's arm bones here were only wings and he said, "Break off my wing and give it to Mother"

púdogo lēne   lāya. Ài ōgoni hōndo lāya.
said (historic tense) said. So that look said.
(said).   So that's all (said).

Appendix 2

Figure 11. *Bì té* by Bebalu (duration: 2:27)—*beginning*. **An audio file of this example can be found in online item 10.**

(heavy rain on roof from here until end)
lā- ya. Ī - ra ì - bi - ra há - ya - go - la ī - ra bí - a - go
e
gā - bi - ya - ri - a hà - ra - ne mbī - ra pú - wa, wā - nda - ri bía-go
3
bé - rea - ri - a pú bi - li - na há - yi - ya lā - ya. Ā - ni
e
bí - ya - go - la mà - nda ā - ga - li bí - a - go - me ī - ra hà - ra - ne
3
3
bí - a - go mò ài ì - bi - ya - ri - a wā-nda - ri bí - a - go há - nda wā - li
3
há - yi - ya lā - ya. Há - nda wā - li há-ya - go - la í - bu
e
mí - ni yá - lu pú - wa í - bu ī - gi - ni dú - ri - a yá-go.
Pā - li - a - gu - ha ú - lu wā - ho - wa ú - lu wā - ho-wa bé - re lā - yi - ya

lā - ya. Bé - re lēa - ri - a ài ī - gi - ri dú - ri - a bá - ru - me
e
tì - a - ge tà - ya pē - ne - ya - go tì - a - bo há - na - lu ì - bi - yi - ya lā - ya.
Tì - a - bo hā - na - lu ì - bi - ya - go - la tì - a bí - a - go
e
3
tì - a - bo há - na - lu ì - bi-ya - go - la tì á - ba í - bu á - ba
í - bu - gua dá - we - lo mí - yi - ya lā - ya. Dá - we - lo
e
mū - wá tì - ni dú - ri - a í - bu á - ba í - bu ò
wā - ra - ga - ne yá - gó ká - ne pó - do wí - yi - yá lā - ya.

Ā - ni bí - ya-go-lá á - ba - o ī - na___ wā - ra - go - ria
e
bé - da - ma - gó dá - go wā - ra - ga - ria bé - da - ma - go dá-go kā - ne
pó - do wé-re-go ài___ na - ga - be lā - ya lā - ya. Ndē___
e
í - ni nō - le lā - ya-go-la ā-ga-li bí-a-go-me pó - do wú - wa
bí - ru - wa mbī - ra - ga ó-re pá - lia hō - ndo nè - ta - ngi wā - nda - ri
bí - a - go___ ò___ wā-nda-ri bía-go tì - a bía-go né - lo
mí - yi - ya lā - ya. Tì - a bía-go né-lo mū-wa
e
mbì___ hā - nu-ni há - ya - go - la hō - wa lā - lu. Ò___ ī - gi - ri

bí - a - go - na - ga ī - gi - ri wā – he - ne bí - a - go - na - ga ò mà

mà - nda - ri___ mà - nda - ri lā - bo mò põ - ngo bī - yi - ya lā - ya.

Dā - mba - le hū - ra - la má - ndi - bu - la mò põ - ngo bī - yi - ya lā - ya.

e̱

e̱

Ā - ni bū - wa lā - lu___ ā - ga - li bía - go - me ò hì - ri - yú - la lā - lu

mbī - ra - ga bí - ru - wa. Ndó gà̱ - wa̱ lā - lu bí - ru - wa bí - ru - wa.

Bí - ru - wa bí - ru - wa lā - lu gà̱ - wa̱ gà̱ - wa̱ lā - lu.

e̱

Ā - ni gà̱ - wa̱ lā - lu lā - lu. Ā - ni bí - a - go - me lā - lu

dí - ndi ā - nda í - ba dá - ya - da. Dí - ndi wā - nda - ri í - ba dá - ya - da. Dá - ra - lu ā - nda í - ba dá - ya - da.

e

Á - mbua-le gì - la bá - li lā - ro. Í - gi - la bá - li lā - ro. Dé - be - la

bá - li lā - ro. Bá - rī - la bá - li lā - ro. Gì - la Gí - la - mbo bá - li lā - ro,

lē - ne lā - ya. Ā - ga - li bía - go - me.

e   e

(spoken loudly)

Ā - ni lā - ya-go-la é-ga ú-ru-bu ngá-we kù - gi - a

lā - lu pù - do - go lā - ya lā - ya. Ĭ - gi - ri mā - ria

e

bía - rua, mā - ria bía - ru dáu - ni bí - a - go____

e

146

í - bu   õ - bia-goha mò   pī - ngi põ-ngo bī - ya - go - me   hè - ya___

àu   hè - yu - a - be   tõ-ba hõ   bé-rea - ri - a.   Hè - ya___ àu

hè - yo - a - be   tõ-ba hõ-wa bé - re - ri - a.   Ò   lī - bu

õ - ne-ne   ā - ga - li - ni - la   hõ-wa hó-no bā - me há - na bi - ni - gõ.

Ò   ī - na bú ká - ma - gó - ni   lā - ga.   Ài   õ - go - ni.

Bì té mbīra lārogo.   *Ndē   húlu   wāndari mbīra-ò, wāndari mbīra béreneya   lāya.*
Story one I'm saying, see. So then person girl   one-o, girl   one   was sitting said.
Listen, I'm going to tell you a story. Once there was a girl, a girl was living there (said).

Ndē   wāndari mbīra béreneyàgo,   ìbu ndē píyiya lāya. Pīalu   hēaria,
And then girl   one   which was sitting, she then went   said.   When she had gone   she stayed,
Then one day the girl who was living there went for a walk (said).   When she had gone, she stopped

ài   nē   lāyagola.   Āgali bālamānda mbīra wīniyago,   hánda wālia hōwa,
then twilight because it was saying. Man   man's house one   which was there when she   found,
because night was approaching.   She found a man's house there with bundles of

ōbíagoha   dù   mbāria mbúla hēago ānda pūwá,   ōbíagoha bírayiya   lāya.
that place   sugar-cane one   tied up there   house when went, that place she sat   said.
sugar cane tied up, and she sat down near that place (said).

Āni   bíaria   āgali wāhe mbīra īra   bòyalu ìbuwa īra   ìbira háyiya   lāya.
Then while doing man old   one   wood carrying came   wood came put down said.
While she was there an old man came along carrying firewood, he came and put it down (said).

Īra   ìbira háyagola   īra   bíago gābiyaria   hàrane mbīra púwa, wāndari bíago
Wood came   when put down wood that one   while he chopped chip   one   went, girl   that one
While he was chopping the wood that he had brought, a chip flew off and struck that girl

bérearia   pú bilina háyiya   lāya. Āni   bíyagola   mànda āgali bíagome īra   hàrane
while sitting go hit   put down said. Then because it did that wig   man that one   wood chip
who was sitting there (said).   Because the chip flew off, the man (*haroli*) went to get it

bíago   mò   ài   ìbiyaria   wāndari bíago hánda wāli háyiya lāya. Hánda   wāli   háyagola
that one   get   then while he went girl   that   found   said. When he   found
and in doing so he found that girl (said).   When he found her, he picked her

ìbu mìni   yálu   púwa ìbu īgini dúria yágo.   Pāliaguha   úlu wāhowa úlu
her picked carried   his sons five were.   Place where to lide down hole found   hole
up and carried her to where his five "sons" (students) were.   He found a hole where she could lie down

wāhowa bére lāyiya lāya. Bére lēaria   ài   īgiri dúria bárume tìage   tàya pēneyago tìabo
found   put   into   said. After putting into then boys five those   cuscus hunt which went cuscus
and put her there (said).   When he had put her there, then thoe five youths who had gone hunting cuscus

hánalu   ìbiyiya   lāya. Tìabo hánalu   ìbiyagola   tìa   bíago tìabo hánalu
carried in bag came   said. Cuscus carried in bag when they came cuscus that one cuscus carried in bag
came bringing cuscus (said).   When they brought the cuscus, that cuscus when they brought it, they gave it

ìbiyagola   tì   ába   ìbu ába   ìbugua dáwelo míyiya lāya. Dáwelo mūwá
when they came, their father he   father he   to cook gave   said. To cook   when had given
to their father to cook (said).   When they had given it

tìni   dúria ìbu ába ìbu ò wāragane yágó káne   pódo wíyiyá lāya. Āni   bíyagolá
they themselves five he father he o sixth   was seventh cut   placed said.   When he did that
to him to cook, he cut five pieces for them, he was the sixth and he cut a seventh (said).   When he did that

ábao   īna wāragoria bédamagó   dágo wāragariabédamago dágo kāne   pódo wérego   àinagabe
"Father we six   we sit (st. v.) see   six   we sit   see   seventh cut   which you put whose?
they said, "Father, there are six of us, six of us, whose is the seventh piece that you cut?" (said).

lāya   lāya. Ndē   íni   nōle   lāyagola   āgali bíagome pódo wúwa, bíruwa
they said said. So then "I myself I will eat" said therefore man   that one cut   put,   waited
            So he said, "I myself will eat it," and he cut it and put it aside, and waited

mbīraga   óre pália hōndo nètangi wāndari bíago   ò wāndari bíago   tìa   bíago   nélo míyiya
night-time very asleep   while   girl   that one o girl   that one cuscus that one to eat gave
until the middle of the night when they were sleeping to give that girl the cuscus (said).

lāya. Tìa   bíago nélo mūwa   mbì hānuni háyagola   hōwa   lālu. Ò īgiri bíagonaga
said. Cuscus that   to eat when he had given midnight   because it was staying said. O boy   that one's
   When he had given her that cuscus to eat, it was midnight.   Then he tied the long

īgiri wāhene bíagonaga ò mà màndari màndari lābo mò pōngo bīyiya lāya. Dāmbale   hūrala
boy   eldest   that one's   o   hair to   hair to   long tied   said. Man's apron grass skirt&
hair of the eldest boy to the others' hair (said).   He tied their *dambale*s and

mándibula   mò pōngo bīyiya lāya. Āni būwa lālu āgali bíagome ò hìriyúla lālu mbīraga   bíruwa.
waist strings& tied together   said. And then said   man that one o *hiriyula* said night-time was sitting.
waist strings together (said).   Then that man sat playing *hiriyula* in the night.

Ndó gàwa lālu   bíruwa   bíruwa.   Bíruwa bíruwa   lālu   gàwa gàwa lālu.   Āni   gàwa
No   *gawa* saying was sitting was sitting. Sitting was sitting saying *gawa gawa* saying. Then   *gawa*
No, he was sitting there playing *gawa*.   He was sitting and playing *gawa*, he played *gawa*. Then he

lālu lālu.   Āni   bíagome lālu díndi ānda íba   dáyada.   Díndi   wāndari
said said.   Then that one   said "Place house water flooded.   Place   girl
played *gawa*. Then while playing that one he said, "Water flooded the houses on the ground. Water flooded the

íba   dáyada.   Dáralu ānda íba   dáyada. Ámbuale gìla báli   lāro.
water flooded.   Place   house water flooded. Yellow   decoration I'm saying.
girl on the ground.   Water flooded the house at Daralu.   I'm decorating in yellow.

Ígila báli   lāro.   Débela báli   lāro.   Bárila báli   lāro.   Gìla Gìlambo
Place decoration I'm saying. Place decoration I'm saying. Pig decoration I'm saying. Places
I'm decorating Igila.   I'm decorating Debela.   I'm decorating pigs.   I'm decorating

báli   lāro,   lēne lāya. Āgali bíagome.   Āni   lāyagola éga   úrubu ngáwe kùgia
decoration I'm saying," he said said. Man   that one.   Then because he said parrots   screeching
Gila and Gilambo," (said).   That man (said it). Then because he said that parrots (in nearby trees)

lālu pùdogo lāya lāya. Īgiri māria bíarua, māria bíaru dáuni bíago íbu ōbiagoha   mò pīngi pōngo
flew away   said said.   Boys four   those four   those fifth that one he in that place which were
flew away screeching.   Those four young men, those four and that fifth, they were all tied together

bīyagome hèya àu hèyuabe?   Tōba hō bérearia.   Hèya   àu   hèyoabe?
tied together raised up how did they rise up? In a line they sat.   Rise up how did they rise up?
so how could they rise up?   They could only sit in a line. How could they rise up?

Tōba hōwa béreria. Ò lību ōnene āgalinila hōwa   hóno bāme hána   binigō.
In a line sat.   O they wife   husband& staying, gave birth spread   everywhere.
They sat in a line. Then those two became husband and wife, and their children spread everywhere.

Ò īna bú kámagóni   lāga.   Ài   ōgoni.
O we are born through   as usually say. Then that's it.
We are descended from them as is said.   That's all.

7. Enga *Tindi Pii*: The Real World and Creative Imagination

Philip Gibbs

Introduction

Found throughout the Enga Province, Enga *tindi pii* are one of the many traditions of chanted tales in the Highlands of Papua New Guinea as discussed in the other chapters of this book. They are lengthy tales, performed at night by a sole performer (man or woman), primarily for entertainment, but at the same time communicating forms of esoteric knowledge. Nowadays, with social change and new forms of entertainment, *tindi pii* are uncommon, but they are still performed occasionally, especially in the western parts of the province.

This paper is based on an analysis of seven performances, recorded in different parts of the Enga Province over the past twenty-four years.[1] The province covers some 12,800 sq km and has over 300,000 Enga speakers. The tales studied come from all the main dialects areas of Enga: Kandepe, Tayato, Yandapo, Mae, Layapo, and Kyaka.[2] The principal issue for this paper is the manner in which the storyteller uses creative language to draw the listeners into an imaginary world. Reaching that ideal world requires a journey beyond, to where the earth and sky meet in people's imagination.

Literature on *tindi pii* and related genres

Some of the early Lutheran and Catholic missionaries circulated private collections of stories. The first Catholic missionary to Enga, Fr. Gerard Bus, has a book in mimeo containing notes on orthography, morphology, syntax, and also twenty stories (n.d.). These are a mixture of short myths and tales—some are almost like what one would call fables or "fairy tales" in English literature.

---

1 Four of the *tindi pii* studied were obtained through the manager of the National Broadcasting Commission in Wabag. He selected them as some of the best that had been aired over the radio in Enga. The other three were commissioned, the writer going to the area, enquiring who was the best person for chanting *tindi pii*, and asking him or her to perform a *tindi pii* for recording.

2 The *tindi pii* were recorded in the following years: Kandepe (Irai Imijo at Taitenges, 1995); Tayato (Andrew Ipakane Pindap at Mulitaka, 1987); Yandapo (Sikulua Waimben at Sirunki, 1984); Mae-Ambumu (Joannes Kepe at Monogam, 2006); Mae-Tarua (Peter Perambi at Keman, 1993); Layapo (Paul Polyo at Wapenamanda, 2006); and Kyaka (Mrs. Jeny David at Yumbisa, 2007). I wish to thank all those who assisted in collecting, translating, and interpreting, particularly Philip Maso, Joseph Lakane, Joseph Tanda, Maku Lungu, and Joseph Berom.

Anthropologist Mervyn Meggitt collected a number of stories which he categorized as myth and legend—the difference being that between cosmology and sociology, respectively—myth and legend both considered as "history" (Meggitt 1976). Meggitt does not say whether his stories were chanted and the nine examples he provides appear more narrative and less poetic that the *tindi pii* studied here.

Historian Roderic Lacey distinguished fourteen main types of Enga oral sources, with a typology based on verbal category, formal structure, manner of transmission, purpose, and significance. Under narratives he includes *tindi pii* and *atome pii* as fables, tales, myths, and legends (Lacey 1975:83). He notes how these two types of narrative are linked, particularly when myths are interpreted as origin stories or when people borrow from *tindi pii* to construct a legend about the origin of their clan or phratry.

In recent times Wiessner and Tumu (1998) have drawn upon *tindi pii* in their project on Enga history. They distinguish between *tindi pii* as myth, and *atome pii* as historical tradition. According to Wiessner and Tumu, *tindi pii* comprise myths and tales, and also origin myths for cults. *Atome pii* include:

a. Tribal origin traditions (*tee pia*). These are free-text stories embellished by narrators, but including historical information such as names of tribal founders and their spouses, places of origin, and subsistence strategies of tribal founders.

b. Genealogical sequences linking the narrator to the tribal founder.

c. Historical narratives in free text concerning any historical events of interest.

d. Metaphorical legends in free text recording historical events.

e. Historical traditions of the colonial era in free text.

Other forms of oral tradition include praise poems from the bachelor cults (*sangai titi pingi*), magic formulas and sacred poetry, songs, and proverbs.

People distinguish between the two narrative forms; for example, *tindi pii* are normally performed only at night, whereas *atome pii* can also be told during the day. However, I have found that in practice storytellers do not keep a strict distinction between *tindi pii* and *atome pii*, and sometimes use both expressions together. For example, the storyteller says, ***Tindi** wane **atome** wanaku ongonya paliu siami* (As legendary figures the boy and girl lived there …) or ***Tindinya atomani** lumu ongope* (As the story goes …). This paper focuses on *tindi pii* and will only consider *atome pii* embedded in the *tindi*.

The plot and the underlying themes

The main plots in the seven *tindi* studied in this paper are the following:

Kandepe: A hero, Ipa Lye Puye, is a small orphan. He eventually meets two women. The elder sister is cursed and lives out her life on earth. The younger sister becomes a Sky Being and Ipa Lye Puye matures into a handsome man and joins her there. We (Kandepe Enga) are descendants of the elder sister.

Tayato: Itali Tamba is a little man who eats lizards and sleeps under trees. His brother goes to the place of the cannibals and Itali Tamba goes hunting. He thinks he is shooting a bird, but it is really a woman. She enters into a sexual relationship with him and after he becomes Ipa Pako Pulyo, the two eventually ascend to a legendary place in the sky by means of vines that descend from above.

Yandapo: The last of twenty children was an ugly little boy who ate lizards. He and his brother climb to the top of a mountain where they discover a beautiful flat plain. There they meet two girls. One puts the ugly little boy into her netbag and using magic takes him away. The boy falls into a pool and is transformed into a handsome man. He marries Tapu Enda Ipali. A cannibal eats him but Tapu Enda Ipali recovers his head and brings him back to life.

Mae-Tarua: There are two brothers Lelya and Lelyapa. One is killed by a cannibal. The other brother finds a magic bow and arrows which allow him to kill the cannibal and avenge his brother's death. He has to fall down a cliff to enter an ideal world from which he ascends to the sky, where he could see all corners of the earth.

Mae-Ambumu: Lelyakali Kimala and Tapu Enda Ipali were not born from a natural mother. They lived in a very beautiful place. A cannibal comes and takes Tapu Enda away. Lelyakali searches after her and ends up marrying the cannibal's sister who bears only birds and possums. Eventually Lelyakali Kimala ascends to the sky.

Layapo: A boy was born from a Sky Woman who had married an earthly man. When the boy was pursued by a cannibal, his mother entered into a pig and carried him away on her back. Eventually the boy along with two girls ascends to the sky.

Kyaka: A mythical hero, Sana Walya Asi Kungyapu, had many women friends. One of them is from present-day Mt. Hagen. Sana is killed in a dispute over land. His Hagen friend comes to see him, mixes her own blood with pig's blood for him to eat with greens, and brings him back to life.

Plots commonly include the following features:

a. A boy who is small and ugly grows to become a strong and desirable man.

b. A boy and girl who have no parents. Often the boy has an advantage. For example, both go to fetch water, but the container given to the girl has a hole in it.

c. A hero figure saves his people from the tyranny of a demon or cannibal.

d. The hero finds or is given a magic bow or a magic package which when used or opened allows him or her to travel immediately to other locations or to have superhuman powers.

e. Often at the end of the *tindi*, the hero and heroine ascend to the sky (*yalya toko* 'sky bridge').

Underlying themes include the seeking of adulthood, a quest for beauty, and the search for a better world. Links to the male initiation rites are common. If, in the tale, a man goes to a house in the forest, the house will be beautiful and the garden well planted and flourishing—but there is no other man present. It is looked after by a young girl who is a Sky Woman. In most cases she marries the man and in the end the woman brings the man to the sky. In the Kandepe tale, there are also obvious links to the Kepele ancestral cult.

The characters and their status as spirit beings or as human beings

Characters in these stories are heroes and heroines, male and female. Very often there is a male or female cannibal or demon. We find contrasting qualities: beautiful and ugly, wild and domestic, younger and older, sociable and unsociable, greedy/selfish and generous. Ipa Lye Puye in the Kandepe tale has never eaten food from a woman or tasted sugar cane from a man and is antisocial and selfish because he eats possums by himself and does not share the meat with others.

Sometimes there is ambiguity about their status as human or some form of spirit being. In the Layapo tale the girls ask, "Is he a real young man or a *pututakali* (dwarf)?" Others seem human but have special origins. We hear in the Mae-Tarua tale how the mother of the two boys became pregnant and bore them after eating birds' eggs. In the Mai-Ambumu tale, Lelyakali Kinane and Tapu Enda Ipali have no mother.

The beautiful young woman Tapu Enda Ipali is portrayed as a Sky Being because the only man to have ever "seen" her was the sun. She is described as a woman who does not walk or do the slightest work: *Tindinya atomani lumu ongope lea oo, tapu enda ipali nikinya pimalenge lumu ongope* (As the myth/story goes, she was the sister of the sun). We hear too that Lelyakali Kimala is *nikinya kaiminingi* (brother of the sun). On other occasions he is called *niki lenge* (sun eyes or bright eyes—an expression used sometimes in political praise songs today). In the Kyaka tale, Sana Walya Asi Kungyapui's wife has the power to bring him back to life by giving him food containing pig's blood mixed with her own. Some characters appear to be ordinary, but in extraordinary situations. For example two boys struggle to the top of a mountain and find two girls already there—suggesting that the girls are spirit beings.

Some figures are larger than life—like supermen. Even the wild dogs couldn't bite the calf muscles of Pandai Akali Lelya, and when he beat his hand drum the earth shook. He could catch three cassowaries at once in the same trap! Horrifying cannibal figures perform supernatural feats or cause unusual events too. When the hero Kimala shoots the cannibal, there is thunder and lightening from the sky and the whole stone cliff breaks into pieces. The superhuman figures will sometimes undergo a transformation in order to beat the cannibal. For example, in one tale the hero disguises himself as a mosquito, then becomes a young boy. As a "mosquito boy" he doesn't have a name. Later he is recognized as the hero Lelyakali Kimala.

There are moments, particularly at the end of the tales where a human being is transformed into a Sky Being. In the Kandepe story we hear how the handsome young man (who initially was classed among the cannibals) and the young woman arrive at a beautiful flat place covered with *nomo* grass and there they turn into Sky Beings. In another tale Lelyapa has to fall down a cliff to enter that ideal place, but then ascends to the sky through a sacred plant. In the Tayato tale, Ipa Pako Pulyo is a human hero who ascends to the sky along with a Sky Woman by climbing *tatali* vines.

The characters are almost always fictional. Among all the tales studied there is only one mention of a living human being whom the listeners would know.

Structure and specialist vocabulary

Enga *tindi pii* are usually chanted in a house at night. The lines are of varying length, with internal rhythms somewhat akin to ordinary speech. Sometimes there are lengthened vowels at the end of each line or after a series of lines followed by a pause to allow the teller to take a breath and a chance for listeners to respond with *ee*, indicating approval (online item 11 is an extract of a performance recorded in the men's house at Mogal, Kandep District, on 11 April 2002). There is repetition either for emphasis, for example, *Poo poo mende* (a strange wind), with the term *poo* (wind) repeated, suggesting that it was stronger than normal or *poto loo poto kaita,* with *poto* repeated for particular emphasis—

an expression referring to where the earth and sky meet. At other times an image may be introduced at strategic points in the story for aesthetic purposes, or even to give the teller a chance to decide what comes next.

The most highly appreciated *tindi pii* use poetic forms quite different from everyday speech. Aside from metaphors and other creative practices (treated in the next section) words used may be particular to a location or any one dialect of Enga. During the study, Enga research assistants had to consult with older persons from the area where the *tindi* was chanted in order to understand many of the expressions. For example, the Kandepe *tindi* refers to the hero arriving at *Kundaki puu Lemeane*. Kundaki is the name of a clan near Ketenge in the Wage region of Kandep and Lemeane a popular name for what would normally be called *tae toko* or *tawe toko* (the 'bridge' or place in the sky) in the rest of Enga. A person from Kandepe would understand this, but outsiders might well experience difficulty.

There is also the use of special names in this genre of speech. Sometimes they are a form of "praise name." Thus in the Mae-Tarua tale a bow has a special name, Sangu Muli, because it is a magic bow with "one end pointing to where it gets dark and the other end pointing to where the sun is shining." The person who holds it can fly. The sky too may have different names, such as Embe or Andakuna. Clans have special names, commonly used in traditional songs.

Occasionally the teller will include popular proverbs, as with the inclusion of the saying *wanakupi akalina loo mandenge* (A woman is born for a man). Most people would recognize the saying, however in this case, the "man" happens to be the cannibal demon.

Creative imagination

Sometimes the teller will mention rivers, mountains, or places that the hearers are familiar with and then will create an extraordinary scene around those points of reference. For example, one hears of a man being chased up Lupamanda mountain (which the hearers would know), but then there is the fantastic image of him laying his spear across from that mountain to another acting as a bridge for him to cross.

Descriptions are laced with imagery that appeals to the senses: sights, sounds, and even smells. Mountains are described as appearing like eagles' beaks or the sharp beaks of *alu* birds. The cannibal monster has ugly brown matted hair and one eye on its forehead—as big as a full moon. In the Yandapo tale, people hear that as one of the girls goes "her cordyline leaves[3] were making crackling sounds in the wind." Moreover, the wind is so strong that "both dry and green leaves fall from the trees." In the Mae-Ambumu tale, Lelyakali Kimala smells smoke and as he came closer to the dance ground "he could smell their bodies, they were so crowded." Such images help stimulate the imagination so that listeners are drawn into the tale.

Tapu Enda is described as beautiful—having no marks on her body from hard work or from being beaten. Other attractive woman are said to have "no signs of death on them." In contrast, the daughter of the cannibal is so ugly that her face looks as though "it had been rubbed with pig excrement." The cannibal monster is huge "like the earth and the sky coming." Lelyakali Kimala is so desirable that four girls dance on each side and others behind him, whereas the little lizard-eater in the Yandapo tale is said to be ugly with his hair, eyes, and jaw like that of a little opossum. The storyteller goes into detail in describing Itala Tambu: "If you tried to cook him in a ground oven, the fern leaves would be dry. If you tried to eat him, your teeth would break. If you tried to cut him, your knife would become blunt. His head was like a native salt packet and his legs as thin as arrow shafts." It seems he is a tough little fellow.

The imagery is not limited to people. Animals and nature are included also. In the Mae-Ambumu tale all the snakes are seen running away with their eggs in their mouths, and birds are flying northwards with eggs in their beaks—signalling that something terrible is going to happen. There are attractive images too. While the hero is dancing, "the sun couldn't decide whether to set or not …, and later, morning was hesitating to come. It was like nature saying 'Will I have/let dawn come or not?'"

At times one image follows another to develop a scene. In the following example, the storyteller describes an unusual night followed by dawn.

> The sky was making strange noises.
>
> The night was filled with something like *yumbi* cherries.
>
> Then there was a very big rain.
>
> He thought there was something happening and he sat in the house.
>
> Now when it was dawning, there were things of all colours moving around.
>
> When the sky was lit and colourful,
>
> When it was dawning, the sky looked like broken firewood being displayed.

---

3   These were traditionally worn hanging from a belt like a loincloth.

It is hard to capture these images in an English translation. The penultimate line above employs words referring to a "spear" and "lighted charcoal" indicating how the sky is not just colourful, but has streaks or shafts of light in the darkness. The underlying meaning is that an extraordinary day was dawning and hunting would be successful.

In another scene we hear how Kupa Lelya and his mother are crying because Lelyapa has not returned from hunting. He was a gardener and had not been hunting before, so they feared for his life and were crying like "rain was falling from a pandanus tree—they were sitting under a waterfall." The listener would know that pandanus trees collect water in their stems, and how when people cut down a wild *wapena* pandanus tree, especially a young one, a large amount of water pours out. Being underneath it at that time would feel like a waterfall. In this way the storyteller illustrates the extent of them being drenched by their own tears.

At times the meaning is apparent only with sufficient cultural knowledge. In the Tayato tale, the Sky Woman who first appeared to Itali Tamba as a bird says:

If a Yali Kuele man brings a kina shell,

A Mai Makepa man brings a huge pig,

I will release the *sane* rope at that time.

I have marked it to break the cobwebs.

Below pigs and dogs die, the *taro* tree dies.

Handsome young men spend time enjoying.

Above I have marked for my Titi clan to live and to care for them.

The woman is referring to herself. She is a virgin and beautiful. Her private parts will be exposed to a man who brings a kina shell or a huge pig. The image of pigs and dogs "dying" refers to bride price as part of the process of marrying a man. In the past, women hid their menstrual blood in moss under a *taro* tree—known to be a very strong tree. Young men should be careful. If her fluids could kill a *taro* tree, then most certainly their lives would be in danger. "Above" refers to her breasts, which will nourish her children.

Sexual imagery may be explicit or implicit. Often sexual imagery is linked to scenes of eating. This appears in a brutal way in the Kandepe tale when, after eating a pig's stomach, a man, described as an *akali opone mende* (newcomer), takes hold of a girl's breast and calls for a knife so he can cut it off and eat it. There are also candid references, such as a comment by the storyteller that "If a man sitting on the men's side would see it (her), he would have an erection," and a woman snapping back, "You come just desiring to see my private parts." Such references add interest to the tale and evoke hilarity among the listeners.

158

What sort of world are the hearers being expected to imagine?

Tindi pii are chanted at night in dark houses, with only the light of embers from the central fireplace. People have eaten, relax, close their eyes, and allow themselves to enter into the imaginary world created in the rhythmic chanting of the storyteller. As noted above, the images appeal to the senses: sight, hearing, smell, touch, but also to people's sense of fantasy. There is geographical depth too. The cannibal asks Lelyakali, "Have you been to the land where rivers reach their destination or the land at the source of these rivers?" The storyteller is putting this question to the listeners as well.

In the Mae-Tarua story, the hero, Kupa Lelya, meets an old man who tests his trust and confidence by telling him to throw himself down a cliff covered with *maku* trees (which have sharp thorns). At the foot of the cliff, he falls into a swamp and finds himself in a wonderland covered with *nomo* grass and other beautiful plants. By following the advice of the old man and summoning enough courage, he arrives at a beautiful land. Kupa Lelya decides to go further, so he gives a cooked bird to the wise old man and asks him to show him the road. He is then told to follow the Pima Limbi road (*pima limbi* being the name of a pandanus tree) and to follow the Lioko road (*lioko* being another tree where beautiful birds gather). He continues on the journey and at a gate is told to stand on the stem of a *lepe* plant. From there he reaches his destiny by ascending to the sky. The "gate" and the *lepe* plant are obvious references to the *sangai* male initiation rite in which young men would symbolically marry a Sky Woman and gain life and well-being symbolized in the *lepe* plant (Gibbs 1988). The storyteller uses known items like trees and plants or the initiation rites to anchor a fantastic journey to an imaginary wonderland somewhere here on earth. Only later is there an ascent to the sky, with little elaboration except that *niki lenge jia* (he becomes "sun-eyes" = the sun).

The imaginary Takapipi Plains are covered in soft *nomo* grass. We hear in the Yandapo story:

> On the top he saw that there was no dirt. It was very tidy.
>
> It was all like *tangopipi* and the *nomo* grasses dancing all the way to the end
>
> *Laki* trees eating and snoring,
>
> *Lapu* trees eating and snoring,
>
> *Konjapipi* flowers watching with bright eyes,
>
> Flat field lying still, did you see?

The listeners are invited to see—with their imagination—the soft grass and the red *konjapipi* flowers, and to sense the calm: so quiet it as if one might hear the trees sleeping (snoring!).

> He saw pearl shells clean without any dirt or blemish
>
> hanging one over top of the other,
>
> parrots with and without bright colours noisily busy near the *lioko* tree.

The silence is broken by the colourful parrots eating the plentiful *lioko* fruit. It is a place of peace and harmony, where one does not have to work. The mythical woman Tapu Enda Ipali has no sign of work on her body. For Enga people who value strength and industriousness in women this may seem incongruous, and maybe it is, because this imaginary world contrasts in so many ways with reality.

The path from reality to the imaginary is accomplished by way of a journey. Occasionally the storyteller reminds the listeners that he is talking about an imaginary world. In the Kandepe story, people are informed, "They didn't have to go all the way as far as the mountain—because this is a *tindi*!"

The storyteller leads the listeners along a familiar path to an imaginary place where something awaits the intrepid traveller:

> He went up and up where pigs turned back from digging around.
>
> He reached the place where young men turned back from initiation rites.
>
> He reached the place where people turn back from collecting mushrooms.
>
> He reached the place where the short pandanus trees grows.
>
> He reached the place where the *tangu* tree grows short.
>
> He reached the place where possums breed.
>
> He reached the place where possums live.
>
> He went on and on.
>
> He reached the place where wild flowers were growing.
>
> He reached the place where short mountain *taro* trees were growing.
>
> "What am I doing?" he asked.
>
> "When I was a boy I went back from hunting here, now what am I doing?"
>
> "Something is going to happen," he said.

Something does happen—either good or bad. Sometimes the hero encounters a woman, but often the cannibal provides an alternative to the dream world of peace and plenty. Ipa Pako Pulyo, tired of hard labour, decided to journey to the land of the cannibals, thinking that it would be a land of beauty and surplus food. He found that it wasn't like that at all. The cannibal woman's father was covered with dirt and drank water from a pool that made him mad. In the Mae-Ambumu story, the cannibal journeys to attack Lelyakali and Tapu Enda Ipali. They have eight palisades to protect them and think they are safe. Keoakali the cannibal comes not just breaking through the palisades, but seizing them and throwing them aside! He carries a bow made of *mimi* timber which others would find impossible to bend. Not only is it *mimi*, but *mimi ii-taka*—from which the waste (*ii*) part on one side has not been removed, making it appear even more primitive!

No matter the difficulties and trials, there is always a happy ending. The Sky Woman saw that Ipa Pako Pulyo was humble and hard working, and when he went to the place of the cannibals to look for a woman, she knew that his life would be endangered, so she came to him in the form of a *lae* bird. She led him to a place more beautiful than he had ever imagined. It was a place of joy with no labour. Typical for *tindi pii*, the Kandepe story ends:

> The place was occupied with *tayakali* (sky people)
>
> Hard to describe.
>
> Everything was seen to be perfect.
>
> There was no dirt or dust.
>
> There were handsome and beautiful people with their bodies shining.

Re-imagining traditional items

Is there a link between such tales and people's lives today? For the most part, *tindi pii* remain as a traditional genre of chanted tales with little reference to the modern world. There is, however, the occasional reference to modern instruments, as in the Tayato tale when the cannibal's daughter is said to hold up the lower part of a pig's leg as though it were a "pistol." Also sporadically there is a re-imagining of traditional items with links to the contemporary world. For example, opening a magic parcel and flying to another location is now likened to using a plane ticket. Possum fur on the floor of a house is thought to anticipate the modern mattress. Gold mines and associated infrastructural development is seen as a new form of "bridge" or "road" that was anticipated in traditional mythic forms.

To draw conclusions and to think of *tindi pii* as a form of revelation which has been fulfilled today with modern developments would be to change the genre from *tindi* into *atome*—from the ideal to the real. In some ways that would go against the spirit of *tindi pii,* which use poetic forms appealing to the imagination to lead people into a world that is very different from the world they experience in their daily lives.

Yet even an imaginary world comes out of a culturally based world view. Material items such as houses or tools, and ideals of beauty or ugliness all draw upon a particular world view. The imaginary ideal world of the *tindi pii* is not simply one of peace and harmony. For example, many of the tales include incidents that seem very violent to an outsider. In the *tindi* from Kyaka the woman who goes to see Sana Walya Asi Kungyapu is beaten by all the other women. The youngest brother in the Yandapo tale is continually mistreated and beaten by his brothers. Gender relations in the tales often reflect the tension and violence that occur in everyday life. In the Mae-Ambumu tale, the storyteller makes a point of Tapu Enda being unique because she has no signs of having been beaten. Even in the ideal land of the Takapipi Plains, Lelyakali beats the cannibal's sister (also called Tapu Enda at this stage in the story) because she bears only animals and not real children. In the Kandepe story, a woman protests: "I am not your wife, so stop beating me!" When the man takes hold of the young woman's breast, she is said to urinate and vomit from the pain. The ideal world of the *tindi* remains a violent world because that is all part of the cultural matter that the storyteller has to work with, be it in a real or ideal world.

Summary and conclusion

This study of the creative language of *tindi pii* remains at the level of manifest content of the tales. A structural or functional analysis could be the task for further study. Even considering the characters, the plots, and the creative imagery one can see how *tindi pii* require great skill on the part of the storyteller, of creativity and facility with poetic forms. It is not only the beauty of language and chant that captures the imagination of the listeners. The skilled storyteller reflects on the human condition of love and fear, fidelity and betrayal. There are scenes of violence between men and women, but there are also moments of tenderness and self-sacrifice, for example when Tapu Enda willingly allows herself to be taken away by the cannibal in order to save Lelyakali from having to fight with the cannibal monster and possibly lose. All Lelyakali could do in response was to weep.

Tindi pii construct an imaginary world based upon and contrasting with life in the real world. That world of Enga, along with people's worldview, is changing rapidly and performances of *tindi pii* are rare nowadays. It remains to be seen whether Enga people will adapt the *tindi pii* tradition as a result of these changes or whether it will gradually be relegated to a tradition remembered from the past but no longer part of the contemporary creative imagination.

References

Bus, Gerard. n.d. "Orthography, Morphology and Syntax of the Wabag Language." Mimeo.

Gibbs, Philip. 1988. "*Lepe*: An Exercise in Horticultural Theology." *Catalyst* 18 (3): 215–34. (also in *Doing Theology with People's Symbols and Images*, edited by Yeow Choo Lak and John C. England, 159–72. ATESEA Occasional Papers, 8. Singapore: Association of Theological Education in South East Asia, 1989.)

Lacey, Roderic. 1975. "Oral Traditions as History: An Exploration of Oral Sources among the Enga of the New Guinea Highlands." PhD dissertation, University of Wisconsin.

Meggitt, Mervyn J. 1976. "A Duplicity of Demons: Sexual and Familial Roles Expressed in Western Enga Stories." In *Man and Woman in the New Guinea Highlands*, edited by Paula Brown and Georgeda Buchbinder, 63–85. Washington, DC: American Anthropological Association.

Wiessner, Polly, and Akii Tumu. 1998. *Historical Vines: Enga Networks of Exchange, Ritual, and Warfare in Papua New Guinea*. Smithsonian Series in Ethnographic Inquiry. Bathurst: Crawford House Publishing.

8. Parallelism and Poetics in *Tindi* Narratives Sung in the Ipili Language

Terrance Borchard and Philip Gibbs

Introduction

The Ipili people of Enga Province, Papua New Guinea, have traditional tales, called *tindi*, which may be told either in ordinary spoken style or as long poetic chanted tales. This chapter focuses on the role that is played by parallelism, which manifests itself in the ordered interplay of repetition and variation in the linguistic and poetic form of the sung versions. Before discussing *tindi* we will first provide some background details concerning the region.[1]

Ipili is the name of the ethnic group living in the Porgera and Paiela valleys, and is also the name of the language that they speak. As is often found to be the case in Papua New Guinea, the name by which they are known was not coined by the Ipili themselves, but others from outside the region, in this case the Huli to the south. The name they coined, Ibili,[2] means 'salt-people' in Huli, the Ipili region being known to them as a source for salt. To the people themselves, Ipili refers only to the Porgera Valley. Paiela refers to a different valley on the other side of a high mountain range. The name "Porgera" comes from the Ipili name for the biggest river in the Porgera valley, which flows into the Lagaipa River. The Ipili called it the Poketa River, but the government officers distorted the pronunciation to "Porgera," and identified the valley on the basis of the biggest river flowing out of it. The origin of the name "Paiela" is unknown.

According to the 2000 government census, the Ipili language is spoken by approximately 26,000 people. There are minimal dialectal differences in the forms of Ipili language spoken in those two areas; for example, the second person plural pronoun in Porgera is *yakama*, but in Paiela, most people say *yakamba*.

Situated at high altitude near the western end of Enga Province, the Porgera and Paiela Valleys drain into the Lagaip River. It joins the Strickland and eventually the Fly River, which flows into the Gulf of Papua. To the north, in lower altitude

---

1 Although this chapter is a joint effort between the two authors, the introduction and conclusion are mainly by Gibbs. The other sections, including the entire discussion of parallelism, are by Borchard, to whom all instances of the pronoun "I" there refer. The texts considered below are from transcriptions made by Gibbs and Frances Ingemann.
2 The letter *b* in Huli orthography is equivalent to the letter *p* in Ipili orthography since both represent an unaspirated, voiceless, bilabial stop; therefore, this word is pronounced the same in both languages.

areas of the Lagaip extending over to the Sepik headwaters, live the semi-nomadic Hewa people, who are culturally very different from the Ipili. The plots of many Ipili chanted tales include depictions of at least some interaction with Hewa, and some Hewa people have intermarried with Ipili people in the border areas, but the Hewa language is related to other languages in the East Sepik Province. It is, therefore, almost entirely different from the Ipili language which, in terms of the latest classification by Ross (2005) and Pawley (2005), belongs to the Engan subgroup of the Trans New Guinea family—a large group of Highlands languages that also includes Enga and Huli.[3]

Over the ranges to the east live the Taiyaro Enga, and to the southeast, the Kandep Enga of the Wake (Wage) valley. To the south, several days walk over rough limestone country, live the Huli of the Tari basin. To the west, also several days walk away, live the Duna people of Lake Kopiago. The Enga and Huli are large, powerful groups and a major force in the region, economically, culturally, and to some extent linguistically. The Duna language belongs to a different subgroup within the Trans New Guinea family, and does not share much vocabulary with Ipili except for a few words borrowed by people who live in the border area between the two language groups. Ipili shares much more vocabulary with Huli and Enga than it does with either Duna or Hewa, due not only to its closer genetic relatedness to them, but to continuing, extensive social interaction, including intermarriage between Ipili and Enga people, especially those who live east of the Ipili area. Many Ipili trace their ancestry back to Enga or Huli origins.

Human contact through visits by hunters in Porgera extends back at least 11,000 years (Jackson and Banks 2002:9). Human habitation goes back more than ten generations. Ipili have been part of trade and ritual networks shared with their neighbours. Salt and axes were traded to the south for tree oil, ochre, and black palm bows. Ritual networks in the Ipili area were linked to the Huli *dindi gamu* cult and the Enga *kepele* ritual. These networks were reinforced by marriage, ensuring an extended network of relatives who could also provide security in time of famine or feud.

First contact with the modern world may have occurred in 1934 when the Fox brothers travelled down the Lagaip River, crossed the Porgera River, continuing through Paiela to the Strickland Gorge area. The next European in the area was Jim Taylor, who passed through Porgera in 1938 during the Hagen–Sepik Patrol. In 1939 John Black crossed the Porgera River again and found gold. That discovery signalled dramatic changes for Porgera. In 1945 an Australian New Guinea administrative unit visited while searching for lost airmen. After the war a number of expatriate prospectors came in search of gold.

---

3   For further details, see chapter 1.

Mission contact started officially with de-restriction of the area in 1962. Four Christian churches came initially and now at least another eight churches are established. Scholars coming to research and write have included Glenn Banks, Aletta Biersack, Alex Golub, Jerry Jacka, Frances Ingemann, and the authors of this chapter.

In a short time Porgera was transformed from a traditional Highlands society living by gardening, hunting, and gathering into the site of one of the largest gold mines in the world. As Golub notes, in less than thirty years the owners of the land on which the mine operates went from their first exposure to money to receiving roughly four million kina (over a million US$) a year in royalties alone (Golub 2001:26).

Today, despite an access road and the nearby Mt. Kare gold deposits, Paiela remains a relatively isolated valley. Porgera, however, is changing very fast with the presence of the gold mine administered by Porgera Joint Venture, of which Barrick Gold is the majority shareholder. The mine employs over two thousand workers, and there are many other contractors and associated industries at the site. The 2000 Census records 11,084 people in Paiela and 22,809 people in Porgera. The Paiela population is increasing at a moderate rate, but the Porgera population is growing at a very high rate of about 8% per annum, mostly due to immigration from other parts of Enga and the Southern Highlands. Now at Paiam in the Porgera Valley, there is a well-equipped hospital, several primary schools, secondary and international schools, a university centre, postal and telephone services, electricity, radio, TV, water and sewage plants, a bakery, car sales, a motel, and guest houses. Not everyone has access to resources to benefit from such facilities, however Porgera today has the atmosphere of an urban centre.

Differences of custom follow a gradation from the east, which is influenced by Enga, to the south, which is influenced by Huli. Ipili people in Porgera make a distinction between the *wakiame* speakers, who are influenced by their Enga neighbours, and the *tumbiame* speakers, who some Porgerans say speak "pure" Ipili. Such a claim might be contested by Paiela people who are more influenced by the Huli. Despite these outside influences, Ipili follow cultural patterns that are distinctively their own—language being one of these.

Ipili have formed their lives from the sources offered by the Papua New Guinea Highlands context. Society is strongly stratified along gender lines, and young men used to go for long periods to the forest to participate in initiation rites. Marriages are formed so as to strengthen or extend alliances, and the exchange of pigs formed the basis of the traditional economy. Today, cultural traditions are changing rapidly as young people attending school choose their own marriage partners and use money both in exchange and to buy the necessities of life.

The Ipili do not have sharply delineated clans, such as in the patrilineal clan society of the neighbouring Enga. Rather, Ipili tend to organise themselves into kindreds—all the people who can claim to be related because they share a common ancestor. In Ipili society one can claim membership in any kindred that one's grandparents were members of. As a result each person has potentially eight cognatic stocks of which they can be a member. Membership of multiple groups is desired as providing a larger security circle, but can have drawbacks today in overcrowding and the risks of illegal mining.

Traditionally sweet potato was the staple food of the Ipili, supplemented by taro. Hunting and gathering was also important, particularly during the season for harvesting pandanus nuts. Pigs were valued as a source of food, but even more for exchange. Today, as the population increases with consequent pressure on the remaining land, many Porgerans rely more on store goods, such as rice and tinned fish.

These life themes—tribal origins, initiation rites, marriage and gender relations, hunting, and gardening—are recurring elements in the chanted tales called *tindi*.

The following section provides background details about some aspects of the grammar of Ipili which especially are relevant for the later discussion of parallelism in Ipili chanted tales.

Aspects of the grammar of Ipili

Ipili is what linguists refer to as an SOV language. The "S" in this formula indicates the normal position of the subject in a sentence or clause,[4] "O" the normal position of the object, and "V" the normal position of the verb. By contrast, English can be referred to as an SVO language because the main verb in a clause is normally preceded by the subject and followed by the object.

For example, for "John hit Peter," an Ipili speaker would say *Joneto Pita pelea*, which puts the subject first, the object next, and the verb at the end of the clause, whereas in English the order is subject-verb-object.

Nouns and other parts of speech are often in the final position in lines of English poetry and songs that rhyme with each other. However, as a result of the fact that Ipili is an SOV language, a verb is almost always in the final position in the lines that are parallel in an Ipili chanted tale. This makes Ipili verbs so important for creating parallelism in Ipili chanted tales that well over 90% of the examples of

---

4 I am using the term "clause" in the linguist's sense to refer to a syntactic construction which has a subject and a verb if it is an intransitive clause, and also an object if it is a transitive clause. A sentence is a potentially more complex unit, which may consist of either a single clause or a series of clauses.

parallelism in this chapter are a result of having the same or very similar verb forms or verbal suffixes at the end of two or more lines. There are more than a hundred different forms of each Ipili verb that can be used to create a variety of very natural forms of parallelism in Ipili chanted tales. In the rest of this chapter, many examples are presented of the different ways the various forms of the Ipili verb can be used to create parallelism.

Ipili verbs are conjugated to show not only the remote past, present, and future tenses, but also the imperfect and perfect aspects, as well as many other finer shades of meaning too numerous to discuss in this chapter. The imperfect aspect is used not only to refer to very recent events, but also to refer to a process which has begun, but is not yet finished. By way of contrast, the perfect aspect is used in situations where an event has been completed. This distinction between actions that have been completed and actions that have not is made not only in sentence-final Ipili verb forms, but also in other forms of the verb that will be discussed in connection with some of the specific examples in the rest of this chapter.

In Ipili sentence-final verb forms, there is a natural interplay between tense and aspect, since events which began recently are less likely to be completed than events which began farther in the past. As a result of this interplay between tense and aspect, the chanter of a tale may chose to use the imperfect aspect rather than the present tense to announce that he is starting to chant a tale because he wants to focus on the fact that he is beginning a process that will not be completed for a while. In another place in the same chanted tale, the chanter of tales may choose to use the perfect aspect to refer to something that he said or to something the listeners heard about only minutes ago, even though those same verb forms are often used to refer to events that happened at least a day ago.

Parallelism: Some general considerations

The poet Gerard Hopkins focused very clearly on the importance of parallelism as an artistic feature when he wrote in 1866 that "The artificial part of poetry … reduces itself to the principle of parallelism" (Hopkins 1959:267). This assertion about parallelism influenced Roman Jakobson who studied it from a linguistic perspective for more than fifty years and stated that "on every level of language the essence of poetic artifice consists of recurrent returns" (Jakobson 1966:399). Parallelism is a poetic feature shared by several genres, including poetry and songs in most cultures in the world, and shared also in the tales chanted in the Highlands of Papua New Guinea, as will be evident not only from this chapter, but from several of the others in the volume, especially chapters 1, 4, 6, 10, and 11.

In my discussion of parallelism in tales chanted in the Ipili language, I have grouped examples of parallelism together on the basis of four main types of parallelism: (*a*) the creation of parallelism by substituting terms within a frame; (*b*) the use of extra non-semantic syllables of the kind known as "vocables," as discussed in chapter 1; (*c*) the creation of parallelism by using medial-verb forms; (*d*) the creation of parallelism by using sentence-final verb forms. Textual examples illustrate all of these types. The terms used to distinguish these four groups will be explained in the individual sections where the examples are given.

Lomas (pers. comm.) notes that these four main types and eight subtypes of parallelism can be found not only in chanted tales, but also in other spoken and sung genres of Huli. He points out that these types of parallelism are consistent with the notions of Hopkins (1959) and others, and that both Hopkins and Hunter (1999:46–61) would have predicted that these kinds of parallelism would be used in this wider range of contexts. I have not systematically studied parallelism in other genres of Ipili, but it is certainly a prominent feature of the traditional songs sung in the Ipili language. Examples of these kinds of parallelism in Ipili songs can be found in a paper by Frances Ingemann (1968), in which she describes the traditional song form, which uses specialized vocabulary and lines that are similar to the repetitive lines in chanted tales.

Parallelism has been studied and discussed by many scholars, but it has taken centuries to make clear distinctions between the various aspects of that term. Lowth defined parallelism very broadly in 1778 when he distinguished between parallel lines and parallel terms by saying, "When a proposition is delivered, and a second is subjoined to it, or drawn under it, equivalent, or contrasted in sense, or similar to it in form of grammatical construction, these I call parallel lines, and the words or phrases answering one to another, in corresponding lines, parallel terms" (Lowth 1843:ix). It seems clear from Lowth's use of the term "equivalent" that he would consider lines that are identical as being parallel.

However, in discussing a chanted tale from the Ku Waru region of the Western Highlands Province of Papua New Guinea, Rumsey notes that "the language is not merely repetitive, it is *systematically* repetitive, making frequent use of parallelism, whereby each instance of partial repetition establishes a framework within which there is significant contrast at equivalent positions from line to line" (Rumsey 2005:49). This recognition of significant contrast as an aspect of lines that are parallel to each other indicates that lines which are identical should not be considered parallel lines. It is better to just refer to them as being identical, and to refer to lines that include both repetition and contrast as being parallel .

Fox (1977) affirms the importance of contrast as a feature of parallelism when he distinguishes between two different aspects of parallelism by saying that one aspect focuses on parallelism as "an extension of the binary principle of opposition to the phonemic, syntactic, and semantic levels of expression" (ibid.:60). He goes on to say that the other aspect focuses on "the specific manifestations of this binary principle as a strict, consistent, and pervasive means of composition in the traditional oral poetry of a wide variety of peoples of the world" (ibid.).

Rumsey (2001:207) points out that in the chanted tale that he is discussing, "partial repetition establishes syntagmatic frames within which there is paradigmatic contrast at equivalent positions from line to line." Contrast between parallel terms at equivalent positions is a feature of parallelism that distinguishes lines that are parallel from those that are not. Fox (1977:75) notes that parallelism can be analysed in terms of whether parallel terms within the verse frame occur in the initial, intermediate, or final position. The examples of parallelism in Ipili chanted tales which I will discuss all have contrast between parallel terms in either the initial or intermediate position. The terms in the final position are either identical, or at least very similar in some way, and therefore function as at least part of the frame within which the parallel terms are contrasted.

Parallelism in Ipili chanted tales

An Ipili chanted tale is referred to as a *tindi*. Magical things can happen in a *tindi*. For example, in the *tindi* named "Kau nala tapeyo," the main character changes from being a small boy to being a big man as a result of eating special sweet potatoes or taro that were given to him by a woman. Then later on he magically becomes a boy again after he eats more of that food. He goes through that magical cycle of change repeatedly. The term *tindi* contrasts with the term *temane* which refers to stories about events that have happened in everyday life. Parallelism in a *temane* would be coincidental, rather than intentional as it is in a *tindi*. The term *tomo* refers to traditional Ipili songs that also have extensive parallelism, but such songs are beyond the scope of this chapter.

The examples used here to illustrate parallelism are taken from four different chanted tales. All four stories focus on the same main character, who eats lizards instead of pig meat, although the degree of emphasis on that aspect of his character varies. His older brother is referred to as Kima and Kimape in three of the tales, and that brother is also said to be from Kengone in three of the tales. Many of the details in each chanted tale are different, but there are many similarities also. The main character goes on at least one long journey during which he meets a young woman. He interacts with the Hewa people and pays bride price to them at some point in each story. After he and the young woman experience many things together during their journey, they finally climb a high mountain until they reach the clouds and enter the sky world.

I have named each of the chanted tales based on the way the main character is referred to in that chanted tale. "Kau nalane akali" in line 57 of that chanted tale

(Yandapake 1964b) means "The man who customarily eats lizards." "Kau nala akali" in line 1022 of that chanted tale (Yandapake 1964a) means "The man who just ate a lizard." "Kau nala tapeyo," which is used many places in that chanted tale (Kale 1974), could mean "The lizard who just ate a lizard." "Kau tali tapeyo," which is used many places in that chanted tale (Kaneanda 1965), could be a subtle play on words to refer to the fact that he offered to share his lizards in that story. His alternate name in that tale, "Kau Tali tane," could mean that he was an inhabitant of the Tari area, which isn't too far from the Ipili area.

An Ipili chanted tale is characterized by a high degree of parallelism of various kinds within some of the paragraphs. Some of the parallelism is created in a very natural way, based on the fact that Ipili is an SOV language that normally places the verbs at the end of each line, as discussed above. The result is that having similar verb forms at the end of two lines can create parallelism. However, some of the parallelism is produced in a very creative way by structuring some of the paragraphs in ways that are not typical in other genres of discourse in the Ipili language. I now turn to a discussion of each of the four types of parallelism that I have distinguished above.

Parallelism created by substituting one or more terms

Some successive lines in Ipili chanted tales are identical. But identical repetition does not seem to be valued as highly as parallelism, which requires more rhetorical skill and creates the impression that the story is moving along, even though it is only by the parallel terms that are changing within the framework established by partial repetition.

Two or more lines in a paragraph may be identical except for one word that may be changed slightly by adding one additional syllable at the beginning, in the middle, or at the end of one of the words in the second line. The two lines in text 1 are exactly the same except that the word *Yongopena* in line 22 contains the additional syllable *-ngo-*, which is not in the word *Yopena* in line 21.

Those two words are parallel terms in the intermediate position set within a framework formed by *Nena ipa* in the initial position and *yoko tepa ya-o* in the final position in both lines.

Text 1. Example from "Kau nala tapeyo."

21. Nena ipa Yopena yoko tepa ya-o.   He cut (trees) down at the Yope River-o.
22. Nena ipa Yongopena yoko tepa   He cut (trees) down at the Yongope River-o.
    ya-o.

Other pairs of lines are identical except for one or two words in the second line that have been substituted for one or two words in the first line. The words may be similar in meaning or refer to the same kind of entity, but they may be completely different in form. The two lines in text 2 are exactly the same except that the words *yuu pokoli* in the intermediate position in line 1181 have been substituted for the word *tunduni* in the intermediate position in line 1180. The words refer to similar kinds of entities, but are not similar in form like the words *Yopena* and *Yongopena* in lines 21 and 22 in text 1.

The substitution of the words *yuu pokoli* for the word *tunduni* is an example of "semantic" parallelism, in which parallel terms are semantically related, but may not have any formal similarity to each other. The repetition of the other words in the initial and the final positions of those two lines serves as the framework within which that contrast is used to create parallelism.

Text 2. Example from "Kau nala tapeyo."

1180.	Iyu tunduni mindi yane okona mee keyea-ko.	He climbed way up on a mountain that was there.
1181.	Iyu yuu pokoli mindi yane okona mee keyea-ko.	He climbed way up on a ridge that was there.

The word or words that are different may be the name of a place, or a kind of plant or animal or bird. Often the information given could have been given more concisely by simply listing these items within a single clause. That is what is normally done in some genres of Ipili when the focus is on giving information as concisely as possible, but in chanted tales, each item is put into a separate line in order to create more extensive parallelism, thereby enhancing the aesthetic appeal of the chanted tale for the listeners and demonstrating the poetic skill of the chanter.

Sometimes the pattern of substitution becomes more complex. In text 3, the word in the initial position in both lines is identical, so it serves as part of the framework for the contrasting parallel terms created by substituting the place name *Anduni* in line 1126 for the place name *Kiyuni* in line 1125. The next word in both lines is identical, so it is also part of the repetitive frame. It is followed by another contrasting pair of parallel terms created by substituting the name *Kimape* in line 1126 for the name *Kima* in line 1125, even though they refer to the same individual. This is another example of the addition of one syllable making the second line different from the first. In both lines, the next four words following the names *Kima* and *Kimape* are also identical except for the addition of the vocable *-o* at the end of line 1126.

Text 3. Example from "Kau nala tapeyo."

1125.	Yuu Kiyuni akali Kima uli atu epeyo ote lea.	"I am coming here with the Kiyuni place man Kima," she said.
1126.	Yuu Anduni akali Kimape uli atu epeyo ote lea-o.	"I am coming here with the Anduni place man Kimape," she said.

In other examples of parallelism, the parallel terms occur in the initial position. The pairs of lines are identical except for one whole word which is added somewhere in the second line. In text 4, the two lines are identical except that the word *eka* 'bird' has been added at the beginning of line 269.

Text 4. Example from "Kau nala tapeyo."

| 268. | Ambi okone peyokale-ko, alo lea. | "I want to kill that one over there," he called out. |
| 269. | Eka ambi okone peyokale-ko, alo lea. | "I want to kill that bird over there," he called out. |

It may seem strange to consider the absence of a term in one line as one of the parallel terms in a pair of parallel terms, but it does create a contrast between lines 268 and 269 within a framework of repetition which is a basic component of lines that are parallel. It may also be more difficult to think of the word and its absent counterpart as being within a "frame" because they occur in the initial position, so all of the words that are identical are on one side. However, it has already been stated that the parallel terms in lines that are parallel can occur in the initial position.

Parallelism enhanced by adding non-semantic syllables or words

Chanters sometimes add a syllable to the end of the last word in a line, even though the addition of that syllable does not change the meaning of the line. Such syllables are sometimes referred to as non-semantic syllables. A whole word may be added at the end of a line even though it doesn't change the meaning of that line. Since they don't change the meaning of the line, it seems that these syllables or words may be added primarily for the aesthetic effect they produce in an Ipili chanted tale.

Parallelism enhanced by adding a single syllable at the end of lines

An additional syllable *-o* is sometimes added at the end of several lines, even when they would already be parallel without adding that syllable. The three lines in text 5 would not be parallel without adding the word *lea* which means 'she said'. However, repeating that word in the final position in all three lines creates a frame within which all of the other words that precede it in each line become parallel terms in a broad sense since those words in each line contrast with the words in the same position in the other two lines.

Therefore, all three lines would already be parallel without adding the vocable *-o*. Vocables are not normally added in several successive lines in other genres of Ipili discourse, and their addition does not affect the meaning of the chanted tale in any way. They are apparently added only to enhance the aesthetic appeal of this genre by allowing the chanter to hold a given musical note for a more extended period of time than would be natural without it.

Text 5. Example from "Kau nala tapeyo."

1375.	Andipa langukale. Ipu napele okonde lea-o.	"Now I want to ask you. What about the fact that you are not coming?" she said-o.
1376.	Yia kee puyale, wanda tewa pii lalawa aŋa napiyainipe lea-o.	"Being about to cut up pig, don't women talk a little?" she said-o.
1377.	Pee, mindimane wua leya lo layango lini lo atelepe lea-o.	"Or by saying that someone is saying that, are you slandering (them)?" she said-o.

In text 6, the same vocable -o is used on two different verbs, *lea* and *epea*. These verbs have very different meanings: *lea* means 'he said', whereas *epea* means 'he came'. Although the verb stems are different, they have the same third person singular remote past suffix -*ea*. It creates a very natural kind of parallelism when two or more lines end with verbs that have the same suffix, even if the meaning of the verbs is different.

It might seem to be stretching the definition of parallelism to say that having the suffix -*ea* in the final position in both lines is enough repetition to serve as a frame for the contrast between all of the rest of the words in those two lines which then function as the parallel terms in this example. However, English speakers immediately recognize the parallelism between lines of poetry and songs in which only the last word in one line rhymes with the last word in another line.

The parallelism is further enhanced by the addition of the vocable -o at the end of many lines in chanted tales in Ipili. This is similar to what is done in chanted tales in many other Papua New Guinea Highlands languages (as discussed by Niles and Rumsey in chapter 1). To create an aesthetic affect, the chanter may continue the -o sound at the end of a line much longer than other syllables would be continued in everyday speech. This expands the final-position repetitive frame from just the verbal suffix -*ea* to a slightly larger frame -*ea-o*. Continuing the sound of the last syllable also helps to draw attention away from the fact that the stem of the verbs at the end of the two lines is different.

Text 6. Example from "Kau nala tapeyo."

466.	Iyu andaka pekaiyu loto, lama epea-o.	Arriving at the house up above, she came saying-o.
467.	Iyu ulia pote yangalo oko patipakale ote lea-o.	"Let's take the *pote* sweet potatoes I just cooked out of the ground oven up above," she said.

The syllable -*ta* is sometimes added at the end of two or more lines in a chanted tale even in contexts where the lines are already identical.

The suffix *-angi* at the end of lines 5 and 6 in text 7 identifies them as dependent temporal clauses. I have never heard the syllable *-ta* used as an addition to the suffix *-angi* in normal everyday speech. Therefore, it seems that it is added to the ends of lines in Ipili chanted tales primarily for aesthetic effect. It may be that these can only be fully appreciated by someone whose mother tongue is Ipili. In ordinary every day speech, lines 5 and 6 would be coalesced into one clause by mentioning the earth and the rivers in the same clause, but they are mentioned in two separate clauses to create parallelism in this chanted tale.

Text 7. Example from "Kau nala tapeyo."

5. Yuu uli oko yoale, ungi mindi lea-angi-ta,	When there was a beginning for this earth to exist,
6. ipa uli tupa yoale, ungi mindi lea-angi-ta,	when there was a beginning for the rivers to exist,
7. akali ote api yale lo makande pua,	comparing, saying, "really like which man?"
8. Iwanaŋa Auwala yale mindi atalane lea.	a small boy like Auwala customarily existed, he said.

The parallelism in a chanted tale is sometimes enhanced by the addition of the suffix *-ko* on the verbs at the end of two or more lines. This suffix often indicates that the previous sentence is the ground or basis for a question, statement, or command that follows that clause, but it does not seem to have that meaning in this context. Ending two or more lines with the suffix *-ko* creates parallelism where it would not otherwise occur because the verbs that precede it are different.

In text 8, lines 159 and 160 are already parallel without adding the suffix *-ko*, because the words *ipa* and *dundu pea* in both lines create a framework of repetition within which the words *Lai* and *Lakai* are parallel terms, along with the word *Nenanga* in line 159 and its absence in line 160 which creates another pair of contrasting terms within a framework. Adding the suffix *-ko* to line 161 enhances the parallelism with lines 159 and 160 by slightly expanding the repetitive framework in those two lines. On another level, adding that suffix also makes line 161 parallel to lines, 159 and 160 even though the content of line 161 and the verb to which that suffix is attached is different from the content and verb in lines 159 and 160.

Text 8. Example from "Kau nala tapeyo."

159. Nenanga ipa Lai dundu pea-ko.	He went along the Lai River.
160. Ipa Lakai dundu pea-ko.	He went along the Lagaip River.
161. Pulu, molo Ewa anda pekayu lea-ko.	Having gone, he arrived at the Hewa house.

Text 9 also includes the suffix *-ko*. The parallelism in this example is very interesting because of its complexity and the way it is structured. Lines 534 and 536 are identical, rather than parallel. However, lines 533 and 534 taken together as a larger unit are parallel with lines 535 and 536 taken together as a larger unit, because lines 534 and 536 create a repetitive framework within which lines 533 and 535 function as parallel terms because they are not identical and therefore contrast with each other. All of line 535 functions as a substitution for line 533 to create the interplay of repetition and variation with these two larger units that is characteristic of parallelism.

In addition to the parallelism at that higher level, line 535 is also parallel to line 533 even though it does not immediately follow it. The repetition of the words *ipa* and *tupa po atalawane-ko* in both lines creates a framework within which the words *Tulini* and *Wakepe* in the initial position and *Wau* and *pete peangolo* in the medial position function as two pairs of parallel terms.

Text 9. Example from "Kau nala tapeyo."

533. Tulini ipa Wau tupa po atalawane-ko.	"Going to the Wau River at Tulini, I customarily stay there," he said.
534. Yawa. Yawape lea.	"Cook (it) in a ground oven. Please cook (it) in a ground oven," he said.
535. Wakepe ipa pete peangolo tupa po atalawane-ko.	"Going to the Wagi water pools, also I customarily stay (there).
536. Yawa. Yawape lea.	Cook (it) in a ground oven. Please cook (it) in a ground oven," he said.

Both lines 534 and 536 could also theoretically be subdivided into two parallel lines with only *Yawa* on the first line. That word can function as a complete sentence by itself, since it is the second person singular imperative form of the verb, indicating that the command should be obeyed immediately. The second line would then say *Yawape lea*, which would introduce variation by adding the syllable *-pe* to create the polite form of the second person singular imperative. This form gives the person to whom the command is given more discretion as to when the command will be obeyed.

Even though it would theoretically be possible to subdivide lines 534 and 536 in this way, it seems unlikely that the chanter intended his listeners to think of the word *Yawa* as a complete line by itself, since no line in any Ipili chanted tale I have ever seen has been that short. He could have chosen to make this line long enough by adding one of the more complex speech orienters that I discuss later in this chapter, and then using that same complex speech orienter at the end of the second line. Instead of doing that, he used *lea* which is the shortest possible speech orienter, so it seems clear that he intended for his listeners to consider both forms of the imperative to be part of the same line.

Parallelism enhanced by adding a whole word at the end of a line

Sometimes a whole word is added at the end of one or more lines of a chanted tale. In text 10, the Ipili word *andoko* is added to the end of lines 82 through 86 and within line 87, but Ingemann (1964:n. 2) reports that the Ipili speaker who helped her translate this chanted tale said the word *andoko* has no meaning in this context. In other contexts it sometimes means 'which one' or 'where' or seems to be intended to elicit agreement from the person to whom the speaker is speaking, but none of those meanings seem to fit here. Lines 82 through 86 certainly would not be parallel if the word *andoko* had not been added at the end of each line, but adding that word makes them all parallel.

Text 10. Example from "Kau nala akali."

82. Amene, nena Kolali ipa tindininga late lauwa andoko.	"Brother, I went in the middle of the Kolali River.
83. Lakae ipa dundu puwa andoko.	I went along the Lakae River.
84. Iyu Uyu mane late lauwa andoko.	I went up to the head waters of the Uyu River.
85. Luyupe mane late lauwa andoko.	I went up to the headwaters of the Luyupe River.
86. Namba amene, napele yala andala baa taimane peke lalo andoko.	Seeing that my brother was not attacked, I have returned quickly.
87. Epeyo andoko lalu, lamaiyane lea-o.	Having said, 'I am coming,' he told him," he said.

The third person singular remote past verb form *lea* in line 87 of this example means 'he said'. This makes it seems like the chanter is telling the tale as though he is quoting or repeating what someone else told him, since the previous word *lamaiyane* serves at the speech orienter indicating what the younger brother told the older brother.

Based on Alan Rumsey's extensive study of Ku Waru chanted tales, he says, "There are other commonly used metanarrational formulas that seem to take as their implicit grammatical subject the tale itself, as if it were an active force making itself manifest in the inner eye and ear of the performer and through him/her to the audience" (Rumsey 2001:208). However, in this Ipili example, it seems to me that the chanter would have used the immediate past tense of the Ipili verb that means 'say' instead of the remote past tense if he meant that the chanted tale itself is the implicit subject that is ultimately telling the tale being given outward expression by the chanter.

My view is based on the fact that the chanter did use the first person singular immediate past tense verb form *lalo* when he announced that he was ready to begin the chanted tale. I would have expected him to use the present tense first person verb form *leyo* to announce this, just as people often use that present tense verb form to announce the fact that they are about to say something in other contexts, such as meetings in which many other people might also want to have a chance to speak.

However, what people say as part of a discussion in a meeting is usually quite brief, whereas some chanted tales are very long and take a long time to tell, so telling one can be thought of as a process that is not completed until the tale is finished. When a tale is finished, the chanter announces that fact by saying *koyo*, which means 'finished', whereas a man who uses the present tense to announce the fact that he is about to say something at a meeting does not announce the completion of what he is saying by using that word. He simply stops talking. So it seems to me that the chanter's choice of the remote past tense of that verb indicates that the implicit subject of the verb "said" in this context is some other chanter who told that same tale at some indefinite point of time in the remote past.

Parallelism created by using medial verb forms

As discussed above, in Ipili the verb normally comes at the end of the clause in which it occurs. There are two different sets of verb forms. One set is referred to as "medial" because they are never used at the end of the final clause in a sentence. The other set, which occurs in that position, is accordingly referred to as "final" verb forms.

The primary function of the medial forms is to specify the relationship between the clause of which the verb is a part and the following clause. However, both medial and final verb forms are often used by chanters of Ipili chanted tales to create parallelism through repetition of either the same verb or the same verb suffix at the end of more than one line in succession. In this section I will show how Ipili chanters create parallelism by repetition of the same medial verb form at the end of two or more lines. In a subsequent section, I will show how they do so by repetition of the same final verb form at the end of two or more lines.

Some medial verb forms indicate that the subject of the next clause is the same as the subject of the one in which they occur, while others indicate that it is different. Other forms do neither. The role of these three kinds of verbs in the creation of parallelism is discussed in the following three sections.

Parallelism created by using same-subject medial verb forms

There are some medial verb forms in Ipili which indicate that the subject of the following clause is the same as the subject of the clause which ends with one of these medial verb forms. These medial verb forms are not inflected, so they do not give any information about the time the event occurred or the person or number of the subjects who participated in it. The number of the subject (singular, dual, or plural) of a medial verb may be indicated in the medial verb itself, but the rest of the information about the event is given in the suffix on a conjugated verb form at the end of some other clause that occurs later in the sentence.

In text 11, the content of line 828 is parallel with the content of line 827 because the words *wana tupa* in the initial position and the word *pituto* in the final position provide a frame of repetition within which the words *iyu yangi Kuma nenenga* is a group of terms in line 827 which is parallel to the words *Kulame wangeanenga* in line 828. Likewise, the content of lines 830 is parallel with the content of line 829 because the words *titikini eka* in the initial position and *yaka-yaka pituto* in the final position in both lines provide a frame of repetition within which the contrasting words *tenda* and *tendekene* function as parallel terms.

Text 11. Example from "Kau tali tapeyo."

827.	Wana tupa iyu yangi Kuma nenenga pituto,	Girls sitting way up on the peak of Mt. Kuma,
828.	wana tupa Kulame wangeanenga pituto,	girls sitting on Mt. Kulame,
829.	titikini eka tenda yaka-yaka pituto,	sitting in a line like *tenda* birds,
830.	titikini eka tendekene yaka-yaka pituto,	sitting in a line like *tendekene* birds,
831.	Patali Tambu Kuapu lalu yane-ta	talked about Patali Tambu and Kuapu.

At a higher level of parallelism, lines 827 through 830 all end with the same medial verb form *pituto*, so all four of these verses are parallel, with the repetition of the medial verb functioning as the frame and all of the words which precede it in each line functioning as groups of parallel terms. This medial verb form is similar to a participle in English and means 'sitting'.

This medial verb form doesn't give any information about the number of the subject or when this event happened, but the third person singular remote past verb form at the end of line 831 retrospectively provides this information. The same subject suffix *-to* at the end of lines 827 and 828 indicates that the subjects of the following lines 829 through 831 are the same as the subjects of lines 827 and 828. That suffix also indicates that the activity of talking took place simultaneously with the activity of sitting.

In text 12 the repetition of the words *lipi ongane* in the initial position and the words *tupa yata wato* in the final position in lines 24 and 25 create a frame within which words *kii pipi* and *kai maukale* function as contrasting parallel terms. In this example also, the medial verb suffix *-to* at the end of lines 24 and 25 doesn't give any information about when those events happened, but the remote past verb form at the end of line 26 provides the information that it was in the remote past. The medial verb suffix at the end of those lines also indicates that the subject who is doing the activity in line 26 is the same as the subject of lines 24 and 25.

Text 12. Example from "Kau nala tapeyo."

24. Lipi ongane kii pipi tupa yoko yata wato,	Cutting down *pipi* (trees), putting them up here,
25. lipi ongane kai maukale tupa yoko yata wato,	cutting down *maukale* (trees), putting them up here,
26. ende pape ima peyalu, yangapia.	having built a stake fence, he burned (the garden area).

The two kinds of trees that are mentioned in text 12 would normally both be mentioned in the same clause in everyday speech, but they are mentioned in separate clauses in this chanted tale to enhance the parallelism within the text. The fact that all of the other words except the names for the trees are the same creates excellent parallelism with lines 24 and 25 both ending with the same medial verb form *yata wato*, which means 'putting them'.

Parallelism created by using different-subject medial verb forms

There is a medial verb suffix which indicates what linguists call "switch reference." That is, it indicates that the subject of the following clause is different from the subject of the clause that ends with the suffix *-kola*. This suffix is not used in two successive clauses very often in everyday speech, but it does create a sense of parallelism when it is used in two successive clauses in a chanted tale given in text 13—the repetition of the suffix *-kola* in the final position serves as a frame for the rest of what is said in lines 858 and 859 which function as parallel terms.

Text 13. Example from "Kau nala tapeyo."

858. Nimba amene-mane pipia-kola,	"Your brother just did (something) and then,
859. namba peyowa tupa yatakawa pitiwasia, ipupi-kola,	while I was still angry, you came and so,
860. peyauwa lea.	I hit (you)," she said.

In text 14, the word *ote* at the end of two or more lines also creates parallelism where it would otherwise not occur. It is often indicates that the line that precedes that word states a critical part of the context or situation in which the events that follow occur. In this example, the young woman would not have met the man if she had not gone to that place.

Lines 284 and 285 would not be parallel at all without the word *ote* at the end of each line since the verbs are different, but repeating *ote* in the final position in line 285 creates a frame within which the rest of what is said in both of those lines serves as groups of parallel terms. Ending both clauses with *ote* indicates that both lines have the same relationship to line 286.

Text 14. Example from "Kau tali tapeyo."

284. Wana ekene kapi molo peka tupa
   tepa mindi ya ote,

That unmarried young woman jumped down to
   get ferns and then,

285. aiyako mane nenanga atea molo pu
   nena lalu, atea ote,

she having gone down to get ginger, was there
   and then,

286. Kau Tali Tane yalua andelepa?

do you see Kau Tali Tane there?

Parallelism created by using medial verb forms that can have either same or different subjects

Conditional clauses are created in Ipili by adding the suffix -*ndo* at the end of the remote past form of the verb at the end of a non-final clause in a sentence. The subject of the clause that follows a clause that ends with this suffix can either be the same or different. Clauses that are marked as being conditional specify the conditions for the consequence that is stated in a following clause, which is usually the last clause in the sentence.

In text 15, line 815 is identical to line 814 except for the addition of *na* in line 815 in the Ipili. *Na* is a shortened form of the first person singular personal pronoun *namba*. This is redundant information because the verb *ateyo* in both line 814 and 815 has a first person singular present tense suffix. The addition of *na* in line 815 contrasts with its absence in line 814, creating a pair of parallel terms within the framework created by the repetition of the rest of the words in those two lines.

Text 15. Example from "Kau tali tapeyo."

814. Ateyoko, na-ipulu mindi peendo,

I am staying, so if you don't come (back),

815. na ateyoko na-ipulu mindi peendo,

I am staying, so if you don't come (back),

816. wua piya mala makipu okomane
   tombo mindi yando,

if there is a dividing line because of what he just
   did,

817. wua piyane andupi okomane lita
   mindi peando,

if there is a boundary because of what he
   customarily does,

818. Kau Tali Tane tingi mialawane,
   yuku-pene lea.

I, Kau Tali Tane, crossing over, customarily take
   fiercely," he said.

819. Kau Tali Tapeyo ipulu, mialawane
   yuku-pene lea.

I, Kau Tali Tapeyo, having come, customarily
   take fiercely," he said.

The repetition of *wua* in the initial position and the suffix -*ndo* in the final position of line 817 create a repetitive frame that makes it parallel to line 816. All of the words in the intermediate position in both lines serve as groups of parallels terms. Even though many of the specific words in those two groups of Ipili words are different, the word 'boundary' (*lita*) in line 817 is very similar in meaning to "dividing line" in line 816. This kind of lexical parallelism further enhances the parallelism of these two lines.

Even though the suffix *-ndo* has been added to three different verbs at the end of four lines, it makes them all parallel by creating a repetitive frame for parallel groups of words which say everything else that is said in those lines. All four of these lines state conditions that relate to the consequence stated in line 819. It would certainly be unusual to have four conditional clauses in one sentence in everyday speech, although several conditional clauses are sometimes strung together in a chain, if many conditions are being stated as leading to the same consequence.

The suffix *-nga* on a verb at the end of a clause identifies that clause as a locative clause in relationship to a following clause which states what event happened, or what situation existed at that location. In text 16, lines 1347 and 1348 are two locative clauses ending with the suffix *-nga* which tell where the scrawny pig was tied up.[5]

The locative word *ambingane* meaning 'over there' in the initial position and the words *palu tupa lolo andi leanenga* in the final position form the repetitive frame within which the contrastive words *one* and *kiwaki* are parallel terms, making these two lines parallel. In everyday speech, there would not normally be two locative clauses in succession in the same Ipili sentence, because the two parallel terms would be included in the same clause. But in this Ipili chanted tale, the parallel terms are put into two separate successive locative lines to create parallelism.

Text 16. Example from "Kau nala tapeyo."

1347. Ambingane one palu tupa lolo andi leanenga,	Over there where the light coloured ones were tied up,
1348. ambingane kiwaki palu tupa lolo andi leanenga,	over there where the grey and tan ones were tied up,
1349. mindiki angu amonga andi leae ya lea.	there was only one (scrawny pig) tied up way over there, she said.

Parallelism created by using the same sentence-final verb form

In this section I will give examples to illustrate how chanters of Ipili chanted tales create or enhance parallelism by repetition of the same sentence-final verb form at the end of two or more lines.

---

5   The suffix *-nga* itself does not mean 'over there'. 'Over there' is the meaning of the first word in the Ipili. Ipili has many specific words which indicate how far away the location is and whether it is lower, on the same level, higher, or on the other side of the river. Rather, it has the different function of identifying the clause as a locative one in relationship to the following clause.

Parallelism created by using speech orienters

Some instances of parallelism in Ipili chanted tales occur quite naturally as a result of the use of the same speech orienter at the end of a series of lines. In text 17 the words "she said" are referred to as a "speech orienter," using one of the terms from a set of terms developed by Beekman, Callow, and Kopesec (1981) to label various kinds of semantic relationships at the discourse level. Using that same set of terms, what she said in this example is labelled as the "content." The terms "orienter" and "content" constitute a pair of terms that normally occur together because it is quite natural to state what a person said along with a verb which indicates that something was said.

This is consistent with what Rumsey (2005:41–42; citing Jakobson 1970) says that, "All narrative uses of language presuppose at least two distinct events: a speech event in which the act of language use is taking place, and another event which is being narrated." The term "speech orienter" refers to the speech event, and the term "orienter" refers to at least part of the event which is being narrated. In text 17, the same speech orienter occurs at the end all four lines.

Text 17. Example from "Kau nala tapeyo."

1154. Ole andipa pele oko naleyo lea.	"I am not including the day that you are going now," she said.
1155. Ole anati atape lea.	"Stay tomorrow," she said.
1156. Ole luma yia peyape lea.	"Kill the pig the day after tomorrow," she said.
1157. Tukunina andaka epope ote lea.	"Come home on the fourth day," she said.

There would be no parallelism between these four lines if the word *lea* had not been added at the end of each line. Repeating this speech orienter at the end of each sentence of quoted material creates a frame for the contrasting content of what she said in each line. The speech orienter at the end of lines 1155 and 1156 would probably be omitted if someone was just telling another person what instructions someone else had given in a daily situation, but this speech orienter is repeated in each line in this example for an Ipili chanted tale to create more parallelism.

The speech orienter that is used most frequently in Ipili chanted tales is *lea*, but the speech orienter *lapia* is sometimes used in two or more successive lines, especially near the beginning of a tale, as in text 18. The main difference in meaning is that *lea* refers to an event that happened long ago, while *lapia* refers to an event that happened more recently. *Lapia* literally means 'he said', but in this example, no character in the chanted tale is being quoted. Rather, it sounds as though the chanter himself is indicating that he is quoting someone else when he chants the tale.

The question is, who might he be quoting? This is the same question that I have already discussed above in relation to text 10. However, the chanter in text 18 has not used the third person singular remote past verb form *lea*, like the chanter of the tale excerpted in text 10 did. The latter performer used *lea* more than eighty lines into the tale, so he is not referring to some other chanter who may have told this tale in the indefinite remote past.

The chanter in text 18 has also not used the first person singular imperfect verb form *lalo*, as the chanter of the tale called "Kau nala tapeyo" did at the beginning of his tale. The chanter of the tale called "Kau tali tapeyo," from which text 18 is taken, has used the third person singular perfect verb form *lapia* at the beginning of his tale instead. Therefore, this chanter seems to be disassociating himself from the process of telling the tale by using the third person instead of the first person.

Ingemann (pers. comm. 2008) notes that the introductory lines quoted in this example were spoken by the performer rather than chanted, so it does seem that he was focusing on the source of the tale at this point. Given the tense and aspect of the verb that this chanter has chosen, he doesn't seem to be focusing on the telling of the tale as an ongoing process, but rather on the completion of each line of the tale as he begins to tell it. For that reason, in this instance, it seems that this chanter may have thought of the tale itself as an active force making itself manifest to the audience through the performer as each successive line was completed.

However, in two of the other chanted tale performances which I used as sources for examples of parallelism, the chanter chose to use the third person singular remote past verb form *lea* in the same position at the beginning of his chanted tale. For that reason, in this instance, it would seem more likely that he was giving credit to another chanter who was the source of the tale that he was now chanting. It seems that each Ipili chanter of tales has the freedom to take the credit for a chanted tale himself, to give credit to another chanter, or even to tell it as though the tale itself is an active force in the telling of the tale.

Text 18. Example from "Kau tali tapeyo."

1. Iwana tepo akali atalaini lapia.	"Three unmarried young men exist," he said.
2. Tepo akali atalaini oko ato yalaini lapia.	"The three men that exist keep on living," he said.
3. Yia tepone lapia.	"A pig is the third one," he said.
4. Yia tepone, iwana lapo atalapele lapia.	"A pig is the third, two young men exist," he said.

In text 18, lines 1 and 2 would have already been somewhat parallel without adding *lapia*, because of the repetition of *tepo akali* in the medial position and the repetition of the verbal suffix *-alaini* in the final position. The presence of *iwana* in the initial position in line 1 contrasts with its absence in line 2, and the presence of *oko ato* in line 2 would contrast with its absence in line 1. This could be thought of as being two pairs of parallel terms. However, lines 3 and 4 would not be parallel with lines 1 and 2 in any way if the speech orienter *lapia* had not been added to make them parallel. At this higher level, *lapia* functions as the repetitive frame for all of the rest of the words in those four lines which serve as contrasting groups of parallel terms.

Two or more lines which would not be parallel in any way by themselves are sometimes made at least somewhat parallel by adding the more complex speech orienter *lo atalu ya* at the end of each of the lines. The word *lo* is the medial form of the same Ipili speech orienter mentioned above. The two lines in text 19 differ greatly in terms of length and content, but adding the words *lo atalu ya* at the end of both of them creates the impression that they are at least somewhat parallel by functioning as a frame for the rest of the words in each line which serve as contrasting groups of parallel terms.

Text 19. Example from "Kau nala tapeyo."

1277.	Iwana epene-ao, lo atalu ya.	"Oh good unmarried young man," she was saying.
1278.	Nimbana palu tambu imane palini pia tupa pitaka pupia lo atalu ya.	"Your relatives and in-laws have all gone," she was saying.

Notice that line 1277 would not be a complete sentence by itself if the words *lo atalu ya* did not occur at the end of that line. The speaker is simply calling the attention of the young man to what she is about to say in line 1278 which ends with the same words as line 1277. It would be overly redundant to have a complex speech orienter like that at the end of both lines in normal speech. It could be omitted at the end of the first line without any loss of meaning, but using it on both lines creates parallelism.

Another way that chanters create parallelism where it would not naturally occur is by adding the words *lama epea* at the end of more than one line. *Lama* is also a form of the verb 'say'. It is normally used to indicate that an action is an ongoing process over a period of time, but chanters of tales seem to use it primarily to create parallelism. The material in each line that precedes *lama epea* is frequently not a complete sentence. It may be no more than a phrase, a clause, or one or two words that are used to describe someone or something, like the description of the old woman given in lines 1354 though line 1356 in text 20.

Text 20. Example from "Kau nala tapeyo."

1353. Okonena anduane wanda mini-yene, lama epea.	"The owner of that (pig) was an old woman," she came saying.
1354. Kama-mane latako-pene, lama epea.	"Covered with grey hair," she came saying.
1355. Lene pata-pene, lama epea-o.	"Flat round eyes," she came saying-o.
1356. Wenene pata-pene, lama epea-o.	"Flat forehead," she came saying-o.

The words *lama epea* literally mean 'she came saying', but there are many contexts like this one in which it doesn't make any sense to understand these words as literally meaning that anyone came saying anything. Therefore, it seems that these words are used primarily as a poetic device to enhance the parallelism of two or more phrase or clauses that might not be parallel without them. These two words are used primarily when stringing those phrases and clauses together would make a line too long.

Sometimes the words preceding *lama epea* form a complete clause including a verb. However, if the words *lama epea* had been omitted from lines 524 and 525 in text 21, neither of the clauses would have been a complete sentence by itself because they both end with medial verb forms. Therefore, another clause that ends with a final verb form had to be added to produce a complete sentence according to the rules of Ipili grammatical structure. Lines 1353 and 1354 in text 20 do not have the added syllable -*o* like lines 1355 and lines 1356, so it seems that the chanter preferred to have two pairs of parallel lines instead of having them all parallel.

In text 21, the word *epea* at the end of lines 524 and 525 has a final verb form, so both seem to be complete sentences, but having the words "she came saying" at the end of both lines does not sound very natural. However, if those words at the end of line 524 and 525 are disregarded, the remaining clauses chain together to form a fairly natural sentence in both Ipili and English. In examples like this, it seems that *lama epea* has been added at the end of each clause in a long complex sentence in order to break it up into shorter pieces that can each easily be spoke as one line.

Text 21. Example from "Kau nala tapeyo."

524. Oo andaipa okone amonga poto, lama epea.	"That one we saw here going over there," she came saying.
525. Atu ambingane pekayu loto, lama epea.	"Arriving over there," she came saying.
526. Ambingane muli-mane kala lamialu, tepa ya.	Having hit (the pig) with a club, let it fall down.

Lines 524 and 525 would already be parallel without adding *lama epea* because the medial verb ending -*to* is the same in both lines and would have served as a very limited frame for the rest of the words in those two lines which function as groups of parallel terms; adding the words *lama epea* creates a larger repetitive frame for those contrasting terms. Sometimes the words *lama epea* are augmented by adding the syllable *-ne*. Adding that syllable to the verb *epea* in normal Ipili might indicate that the person who is speaking actually witnessed the event being mentioned, but it does not seem to change the meaning in that way in all cases in a chanted tale.

Parallelism created by using sense orienters

Some verbs function as orienters that indicate which one of the five senses people have used to gain information about their environment. The rest of the clause or sentence states what information is being gained. The three lines in text 22 all end with the Ipili words *ale ya*, which mean 'he heard'.

Text 22. Example from "Kau tali tapeyo."

251.	Kuaka puli toko pulu yanga ale ya.	He heard laughing like the cutting of a *puli* tree
252.	Wana tupa kuaka waiyawe toko pulu yanga ale ya.	He heard the girls laughing like the cutting of a *waiyawe* tree.
253.	Wana tupa kuaka puli toko pulu yanga ale ya.	He heard the girls laughing like the cutting of a *puli* tree.

Text 23 is another illustration of using a sense orienter to create parallelism, since the ability to see is another one of our senses. A chanter sometimes uses either the singular or plural interrogative form of the verb "see" to ask the listeners if they envision what he is telling them. He may ask whether they envision not only characters and other physical objects, but also events in the chanted tale as illustrated by text 23.

In the following example, the use of the Ipili first person plural interrogative verb form *andeyaipe* at the end of each of the six lines illustrates the use of the same verb form at the end of more than one line to enhance the parallelism between lines. Lines 9 and 10 would obviously be parallel already without the word *andeyaipe* because the words *amene kayane* in the initial position and the words *mialane yalua* in the final position would function as the frame, and the words *aŋa sia* in the medial position in line 9 and the word *ipa* in line 10 would serve as contrasting parallel terms.

In the same way, lines 12 and 13 would already be parallel without the word *andeyaipe* because the word *aŋa* in a medial position and the words *yale yalua* in the final position would function as the repetitive frame. The contrastive words *kene* and *kini* in the initial position would serve as parallel terms along with the contrastive pairs of terms *kengali kapu* in line 12 and *aŋa peya-peya* in line 13 in another medial position.

Text 23. Example from "Kau nala tapeyo."

9.	Amene kayane aŋa sia mialane yalua andeyaipe.	Do you see that the little youngest brother customarily gets firewood?
10.	Amene kayane ipa mialane yalua andeyaipe.	Do you see that the little youngest brother customarily gets water?
11.	Aŋa Kau Nala Tape yalua andeyaipe.	Do you see little Kau Nala Tape?
12.	Kene aŋa kengali kapu yale yalua andeyaipe.	Do you see (his) little legs like dry Piper trees?
13.	Kini aŋa, aŋa peya-peya yale yalua andeyaipe.	Do you see (his) little arms like *peya-peya* trees?
14.	Kawane itini yaiyapia yoko mina pelene yale yalua andeyaipe.	Do you see (his) hair like *yaiyapia* tree leaves which have been held and hit?

It would be quite unusual to have such a long series of questions in any other genre or type of discourse in the Ipili language, so this long series of questions can be considered a creative poetic feature intended to encourage the listeners to envision what he is describing to them. Text 23 occurs near the beginning of a performance, whereas text 24 occurs much later in another performance.

Text 24 and the next four are consistent with Rumsey's report that many Ku Waru people have pointed out that all performers of chanted tales seek to keep the attention of their listeners focused on the story and by presenting it in a way that "makes them see and hear it happening in their own minds as the performer does in his or hers" (Rumsey 2001:215).

Text 24. Example from "Kau nala akali."

240.	Epo peapele oko iyunga ote tupa yalua andelepa.	Do you see that the two went back and forth up there?
241.	Kesa minaka kesa minaka epo peane oko yalua andelepa.	Do you see that the one went back and forth trying to grab it?

The chanter in text 24 uses the second person singular interrogative form of the verb "see," even though it is almost certain that many people were listening to his tale. This is an example of addressing his listeners as individuals, which may further enhance their sense of personal involvement. In both texts 24 and 26, the chanter asks the listeners if they can envision what the chanter is describing.

Lines 240 and 241 would be parallel already without the word *andelepa* because *yalua* would function as a frame for the rest of the words in each line which would therefore serve as groups of parallel terms; adding the word *andelepa* to the repetitive frame makes the parallelism more obvious because it then consists of two words instead of just one.

Text 25 is another illustration of the use of an Ipili first person dual verb form to reinforce the connection between himself as the chanter of the tale and each one of his listeners as individuals. He is telling each listener to join him in envisioning what he himself is seeing in his own mind. The words *itai eka* in the initial position and *longone taka mindi epeya andeyapa* in the final position provide a very big repetitive frame within which the contrasting terms *lewa* in line 1815 and *puluma* in line 1816 serve as parallel terms to create a high degree of parallelism.

Text 25. Example from "Kau tali tapeyo."

1815. Itai eka lewa longone taka mindi epeya andeyapa.	We two are seeing that many *lewa* doves are coming together.
1816. Itai eka puluma longone taka mindi epeya andeyapa.	We two are seeing that many *puluma* doves are coming together.

Sometimes a chanter uses the past tense of the verb "see" to ask whether the listener "saw" what he has already mentioned in previous lines of the chanted tale. In text 26, the chanter uses the first person singular verb form *lauwa*, which literally means 'which I said', to establish a link between his telling of the story and the listener's visualization of what he is referring back to at this point.

The chanter also uses the singular form of the verb in his question, even though it is likely that many people were listening to his tale. There would be minimal parallelism between lines 24 and 25 in this example without the words *lauwa andapipa*, but adding those two words at the end of these two lines enhances the parallelism.

Text 26. Example from "Kau nala akali."

24. Yia piango-la lapo lauwa andapipa.	Did you see the dog and the pig I mentioned?
25. Iwanaŋa lapo lauwa andapipa.	Did you see the two boys I mentioned?

In text 27, the first person dual perfect verb form *andaipa* literally means 'which you and I have seen'. Chanters use it to refer back to a character or other information that has previously been mentioned. The first person dual form of the verb in this context stresses the connection between himself as the story teller and each of his listeners as individuals. The use of *lauwa andaipa* at the end of two or more lines in succession enhances parallelism.

Even without the words *lauwa andaipa*, the words *yale mindi* in lines 179 and 180 would function as a repetitive frame for the rest of the words in those two lines which serve as groups of parallel terms. However, the use of the words *lauwa andaipa* at the end of all three of the descriptive lines makes them all more parallel, even though line 181 is slightly different because it has the additional syllable -*o*. Adding the words *lauwa andaipa* once again encourages the listeners to envision the main character or the action in which he is involved.

Text 27. Example from "Kau nalane akali."

179. Kawane itini yaiyapia yoko yapiane yale mindi lauwa andaipa,	The one I mentioned who we two saw who looked like he had *yaiyapia* tree leaves for hair,
180. inga munini panjea komani yale mindi lauwa andaipa,	the one I mentioned who we two saw whose nose was like dry bamboo,
181. kau one neenga atene mindi lauwa andaipa-o,	the one I mentioned who we two saw with light skinned lizard skin on his teeth-o,
182. oo andaipa okomane lakea ekapu jaa lo leangato, yalua andalaini.	they customarily see that one who we two saw here (walking with his) cordyline leaves flapping.

There is a sense in which an Ipili *tindi* could be compared with television, since the chanter tells a story and then repeatedly asks his hearers to envision the characters and events in the story.[6] We could say he "tells-a-vision" and uses the verb "see" in its various forms to encourage the listeners to visualize what he is saying.

Parallelism created or enhanced by using other sentence-final verbs

Many other verbs occur at the end of two or more successive lines in Ipili chanted tales. The verb *ya* is used when referring to objects or creatures like snakes that are often in a horizontal position. This verb means 'was' or 'were' in the past tense. In text 28, even without the word *ya* at the end, lines 183 and 184 would be parallel because the word *ima* in a medial position and the words *eyaka palene* in the final position would function as a repetitive frame. The words *napi kene* in line 183 and *kini* in line 184 in another medial position would serve as parallel terms along with *nimapu* in line 183 and *momapu* in line 184 as a second pair of parallel terms. Adding *ya* at the end of both lines enhances the repetitive frame by making it bigger.

Text 28. Example from "Kau nala tapeyo."

183. Napi kene ima nimapu eyaka palene ya.	Down below (his) legs were (like they) had *nimapu* vines inside of them.
184. Kini ima momapu eyaka palene ya.	(His) arms were (like they) had *momapu* vines inside of them.

In text 29, even without the final word *yane*, the two lines are already highly parallel, since *pati mialu* in the initial position and *nuu mindi yane* in the final position create a large repetitive frame for the contrasting parallel terms *upe* in line 651 and *lombami* in line 652, which refer to different kinds of netbags. The verb in the final position is formed by adding the suffix *-ne* to the end of the verb *ya*.

---

6   Note the comparison that is made by Yuna man Kenny Kendoli (chapter 2) between the experience of listening to *pikono* chanted tales and watching exciting action films.

Text 29. Example from "Kau nala tapeyo."

651.	Pati mialu, ambi upe nuu mindi yane.	Having taken (the food) out of the ground oven, there was an *upe* net bag nearby.
652.	Pati mialu, ambi lombami nuu mindi yane.	Having taken (the food) out of the ground oven, there was a *lombami* net bag nearby.

The suffix *-ne* which occurs at the end of the verb in text 29 can also be added to most other verbs. In text 30, it has been added to *atea*, which is the remote past form of the Ipili verb which is used with masculine subjects, subjects like trees that stand upright, and many other subjects including dogs. It means 'was' when it is in the past tense.

Text 30. Example from "Kau nala akali."

790.	Piangone Waleya atu ateane.	The dog Waleya was along.
791.	Iwanaŋa piako atu ateane.	That young boy was along.

Conclusion

This chapter has explored parallelism and poetics in sung narratives among Ipili speakers in the Papua New Guinea Highlands. Using examples from several chanted tales based on the same general theme, the chapter illustrates four principal means by which narrators use parallelism in Ipili tales. Parallelism follows the binary principal whereby meaning comes from both repetition and contrast. There is systematic repetition between lines, but with variation due to the inclusion of contrasting elements.

Four types of parallelism have been discussed and exemplified. Firstly, parallelism may involve substituting terms within an unchanging frame, such as referring to the same mountain, tree, or animal by different names in successive lines. Thus words change though the meaning remains the same. English speakers are familiar with poetic parallelism between lines of poetry and songs in which the last words of two lines rhyme. Ipili speakers recognise such linguistic practices also, as seen in the second type parallelism, in which the aesthetic appeal of the tale is enhanced by the use of line-final verbs that rhyme or similar non-semantic syllables. A third form of parallelism involves the repetition of a medial verb form or a suffix linked to a medial verb over several lines functioning as a frame, with all of the preceding words in each line functioning as groups of parallel terms. The fourth type of parallelism makes use of a frame which is formed through the repetition of the same sentence-final verb form at the end of two or more lines. Each of these four means of creating parallelism involves the interaction of contrasting parallel terms or syllables within a repeated frame in a systematic and creative way, so as to produce a performance that adults as well as children listen to with rapt attention.

In ordinary speech, where the focus is on providing information, people will speak concisely, listing different items in a single clause. However, the narrators of Ipili sung narratives place different terms in separate lines, leading to the parallelism and poetics of the genre of *tindi*. At times the meanings may change to provide semantic parallelism, while at other times there may be lexical parallelism that makes no difference to the meaning. The purpose of such creative parallelism is to produce a narrative with aesthetic appeal that will draw the listeners into the tale.

This chapter helps to show the complexity and poetic creativity found in Ipili *tindi*. However, it is difficult to capture the dynamism of *tindi* performances in a textual analysis such as this. The narrator appeals to the listeners' senses, calling on them to hear or envision the characters or events referred to. This may involve a series of questions addressed to the listeners to involve them so that they become participants in the tale. In this way, the chanted narrative takes on an active force manifest in the hearers through the performer.

Performances of *tindi* are an important part of Ipili tradition. However, the Ipili context is changing rapidly, particularly with the influx of outsiders due to the presence of the Porgera gold mine. English is the official language for young people taking part in formal education. In market places in Porgera, one may hear as much Enga and Tok Pisin spoken as Ipili. Modern music and television are the most common forms of evening entertainment. Yet the poetics of *tindi* discussed in this chapter still fascinate Ipili speakers young and old on rare occasions when *tindi* are heard live or even over the radio. The older generation who grew up with the tradition are passing away and prospects for live performances of the tradition of chanted narratives will depend on the degree to which future generations of Ipili speakers can maintain the linguistic skills and poetic imagination to create *tindi*.

References

Beekman, John, John Callow, and Michael Kopesec. 1981. *The Semantic Structure of Written Communication*. Dallas: Summer Institute of Linguistics.

Fox, James J. 1977. "Roman Jakobson and the Comparative Study of Parallelism." In *Roman Jakobson: Echoes of His Scholarship*, edited by Cornelis H. van Schooneveld and Daniel Armstrong, 59–90. Lisse: Peter de Ridder Press.

Gibbs, Philip. 1978. "*Kaunala Tape*: Towards a Theological Reflection on a New Guinea Initiation Myth." MA thesis, Catholic Theological Union (Chicago).

Golub, Alex. 2001. *Gold Positive: A Short History of Porgera 1930–1997*. Mt. Hagen: Porgera Development Authority.

Hopkins, Gerard. 1959. *Poetic Diction: The Journal of Papers of Gerard Manley Hopkins*. Edited by Humphrey House; completed by Graham Storey. London: Oxford University Press.

Hunter, Alistair G. 1999. *Psalms*. London: Routledge.

Ingemann, Frances. 1964. Unpublished transcription of a chanted tale told by Yandapake.

———. 1968. "The Linguistic Structure of an Ipili-Paiyala Song Type." In *Proceedings: 8th International Congress of Anthropological and Ethnological Sciences, Tokyo and Kyoto, Vol. 2: Ethnology*, 398–400. Tokyo: Science Council of Japan.

Jackson, Richard, and Glenn Banks. 2002. *In Search of the Serpent's Skin: The Story of the Porgera Gold Project.* Port Moresby: Placer Niugini Ltd.

Jakobson, Roman. 1966. "Grammatical Parallelism and Its Russian Facet." *Language* 42 (2): 398–429.

———. 1970. "Shifters, Linguistic Categories, and the Russian Verb." In *Selected Writings*, Vol. 2: *Word and Language,* 130–47. The Hague: Mouton.

Kale. 1974. "Kau nala tapeyo." Text of transcribed *tindi* recorded in 1974 and included in Gibbs 1978.

Kaneanda. 1965. "Kau tali tapeyo." Unpublished manuscript provided by Frances Ingemann.

Lowth, Robert. 1834. *Isaiah: A New Translation with a Preliminary Dissertation and Notes, Critical, Philological, and Explanatory.* Boston. (Orig. pub. in 1778.)

Pawley, Andrew. 2005. "The Chequered Career of the Trans New Guinea Hypothesis: Recent Research and Its Implications." In *Papuan Pasts: Cultural, Linguistic and Biological Histories of Papuan-Speaking Peoples*, ed. Andrew Pawley, Robert Attenborough, Jack Golson, and Robin Hide, 67–107. Pacific Linguistics, 572. Canberra: Australian National University.

Ross, Malcolm. 2005. "Pronouns as a Preliminary Diagnostic for Grouping Papuan Languages." In *Papuan Pasts: Cultural, Linguistic and Biological Histories of Papuan-Speaking Peoples*, ed. Andrew Pawley, Robert Attenborough, Jack Golson, and Robin Hide, 15–65. Pacific Linguistics, 572. Canberra: Australian National University.

Rumsey, Alan. 2001. "*Tom Yaya Kange*: A Metrical Narrative Genre from the New Guinea Highlands." *Journal of Linguistic Anthropology* 11 (2): 193–239.

———. 2005. "Chanted Tales in the New Guinea Highlands of Today: A Comparative Study. In *Expressive Genres and Historical Change: Indonesia, Papua New Guinea, and Taiwan*, edited by Pamela J. Stewart and Andrew Strathern, 41–81. Anthropology and Cultural History in Asia and the Indo-Pacific. Hants: Ashgate Publishing.

Yandapake. 1964a. "Kau nala akali." Unpublished manuscript provided by Frances Ingemann.

———. 1964b. "Kau nalane akali." Unpublished manuscript provided by Frances Ingemann.

9. The Structure of Chanted Ipili *Tindi*

Frances Ingemann

Introduction

The Ipili people of the Porgera and Paiyala valleys of Papua New Guinea have traditional tales, called *tindi*, which may be told either in ordinary spoken style or as long poetic chanted tales. Information about the Ipili people and *tindi* can be found in the chapter 8 of this volume.

Spoken versions of *tindi* are shorter and less elaborate than the chanted versions. Chanted *tindi* are not memorized poems, but are recreated from traditional elements in each performance. While anyone may tell a spoken version, only skilled tellers are capable of performing chanted versions. The fact that great skill is required for the performance was demonstrated by unsuccessful attempts of two men who were not traditional tellers. They were able to imitate the chant melody, but were excessively repetitive and could not produce the rich poetic language of a skilled chanter.

The chanters I recorded were all men and mostly middle-aged, three of whom performed more than once. The observations in this article are based on seven *tindi* chanted by four men from the Paiyala in 1964–65: Alua, Kaneanda, Pinyati (two tales), and Yandapake (three tales). As might be expected, there are minor differences in style among the chanters.[1]

The *tindi* were not performed in natural storytelling settings, but under field conditions specifically for the purpose of making a recording. The teller typically sat cross-legged on the ground inside a house and rocked back and forth during the performance without attempting to make eye contact with the listeners or accompanying the chanting with gestures. In order to make recordings that would be clear enough to transcribe later, the number of people present was limited, and they were instructed not to speak during the recording. The recordings, therefore, do not provide information as to what the normal interactions between the teller and the audience might be.

---

1   One chanted *tindi* was recorded in 2000 in the Porgera region. Although there are many similarities with the 1960s *tindi*, there are greater differences than among the 1960s versions. Since only one tale was collected in 2000, it is not possible to know to what extent the differences are due to the stylistic variation of a single chanter, regional differences, or developments in chanting style since the 1960s. The 2000 chanter learned to chant *tindi* from his father, who was also a chanter. His skill is recognized among the Ipili people by the fact that he has been able to charge admission to his performances.

Tindi have an internal structure which divides the long tale into segments and lines determined largely by the chant melody but also by a limited number of conventional phrases at the end of segments and lines. These structural elements will be described in the following sections.

Segments

Segments are delineated by pauses and the chant melody of the line immediately preceding the pause, which differs from a normal line by having a slightly different melody at the end and a greater-than-normal lengthening of the final syllable. All the chanters ended the segment with a lengthened, semantically empty final *o* (as discussed in chapter 1 under the rubric of "vocables"). There is also usually a final phrase, meaning that the teller is repeating what has been passed down, which is added to an otherwise normal line. The most common such ending is *leai tupa ya-o* 'this is what they said'.

The length of a segment is not fixed, with some chanters preferring shorter segments than others. There were segments as short as three lines and others well over a hundred. Segments do not necessarily coincide with episodes in the story. Although an episode may end before a pause, the pause may also be inserted at a suspenseful moment or elsewhere in the narration. Repetition sets of the sort described by Borchard and Gibbs in chapter 8 often occur before a pause and are never interrupted by a pause.

Pauses between segments also varied in length. Some chanters took the opportunity to relax for a moment, clear their throats, or engage in chitchat with listeners. At other times the pauses were only long enough to take a breath. In general, short pauses followed short segments, and longer pauses followed longer segments.

As the tale resumes following a pause, there is frequently an introductory phrase such as *de ote*, which corresponds to something like the English 'well', or *ondo atape* 'wait'. Another common way to resume the narration is a brief recapitulation or reference to what has happened just before the pause. For example, the beginning of the second segment in the tale told by Pinyati is:[2]

```
74.  uane    peane-ko    yalua    andele-pa
     thus    did.3sg-def seems    you.see-?
     It seems he did that; do you see?
```

---

[2] The numbers in examples refer to lines in the *tindi*. The transcription used here is similar to the orthography developed by Terrance Borchard. Minor differences are the use of single vowels for all monosyllabic words (there is no vowel length distinction in Ipili) and word divisions. Abbreviations used in the interlinear translation are: 3sg (third-person singular); aux (auxiliary); def (definite marker); emph (emphatic); loc (locative); T (poetic word not used in ordinary speech); V (variety of); ? (interrogative marker). No attempt has been made in the translation to identify individual inflectional and derivational morphemes.

Lines

Lines of a *tindi* are marked by the chant melody. There are usually slight pauses between lines, but occasionally two or more lines may be chanted without such a break. Lines may optionally be embellished with a final *o*, but it is not lengthened as much the *o* at the end of segments. Lines are variable in length with no rhyming, alliterative, or metrical structure. The principal poetic device is the parallelism described by Borchard and Gibbs in chapter 8. Some chanters subdivided lines by lengthening an internal part of the line, usually at a syntactic constituent boundary.

A line may equal a sentence, but a sentence may also be spread out over several lines. Although a line may consist of what could be a normal spoken utterance, it usually is more elaborate.

Lines usually contain words which have no relevance to the story line. Interpreters omit them in translation and when asked, say they have no meaning even though the words may have literal meanings elsewhere. For example, *mindi* 'one, a' has no meaning in the line from Yandapake (1964c):

38. yawo   yapu   lo   amo   nana   mindi pea   ote
    baking   divide   aux.-ing across   down   one   went.3sg   emph
    Baking [food], he went around dividing it up.

Many lines end in formulaic expressions to indicate that the story comes from what someone else has said. Examples of this are *lea* 'said' and *lama epea* 'came to say'. Another type of formulaic line ending is one that evokes involvement of the listener. Examples of such expressions are *yalua andele-pa* 'it is, do you see/know?'[3] and *andoko* 'see'.[4]

The passage below of some typical *tindi* lines comes from a tale performed by Alua in 1965 (an audio file of this example can be found in online item 12).[5]

Line 22 consists of a clause embedded in a locative phrase followed by a formulaic ending *lama epea* 'he came to say', indicating that this is not something that the teller knows from personal knowledge. The sentence is continued in line 23. Again there is a reference to this having been told by someone else: *lea* 'he said'. It should be noted that in ordinary Ipili speech there is an affix *-pia* added to remote past inflections to indicate that the speaker does not know of the event from personal knowledge. This affix does not occur in the chanted *tindi*.

---

3   The verb *anda*, having the basic meaning 'see', also means 'know'.
4   The word *andoko* also means 'where', but here seems just to be a means of involving the listener, like the colloquial English tag 'see'.
5   Readers who listen to the online recording of these lines should note that there is a false start before line 32, in which the performer mistakenly repeats part of line 31.

22.   wamba   yale   pua   yandeane-sia   lama   epea
      before   like   doing   planted.3sg-loc to.say came.3sg
      Where he planted as he had done before, it was said,

23.   komba   iyu   kiya-laliya   tupa   yo   peane   lea
      komba   up   komba   plural   putting did.3sg said.3sg
      He planted *komba* [a cabbage-like edible leafy plant], it was said.

24.   komba   iyu   kiyala   tupa   yo   peane   lea
      komba   up   komba   plural putting did.3sg   said.3sg
      He planted *komba*, it was said.

25.   wamba   yale   pua   yandeane-sia   lama   epea
      before   like   doing   planted.3sg-loc to.say came.3sg
      Where he planted as he had done before, it was said,

26.   tikili   ulia   mole   mokea   lama   epea-o
      Tsweet.potato sweet.potato Vsweet.potato   Vsweet.potato   to.say came.3sg-o
      Mole and *mokea* sweet potatoes, it was said,
      ["T" indicates that this is poetic vocabulary not used in ordinary speech.
      "V" indicates a variety of plant for which I do not know an English equivalent]

27.   papo   upapo   lama   epea-o
      Tsweet.potato Vsweet.potato to.say came.3sg-o
      Upapo sweet potatoes, it was said,

28.   utupane ote   poli   poko   ne   tete   pima   epeane   ya   lea
      them   emph   Trat   bush.rat tooth   chew   to.do came.3sg was   said.3sg
      bush rats came to chew them, it was said.

29.   poloko   ne   tete   pima   epeane   ya   lea-o
      house.rat tooth   chew   do   came.3sg   was   said.3sg-o
      House rats came to chew them, it was said.

30.   de   ote   atu   ote   yoko   yandauwa-ko   o   de   lo
      well   emph   enough emph   cultivating I.planted-def   o   well   saying
      Saying, "Well, I have planted enough."

31.   kope   yale   anda   mindi   pukale   piako   o   de   lo
      Tbig   like   house   a   I.will.do that   o -   saying
      Saying, "I will build a big house."

32.   anda   mindi pukale   ondo   atape   lea
      house   a   I.will.do wait   be   said.3sg
      He said, "I will build a house, wait."

Line 23 also illustrates another characteristic of *tindi* language: specialized vocabulary not used in ordinary speech. *Kiya-laliya* is used only in poetic language and has the same meaning as the normal word *komba*, an edible leafy plant in the cabbage family. Many of these poetic words are well known to everyone, but some are obscure, and Ipili speakers were sometimes unable to translate lines because they did not understand them. At times, as in line 23, the use of the ordinary word in addition to the poetic vocabulary aids in understanding the meaning.

Although the use of words indicating location is common in ordinary Ipili speech, it is much more frequent in *tindi*. *Iyu* 'up' in line 23 would probably not be used this way in an ordinary sentence, but here provides an embellishment.

Line 24 illustrates the repetition discussed by Borchard and Gibbs (chapter 8). In this line, only a single word is changed from line 23: *kiyala*. In this instance the substituted word is derived from a word used in the previous line, *kiya*, by adding the syllable *la*.[6] It also bears some phonetic resemblance to *laliya*, one of the words in the two-word expression in the previous line for which it substitutes.

Lines 25–28 form another sentence. Line 25 is a repetition of line 22. Lines 26 and 27 again use poetic vocabulary and the formulaic *lama epea* of line 25, but this time embellished with a final *o*. Lines 28 and 29 form another pair of parallel lines with partial repetition. In line 28, *ote*, which ordinarily is an emphatic particle, seems to be here a simple embellishment.

Line 30 has embedded direct discourse, beginning with an introductory interjection *de* 'well' and ending with *o de*, which seems to be an expression to invite a response from the listener. Line 31, because it is continuing the thought in line 30, omits the introductory expression in 30. It should be noted that the *piako* of line 31, normally translated as 'that', has the function here of making the clause of line 30 the background for line 31 and could be translated 'since' or 'and so', giving the two lines the meaning 'I have planted enough, and so I will build a big house'.

Line 32 contains the phrase *ondo atape*, which was translated 'wait', but occurs in *tindi* much more commonly than in ordinary speech. Its function is not clear.

Chant

The chant melody is a general pitch contour for a line. The pitch range varies from one chanter to another and is within the chanter's normal speaking range. The chant typically begins with a rising pitch on the first syllable. Within the line there are normally a series of syllables at more or less the same pitch, but there may also be rises and falls internally. Often lines are chanted in pairs with the

---

6   Sets of such poetic words are also used in traditional songs. See Ingemann 1968 for further examples of sets of these words.

first of the lines rising at the end and the second falling. These pairs of chanted melodies do not necessarily coincide with the repeated parallel lines of the text. Figures 1 to 6 represent pitch movements in lines from three different chanters.[7]

Figures 1 and 2 represent the pitch change in the first two lines of the sample passage given above. Note that in the first line the pitch rises on the first syllable, drops in the middle portion to a sustained mid level, drops towards the end and then rises. At the beginning of the second line the pitch contour is similar but at the end has a high pitch followed by a low one.

Figure 1. Alua (1965:line 22): *wamba yale pua yandeane-sia lama epea* **'where he planted as he had done before, it was said'. An audio file of this example can be found in online item 12.**

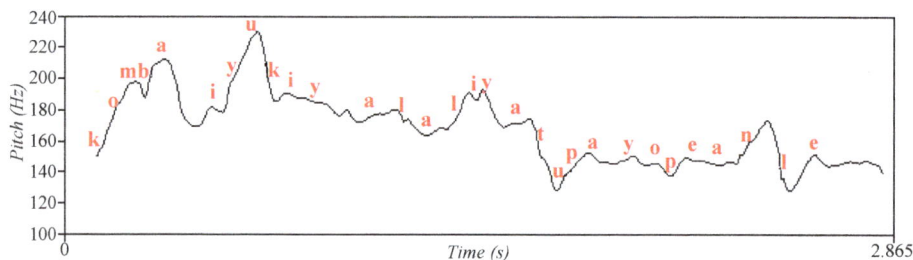

Figure 2. Alua (1965:line 23): *komba iyu kiya-laliya tupa yo peane lea* **'he planted** *komba*, **it was said'. An audio file of this example can be found in online item 12.**

---

7   These figures were produced by the Praat acoustic analysis program. Minor fluctuations in pitch should be ignored since they represent influences of consonant and vowel articulations. There may also be other fluctuations attributable to lexical tone, which has not been fully analysed and is not marked in the transcription.

Figures 3 and 4 show the chant melody as produced by another *tindi* teller. These are the first two lines in Borchard and Gibbs's figure 11 in chapter 8. Like the contour in figure 1, figure 3 displays a rise to high pitch at the beginning, a gradual descent, and a rise to a higher level at the end. Figure 4 has a similar contour but the end does not have a rise.

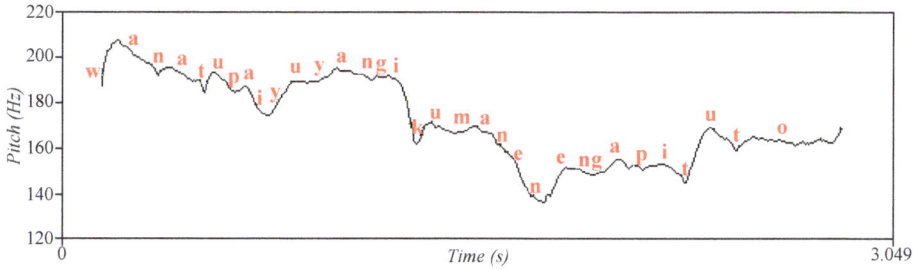

Figure 3. **Kaneanda (1965:line 827):** *wana tupa iyu yangi kuma nene-nga pitu-to* **'girls sitting up on Mt. Kuma'. An audio file of this example can be found in online item 13.**

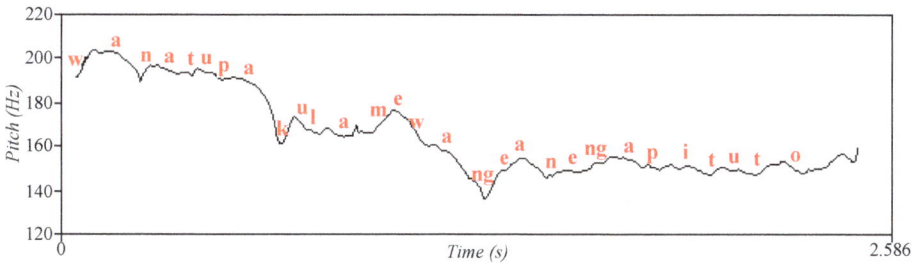

Figure 4. **Kaneanda (1965:line 828):** *wana tupa kulame wangeane-nga pitu-to* **'girls sitting up on Mt. Kulame'. An audio file of this example can be found in online item 13.**

Figure 5 represents the pitch contour of a third *tindi* chanter. The line is the first one in text 26 in Borchard and Gibbs (chapter 8). This chanter has a lower pitch range than the previous two, but the contour is much the same as in figure 2, with a rise and a fall at the end.

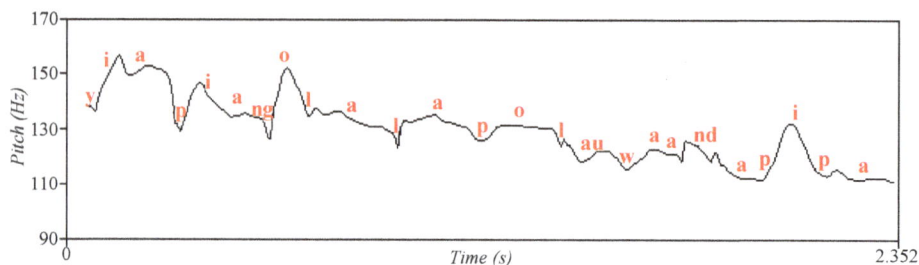

Figure 5. Yandapake (1964b:line 24): *yia piango-la lapo lauwa andapi-pa* **'both previously mentioned pig and dog'. An audio file of this example can be found in online item 14.**

Figure 6 represents a line at the end of a segment as chanted by the same man whose lines are shown in figures 3 and 4. The main part of the line is similar to non-final lines, but ends with the level final phrase *leai tupa ya* and a very long *o* with a rise at the very end.

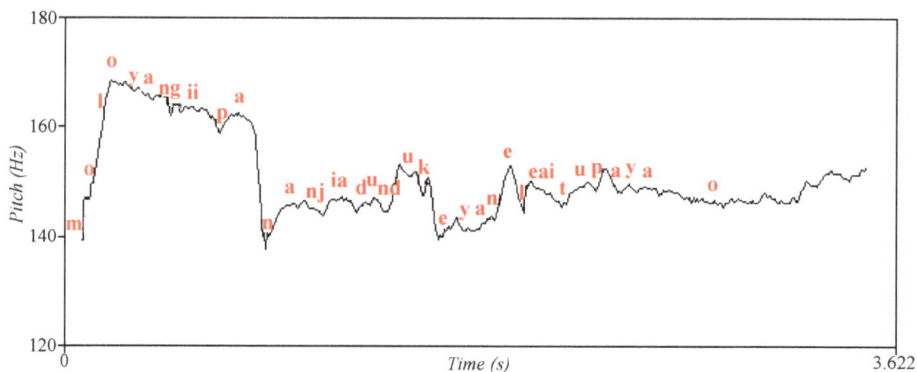

Figure 6. Kaneanda (1965:line 68): *molo yangi ipa nanjia dundu keyane leai tupa ya-o* **'he climbed up over along Nanjia River, they said'. An audio file of this example can be found in online item 15.**

Sets

Sets of lines based on repetitions have been discussed by Borchard and Gibbs (chapter 8). These sets are usually two or three lines in length, but there are some longer. There is one place within the line where one or more words differ, but the end of the lines normally remains the same. Such sets are illustrated by lines 23–24, 26–27, and 28–29 in the passage from Alua given above. The word that changes may be normal vocabulary or a poetic word used only in tales and traditional songs. Often the portion that changes is the name of a place, clan, or person. Some of the specialized poetic vocabulary is well known and understood by all listeners. For example, *lanema* is frequently used in place of *yia* 'pig', and *gulupi* and *maiyala* are used in repetition sets in place of *ana* 'stone, moon'. Other words or phrases were not understood by Ipili speakers who helped translate the stories. At times the *tindi* teller helps the listener by adding a classifier word such as *sia* 'tree'.

Frequently in the first two lines of a set, there is phonetic resemblance between the words that alter the line. The most common way of forming the second of these words is by adding a syllable. For example, *Kima,* the name of a main character in *tindi*, becomes *Kimape* in a repetition set.

Content

Although *tindi* stories differ in detail, there are a number of events and descriptions which occur in more than one. The main story line usually recounts how a young man develops into an adult, gets a wife, and eventually disappears into the clouds, which those helping translate the *tindi* explained meant going to heaven. The young man is usually living alone in an isolated area, sometimes with a brother and occasionally an aging mother. Frequently, the young man is described as being scrawny and unattractive. At some point in the story, he meets a young woman up in the mountain forests. After spending some time with her, he turns into a strong, good-looking man and receives from her items of personal adornment so that he returns home a well-developed and well-outfitted man. This part of the story is a reference to the time when boys at puberty would leave inhabited areas to live in the mountain forests, undergo ritual cleansing, perform magic spells so that their hair would grow long enough to form the large traditional hair style, and return to the inhabited area as adults.

Tindi usually include passages about making a garden, going hunting, meeting a young woman, paying compensation to the bride's family, and going to a dance. These events contain similar details and descriptions from one *tindi* to the next. The interweaving of these conventional elements and descriptions facilitates the recreation of the tale.

Conclusion

Melodic lines, segmentation, conventional phrases (particularly at the end of lines and segments), repetition, and poetic vocabulary are all features of an Ipili *tindi*. *Tindi* tellers differ slightly in style, but they have enough in common to make the Ipili *tindi* a well-defined genre. The use of conventional themes, stock phrases, and repetition facilitate the recreation of a *tindi* each time it is performed.

Acknowledgements

I am deeply grateful to all the Ipili speakers who at various times over a period of more than forty years have helped me to understand their language and culture. In particular, I thank the *tindi* tellers, whose performances formed the basis for this chapter, and the interpreters who helped me in the laborious task of transcribing and understanding the tales. My work on the Ipili language in the 1960s was funded in part by the Lutheran Church Missouri Synod, the Wenner-Gren Foundation, the National Science Foundation, and the University of Kansas. I also appreciate the help that I received from the Papua New Guinea mission of the Lutheran Church Missouri Synod in getting to and from the Ipili area, as well as housing and support while living there. Many New Guineans are to be thanked for providing housing and other assistance as I hiked around, recording language samples as well as the *tindi* analysed in this chapter. I have greatly benefited over the years from insights into the Ipili language generously provided by Terry Borchard. Also, I cannot thank him and his wife, Janet, enough for their hospitality and assistance with travel arrangements in recent years, without which I would not have been able to continue to work with Ipili speakers to unravel the complexities of the *tindi*.

References

Alua. 1965. Recording transcribed and translated by Frances Ingemann.

Ingemann, Frances. 1968. "The Linguistic Structure of an Ipili-Paiyala Song Type." In *Proceedings: 8th International Congress of Anthropological and Ethnological Sciences, Tokyo and Kyoto, Vol. 2: Ethnology*, 398–400. Tokyo: Science Council of Japan.

Kaneanda. 1965. Recording transcribed and translated by Frances Ingemann.

Pinyati. 1964. Recording transcribed and translated by Frances Ingemann.

———. 1965. Recording transcribed and translated by Frances Ingemann.

Yandapake. 1964a. Recording transcribed and translated by Frances Ingemann.

———. 1964b. Recording transcribed and translated by Frances Ingemann.

———. 1964c. Recording transcribed and translated by Frances Ingemann.

10. Skywalkers and Cannibals: Chanted Tales among the Angal

Hans Reithofer

Preface

In this chapter I provide a general introduction to the art of chanting tales as practised and valued among Karinj speakers (a West Angal, or Wola, dialect) in the Southern Highlands of Papua New Guinea. Apart from discussing aspects of form and performance as well as content, the social significance of this verbal art and of the stories themselves will be considered in some detail. Why folk tales about skywalkers and cannibals should be important at all—beyond the aesthetic pleasure and entertainment afforded by their skilful performance—is a question that is answered by looking at the influence these stories had on the interpretation and widespread adoption of Christian teachings. As it turned out, Karinj speakers discovered a close correspondence between Christian moral teachings and their own folk tales.

Since this is the only chapter on Angal chanted tales in this volume, I will open with an ethnographic sketch of the wider language area before situating the Karinj speakers within it. This should also help to familiarize non-Melanesianists with the larger sociocultural context. To appreciate the distinctive quality of Karinj chanted tales as compared with other kinds of stories they have, a brief discussion of narrative categories and genres will preface the main section on chanted tales, their properties and significance. The chapter will conclude with some reflections on the current state and possible medium-term development of this verbal art in that area.

It is appropriate to clarify at the outset some aspects of the research context which have affected to some extent the nature as well as some of the limitations of the data and findings presented here. My research on chanted tales among Karinj speakers was not conducted systematically for any appreciable period of time, but instead was a by-product of my research on other topics such as pre-colonial ritual life and processes of Christianization. The invitation to the second Chanted Tales Workshop in Goroka in 2006 did provide some opportunity for me to follow up on relevant points and collect some more stories, but for a proper research project on this topic I would have needed more time and funds than were available. The majority of chanted tales were related to me by one very gifted narrator, Josep Haip (figure 3), and recorded either at my field house or in houses of common friends. Since I worked so extensively with him, or he with me, it is appropriate that he features prominently in this account. Whether chanted or related in prose, almost all of the stories were told or performed because I had signalled my interest in recording (and later transcribing and analysing) them, not because they would have been told anyway at that particular moment. In other words, with very few exceptions I did not hear the stories in their typical social setting, that is, when men or women tell them at night to their various audiences. This has some important implications: I do not know whether performances by women tend to differ from those by men with regard to performance style, choice and composition of stories, exegetical comments, and so forth. Nor can I say how much these variables are determined or influenced by a particular audience and the specific circumstances of a given performance. My data are also too limited for me to be able to differentiate in every instance between standard performance style and individual peculiarities. This would necessitate the analysis of a range of (both male and female) performers.

The Angal language area

The linguistic situation

As the linguistic situation is potentially confusing, it seems best to begin here, even though the reader should not expect language borders to coincide with sociocultural boundaries—a point that will be argued shortly. The Angal language group,[1] variously subsumed under other umbrella terms such as Wola and Mendi, comprises about 80,000 speakers (Gordon 2005) occupying five valleys in the Southern Highlands Province of Papua New Guinea that are drained by the following rivers (from east to west): the Mendi, Lai, Nembi, Was (or Wage), and Ak (or Augu). For the three main Angal "languages,"[2] their approximate numbers of speakers and boundaries, see figure 1 in this chapter and figure 2 in chapter 1. The principal terms given to the "languages" (in bold italics in figure 1 here) may each be translated as 'the normal language' or 'the true talk', since *angal* means 'word, talk, language' and the cognate terms *heneng, enen,*

---

1 See chapter 1 for details and references on the classification of Angal languages within the Engan group of the Trans New Guinea family.

2 Although *Ethnologue* (Gordon 2005) treats the three members of the Angal group as separate languages, the question whether they are to be classified as dialects rather than languages remains as unanswered as it was forty-five years ago (Rule 1965:98). This has certainly to do with the fact that, apart from one rather preliminary paper (Rule 1965) and one linguistic study on Nembi narrative and procedural discourse (Tipton 1982), no academic analyses of any of the three Angal languages have been published so far. The main "dialects" are quite distinct, but only to some extent mutually unintelligible. It appears that communication is most difficult (but not impossible) between the western and southern "dialects" (Schlatter, pers. comm., 29 April 1999; Sillitoe 1979a:13 n. 8).

and *henen* 'true' or 'real' or just 'normal, everyday, standard'.[3] Figure 1 also lists Karinj (sometimes spelled Katinja in accordance with Enga orthography), a dialect variant of (West) Angal Heneng or Wola spoken in the northwest corner of the language area. That area and its inhabitants are the main ethnographic focus of this chapter.

ANGAL LANGUAGE GROUP	
Dialect variant: **Karinj / Aklal Heneng / Pi Heneng**	*Angal (Henen)* aka East Angal, (North) Mendi 22% (c. 18,000 speakers)
Angal Heneng aka Wola, West Angal Heneng, West Mendi 50% (c. 40,000 speakers)	*Angal Enen* aka Nembi, South Angal Heneng, South Mendi 28% (c. 22,000 speakers)

Figure 1. The Angal language group, based on Gordon (2005) and Vic Schlatter (pers. comm., 29 Apr 1999).

The term *karinj* may be rendered as 'west' or 'western'[4] and is a term with shifting referents within the Angal language area. The Mendi in the east would call the West Angal area and its inhabitants *Karinj*, while the Karinj speakers I worked with, in turn, reserved the term for the people and area to *their* west, that is, to the Wage valley and its population around Margarima. Karinj speakers refer to their specific dialect as *Aklal Heneng* (in distinction to *Angal Heneng*) or—more often—as *Pi Heneng* (again 'the true/normal language'), a term that already indicates the influence from, and proximity to, Enga (*pii* = Enga for 'word/talk') and Huli (*bi* = 'word/talk').

Although Angal speakers of all shades would certainly acknowledge the relatedness of their respective languages,[5] ethnographers caution against the assumption of sociocultural homogeneity on linguistic grounds (e.g., Lederman 1986a:8–9; Sillitoe 1979a:24–30). Studies from different parts of the language area (Sillitoe 1979a; Lederman 1986a; Nihill 1996; Reithofer 2006) provide

---

3   Theodore Mawe, a Mendi (East Angal) speaker, offered another etymology at the 2006 Goroka workshop: translating *enen* as 'lower' in the sense of downriver or lower altitude, *Angal Enen* could rather be rendered as the 'Lower Language'. The anthropologist Michael Nihill used the term *Anganen* for the people of the Lower Lai and Nembi Rivers and accounted for it in yet another way—as 'talk' (*anga*) of this 'general region' (*nene*) (Nihill 1999:70).

4   In Angal, the term *karinj* is used, together with its counterpart *aron*, to refer to opposite sides of a valley; given the general north-south-flow of the main rivers, these terms thus denote 'west' and 'east', respectively (cf. Sillitoe 1979a:26–28).

5   See Nihill (1999:84 n. 7) for a Lower Nembi perspective on this linguistic commonality.

enough evidence to conclude that there is as much exchange, borrowing, and mutual influence with speakers of other languages as between Angal-speaking groups themselves, giving rise to an internal heterogeneity that manifests itself in various domains of the social, economic, political, and religious life (e.g., land tenure, leadership, marriage, exchange, ritual).[6] Linguistic boundaries, in other words, matter little, and commonalities may be greater between groups with adjoining territories and different languages than between widely spaced groups of the same or closely related language. This should be kept in mind for the following sociocultural notes. The intention is to point out some relevant features of the language area, not to suggest a sharply bounded cultural region.

Ethnographic sketch

Much of the Angal language area is limestone country characterized by heavily forested mountain ridges and roaring rivers, on the one hand, and neatly patterned gardens and extensive cane grassland in the settled parts, on the other. The entire area is divided in territories associated with larger kin-founded groups variously rendered as clans, clan clusters, tribes, or clan/tribal alliances in the ethnographic literature.[7] These larger territorial groups are invariably divided into smaller localized kin-based groups that have an agnatic bias (i.e., exhibit a preference for membership following the male line), both in practice and in ideology (Sillitoe 1999:336–37). Notwithstanding this patrilineal preference, these smaller local communities living in more or less scattered settlements are very much bilaterally constituted, and all researchers stress the absence of discrimination against people who have joined the group on the basis of other (kin) connections—for example, through their mother or wife. By virtue of the blood ties between their members, local groups are usually and ideally exogamous (i.e., strictly out-marrying). This requirement of exogamy, in conjunction with the fact that most married women live with their husband's group rather than their own, is clearly mirrored in the standard plots of chanted stories in Angal. Each "clan" territory contains one or more ceremonial grounds, the centre of social and political life. These carefully levelled and cleared areas surrounded by tall casuarinas (*Casuarina oligodon*)

---

6   A number of recent volumes in the comparative vein (A. Strathern and Stürzenhofecker 1994; Biersack 1995a; Goldman and Ballard 1998; Ballard and Clark 1999; A. Strathern and Stewart 2000) have shown that this pattern of intense intercommunication and interdependence through history and across "cultures," linguistic and physical boundaries applies to the broader western Highlands region of Papua New Guinea more generally.

7   The terms are problematic for suggesting a social organization heavily premised on unilineal (in this case, patrilineal) descent, giving rise to patrilineal descent groups and descent-based political corporations that are both inappropriate to capture the socio-political realities of the Highlands region more generally. But this is not the place to broach this rather large debate; see Sillitoe (e.g., 1979a:30–33, 1999) for a critical discussion from a Wola (West Angal) perspective. The terms are appropriate, however, for reflecting the descent *ideology* that pervades people's representations of the structure and solidarity of their groups (A. Strathern 1968; Lederman 1986a:19–61), and it is in this sense that I use these terms.

have a park-like appearance and set the stage for dances and pig-feasts, general meetings and chatting. Scenes of a pig-kill and a dance are almost a required part of every chanted tale, as we shall see.

The Angal are largely swidden agriculturalists, cultivating sites within an altitudinal range from 1,300 to 2,600 metres. The staple is sweet potato, supplemented by crops such as bananas, various cucurbits, greens and beans, sugar-cane, and taro. Coffee has gained importance in recent years as a cash crop, notably in eastern and southern parts of the area. Like other Highlanders, the Angal keep pig herds of considerable size, which they channel into an extensive exchange system, a point I will return to presently. Hunting (mainly of marsupials, cassowaries, and other birds) is culturally valued, but does not contribute to the daily diet in any significant way (Sillitoe 2003). This contrasts with the hunting as portrayed in many stories, a possible reflection of older subsistence strategies in which hunting may have complemented agriculture to a greater extent (but see Sillitoe 2002). As elsewhere in the Highlands, subsistence activities are strongly gendered, with men being responsible for the heavy work of clearing and fencing garden land and claiming hunting as their domain, while women assume largely the tasks of routine cultivation and harvesting as well as pig-rearing.

All Angal communities have elaborate systems of exchange, both in the form of everyday and comparatively small-scale exchanges carried out between individuals or families, and in the form of large-scale public events sponsored by local groups. It is certainly not merely a reflection of the prevailing zeitgeist that anthropological research in all three Angal "language communities" has produced monographs focused on exchange (Ryan 1961; Sillitoe 1979a; Lederman 1986a; Nihill 1986). Large public exchanges in the contexts of warfare reparation payments and pig-killing festivals are the more prestigious and conspicuous events; the latter may culminate in massive pig kills involving up to 2,000 pigs killed within a few days and pork distributed to thousands of people, as has been reported for the *mok ink* festival of the Mendi area (Ryan 1961; Lederman 1986a). It is the everyday form of exchange, however, that is the backbone of Angal social life. Constituting an interminable series of exchanges notably in the contexts of marriage and death, it involves more transactors and more (kinds of) wealth than its more conspicuous counterpart: pigs and pearlshells in the past, along with other sea shells, *tigaso* decorating oil from the Kutubu region and other valuables, nowadays mostly pigs and cash. These quotidian and multiple exchange transactions create and sustain durable relations between individuals of different local groups, most often between affines (in-laws). Everyday exchange thus fosters extra-group ties and challenges intra-group solidarity, but without these personal networks of exchange partnerships, large-scale exchange displays foregrounding the group would be all but impossible. In social practice, the two forms of exchange are indissolubly linked, both hierarchically and complementarily (see, especially, Lederman 1986a, 1990).

The staging of pig-kills, a standard theme of chanted tales, was done not only in the context of large-scale public prestations. While the history of ceremonial pig-killing festivals such as the *mok ink* of the Mendi may be less than a century long, major pig-kills with a probably longer history were held in association with a number of fertility cults (Mawe 1982; Lederman 1986a:181–82; Nihill 1996). Invariably controlled by men, these fertility cults were concerned with the continued or improved reproduction of people, pigs, and the land. Female participation in these cults, even as spectators, was severely limited. But even most of these cults were not simply autochthonous to the area but imported from other groups and subsequently adapted and also transmitted to others, much in the same way as other trade items (such as shells, oil, axes and adzes, pigs, salt, fur and feathers, drums, bows, and so on) as well as stories and beliefs were circulated along the trading routes that criss-crossed language borders and physical boundaries (e.g., Crittenden 1991). A famous case in point is the Timp (or Rimbu) fertility cult: while it attracted much colonial attention in the then Southern Highlands District when it swept like a bushfire through the Mendi area in the 1950s and 1960s, it had been adopted from southern Angal speakers in the Lower Lai and Nembi valleys who, in turn, had been introduced to it by their trading partners to the south some fifty years earlier (Lederman 1986a; Nihill 1996:277).

While participation in these fertility cults cut across "clan" lines, thus emphasizing—according to some researchers (e.g., Lederman 1986a:58–59)—the importance of a general male solidarity over "clan" solidarity, there is also evidence of a patrilineal ancestral cult of longer standing which was inwardly oriented, concerned with preserving the viability and strength of local kin-based groups (A. Strathern 1994:240; Wiessner and Tumu 1998:199; Reithofer 2006:122–33). Ritual practices involved the handling of sacred stones and the occasional sacrifice of a pig to ancestral spirits believed to cause sickness and death, on the one hand, and to confer blessing and assistance on their living descendants, on the other. Both basic templates of cults were practised in a bewildering array of local and regional variants until Christian missionization, which for most parts of the language area began in the 1960s—except for the Mendi area proper, where the Methodist Overseas Mission founded a station in 1950.

Another common feature salient to a large group of sung stories involving a cannibal ogre is related to the fact that the Angal area, as part of the Highlands region, borders on the Papuan lowlands inhabited by groups with markedly different languages and customs. The social universe of Angal groups is thus more heterogeneous than that of more central Highland communities, and there is a prevailing image of the south as feared and dangerous (Nihill 1999:75), populated by powerful sorcerers and cannibals. The malarial climate of the lowland forests certainly contributed to this perception (Crittenden 1991:135–37). This did not prevent southern Angal groups from sustaining trading relationships with these groups, even to the point of hiring sorcerers or purchasing sorcery techniques for their own use, but they always did so with caution (Crittenden 1991:136; Sillitoe 1979b:42–43). The same perception of the south also obtained among the northernmost Angal communities, the Karinj speakers, and proved a rich inspirational source for their popular cannibal stories.

The Karinj and the Somaip "tribe"

The Karinj-speaking groups occupy the high country of the upper Wage and Lai Rivers of the Enga and Southern Highlands Provinces. From the Wage, the land rises sharply into a folded range of mountains reaching over 3,000 metres, but gives way to a series of foothills and rolling grassland as it descends towards the swamps of the Lai valley. Virtually all of the land lies above 2,300 metres. Both culturally and linguistically, this is a transitional zone. Three major languages intersect here: Enga, Huli, and Angal (in the Karinj dialect). The larger territorial groups or "tribes" that live here (such as the Timitopa, Yalipuni, and Maulu)[8] reflect this border situation as they typically comprise not only Karinj but also Enga- and/or Huli-speaking groups—the result of migration, dispersal, and a wide variety of exchange networks across language boundaries. Not surprisingly, many Karinj individuals are bilingual, and not a few trilingual.

This applies also to the one Karinj "tribe" with which I have worked more specifically: the Somaip, known as Yamape in Enga and Yamabu in Huli. Notwithstanding the linguistic diversity existing among them, their sense of tribal unity and identity is securely anchored in their origin myth and was regularly reinforced—in pre-Christian times—by cult performances in which representatives of all Somaip "clans" participated to appease the "Python Spirit," their founding ancestor, in order to renew the world. The same cult also had a strong centrifugal dimension, as it was performed at a site the Somaip viewed as the centre of a wide-reaching ritual network connecting them to the Huli, Ipili, and Enga.[9] This illustrates the point made above: the Somaip's primary allegiances were with neighbouring Enga- and Huli-speaking groups to their north and west,

---

8   I use here the Enga orthographic transcriptions (cf. Wiessner and Tumu 1998); the Karinj pronounce the names more like Timorop, Salupisi, and Maul.

9   See Reithofer (2006:163–77) for a detailed discussion of this Tunda cult, known as Tondaka by the Enga and Tuandaga by the Huli.

rather than with other Angal speakers to their south and southeast. They also vigorously opposed the aforementioned Timp fertility cult as incompatible with their own ritual practices and halted its rapid spread at their territorial borders.

As keepers of what they regarded as the world's ultimate sacred site, the Somaip perceived themselves as being at the ritual hub of a multi-ethnic universe. Their self-description as the world's 'centre-people' (*hoinyal el*) was also explicated in linguistic terms: "We live right in the middle, where three big languages converge which we can understand, while we also have our own local language [i.e., Karinj]." Like other Karinj "tribes," the Somaip were, in pre-colonial times, acutely aware of the many differences existing between the various groups in terms of language, dress, customs, etc. Yet they also shared the sense of an underlying, fundamental commonality that was mythologically grounded in the figure of Hela, the "father of all people"—of all people, that is, that were considered 'true humans' (*ol heneng*). Hela gave birth to Hela-Hul (the Huli), Hela-Tuna (the Duna), Hela-Tukupa (comprising groups west and south of the Tari Basin), and Hela-Open (comprising the Wola, Karinj, and Enga).[10] This social universe, which relegated the feared populations in the far south to a periphery outside "true humanity," was expressed in various ways in the chanted tales, as we will see.

Enj: Chanted tales among the Karinj

Genres of story

Karinj speakers make a basic distinction between narrative and non-narrative discourse by referring to the former as *enj* (story, tale) and to the latter as *pi* (word, talk). Within the narrative domain, the Somaip recognize, as do other Karinj speakers, several categories, which may be labelled as *enj* or *arman* or a combination of both—*enj-arman*. But the categorizations are in fact quite fluid as there are at least two cross-cutting axes of distinction that may be employed. Consequently, the labels too vary in their meaning (see figure 2 for a summary of this argument).

One axis of distinction emphasized by the Somaip men with whom I discussed the matter in the run-up to the 2006 Goroka workshop, focuses on the historical, social, and political relevance of stories and leads to the basic distinction between rather irrelevant 'fiction' (*enj*) and more significant 'history' (*arman*). From this perspective, the two categories may encompass the following types of narratives:

---

10 Again, this is an idea that connects the Karinj to the Huli, Duna, and Ipili to their west, who entertain very similar ideas about a mythical father figure of "all people" (cf. Frankel 1986; Ballard 1994; Biersack 1995b), rather than to other Angal speakers, who do not seem to hold such a notion (Sillitoe, pers. comm., 25 April 2008).

Enj as 'fiction' may be translated as 'folk tales' and refers to the sung stories this chapter (and volume) is concerned with.

Arman as 'history' comprises narratives that 'have a base' (*te hai*), that is, a grounding in reality. Among them:

- *Origin myths* of social groups (such as the Somaip "tribe") and cult practices: Despite their fantastic elements and primordial settings, these "myths" belong to the historical *arman*-category, it was argued, because they were not just *enj* or Tok Pisin *stori nating* ('mere stories') but "true stories—our history."[11] These origin myths thus stand in a hierarchical relationship to chanted tales or *enj*. They are "emplaced" in the local or regional landscape and record the deeds of primordial ancestors who have shaped this very landscape (cf. Rumsey and Weiner 2001). Only the people whose history is recorded in these origin myths will really know them, that is, in their details, hidden meanings, and the like. Regarded as important and also potent stories/knowledge, they are not readily disclosed to outsiders; when I was told them, it was typically with considerable reluctance and secrecy.

- *Genealogies*: While most Karinj speakers do not use a specific genre to recite genealogies, these are certainly considered important as individual "historical" knowledge and hence *arman*, even though they typically extend back into mythical origin times.

- *Remembered history*: Stories relating events of a more recent or "historical" past as they involve persons that can be firmly placed genealogically. These may concern outstanding exchange events, cult performances, warfare, extraordinary feats of men of renown, famines, and the like.[12]

- News or stories from other places concerning supposedly true incidents (also referred to as *tema*).

Another type of narrative may be called fables or etiological stories, as they explain, for instance, the contrasting "lifestyles" of flea and cockroach. Initially classified as *arman* because they were "true," they were then placed in the *enj* category and finally slotted in between as *enj-arman*, a further indication of the fluid nature of story categorization.

Following another axis of distinction based on formal criteria of performance, *enj* are those stories delivered in a distinctive melodic recitation style, while *arman* are those presented in relatively unembellished prose. From this

---

11 In line with the general argument of fluid story categorizations, the neighbouring Wola use the term *injiy* (= *enj*) in reference to such origin stories: *ol maerizor injiy* (lit., 'man borne story') (Sillitoe 1999:336). They also often refer to stories more generally as *injiyatmaen* (= *enj* + *arman*), thus conflating the two labels and abrogating a categoric distinction between the two (Sillitoe, pers. comm., 25 April 2008).

12 A good discussion of Mendi "historical" story genres and historical consciousness more generally is provided by Lederman (1986b).

perspective, different narrative genres may be either categorized as *enj* or as *arman*, depending on the performance, as illustrated by figure 2. While it is true that the only stories *typically* chanted are folk tales, the boundaries become blurred, once again, for various reasons. First, gifted storytellers often employ elements of *enj*-performances (clearly demarcated lines, line-final vowels or vocables) when relating origin stories of their own or other social groups. One remarkable Karinj performer, Josep Haip, claims that he can perform any story in *enj*-fashion. Second, *arman* origin stories also share many elements with *enj* folk tales: certain themes and motifs, such as elaborate dress-up and decoration before taking off for a journey, marvellous pig-kills, things or persons disguising their true nature or character. Third, even the most paradigmatic folk tales are often told in prose, and would then be described as being told 'just so, in *arman*-style' (*pahame arman was*).

Narrative vs. non-narrative discourse:

Narrative genres:	**enj** = story (generic term)
Non-narrative genres:	**pi** = talk (generic term)

Historical/social/political relevance:

Least relevant:	**enj** = "fiction" (folk tales)
True, but of little relevance:	**enj-arman** = fables, etiological stories
Most relevant:	**arman**: 1. origin myths/stories of clans, tribes, cults, etc. 2. genealogies 3. accounts of historical and contemporary events 4. biblical stories

Performance style:

Distinctive melodic style (chanted/sung):	**enj**: 1. folk tales 2. fables, etiological stories 3. origin myths/stories of clans, tribes, cults, etc. 4. biblical stories
Narrated in prose:	**arman**: 1. folk tales 2. fables, etiological stories 3. origin myths/stories of clans, tribes, cults, etc. 4. genealogies 5. accounts of historical and contemporary events 6. biblical stories

Figure 2. Karinj narrative terms and distinctions according to different criteria.

The social significance of *enj* folk tales

The etymology of the term *enj* is unclear. Questions in this regard were met with shrugs.[13] The term is possibly related to the far past tense of the verb *la* (speak/tell): *inja*; both the verb and the tense are prevalent in sung stories. If the suggestion has some merit—Somaip friends neither denied nor affirmed it— the term would encapsulate the general knowledge and expectation that chanted tales are "stories from a distant past."

Enj folk tales are primarily told for entertainment (*turi te*: to make people 'feel happy'), but also—according to catechist Alois Along (Goroka Workshop 2006)—to let listeners settle down from a sad or turbulent experience or gain a new perspective on their current life situation. Most stories contain fairly explicit moral messages which may be further explicated in exegetical commentaries proffered by performers as a kind of postscript at least in some instances.[14] The morals of folk tales (discussed in the following section) point to an educational aspect and potential of *enj* storytelling and make it appropriate to view the verbal art as a form of "edutainment." Entertainment is the dominant factor, though, and it is for this reason that *enj* storytelling is so much more appreciated when delivered in a rather definite melodic style, which is typically done indoors at night.[15] The reputation enjoyed by accomplished performers is correspondingly high, not least because there are few who acquire this special skill which takes a good deal of time and dedication to train and develop. Josep Haip (figure 3) is such a specialist. A man in his fifties when we met in 1998, he was widely known for his performance skills which he had learned from various local bards over long years of exercise in his teens. The art of singing stories had fascinated him since his childhood days. Without this strong interest, he said, it would be impossible to persevere and become a master bard. In the course of his career, Haip had created his own distinctive performance style and commanded a seemingly inexhaustible pool of stories and episodes to draw upon. Performers like him expect (or demand) some sort of payment that commonly consists of tobacco, some money, or a drink in appreciation of their strenuous performance (said to cause backache and a dry throat) and their demonstrated skill as entertainers captivating their audience. Like other bards, Haip has on occasion been hired

---

13 Theodore Mawe at the 2006 Chanted Tales Workshop pointed out that the cognate Mendi (East Angal) term *inj* refers also to a leech and suggested this as an etymology. The same homology applies to the term *enj*, but my Karinj interlocutors viewed this as a coincidence, without any etymological import.

14 As noted earlier, my data are insufficient in this regard. Narrators sometimes added commentaries after relating a story to me without any prompting, but they possibly did so in anticipation of curious questions I usually asked in such situations.

15 Whether told in prose or chanted, the basic verb *la* ('speak/tell') is used for the act of delivering an *enj*— and any other story genres, speeches and talk, for that matter. By adding certain conjunctions or adjectives, however, one can express the fact that an *enj*-story was chanted 'in style' (*mo hain*) or told 'just so' (*pahame*); but neither of these expressions is exclusive to the semantic domain of *enj*. One can also build a house or deliver a speech 'in style'.

also by political candidates to perform in the context of their campaigns in order to make their voters "feel happy." In such cases, the enlisted narrator expects a payment of a suitably higher amount of money. While both men and women may chant *enj*, there are more male than female performers known in the region.[16]

Figure 3. Narrator Josep Haip enjoying a smoke on his pipe, August 1998 (photo by author).

Since anyone—men, women, or children—may hear these stories, the actual audience will depend primarily on the type of house in which a story is performed (men's houses, women's or family houses, nowadays also church-related community houses) and on the overall context (such as a *singsing* or a political campaign). Through extensive use of parallel repetition and synonym substitutions, and the insertion—or omission—of stock episodes, performances using the "same" story plot may vary greatly in length and span several hours. One performance by Josep Haip lasted well over two hours, interrupted by a meal that was part of his payment. He claimed that he could have made it last much longer.

A novel performance type is the enactment of folk tales (and other stories) on public occasions, such as church feasts and school-sponsored cultural days. I have witnessed—and unwittingly facilitated—Karinj enactments of *enj* folk tales

---

16   I have never attended a woman's *enj*-performance nor inquired whether stories told by women tended to be more educational than those told by men, as has been pointed out at the 2006 Goroka workshop for the Duna, for instance.

on two occasions when I sponsored a communal day of sports and performances at Ipisam, my fieldwork base. Not surprisingly, it was Josep Haip who persuaded his group to enact a popular folk tale featuring the cannibal figure Wan Heyo (figures 4–5) on the first occasion in 2000. While he assumed the role of the narrator, he presented the storyline in prose and as a kind of running commentary to the enactment. The innovation extended also to the interpretation of the story, as discussed in the section on Christianization below. The audience liked it, and there were more such performances years later on the second occasion. Such enactments of popular stories and pre-Christian ritual performances are known to the Karinj through various other contexts in which the representation and celebration of one's cultural traditions are encouraged. Aside from school and church festivities, the most prominent ones are state-sponsored events, such as cultural shows and Independence Day celebrations.

As is common throughout the region, *enj* folk tales do not have individual authors. There is a pool of stories from which any performer might draw and to which he or she may add new ones from other regions. Variations between different performers concerning the "same" story pose no problem. The standard reply to queries about variations is also a typical expression of valued individuality: "That's how he or she has heard the story, and that's how I have heard it. That's all." Many of the stories are widely known within a given region, but there are no definite "titles" associated with them. If a particular story is requested from a listener, he or she would summarize the most typical features of it in a few words or refer to the predominant protagonist and say something, such as, "tell us about what so-and-so did long ago."

My Karinj interlocutors claim that the art of performing *enj* in style is restricted to their area and does not extend to other areas like Nipa or Mendi. (They are aware, however, of equivalents among the Huli—*bi te*—and Enga—*tindi pii.*) This claim bespeaks some ethnocentric pride but does not entirely hold up against other evidence. Ruth Tipton collected several 'ancestral stories' or *inji* during her linguistic research on the Nembi Plateau and in the Nipa area in the early 1970s, and these appear to be very much akin to Karinj chanted tales in content, form, and performance (Tipton 1982; email, 20 Oct 2009). Subsequent re-visits in the years 2005–7 suggested to her "that the stories are still told" in those southern and southwestern areas of the Angal language area (Tipton, email, 20 Aug 2009).[17] A different development is attested for the Mendi region by Theodore Mawe, who was born in the early 1950s near Mendi. He related at the 2006 Chanted Tales Workshop that he still remembered *inj* (= *enj*) being told in his childhood days,

---

17 Asked whether southern Angal narrators indeed "chanted" their stories, Tipton replied (email, 20 Oct 2009) that "the intonation patterns for the entire story were pronounced"; the opening part of the story may have "sounded more like normal prose, but when the [narrators] were working up to a climax, or when the words were repeated a lot, it was more like singing."

but that the practice has been abandoned since. This storytelling seems to have been associated more with a family setting, that is, with mothers telling tales to their children. Cannibals (*keo*)[18] frequently featured in these stories, just as in the Karinj *enj*, as we will see. For Wola speakers in the west of the Angal language area, the status quo of the art form could not be ascertained. While sharing much the same corpus of popular folk tales and motifs, it is noteworthy that Sillitoe (email, 1 Dec 2010), over the *longue durée* of his involvement with the Wola since the 1970s, has never witnessed performances that would qualify as sung or chanted narrating.

Typical plots and cast of characters

Two very popular basic plots used in *enj* folk tales make it feasible to speak of two subcategories of stories, even though they are not formally labelled as such and some stories do not fit into this simple scheme.

A typical plot of what I have labelled **ascension stories**, the first subcategory, centres on the alliance between a young male protagonist and a young woman, a Female Spirit figure from the sky world who assists the young man in becoming a successful and renowned big man. The theme of the boy's transformation—more dominant in Enga and Ipili male puberty rites and stories (Gibbs, chapter 7; Ingemann, chapter 9)—is often attenuated, however. The stories typically culminate in an ascension to the sky whence the young woman hailed.

A second subcategory may be called **cannibal** or **Wan Heyo stories**, since they revolve around a cannibalistic male ogre of that name (Wan Heyo) with whom the male or female protagonist must contend. A variation of this cast is the contest between the male protagonist and a Heyo *woman*, or the rivalry between a Heyo woman and a sky woman for the same male protagonist.

These plots may also be combined. It is interesting to note here that when Somaip (or Karinj) narrators sing stories in the Huli language, as Pita Tapuli (present at the 2006 workshop) commonly does—preferring it to the Karinj language—the tales are similar in form and content to *enj* rather than Huli *bi te* proper. That is, his heroes and heroines have to face Wan Heyo rather than his Huli counterpart Baya Horo. This is another indication that in this transitional zone, cultural communalities are stronger than language differences.

There are also other stories that are more entertaining or hilarious than the standard folk tales and may not involve a sky woman or a cannibal at all. One example is the story I titled "Con Man Imakan," a "rubbish" man who tricks a

---

18   *Keo* is clearly cognate to the Karinj term *(Wan)Heyo*, conforming to a well-attested (if irregular) pattern of phoneme-switching between West and East Angal/Mendi (Rule 1965).

beautiful woman into marrying him, another the tale of a man who at first has no penis at all and later is endowed, through ancestral assistance, with an organ of unmanageable length.

Narrators may refer to the protagonists of their stories either in a more generic way ("that old woman," "the younger brother," and the like) or assign them names, in which case they choose from a stock of names which are also known to their listeners or self-explanatory. Following conventional usage, these are double names (hyphenated in my transcription) in which the first part usually refers to a place or an ethnic group, in some cases also to a qualifying trait such as 'pretty' (*tambuan*) or 'skinny' (*kulkul*), and the second part to the name proper. Place names often refer to real places known to the audience from personal experience or hearsay, but may also refer to imaginary topographical features; a favourite example for the latter is Ipulup, an imaginary border river (in some stories, a lake) to the sky world and hence a name commonly given to sky people or the male protagonist destined to ascend to the sky world.[19] In ascension stories, the protagonists will often be associated with places or ethnic groups that are further north or higher up altitudinally, such as the groups occupying the Wage headwaters or locales in the high forest. This has to do with a general cosmological opposition between the sky (*har*) and the ground (*su*) and with the fact that high altitudes are associated in various ways with the sky world. Female protagonists named after the Lake Kutubu (Ip Kutup) in the far south are either disguised sky women (and thus "goodies") or Heyo women, associated with the cannibal Wan Heyo and expected to fare badly in the story. The reason for this ambivalence will become evident in the discussion of the Somaip social universe below.

Karinj chanted tales are often set in the real world of the local and regional setting, but not in a contemporary world of Tok Pisin schools, markets, aid posts, and the like. Only the imagery may be inspired by the "modern" world: a dance ground or the fabulously rich "waterworld" of Lake Kutubu may be described as "magnificent like a city," and a special light as being as bright as electric light (*pawa*). In this sense sung stories evoke and celebrate, like Duna stories (Goroka workshop 2006), an *idealized* pre-colonial past. The real-world setting is often complemented by standard imaginary topographical features and places such as the above-mentioned border river to the sky world (Ipulup), forested mountains, or steep cliffs which have to be climbed to reach the sky world. The intertwining of both real and imaginary places is also done through the use of what Merlan (1995) has called "techniques of verisimilitude": performers may

---

19 No etymology was volunteered for the name/term Ipulup which, incidentally or not, is the immediate plural imperative of the verb 'to come', but also contains the morpheme *ip*, which is the word for 'water/river' (additionally, distinguished by tone only, the immediate singular imperative of the verb 'to come').

use comparative terms such as "like" or "resembling" to mediate real places and persons with imaginary ones—a valley 'like' (*upi*) this-or-that valley, a poor old man 'like' (*nonpi*) so-and-so.[20]

Themes and motifs

I will first discuss and elaborate on the two identified subcategories of stories and their most conspicuous themes before considering motifs prevalent in chanted tales more generally, across diverse categories and plots.

Skywalkers and the opposition between sky and ground

Ascension stories focus and elaborate on a fundamental opposition between ground (*su*) and sky (*har*), between the human world here on earth and the sky world above. Basically, the narratives depict the terrestrial as a realm of toil and hardship, death and decay, while the celestial is portrayed as a paradise of peace and plenty, immortality and ease. This is a central cosmological orientation not only among the Karinj but also in the wider region (cf. Reithofer 2006:37–63, with further references). We can note a great many standard features and forms to depict this cosmological opposition and the ascension itself, even across individual narrators. The more common ones are discussed here.

In contrast to the mountainous—and hence strenuous—topography of the ground, the sky world is depicted as a 'raised and level place in the clouds' (*sa to* or *sa piyun to*),[21] flat and comfortable like a platform. Levelness and beauty of the sky world are also conveyed in the circumscriptive term *iyu hama*—the 'ceremonial ground up there'. The fundamental opposition to this ground here (*su*) is expressed bluntly when narrators refer to the sky as *su epe*—the 'good ground'.[22]

Celestial abundance and ease are routinely illustrated by the food that awaits the skywalkers: always plentiful and ready-to-eat, it is also distinctly celestial

---

20 Such comparisons are commonly used also by southern Angal (Tipton 1982:18–19) and Wola or West Angal narrators (Sillitoe, pers. comm., 25 April 2008).
21 *Sa* denotes sky or clouds, *to* a raised platform.
22 It is possible, however, that the latter two phrases originated more recently in the context of Christianization: Sillitoe (pers. comm., 25 April 2008) claims that the term *iyu hama* was introduced in the Was/Wage valley for heaven, and Tipton (email, 21 Sep 2009) suggests for the phrase *su epe* ('the good ground') that it was originally coined by missionaries as *su epen* ('ground heaven'), where *epen* was a transliteration of heaven. After a while the *n* was dropped and 'heaven' became, quite fittingly in Christian eyes, 'the good ground'. While Tipton refers to the work of the Christian Union Mission among the Nembi people in the 1970s, such phrases may travel quickly and widely, and it is quite possible that Karinj narrators have adopted here phrases originating in Christian discourse. A careful reading of the early ethnographic literature of the region provides consistent evidence, however, for the pre-Christian (and pre-colonial) existence of a cosmological opposition between sky and ground as outlined in this chapter. How much it has been reinforced or altered in the course of Christianization is another matter.

as it comprises high-altitude pandanus varieties (poetically termed *aluweip nem* = 'the sun's food') and animals associated with the sky rather than the ground (marsupials and birds). Likewise, pure and tasty drinking water (*yuli-ambi*) can simply be sucked from a bush vine always dangling within one's reach. In commentaries, this sky water was likened to water taken from a tank or a fridge, that is, to cool, tasty, and readily available water. The outstanding beauty, power, and fertility of the sky world are manifest also in the houses of the sky people (poetically referred to as *tikipir anda* or *oukmar anda*) and the prolific growth of ritually and magically significant plants such as ginger (*sambi*) and bog iris (*lep*). Most crucial, however, is the celestial abundance of pigs and pearlshells, the two most valuable exchange items in the pre-colonial past. The sky women are identified in many stories as the "mothers" of pigs and pearlshells, that is, as their true owners and ultimate source. The recurring image used here is that of two trees bearing pigs and pearlshells respectively.[23] The image and the maternal idiom also point to an intimate association indigenously established between wealth and fertility.

In one story, the 'pig tree' (*tas isa*) and the 'pearlshell tree' (*momak isa*) are identified with two sisters, one living high up in the north, the other down south on the shore of Lake Kutubu. They eventually ascend to the sky together with a bachelor, leaving behind for the "ground people" only offcuts of pearlshells and a small "rubbish" pig and a female pig for breeding.

This etiological explanation for the paucity and scarcity of these two valuables here on earth was also elaborated by narrator Josep Haip in a commentary. While the identification of (sky) *women* as the true origin of pigs and pearlshells is not ubiquitous—in some stories, two brothers are identified as "pig tree" and "pearlshell tree"—it does suggest that a notion of the "mythical primordiality of females" (Goldman 1983:96, in reference to the Huli) was current among the Somaip as well.[24]

Another important feature of ascension stories is the alliance between a young man and a sky woman, the Karinj version of the Female Spirit. As indicated above, the liaison may result in an encompassing transformation of the male protagonist that pertains to physical health and attractiveness as much as to moral integrity, power, and wealth. However, this theme of a (celestial) Female Spirit facilitating the transformation of ugly bachelors or 'rubbish little men' (*ol teir kang*) is not as dominant as it appears to be in the wider region (as discussed in

---

23   The notion of a pearlshell tree was also held by Wola or West Angal speakers (Sillitoe 1979a:302) and beyond the Angal language area (e.g., Meggitt 1965:109; Clark 1991).

24   The theme is certainly also a reflection or recognition of the fact that women—as sisters and wives—open up roads of exchange that are among the most important in any man's personal exchange network. "Women in between" (M. Strathern 1972) open the roads on which pigs, pearlshells, and other valuables travel between exchange partners.

chapter 1 for the Duna, Enga, and Ipili; see also Clark 1999 and A. Strathern and Stewart 2000:80–94 for good overviews). In many a tale, the male hero may be a lonely bachelor, but he is able and strong and handsome from the beginning— and a perfect match for the attractive young woman. The emphasis, then, is more often on courtship, so that Karinj tales can be placed half-way between those in the west of the sung-tales region stressing tutelage and guardianship, and those in the east (Ku Waru and Hagen) privileging the courtship motif (cf. Rumsey, chapter 11). The following are examples where the transformative aspect is stressed:

- A leprous man and his son live in the forest somewhere to the south; their gardens are planted by a woman who also brings them all kinds of adornments they didn't have before, thus facilitating their transformation into handsome dancers.
- Bodies of lepers become whole and good again upon their ascension to the sky.
- A poor and ugly man is transformed into a handsome young man after being thrown into the black-coloured Ipulup lake (a celestial body of water) and then into a yellow-coloured pool.

It is revealing that narrators who elaborate the courtship scenario commonly emphasize also the asexual character of the relationship, the need to abstain from sex (until after ascension, at least). This theme is obviously linked to bachelor cults as they were practised by neighbouring groups such as the Enga, Ipili, Huli, and Duna (and eventually adopted by the Karinj as well), in which contexts stories about the asexual liaison between spirit brides and bachelors were disseminated widely (chapter 1; see also Wiessner and Tumu 1998:215–44 for a thorough overview and further references).

With regard to the ascension scenarios, various images may be employed, sometimes in combination. The skywalkers may ascend along giant hardwood trees (e.g., *hapol* brown pines (*Podocarpus neriifolius*)), growing out of or materializing next to the king post of the house in which the couple is staying, or climb a stone wall or a high mountain, sometimes with the help of vines or the long hardy stalks of a certain grass (*tein win*) dangling from the summit. The male hero may also grab hold of the sky woman's sedge skirt (unthinkable under normal circumstances) or a marsupial's tail. As the couple ascends to the sky world, the house beneath them frequently bursts into flames and is consumed by fire. In the words of one commentator (Alois Along), the fire functions like a rocket, propelling the two upwards and facilitating their transition from one cosmic realm to the other.

Wan Heyo cannibal stories and the Somaip social universe

Karinj folk tales featuring the cannibal ogre Wan Heyo (figures 4–5) are almost invariably linked to the enormous Lake Kutubu (Ip Kutup) in the far south, situated at the extreme periphery of the Somaip social universe. Although few Somaip have ever seen its expanse with their own eyes, the lake inspired narratives about an aquatic land of plenty (called "waterworld" hereafter) that in many ways appears equivalent to the sky world. In these tales, it is the fabulous waterworld of Lake Kutubu which is portrayed as the true origin of all pigs and pearlshells. (The lake lies indeed in the direction from where pearlshells arrived in the region in pre-contact times.) It is evident that we have here another instance of the point raised by A. Strathern and Stewart (2000:71) with regard to Duna imagery: "lakes and sky are often conflated or regarded as mirror images of each other, so that below the lake could be thought of as an inverted equivalent to up in the sky."

Access to this waterworld is jealously guarded by the cannibal Wan Heyo, a non-human monster who traps humans like marsupials, breaking their legs to prevent escape before carrying them home in netbags to store and eventually consume them.[25] Most tales end with a deadly showdown that has Wan Heyo stripped of his magical powers or killed, and his victims rescued/revived. Apart from his cannibalistic appetite, a trait simultaneously signifying his inhuman nature and superhuman strength (Goldman 1998:214–19), Wan Heyo lives very much like other humans. But his privileged access to the waterworld as the source of all wealth enables him to pay bridewealth for many wives and to line up hundreds of pigs for this purpose if need be.

A brief look at one of the stories reveals not only further resemblances between the sky world and the Lake Kutubu waterworld but also, in this case, between a Wan Heyo story and other ascension stories. It is the folk tale I dubbed "The Kutubu Kwin" (The Kubutu queen):

---

25 There are clearly parallels here—but also structural differences—to Huli tales about a subterranean land of plenty controlled by Baya Horo cannibal ogres (cf. Ballard 1998:71; Goldman 1998:219–20).

Figure 4. The Wan Heyo cannibal figure as represented in a Karinj performance of a Wan Heyo folk tale at Ipisam, October 2003. Note the coil of rope in his hands for trapping his human victims (photo by author).

Figure 5. Contravening the aesthetics of self-decoration with the sloppy and profuse application of brown and black paint, and the use of uncomely botanical materials, a Karinj actor captures Wan Heyo's inhuman nature and dangerous/ powerful wildness. Ipisam, October 2003 (photo by author).

The male hero, having outwitted Wan Heyo and usurped his magical powers, meets the young beautiful (spirit) woman who is the true "queen of the lake" and its riches, and speaks to him from inside a bright light [the Sun?]. Her name is Ipkutup-Wankwank (Lake Kutubu-Wankwank), and she agrees to follow her new protégé, rather in the manner of a wife moving to her husband's place. Lake Kutubu with all its paradisical qualities moves with her, transforming the cane grass–dominated natal place of the hero into a "magnificent city." The spirit woman provides an abundance of everything, looking after the man like a sister, like a mother. The asexual relationship between the two is also the condition of this "dream come true," and when the young hero rapes her despite her protest and warnings, Lake Kutubu vanishes the very same night, together with the "queen," the glorious city and the endless supply of wealth items and fertility.[26]

Here, too, narrator Josep Haip added in an etiological and moralizing comment that the story explained why the Somaip, descendants of the foolish male hero, found themselves in an economically inferior position and why the Lake Kutubu groups fared so well. Their affluence is not a mere mythological contrivance. The forests around the lake are said to abound with wild pigs and cassowaries, and in the past, many valued trade items came from there, most notably pearlshells and the sought-after *tigaso* decorating oil (termed *wambol* in Karinj). But the Heyo and Tukup people (ethnographically known as Foi and Fasu) living there and controlling access to this wealth were cast by the Somaip into a role very much akin to Wan Heyo: they were feared as cannibal witches and powerful sorcerers. From a Somaip-centric perspective, the Heyo and Tukup lived at the edge of their social world, at the edge, in fact, of humanness (figure 6). In contrast to 'true/normal humans' (*ol heneng*), the Heyo and Tukup were said to combine superhuman power and wealth with an almost subhuman physical appearance: "rubbish" decorations, a skinny body and a dull skin riddled with lesions. The Somaip and other "true/normal humans" tapped their riches—with all due precaution—but did not intermingle with them. This maxim of social avoidance was also reinforced by *enj* folk tales featuring Heyo *women*, who are often poised in rivalry against sky women as they compete for the attention of the same male bachelor. The bachelor must resist the temptations of the Heyo woman in order to ascend to the sky world, a destination the Heyo woman never attains.

The cannibal ogre Wan Heyo epitomizes the ambiguity of these people at the fringe, their powers as well as their dangers. Various commentators pointed out that the Lake Kutubu people's privileged access to wealth has survived into modern times through the extraction of oil reserves found on their land. If the

---

26   See chapter 11 for a similar tale from the Hagen area discussed by Rumsey.

lake was considered the true source of pigs and pearlshells in the pre-contact past, it was now said to be the origin of money, the modern wealth item (Tok Pisin *mani i kamap long dispela ples*). When whites entered the Somaip universe, there were speculations that they had come from Lake Kutubu, the "true source of power, wealth, and danger."

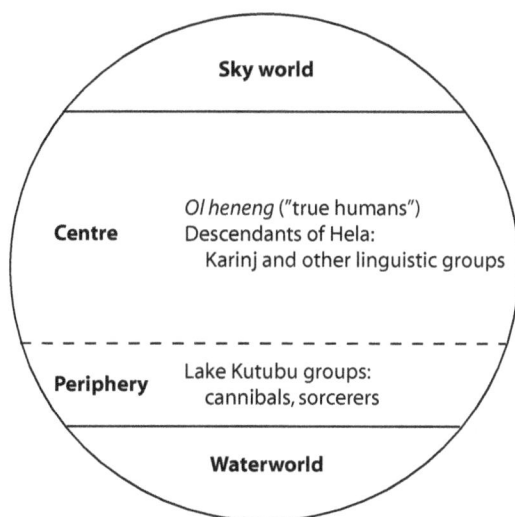

Figure 6. The Somaip cosmos and social universe.

Adherence to a moral order, punishment of wrong-doers

Karinj folk tales of either category typically convey the message (wrapped up in very good entertainment) that success and social esteem, even immortality, are only for those who adhere to a moral order, as exemplified by the young protagonists who obey their sky-woman friend and do as they are told. It is precisely because the sky people (*har kem tenel*) adhere strictly to a moral order that their sky world is the place of abundance depicted in the stories. Conversely, those who violate this order or behave grossly antisocial can only expect severe punishment or, if they have already ascended to the sky world, a fall from grace—a fall, alas, that brings about the fundamental imperfections of contemporary life or human existence more generally.[27] Some stories do end on this pessimistic note (e.g., "The Kutubu Kwin" outlined above), even though the majority of the tales I collected feature a happy ending.

---

27 Tipton (1982:26–27) suggests for the southern Angal that a moralizing comment on the dire consequences of disobedience is one of three methods of closing an (ancestral) narrative.

The ambivalence of exogamy

The rule of exogamy gives rise to the popular motif of courtship between a man and a (spirit) woman from faraway places, a theme present in most Karinj folk tales, and often central in ascension stories (as has already been noted). A. Strathern and Stewart (1997:4) have called this the "romance of exogamy." One recurring image of this romance is the way in which the decorated couple's splendid dance on the ceremonial ground attracts the admiring gaze of all onlookers. The depth of affection is indicated by intense emotions: a sky woman slices her earlobe and lops off a finger joint out of grief for her boyfriend who comes late to the dance and the subsequent ascension to the sky. In other stories, the same inflictions are attributed to brides who have to leave their natal place and people and must go with their husband to a new area and new kinsfolk, thus putting the emphasis on the darker side of exogamy (from a bride's perspective): the general rule of taking up residence with the husband's group. The sadness may be exacerbated by the fact of a more or less forced marriage with Wan Heyo, the trickster cannibal. In the folk tale "The Kutubu Kwin" outlined above, the bride's sadness is projected on to Lake Kutubu itself. Its grief for having to leave its place and follow its "queen" is expressed by heavy rain setting in—as if the sky, too, wept in grief.

Some stories present a burlesque twist of this theme; in the story of the "Man with the Long Penis," it is the cut-off penis which "goes on a journey" and visits women in a far-away place.

Dance and pig-kill

The popular themes of dance and the pig-kill, not restricted to folk tales, are a favourite ingredient because they enhance the effect of entertainment and evoke memories and fantasies that are likely to make the audience "feel happy." Performers use a number of stock features and images to portray the scenarios as outstanding:

- The dance ground is nice and beautiful like a "city."
- The dancing sky woman is flanked by admiring men like the *op* tree by its branches.
- The hero butchers his pig(s) first and fastest, and generously distributes to everyone, so that no one is wanting and everybody praises his name. It is interesting to note here that although pig-kills are collective affairs, the focus is very much on individual participants and the internal competition that exists between them. While this focus is related to the narrative "need" of foregrounding individual protagonists, the tension between group cooperation and internal rivalry is also noted in ethnographic accounts (e.g., Sillitoe 1979a; Lederman 1986a).

- The butchering of pigs is often done with special magical knives (*olsomp ne, mur hari, hari wano*) provided by sky people or deftly wielded by the cannibal-sorcerer Wan Heyo. This motif serves to reinforce the lightness and ease of celestial existence as opposed to the hard work of human life on earth. It also contains etiological and moral aspects, as the magical dissection of pigs is often presented as an ability lost to normal humans through some protagonist's immoral, foolish act.

- When the heroes make their appearance on the dance ground, people move aside respectfully and remove obstacles and faeces from their path.

Travelling

Travelling is ubiquitous in folk tales. There are many reasons for going on a journey: the wish to participate in a dance staged in a far-away place, to visit a girlfriend, to visit the sister who has married someplace else. Standard motifs used by *enj* performers in this context include the collection and preparation of all kinds of steam-cooked food to carry along or the work that goes into a truly impressive decoration before setting out.

Disguise and deception

The popular themes of disguise and deception are not restricted to *enj* folk tales. In ascension stories, a sky woman will often disguise herself as an old, ugly woman or turn into all kinds of disgusting things in the hands of the male hero before revealing her true nature. In cannibal stories, the fearful Wan Heyo may give himself the appearance of a poor and weak man who does not even defend himself when attacked. The themes are played out not only with personae; in one story, for instance, the protagonist urges his mother to bake a seemingly intact taro corm which he had previously hollowed out and filled with ashes.

Lines, melody, and pitch

Karinj *enj* are divided into non-metrical lines of varying length, but with a very regular melodic shape. Lines are clearly identifiable on melodic grounds, but also by line-final vocables such as *e, la e, la, la o, la la o*, or formulae such as *inji* ('it's been told'). Lines are grouped into melodic units or cycles that have relatively fixed pitch contours, but may vary according to the performer. It seems that each melodic unit comprises a scene or episode of a story and typically ends in meta-narrational locutions that also exhort the audience to respond with a melodic 'oh yes!' (*ehe*). Two examples follow (A = Audience):[28]

---

[28] A note on the transcription of Karinj (Aklal Heneng) texts: As no language manual or grammar exists for Aklal Heneng, I have worked out, together with Somaip friends, a phonetic system of spelling that lacks the refinement of professional linguistics, but worked well enough for the Somaip themselves. To facilitate their skills in reading their own language, I have more or less limited the system to those characters that are also used in Tok Pisin, the lingua franca with which literate Somaip are most familiar.

1. ... gup lo peyo o. [A:] Ehe!   ... like this I'm telling you. [A:] Oh yes!
2. ... gup inja lo pereyo. [A:] Ehe!   ... like this it's told and I sit (here) telling you. [A:] Oh yes!

Ruth Tipton relates from her research in the Nembi and Nipa areas in the 1970s that southern Angal speakers "expected the audience to respond with a grunt. It was one syllable only, and came out like a nasalized grunt. It had no vowels. If the listeners did not respond, the speaker would repeat the lines until he or she got the appropriate audience response" (Tipton, email, 20 Aug 2009).

Accomplished performers command different melodies and may employ them consecutively within the same story in order to enhance their listeners' interest or attention, especially if the performance lasts for hours. Josep Haip, for instance, uses three different melodies, and in the accompanying audio sample (online item 16)—an extract from his performance at the 2006 Goroka workshop—one can hear such a change in melody at 0:29 into the recording (corresponding to 3:43 of his ten-minute performance). As ethnomusicologist Don Niles noted (email, 23 Feb 2011), one can hear a melodically rather unclear line before Haip shifts to a new, higher range of singing. The new melody exhibits a strict alternation of phrase endings: While all lines end on the meta-narrational formula *inji* ('it's been told'), Haip ends the two syllables on one pitch in one phrase, and on a pitch a step higher in the other. This strict alternation of different phrase ending pitches is very distinctive and might be seen as having some sort of structural similarity to Hagen performances, where a continually repeated melody is divided into two half-melodies, with many of the notes of one half-melody being separated by a step from the other half-melody (see also Niles, chapter 12). The audio sample also features extended melodic phrases (using the formula *gup inja lo pereyo*) with which Haip ends larger sections of his story and invites the audience to respond with an affirmation of their interest (*ehe*). The phrases appear at 0:28, 1:08, and 2:07 into the recording; the response is rather timid at the final instance and missing at the second one, but this is due to the predominantly non-Karinj audience. The audience picked up quickly on Haip's prompts, however, and performed much better during the remainder of the narrative.

Textual parallelism

The language of *enj* storytelling is clearly *systematically* repetitive, as Rumsey (2005:49) has demonstrated for the Ku Waru *tom yaya kange* and as is probably the case for most if not all genres of sung stories, in Papua New Guinea and elsewhere. Repetition in Karinj *enj* does not, however, attain the high density it has in Ku Waru (cf. ibid.). Its most typical form is textual parallelism, that is, two or even three or more successive lines which remain the same except for the substitution of one or a few words. The first example is a motif often used to highlight the sense of awe that the splendidly decorated protagonist arouses as he makes his appearance on the ceremonial ground; the gathered people hurry to remove all things dirty and filthy from his path:

1.	Ten konwi saim umu tas ii hama-on pirisa la	The women [covered up] the pigs' faeces on the dance ground,
2.	ol konwi saim san ii hama-on pirisa la	the men [covered up] the dogs' faeces on the dance ground,
3.	nonak mari umu nonak ii hama-on pirisa la	the mothers [covered up] the children's faeces on the dance ground.

The motif illustrates nicely the cultural associations made between women, children, and pigs on the one hand, and men and dogs (used for hunting), on the other. The second example of textual parallelism demonstrates various possibilities for referring to other groups of their social universe in the context of a pig-kill. In accordance with a standard theme, the protagonist manages to distribute first raw strips of pork (*poke*) and subsequently steam-cooked pork to all attending visitors faster than any of the other hosts:

1.	Kulwap nak hal kalisa la	He gave [*poke*] to the men from Kulwap [a place in the Enga-speaking north],
2.	iyu Ipilpap nak hal kalisa la e	gave to the Ipili men from up there,
3.	inyu Hond Moint nak hal kalisa la e	gave to the Mendi Lake [Lake Egari] men from down there,
4.	Karinj Hak nak hal kalisa la e	gave to the Karinj men with their white cockatoo headdresses [Huli from Margarima].

Having quickly cut up the cooked pork shortly thereafter, he distributes the pieces:

5.	Ank-Lirili nak hal pe	... to those men from the Pandanus-Aplenty place,
6.	Pipi-Lerela nak hal pe	to those men from the Frosty place,
7.	Ssei Tandak-Marela nak hal pe	to those men from the Hailstorm place,
8.	Hond Moint nak hal pe	to the Mendi Lake men,
9.	Karinj Pol nak hal pe	and to the Karinj men with their white cockatoo headdresses [from Margarima].

The stylized circumscriptions in lines 5–7 refer to places like Yumbis, Longaip, and Gereng at the Wage headwaters, where the climate is even more severe than in the Karinj area and where the high-altitude groves of wild pandanus palms (*Pandanus brosimos*) are said to regularly produce bumper harvests. References to place names or topographical features (lines 1, 3, and 8) or to distinct styles of dress and decoration (lines 4 and 9) are another possibility to denote particular social groups.[29]

---

29 The synonymous terms (Karinj) *Hak* and (Karinj) *Pol* refer to a headdress of typical Huli fashion: white cockatoo feathers mounted on some form of wire or springy slivers and pinned to the hair (cf. Sillitoe 1988:320–22).

Repetition is manifest in other ways as well, as when a certain motif is repeated refrain-like within the same story (in ascension stories, this may be the formula that the earth is a place of decay and death, "where the *lindil* mushroom grows and decays" and people die) or when certain themes are used again and again *across* various stories and even story genres (such as *enj* and clan origin myths classified as *arman*), as has been noted in the discussion of themes and motifs. Across stories and story genres, repetition is also evident in the use of a stock of standard expressions and attention markers. If, for instance, a narrator begins a line with the words "When an extended spell of fine weather came" (*urpoin ipisa tomben*), his or her audience will know that something new and decisive is going to happen.

Special vocabulary and imagery

The art of good storytelling also hinges upon the use of an adequate and well-established vocabulary that is different from everyday speech. Most of the expressions or lexemes used are not exclusive to *enj* but indicative of a "higher" and more poetic style of language that is said to enhance the overall quality and attractiveness of a performance. The special terms do not pertain to any kind of secret language, however, or make borrowings from what is called the "pandanus language," the language people use when they are in the high forest.[30] Some of the special terms are obviously from an archaic stock or borrowed from neighbouring languages,[31] others have referents that are themselves things of the past and hence outside everyday language, such as stone axes and the types of decoration associated with them. Knowledge of this special vocabulary is simply a matter of exposure and growing familiarity, so that older children will have no problem sorting them out. Typical examples for special vocabulary and high stylistic lexemes include the following:

- The protagonists of stories are never simply called *nak* (lad/man) or *nong* (girl/woman) but *hump nak* and *hump nong*, terms that connote physical attractiveness (rendered as *smatpela* in Tok Pisin) and establish the persons in question as the main characters of the story.

- Likewise, their houses are never simply called *anda,* but *tikipir anda* or *oukmar anda*, if only to make them stand out from other houses and comply with the stylistic prerogatives of *enj* storytelling. (The words *tikipir* and *oukmar* themselves are not really translatable.)

---

30 Out of fear and respect towards forest spirits—and often also ancestral spirits believed to dwell in high forest pools—people staying temporarily in the high forest will replace terms for things or entities typical of human habitation and village life (such as dogs, pigs, wooden tongs, or axes) or typical of the forest (such as possums or cassowaries) with circumscriptions. Possums, for instance, would be referred to as 'the furry ones' (*iri hai*) or an axe as 'the sharp one' (*ne hai*).

31 The *enj* term for 'sun' (*aluweip*), for instance, is clearly cognate with the Duna praise name for it, *alu(lu) wape*.

- Neighbouring groups will be referred to by descriptive terms that are also used in other stylized speech genres (cf. examples above).

- There is a whole battery of high stylistic lexemes used for pigs, each referring to a different skin colour or simply to a "huge pig" (cf. Sillitoe 2003:part 3 for Wola pig lexicography).

- Similarly, special lexemes are often used also for adornments and attire more generally as well as for weapons.

If the special vocabulary serves to create some distance between the narrated events and ordinary or unembellished everyday experience, the effect is heightened by a certain imagery in which actions or events are routinely presented. Exaggeration is one technique employed to this effect. Protagonists usually 'jump' (*ponge*) rather than simply 'walk' from here to there, and on their journeys they always travel on the more comfortable ridge paths (*kunk haret*) that are also visible from far away rather than on muddy tracks deep in the forest. Some heroes are even spared the walking and move to a distant place in the wink of an eye with the help of magic ginger (*sambi*). Here the imagery emphasizes ease where the normal human experience is strenuous walking. The ascension to the sky is routinely described as a gracious dance despite the fact that the skywalkers have to climb a vertical rock wall or a towering tree in order to reach the celestial paradise. Other aspects of this imagery have been pointed out in the above discussion of themes and motifs.

The truth of folk tales

Compared to clan origin myths classified as *arman* or 'history,' *enj* folk tales may be downgraded as 'mere stories' (Tok Pisin *stori nating*), of little value and import beyond the entertainment factor that inheres in their performances. But if viewed in their own right—and the Goroka Chanted Tales Workshop in 2006 provided a platform and many good reasons for doing so—folk tales have other merits that few Somaip would contest. These stories have *te* (a foundation, basis or root), their message or teaching is true (*pi go heneng*), Somaip participants asserted at the workshop. Alois Along viewed the stories as a kind of prophetic talk, as carrying a "promise" within them which will eventually come true or bear fruit. This "promise" concerns the basic moral tenet conveyed in almost all stories, especially of the ascension type. Put simply, it says:

> If you follow the "law" (a given moral order), you will have a good life!
>
> If you disobey or disrespect the "law," your life will be miserable!
>
> Therefore, do not disrespect (Tok Pisin *sakim*) the "law"!

Somewhat less encompassing promises or prophecies contained within folk tales have already come true and thus indicate further the truthfulness of these stories, as others pointed out. The high stylistic lexeme *kusmen mapen* (pigs), for instance, is now seen by many as a hidden prophecy of the large "pigs" that have indeed arrived now in the form of cows and horses! Another example is the sky water *yuli-ambi*, which is one standard image of celestial comfort and ease; white technology in the form of water tanks, electric power, and refrigerators has made it a part of contemporary human life.

Beyond such particular examples, the truthfulness of folk tales is indeed of a very basic and rather unshakeable kind, as these stories reiterate foundational cosmological and social truths. In so far as these truths guide social behaviour between individuals and among groups, it is social practice—between Karinj and Lake Kutubu groups, for instance—which undergirds the wisdom of these truths. The truth of folk tales is also evident for just about everyone (with the possible exclusion of singular big men) because of the near-universal experience that pigs and pearlshells (and nowadays, money) are always short: too few, too small, too wretched. The true owners and sources of these valuables must have disappeared from the face of the earth long ago. Evidence for the truth of the notion that women are the ultimate origin of these wealth items was also found: in the perception that the true basis or source behind all the white-man's wealth and power is also a woman—Queen Elizabeth!

In important respects it was (and still is) Christianity that provided ample evidence for the truthfulness of folk tales and the appropriateness of their moral messages. It is to this relationship that we now turn.

Chanted tales and Christianization

Interpreting Christianity

There is today among the Somaip (as among so many other groups in Papua New Guinea) a pervasive rhetoric of a radical break between their ancestral, "pagan" past, on the one hand, and their enlightened Christian present, on the other. With Christian missionization beginning in the mid-1960s, the Somaip have by and large opted for Christianity in its various forms (Methodist, Catholic, Seventh-day Adventist, amongst others) and turned their back on many things of the past, thus reinforcing this break and widening the gap between the past and the present themselves. But there is a counter-rhetoric to this one, and the processes of interpreting and adopting the Christian message also involved substantial efforts to compare Christian and ancestral traditions, and to sound out their compatibility. Narrative traditions constituted one important body of material that was examined in this way, and folk tales featured strongly here. *Enj* folk tales and a number of origin myths were found to correspond very closely with biblical stories and the Christian message, and thus furnished an important link of continuity between past and present (cf. Reithofer 2006:271–91). These findings had the double effect of validating the truths of indigenous myths and folk tales, and facilitating the acceptance of the Christian narratives as truthful and meaningful. The two narrative traditions were interpreted as mutually reinforcing in many ways.[32]

The category of ascension stories was especially critical here. Somaip friends made this clear to me on several occasions, one of them is still very vivid in my mind. After the memorable performance of one such tale by Josep Haip, the male audience related that when they were told the biblical stories, they perceived them as 'one' (*pombor*) with their own stories. The parallels were found particularly striking with ascension stories which, according to the men, emphasize the correlation between morality and a good life, and reiterate the point that only a few will ever ascend to the sky, that is, attain a good life. The same message is felt to be expounded in Christian teachings and biblical stories, as a summarized account of their statements makes clear (Reithofer 2006:272):

> We Christians have commandments (*lo*). If we follow them, we will go to heaven and have a good life. If we don't, we won't go to heaven and won't have a good life. Who of us will go to heaven will become apparent only at the end. In any case, those lucky ones will only be a few, while the majority does not ascend to heaven. We can see today, as Christians, that our ancestors too were trying to find God and the way to heaven. It's all too apparent in the stories they told and handed on to us. (29 June 2000)

We can note the following interesting points:

- While some laws/commandments are acknowledged to have changed with Christian teachings, the underlying principle has remained constant: to attain a good life, a moral order has to be upheld and adhered to. The best-known biblical narrative encoding this principle is the fall of Adam and Eve, as Somaip Christians have pointed out to me: The primordial parents' disobedience vis-à-vis God's established order introduced death and immoral behaviour into the world.

- The autochthonous notion of a sky world is blended with the Christian one of heaven, a process that leaves neither notion unaffected (see below).

- A temporal shift is indicated: Whereas adherence to the ancestrally devised moral order was supposed to translate into a good life in the here and now,

---

32   It is quite likely that some appropriate contemporary editing of indigenous stories was carried out which furthered the perception and representation of mutually reinforcing narratives, as Sillitoe (pers. comm., 25 April 2008) pointed out to me. A reliable assessment of these processes of rapprochement is difficult, however, and would necessitate a database of stories from the early years of missionization.

the Christian worldview presupposes a gratification retardant: the chosen few will be revealed only at the end—and perhaps only in what Western tradition calls the afterlife.

• The statements indicate a perception of the Christian religion very much in terms of rules and interdictions.

• They also indicate an interest in vindicating the ancestors as some kind of "anonymous" Christians, if I may borrow this term from Christian theology (Karl Rahner).

The celibacy of Catholic missionaries (priests, clerical brothers and sisters)—working in the Angal language area since 1958—reinforced the perception that Christian teachings and ancestral wisdom shared fundamental truths. As noted earlier, one typical feature of ascension narratives is the emphasis on sexual restraint on the part of the male protagonist. According to catechist Alois Along, Catholic missionaries were perceived to follow the example of the mythical skywalkers as they sacrificed themselves and forwent marriage for the sake of a greater good—heaven.

Ascension stories with their popular and standardized depictions of the sky world clearly influenced the Somaip interpretation and imagination of the Christian heaven (*heven, har kem*). The imagery used in various (Catholic) church songs combines indigenous and biblical/Christian elements: heaven is paraphrased as *heven hama* or 'heavenly ceremonial ground', an image associated with levelness (and, hence, effortlessness, comfort, and ease), decorative beauty, and centrality; as 'Jerusalem' or 'God's heavenly city' (*Goden heven siti*), which is said to be huge and connotes a world of plenty, modernity, and richness—just as the "city" of the Lake Kutubu waterworld. According to one hymn, 'water of life' (*ip laip*) is flowing everywhere in God's house (heaven), an image that was explicitly linked to the sky water *yuli-ambi*. The image establishes God as the source and provider of good water, the quintessential element of all growth, fertility, and indeed life itself.

The Christian notion of angels, too, resonates with a recurrent feature of *enj* folk tales: the messenger bird (*ek pip*)[33] which brings important news to isolated or ignorant protagonists. This is also an important function of angels in biblical stories, as Somaip Christians have been quick to notice. In some church skits, men played the role of a *pip* messenger bird to convey a divine message to humans, thus fusing the notion of a messenger bird with that of angels.

Much more importantly, however, ascension stories with their nostalgic depictions of a limitless and abundant sky world have also facilitated among the Somaip a millennial interpretation of the changes they witnessed and shaped, resisted

---

33 Alternative terms are *ek piauwi* and *ek pipol*. All terms contain the morpheme *pi* for 'word/talk/language'.

and reinforced over the last fifty years or so. To many Somaip who have been to Mendi or Mount Hagen, modern town life appeared to closely approximate the unlimited and carefree life in the mythical sky world. As one Seventh-day Adventist put it: "When the Europeans came, we thought that we had gone to the sky at last!" It is difficult to overestimate the ramifications of this interpretation, which still has a strong currency among contemporary Somaip and reached a peak just prior to the turn of the millennium (Reithofer 2006:310–30). With ascension stories in mind, it was easy to read the Christian heaven as a code or vision of a radically different and better world to come.

Of course, the sung stories are themselves only part of a wider context facilitating this millennial reading of their recent history; elsewhere I have discussed other important factors such as a basically "entropic" worldview, indigenous notions of apocalyptic events believed to terminate one earth cycle and inaugurating a new one, and the various speculations about the true origin and nature of the white people, who were widely associated with the sky world (Reithofer 2006:49–61, 224–38).

Reinterpreting chanted tales

The comparative endeavour stimulated by missionization has established a basic compatibility between indigenous folk tales (and other narratives) and Christian teachings. This perception is apparently shared by the Christian churches as well, since chanted tales have not been—like so many other traditional practices—tabooed for baptized Christians. Somaip participants at the 2006 Goroka workshop even viewed their chanted tales as a part of the biblical Good News (Tok Pisin *olsem hap gut nius*). At the least, they can give support and strengthen the biblical message. The men considered it appropriate, therefore, that in some areas Bible readings were occasionally delivered in the melodic recitation style of *enj* performances. While I have not witnessed such performances, I have seen other instances of articulating *enj* stories with the Christian message, of reinterpreting them in a Christian cast. One particularly noteworthy instance involved a rather typical Wan Heyo story that was enacted as a "drama" at a (Catholic) church feast in the so-called Jubilee Year 2000.

> Two brothers live together, one a horticulturalist, the other a hunter. One day the hunter gets himself caught in a trap set up by Wan Heyo. When the other brother finds him but cannot disengage the trap, he leaves him with food and turns himself into a mosquito at a place where young women come to drink water. One of the women swallows the mosquito, becomes pregnant and eventually delivers a baby boy. He grows up and later travels to the abode of Wan Heyo, his brother-in-law, with whom he stays for some time. Having detected the hideout in which the cannibal

ogre kept his victims for later consumption (their legs broken to prevent escape), the young man, aided by a young woman, succeeds in killing Wan Heyo and setting the prisoners free—his brother included.

After the drama, narrator Josep Haip proceeded to give the audience a Christian reading of the story. (Having been the first local Catholic catechist for many years, Haip was well versed in these matters.) The boy being reborn of that young woman is Jesus. The woman, who conceives without the help or assistance of a man, is St. Mary, the mother of God. Wan Heyo's prisoners are to be interpreted as Christians trapped and immobilized by their own sins. Jesus is the saviour who has come to liberate us from our sins. Wan Heyo, finally, is recast as Satan, who has much power over us humans, but is overcome by the greater powers of Jesus.

The enactment and Haip's subsequent interpretation found general approval among the assembled Christians. The example certainly gives an idea of the extent to which chanted tales and Christian teachings may be merged and presented as mutually illuminating and reinforcing. This is true also for other parts of the Angal language area. Very similar biblical reinterpretations of (much the same) ancestral tales and motifs have been proffered by southern Angal speakers in the 1970s (Tipton 1982:27) and by attendants of a Tok Pisin Bible school in the years 2005–7 (Tipton, email, 20 Aug 2009)—another piece of evidence for the ongoing salience of chanted tales in that region.

Conclusion

Enj storytelling is a verbal art still alive and enjoyed among Karinj speakers in the northwestern part of the Angal language area (and beyond, as we have noted). This chapter has highlighted—to varying degrees—three dimensions of the significance of this art form and the chanted tales themselves. First and foremost, *enj* performances are a popular form of entertainment, to make people "feel happy," either in the more private settings of men's and women's houses or in the more public contexts of *singsing*-events or political campaigns. The entertainment factor critically depends on the performer's skill and ability to captivate his or her audience. Secondly and secondarily, chanted tales have educational potential as a means of transporting moral messages that may be further explicated in exegetical commentaries in certain settings. The key theme here is the need to submit to a given moral and social order and its authorities. Thirdly, *enj* folk tales are valued as a means to reflect on this world as it is represented, ordered, and experienced, and also, as it could be or could have been. Many stories contain etiological aspects that not only provide explanations for certain facts of human life or the nature of the social world, but also help to understand and come to terms with major changes and new developments.

This latter dimension of significance is evidenced by the way Somaip people have brought their folk tales into dialogue with important events and changes of their recent history: the arrival of white people, colonial rule, the teachings of missionaries and the subsequent adoption and adaptation of Christianity, the oil drilling in the Lake Kutubu region, modern town life, to name a few. *Enj* folk tales (in conjunction with other narrative traditions) have provided them a measure of orientation as they faced events and new knowledge that were challenging in many ways, to say the least. Conversely, folk tales were themselves subject to reinterpretation in the light of new developments and new knowledge.

The arguments presented in this chapter hopefully conduce to an appraisal of *enj* storytelling among Karinj speakers which neither exaggerates nor underestimates its social significance in the recent past and at present. They are still a popular form of entertainment, and more than that. Unfortunately, I cannot make a controlled comparison with the significance of this verbal art, say, fifty years ago. This would perhaps make it easier to speculate on its development in the near future. We have some evidence for the North Mendi area that the art of chanting tales has declined over the last fifty years or so, perhaps to the point of being discontinued altogether. The available evidence for the Karinj area (and the southern Angal area) does not suggest such a course at least in the medium term. There is still a widespread appreciation of these tales and their performances "in style," enough to encourage interested and talented individuals to train and develop their performative skills in accordance with local standards and expectations. Josep Haip, for one, has pinned his hopes on his youngest son Samuel, whom he judges to be not only talented but also interested enough to follow in his footsteps. If the Chanted Tales Project orchestrated by Alan Rumsey and Don Niles and this publication have the effect of stimulating interest as well as pride in this verbal art form, this would be not the least of their accomplishments.

Acknowledgements

I wish to thank Rena Lederman, Paul Sillitoe, and Ruth Tipton for many helpful comments on earlier versions of the paper. By sharing pertinent data from their own research in various parts of the Angal language area, they made it possible for me to include some comparative notes concerning chanted tales among Angal speakers more generally. Many thanks also to Alan Rumsey and Don Niles for inviting me and three Karinj experts to the 2006 Chanted Tales Workshop in Goroka, a platform for stimulating discussion and memorable performances by narrators from across the Highlands. I am especially grateful to Josep Haip, a resourceful Karinj performer who never grew tired of telling me one of his stories, both in prose (*pahame*) and 'in style' (*mo hain*), and to Alois Along for his unwavering support and friendship throughout my fieldwork. I gratefully acknowledge also the invaluable assistance of Henry Palip and Toni Joneli in translating recorded stories and clarifying countless idiomatic and cultural particularities. For financial support during my principal research among the Karinj (1998–2000), I acknowledge the Catholic congregation of the Society of the Divine Word (SVD), of which I was a long-time member, and the late Bishop Hermann Raich of the Enga Diocese.

References

Ballard, Chris. 1994. "The Centre Cannot Hold: Trade Networks and Sacred Geography in the Papua New Guinea Highlands." *Archaeology in Oceania* 29 (3): 130–48.

———. 1998. "The Sun by Night: Huli Moral Topography and Myths of a Time of Darkness." In *Fluid Ontologies: Myth, Ritual and Philosophy in the Highlands of Papua New Guinea,* edited by Laurence R. Goldman and Chris Ballard, 67–85. Westport: Bergin and Garvey.

Ballard, Chris, and Jeffrey Clark. 1999. "Blurred Boundaries and Transformed Identities: Myth and Ritual in the Southern Highlands of Papua New Guinea." *Canberra Anthropology* 22 (1): 1–5.

Biersack, Aletta, ed. 1995a. *Papuan Borderlands: Huli, Duna, and Ipili Perspectives on the Papua New Guinea Highlands.* Ann Arbor: University of Michigan Press.

———. 1995b. "Introduction: The Huli, Duna, and Ipili Peoples Yesterday and Today." In *Papuan Borderlands: Huli, Duna, and Ipili Perspectives on the Papua New Guinea Highlands.,* edited by Aletta Biersack, 1–54. Ann Arbor: University of Michigan Press.

Clark, Jeffrey. 1991. "Pearlshell Symbolism in Highlands Papua New Guinea, with Particular Reference to the Wiru People of Southern Highlands Province." *Oceania* 61: 309–39.

———. 1999. "Cause and Afek: Primal Women, Bachelor Cults and the Female Spirit." *Canberra Anthropology* 22 (1): 6–33.

Crittenden, Robert. 1991. "The Back Door to the Purari." In *Like People You See in a Dream: First Contact in Six Papuan Societies,* edited by Edward L. Schieffelin and Robert Crittenden, 125–46. Stanford: Stanford University Press.

Frankel, Stephen. 1986. *The Huli Response to Illness.* Cambridge: Cambridge University Press.

Goldman, Laurence R. 1983. *Talk Never Dies: The Language of Huli Disputes.* London: Tavistock Publications.

———. 1998. *Child's Play: Myth, Mimesis and Make-believe.* Oxford: Berg.

Goldman, Laurence R., and Chris Ballard, eds. 1998. *Fluid Ontologies: Myth, Ritual and Philosophy in the Highlands of Papua New Guinea.* Westport: Bergin and Garvey.

Gordon, Raymond G., Jr., ed. 2005. *Ethnologue: Languages of the World.* 15th ed. Dallas: SIL International. Accessed 15 February 2008. Online version: http://www.ethnologue.com/.

Lederman, Rena. 1986a. *What Gifts Engender: Social Relations and Politics in Mendi, Highland Papua New Guinea.* Cambridge: Cambridge University Press.

———. 1986b. "Changing Times in Mendi: Notes towards Writing Highland New Guinea History." *Ethnohistory* 33 (1): 1–30.

———. 1990. "Big Men, Large and Small? Towards a Comparative Perspective." *Ethnology* 29 (1): 3–15.

Mawe, Theodore. 1982. *Mendi Culture and Tradition: A Recent Survey.* Port Moresby: Prehistory Department, National Museum and Art Gallery.

Meggitt, Mervyn J. 1965. "The Mae Enga of the Western Highlands." In *Gods, Ghosts and Men in Melanesia: Some Religions of Australian New Guinea and the New Hebrides*, edited by Peter Lawrence and Mervyn J. Meggitt, 105–31. Melbourne: Oxford University Press.

Merlan, Francesca. 1995. "Narrative Genres in the Western Highlands of Papua New Guinea." In *SALSA II: Proceedings of the Second Annual Symposium about Language and Society, Austin*, edited by Pamela Silberman and Jonathan Loftin, 87–98. Texas Linguistic Forum, 34. Austin: University of Texas.

Nihill, Michael. 1986. "Roads of Presence: Exchange and Social Relatedness in Anganen." PhD dissertation, University of Adelaide.

———. 1996. "Alternating Ontologies: Exchange and Ritual in Anganen History." *The Australian Journal of Anthropology* 7 (3): 275–98.

———. 1999. "Time and the Red Other: Myth, History and the Paradoxes of Power in Anganen." *Canberra Anthropology* 22 (1): 66–87.

Reithofer, Hans. 2006. *The Python Spirit and the Cross: Becoming Christian in a Highland Community of Papua New Guinea.* Göttinger Studien zur Ethnologie, 16. Münster: LIT Verlag.

Rule, Joan. 1965. "A Comparison of Certain Phonemes of the Languages of the Mendi and Nembi Valleys, Southern Highlands, Papua." *Anthropological Linguistics* 7 (5): 98–105.

Rumsey, Alan. 2005. "Chanted Tales in the New Guinea Highlands of Today: A Comparative Study." In *Expressive Genres and Historical Change: Indonesia, Papua New Guinea, and Taiwan*, edited by Pamela J. Stewart and Andrew Strathern, 41–81. Anthropology and Cultural History in Asia and the Indo-Pacific. Hants: Ashgate Publishing.

Rumsey, Alan, and James F. Weiner, eds. 2001. *Emplaced Myth. Space, Narrative, and Knowledge in Aboriginal Australia and Papua New Guinea.* Honolulu: University of Hawai'i Press.

Ryan, D'Arcy. 1961. "Gift Exchange in the Mendi Valley." PhD dissertation, University of Sydney.

Sillitoe, Paul. 1979a. *Give and Take: Exchange in Wola Society.* Canberra: Australian National University Press.

———. 1979b. "The Menstruating Tree." *Cambridge Anthropology* 5 (2): 32–47.

———. 1988. *Made in Niugini: Technology in the Highlands of Papua New Guinea.* London: British Museum Publications.

———. 1999. "Beating the Boundaries: Land Tenure and Identity in the Papua New Guinea Highlands." *Journal of Anthropological Research* 55 (3): 331–60.

———. 2002. "Always Been Farmer-foragers? Hunting and Gathering in the Papua New Guinea Highlands." *Anthropological Forum* 12 (1): 45–76.

———. 2003. *Managing Animals in New Guinea: Preying the Game in the Highlands.* Studies in Environmental Anthropology, 7. London: Routledge.

Strathern, Andrew. 1968. "Descent and Alliance in the New Guinea Highlands: Some Problems of Comparison." *Proceedings of the Royal Anthropological Institute of Great Britain and Ireland* 1968: 37–52.

———. 1994. "Lines of Power." In *Migration and Transformations: Regional Perspectives on New Guinea,* edited by Andrew Strathern and Gabriele Stürzenhofecker, 231–55. ASAO Monograph, 15. Pittsburgh and London: University of Pittsburgh Press.

Strathern, Andrew, and Pamela J. Stewart. 1997. *Ballads as Popular Performance Art in Papua New Guinea and Scotland.* Centre for Pacific Studies Discussion Papers Series, 2. Townsville: James Cook University of North Queensland.

———. 2000. *The Python's Back: Pathways of Comparison between Indonesia and Melanesia.* Westport, Connecticut: Bergin and Garvey.

Strathern, Andrew, and Gabriele Stürzenhofecker, eds. 1994. *Migration and Transformations: Regional Perspectives on New Guinea.* Pittsburgh and London: University of Pittsburgh Press.

Strathern, Marilyn. 1972. *Women in Between: Female Roles in a Male World; Mount Hagen, New Guinea.* Seminar Studies in Anthropology, 2. London: Seminar Press.

Tipton, Ruth A. 1982. *Nembi Procedural and Narrative Discourse.* Pacific Linguistics, B 82. Canberra: Australian National University.

Wiessner, Polly, and Akii Tumu. 1998. *Historical Vines: Enga Networks of Exchange, Ritual, and Warfare in Papua New Guinea.* Smithsonian Series in Ethnographic Inquiry. Bathurst: Crawford House Publishing.

11. Style, Plot, and Character in *Tom Yaya* Tales from Ku Waru

Alan Rumsey

Introduction

This chapter is about sung stories and associated modes of performance in the Ku Waru region of the Western Highlands of Papua New Guinea, which are known as *tom yaya kange*. This region lies within the broader one referred to by Don Niles in chapter 12 of this volume as the "Hagen Area," which also includes Melpa as discussed both by Niles and by Strathern and Stewart in chapter 13. The chapter will open with a brief introduction to the Ku Waru region and its genres of verbal art. I will then turn to *tom yaya kange* in particular and describe their distinctive features. The linguistic and musical properties of *tom yaya kange* and their narrative framing are matters that I have treated in detail in other publications (Rumsey 2001, 2005, 2007, 2010) and which I will accordingly deal with in summary form here. I will then turn to a more detailed consideration of two issues that I have not yet treated systematically in print: (1) the question of how to translate *tom yaya kange* into English, and (2) the full range of plots of the *tom yaya kange* that I have recorded, what they have in common, and how this relates to their poetic form and modes of performance. Discussion of the latter point will involve comparison with the range of plots that are found among Melpa *kang rom* to the west, as described by Strathern and Stewart (1997, 2005b, chapter 13 (this volume)) and by Stewart and Strathern (2002). Since 1965 at least, all *kang rom* have been tales of courtship. Showing that there is also a strong tendency in that direction in the Ku Waru region, I conclude with a discussion of why that should be the case.

The Ku Waru region and its genres of verbal art

Ku Waru and Melpa are regional speech varieties within a larger group that also includes Meam, Umbu-Unggu, and Imbonggu as shown on figure 2 in chapter 1.[1] Ku Waru and Melpa are about as closely related to each other as, for example,

---

1   This group comprises a regional continuum within which there is no single set of mutually exclusive names for the dialects or "languages," or for the continuum as a whole. In keeping with the current *Ethnologue* classification (see chapter 1 for details), the name Umbo-Unggu (meaning literally 'indigenous language') is used here for roughly the same dialect range that is also called Kaugel (or, in Melpa, Köwul/Gawigl), after the valley in which it is spoken and the eponymous river that flows through it. Ku Waru is an intermediate variety between Umbo-Unggu (Kaugel) and Meam (Temboka), the latter being more similar to Melpa. Not shown on this map is the so-called Awa (Aua) dialect, which is spoken by a few hundred people in an outlying region of otherwise uninhabited territory to the east of Meam.

Spanish and Italian. People's way of life is similar across the entire Hagen area, especially in the rural parts that comprise most of it. The local economy is still largely a subsistence one, based on the intensive cultivation of sweet potatoes, taro, and a wide range of other crops. Most households nowadays also grow coffee, which is the main source of cash income. This is used largely to pay school fees[2]—most children attending local schools through grade six—and for non-market-based transactions such as bridewealth, compensation, and ceremonial exchange. Nowadays it is also used to a considerable extent for store-bought food, such as rice, packaged noodles, and tinned fish, but sweet potatoes remain the staple food of nearly everyone, especially in the rural districts where the great majority of Ku Waru people still live.

Across the entire Hagen Area, social life, including residence patterns, marriage, wealth exchange, and warfare is still to a great extent organized in terms of segmentary units called (in Ku Waru) *talapi* ("tribes," "clans," "sub-clans," etc.), which range in size from a few score of people to over 10,000. The system of wealth exchange among *talapi*—called *moka* (in Melpa) or *makayl* (in Ku Waru)—has become a textbook case of such systems through the work of Andrew Strathern (e.g., 1971, and refs. therein; cf. Merlan and Rumsey 1991 on *makayl*). In some parts of the Melpa region, this system has wound down (Stewart and Strathern 2005),[3] but it is still in operation throughout much of the Ku Waru region.

Throughout the Ku Waru region, as elsewhere in the central and western highlands, men and women formerly lived in separate houses, boys sleeping in their mother's until they were about twelve years old, then moving into their father's. This has changed over the past generation or two—partly under the influence of Christian churches, which are active throughout the region—but men and women still do much of their indoor socializing in separate 'men's houses' (*lku tapa*) and 'women's houses' (*ab lku*). Many of their working hours are also spent apart in more-or-less gender-specific tasks, men making the new gardens, building the houses, chopping the firewood; women growing and harvesting the sweet potatoes, tending the pigs, cooking the everyday meals, etc. Nowadays, although there are no towns within the Ku Waru region, many people from there, especially young men, travel frequently, usually by "PMVs" (licensed "public motor vehicles") to the provincial capital of Mt. Hagen (which lies within the southwestern reaches of the Melpa region), to bring their coffee and other cash crops to market, purchase trade goods, drink beer when they can afford it, and generally enjoy the buzz that town life is felt to offer.

---

2   The Papua New Guinea state does not offer free public education; fees are charged at all levels.
3   More recently, with reference to the main Melpa group that Andrew Strathern has worked with over the past forty-five years, he and his collaborator Pamela Stewart (pers. comm., July 2010) say, "We have discovered over the past five years that moka-type exchanges / compensation payments actually continue among the Kawelka, so the point itself has transformed over time."

Below a certain level of socio-territorial segmentation, marriage is strictly exogamous with respect to *talapi*, but with no particular relations of prescribed marriage. Finding a wife (or wives) is a demanding task for a young man and his close kin, as it requires them to assemble a bridewealth payment of, roughly, twenty to thirty pigs (more than are raised by most households in five years) and the cash equivalent of about US$ 2,000–3,000 (K 5,000–6,000, well beyond most families' total annual cash income; formerly this part of the payment often consisted of gold-lipped pearl shells, then equally hard to attain). Given the continuing practice of polygyny, marriageable women are in short supply relative to the number of men looking for them. Though she does not have the only say as to whom she will marry, a young woman who is being courted is usually allowed a final power of veto in the matter, which she can exercise in the almost certain knowledge that other prospective suitors are waiting in the wings. As we shall see below, the challenges this presents to a young man, and what Stewart and Strathern (2002:123) call the "romance of exogamy," provide one of the main subjects of *tom yaya kange.*

Skilled use of language is highly valued by Ku Waru and other New Guinea Highland people. There were no inherited political offices in the area and the leadership status of 'big man' (*yi nuim*; now to some extent correlated with success in electoral politics) is one that men are said to have always achieved in part through their oratorical ability.

Men and women alike are also composers of songs in several different genres (for examples and discussion see Strathern (1974) and Stewart and Strathern (2002)). There are also several recognized genres of story, all performed both by men and women. There is a primary division between kinds of story which in Ku Waru are called *kange* and *temani* (= Melpa *kang*, *teman*). As Francesca Merlan (1995) has shown (see also Rumsey 2005), the difference between these types has to do with the kind of relationship which is set up between the world of the narrated events and the here-and-now world from which they are being narrated. In neither genre is the narrated world necessarily presented as "factual," but the world of *temani*, even if only by default, is presented in ways that invite the audience to imagine it as continuous with the here-and-now, while that of *kange* is presented as very different from the here-and-now, but using what Merlan (ibid.) calls "techniques of verisimilitude" by which the audience is invited to imagine themselves into that world—for example by drawing explicit parallels between the characters and places in the story and familiar ones from the local scene in which he or she is telling it: "Once there were two brothers, just like my sons Don and Pai"; "They came to a little hill, like over there at Ambukl," etc. These and other generic features of *kange* will be exemplified by the stories presented below. First, I will turn to the question of what makes them *kange* of the more specific sort known as *tom yaya kange.*

Distinctive features of *tom yaya kange*

The features which are common to all performances of *tom yaya kange* / *kang rom* that have been analysed so far[4] are:

1. Clear division into lines, each ending in an added vowel *e*, *o*, or *a*
2. Use of formulaic expressions, each comprising one or more whole lines
3. Organization of the lines into repeating two-part melodies, the second part being a pitch-by-pitch variation on the first
4. A strong tendency for each line to comprise an integral syntactic unit
5. Extensive parallelism across lines

In addition to these five features, some but not all *tom yaya kange* display two others, always in conjunction with each other:

6. Rhythmic organization of each line into a fixed number of beats or feet
7. A strong tendency for each beat except the final one to be associated with a single word.

Features 1, 3, and 6 are discussed and exemplified in detail by Niles in chapter 12. They are further exemplified, along with features 2, 5, and 7, in text 1,[5] which presents in bilingual form the opening lines of a story by one of the most renowned composer/performers of *tom yaya kange* in the western Nebilyer Valley, Paulus Konts (figure 1).[6]

The text begins with a standard opening line which is frequently used in *tom yaya kange*. The expression *ama* 'oh mother!' is a frequently used exclamation in Ku Waru, roughly equivalent to "wow!" in English. This line differs from all the following ones in consisting of only four syllables and in not having a vocable at the end. For this and other reasons discussed below, it is best seen as prefatory to the main flow of the *tom yaya kange* rather than as a part of it. In terms of rhythmic structure, the main flow of the performance begins with line 2. As can be seen, from then on, almost every line consists of four words plus the line-final vocable. As I have demonstrated elsewhere with instrumental-phonetic evidence (Rumsey 2007), depending on the number syllables in each word, when used in these lines of metrical *tom yaya kange* they tend to be stretched or contracted in order to make all the words in the line of roughly the same audible duration, which also roughly matches that of the vocable at the end of the line. This and

---

4   These include some thirty performances of twenty-five different tales that my assistants and I have made and transcribed during 1983–2004, totalling approximately 18,000 lines. For further details concerning the way in which these recordings have been made and transcribed, see Rumsey (2001:203–5). I have also heard perhaps another thirty performances during that time, which, as far as I could tell, were consistent with the generalizations offered here.

5   For discussion and evidence regarding feature 4, see Rumsey (2007:258–61).

6   For biographical details and a character sketch of Paulus Konts, see Rumsey (2006b).

other factors discussed below establish a regular rhythm to the line with a fixed number of beats or "feet"—in this case five of them, one filled by each of the four words and one by the vocable.[7]

Figure 1. Paulus Konts in Kailge, 2004 (photo by Don Niles).

---

7 For the occasional lines which do not have enough words or readily separable bound morphemes, one of the words may be stretched over two beats to fill out the line. There are two instances of this in this in text 1, in line 23, where *mepa* is stretched out over two beats, and line 25, where *kela* is.

Text 1. Opening lines from the story of Rosa and Koka as performed by Paulus Konts, 2 March 1997. An audio file of this example can be found in online item 17.

1.	ama na na	Oh mother, oh me!
2.	puku to pena purum e	He jumped and rushed outside.
3.	puku to lkud urum e	He jumped and ran to the house.
4.	olu-ma ngil nyirim e	The flies began to buzz.
5.	lupal-ma tom turum e	The mosquitoes began to drone.
6.	nu takan mului nyib a	"Now you just keep quiet," he said.
7.	kanab a taka nyiba a	In my mind's eye the story unfolds.
8.	kayi nga we kaniyl e	A fine looking fellow was he.
9.	mong-ne kubi kel e	His eyes made his nose look small.
10.	kubi-ne mong kel e	His nose made his eyes look small.
11.	kanab a taka nyiba a	In my mind's eye the story unfolds.
12.	kayi nga mon kaniyl e	A very fine fellow indeed.
13.	puku to pena pupa e	He jumped and rushed outside.
14.	puka topa lkudu urum e	Then jumped and rushed to the house.
15.	madi luyiya tok piring e	"In Mendi they're having a feast.
16.	na ultuk pubu nyirim e	I'll go there tomorrow," he said.
17.	ab rota ab nayi e	"Rosa what woman are you?
18.	nu nanga kuk wanyayl e	My brightly coloured hat,
19.	lumayia tunjan pui nyirim e	Please get it and wash it," he said.
20.	puyl wang manya purum e	Down she went to Puyl Creek.
21.	abulka menayl poyibi turum e	She carefully washed it off.
22.	nui-nga nai tirim e	It really did look fine.
23.	mepa ola oba a	She brought it back from the creek
24.	ena-nga depa mulurum e	And laid it out in the sun
25.	kapola kela purum e	And then she turned and left
26.	na uj mong tulab e	"I'll cut some growths from tree trunks"

The use of formulaic expressions is exemplified by: the figure in lines 2–3, which is repeated in lines 13–14 and ten more times later on in the performance; the figure in line 7, which is repeated in line 11 and thirty times later on; the figure in lines 9–10, which is repeated once in this performance in a variant form and often used in other performances; and the figure in line 22, which is repeated once in this performance and also commonly used in others. Note that in each case the figure comprises one whole line or two of them in sequence. By way of explanation, the standard two-line figure in lines 9–10 in effect amplifies on what is said in line 8, that the young man who is being referred to is very good looking—large eyes and noses being considered attractive features.

The use of parallelism—repetition with variation—is exemplified in lines 2–3, 4–5, 9–10, and 13–14. Note that in each case, the unit within which this variation is found is the line. That is, both the elements that are repeated and those that are varied occur at corresponding positions within adjacent lines. As discussed in Rumsey (2007:261–66, 269–70), this both contributes to the salience of the line as the basic building block of *tom yaya kange* in general (as in all the other sung story genres treated in this volume) and draws on the enhanced possibilities for parallelism that are afforded by the fixed line-length in metrical variants of *tom yaya kange* such as Konts's. As is true of parallelism in other regional genres discussed in this volume (in chapters 4 and 8) and in many other genres of verbal art around the world (Jakobson 1960, Fox 1977, Fabb 1997), the terms that are placed in a parallel relationship with each other typically are ones with meanings that are closely related to each other, either as antonyms or as other kinds of contrasting terms within a given semantic domain (so called "semantic parallelism"). This is true of all the parallel terms in text 1, that is, *pena* 'outside' / *lku-d* 'into the house'; *olu-ma* 'flies' / *lupal-ma* 'mosquitoes'; *ngil* 'buzz' / *tom* 'drone'; and *mong* 'eye' / *kubi* 'nose'. Note that the parallelism in lines 9–10 is of a more elaborate kind known to classical rhetoric and poetics as "chiasm" (lit., 'shaped like the letter X'), in which both of the contrasting terms occur in each of the two parallel lines, in reversed positions as between the two (eye … nose / nose … eye).

In addition to the occasional grouping of lines into parallel pairs (and sometimes larger sets; see Rumsey 2007:264–66 for examples), *tom yaya kange* are musically organized into repeating melodies consisting of an even number of lines of text, each of which can be considered to comprise, in musical terms, one measure. The general form of the melody used by Konts in the performance associated with text 1 is shown in cipher notation in figure 2 and in musical notion in figure 3.[8]

1	1	1	5	5
5	5	6	5	2
5	5	3	4	4
2	2	3	2	2
2	2	2	5	5
6	5	5	4	1
3	3	2	3	3
1	2	2	1	1

Figure 2. Basic form of 8-line *tom yaya kange* melody shown in cipher notation.

Figure 2 is useful for showing how Konts's melody maps on to individual lines and the words within them. In this particular performance, the melody begins in line 3. Line 1 stands outside of the melody, by having only four beats and no final vocable as discussed above, and also by having all of the words intoned on a single pitch, the same one on which the melody begins and ends. Line 2, although it has the same rhythmic structure as the following ones, differs from all of them

---

8   This melody, which is used by Konts in all of the performances of his that I have recorded, is very similar the one used by the renowned Melpa *kang rom* performer Paul Pepa as described by Niles in chapter 12, and indeed is modeled upon it. For details of the relationship between Pepa's work and Konts, see Rumsey (2006b). Note that the representation of this melody in figures 2 and 3 differs in some details from the one presented in Rumsey (2001:212) and Rumsey (2006b:326). This is a result of the instrumental-phonetic analysis that was done for Rumsey (2007) and of collaboration with Don Niles. The representation of the melody presented here and in Rumsey (2007) supersedes the earlier one.

in being sounded at a single pitch—the same pitch as in line 1. Beginning with line 3, each of the four words in each line and the final vocable are sung on the six respective pitches shown in each line in figure 2 and in each measure in figure 3. This same eight-line melody is repeated through Konts's performance, in lines 3–10, 11–18, 19–26,[9] and so forth.

Figure 3. Basic form of 8-line *tom yaya kange* melody shown in musical notation.

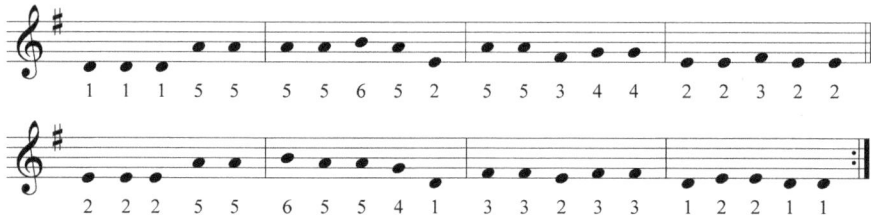

While the notes in these figures are not shown with any specific time values, as described above, each word or vocable with which they are associated is sounded over roughly same duration. So while figure 3 represents the general form of the melody, a musical transcription of, for example, line 19, would have a triplet on the first beat of the measure, pairs of quavers (eighth notes) on the second, third, and fourth, and crotchet (quarter note) on the fifth (along the lines of Niles's transcription of Paul Pepa's *kang rom* melody in chapter 12; for musical transcriptions from one of Konts's performances, see Rumsey 2007:246). The fact that the pitch movements within this melody generally map on to whole words or beats provides a further audible trace of the primary division of the line into five integral units.

Turning now to the overall shape of the melody, note that in figure 2 there is a close resemblance between: lines 1 and 5; 2 and 6; 3 and 7; and 4 and 8. This can also be seen in figure 3, where the corresponding musical measures are shown directly above and below each other. From both of these figures it can be seen that the second half of the melody is a variation on the first half, with some of the notes in equivalent positions being identical and all the others being either one note higher or one note lower. As detailed by Niles in chapter 12, this elaborate form of musical parallelism has been found in all of the *tom yaya* and *kang rom* performances that have been analysed to date, in all song genres that have been analysed to date in the Melpa region, and in all but one genre in the Ku Waru region.

---

9 Note that although line 26 comes at the end of the melody, it does not come at the end of a textual unit. Rather, in terms of textual coherence, it goes with the following line (not shown in text 1), which is "'You count them,' her brother told her." The frequent lack of fit between melody and textual units in sung tales is also discussed by Niles in chapter 12 (n. 15).

The translation of *tom yaya* style

Given the range of linguistic and musical features discussed above, a major concern in my work on *tom yaya kange* has been to develop a way of translating them that will allow some of the effect of the original sung Ku Waru version to be carried over into written English, as per Dennis Tedlock's (1983:31–61) concept of the "translation of style." As in any attempt of this kind, there are at least two kinds of problems to be faced, one at the level of sound and the other at the level of sense.

At the level of sound, at least when translating the metrical varieties of *tom yaya* performance such as those of Konts, there is the problem that their metrical form is different than any of those used by poets working in English, insofar as it is based not on a distinction between strong and weak syllables, but on syllable timing and word boundaries as discussed above.[10] Notwithstanding this difference, a basic fact about the *tom yaya kange* of Konts and almost all other bards within the Ku Waru region is that it does have a regular rhythm to it (as do all Melpa *kang rom*), with a fixed number of beats per line (albeit with different numbers of them in different styles). For that reason it seems to me most appropriate to translate their work into lines of English which also have a fixed number of beats per line.

What must differ as between English and Ku Waru is the way in which those beats are realized. Given the very different prosodic patterns of the two languages, any attempt to realise them solely by means of syllable timing and word placement within the line would fall flat on its face. Rather, I have found that what works best is to organize the lines into a fixed number of feet per line, each with one strong syllable, followed and/or preceded by up to two weak syllables.

But how many feet should there be in each line of the English translation? The same number as in the corresponding line of *tom yaya kange*? The answer to that question must depend in part on what we do about the vocable at the end of each line of *tom yaya kange*. As a vocable it is by nature not something that could have a literal "translation": it has no sense that we could attempt to capture with one. All that we could do would be to render it with another vocable, that is, to end with a corresponding sound at the end of each line of English, for example:

2.	puku to pena purum e	He jumped and rushed outside e.
3.	puku to lkud urum e	He jumped and ran to the house e.
4.	olu-ma ngil nyirim e	The flies began to buzz e.
5.	lupal-ma tom turum e	The mosquitoes began to drone e.

---

10   For further details concerning this difference and its implication for theories of poetic metre, see Rumsey (2010).

But this is far too literal an approach to work in English. Paradoxically, it fails to capture the spirit of the original by reproducing it "to the letter" at the end of the line. So I have chosen to leave out the line-final vocables, allowing the fixed length and prosodic structure of the English line to serve as sufficient markers of the passage from one to the next.

Since the line-final vocable in the Ku Waru line fills one whole beat, if it is omitted from the English line, should that line include the same number of beats as the Ku Waru line minus one? Again, I have treated this as a matter to be settled by trial and error. The answer depends in part on the question "How long a line of English does one need in order to translate a line of *tom yaya kange*?" This in turn depends on the kind of English that one translates with. Different answers to that question are possible and viable in their own ways. An interesting approach which is quite different from mine is the one used by Dr. Joseph Ketan, a political scientist-cum-anthropologist who comes from the Hagen area, is a native speaker of Melpa, and has done extensive translation of *kang rom* sung tales from the region. Treating *kang rom* as a kind of "high art," Ketan attempts to capture that aspect of its style by translating it into relatively "high" sounding English, making frequent use of three- and four-syllable, often Latinate words, in preference to shorter Anglo-Saxon ones. This is exemplified by the following lines of his translation from the story of Kuma Pököt and Kopon Morok:

> The Kumanian grasped the menacing club tightly
>
> His rock-like knuckles curved in, forming an out of proportion ball;
>
> Lifting the club with ease he let it fall;
>
> The impact was devastating;
>
> The skull of the pig was literally smashed to pieces. (Strathern and Stewart 1997:10)[11]

Would a similar "high style" of English be appropriate for translating *tom yaya kange*? In order to answer that question it is necessary to say more about the varieties of Ku Waru that are used in *tom yaya kange* performances. As discussed above, the performers make frequent use of parallelism and of formulaic expressions, many of which are themselves cast in parallel form. While neither of these features per se is unique to *tom yaya kange*, they are used there in ways that are highly distinctive of the genre. An example is the expression used in lines 7 and 11 of text 1: *kanab a taka nyiba*. As far as I know, this expression is never used except in *tom yaya kange*. What it literally says is 'As I see/watch,

---

11   These lines come from a translation that Ketan prepared from audio recordings and transcriptions of *kang rom* that he had produced with grants from the Institute of Papua New Guinea Studies in 1981 and 1982. The translation won an award in the lyrics section of the Papua New Guinea National Literature Competition (Joseph Ketan, pers. comm., 2006). During 2003–4 Ketan worked in association with the ANU based Chanted Tales Project, producing transcriptions and translations of *kang rom* performances by renowned Melpa bard Paul Pepa that were recorded during those years.

quietly …'. This is a standard formulaic line of the kind known to ethnopoetics as a "metanarrational" (Babcock 1977) formula, used by the performer to frame his narrative from the point of view of the performance event. My very free translation, "in my mind's eye the story unfolds," is based on the few exegeses I have been able to elicit concerning the precise import of this oft-repeated line (many other people giving answers like "It's there to make it sound good; to make it sound like *tom yaya kange*").[12]

What is difficult about this line is not any of the words in it, all of which are perfectly ordinary ones in Ku Waru. Rather, what is difficult to understand is the sense of the line as a whole, as given in my literal translation above. There is a large-ish set of such metanarrational formulae that are used in *tom yaya kange* (as in *kang rom*), many of which are distinctive to the genre in the same way that this one is, that is, not in the words used in them, but in what the particular combinations of those words are used to mean within the context of *tom yaya kange*. (For further discussion, see Rumsey 2001:207–8.)

Some of the other expressions used in *tom yaya kange* include words that are not ordinary Ku Waru, but, rather, are said to be used only in *tom yaya kange*. An example occurs in text 1, line 21: *menayl poyibi turum*. The word *turum* is ordinary, being the third-person singular remote past form of the verb *to-* which when used by itself means 'to hit', but which also occurs regularly in combination with a preceding "verbal adjunct," in which context it means simply 'do'.[13] But unlike *turum*, the preceding two words (*menayl* and *poyibi*) are said to occur only in *tom yaya kange*, where, in combination with *turum* and *abulka* 'holding',[14] they can be glossed as 'she scrubbed till the dirt all came out'—the usual way of saying this would be *no lelka kalaru-ma purum*. Another example occurs in line 22: *nuinga nai tirim*. Again, the final verb—in this case *tirim*—is ordinary, being glossable in this context as 'did'. But the two preceding words *nuinga nai*—in the sense in which they are used here, 'to look exceedingly fine'—are said to occur only in *tom yaya kange*.

Totally genre-specific expressions such as this are relatively rare in *tom yaya kange*. In the great majority of lines, every word comes from everyday Ku Waru, from a more ordinary level of what literary scholars call "diction" than do expressions such as Ketan's "grasped the menacing club," "rock-like knuckles," or "out-of-proportion ball" in English. And as noted among the features of *tom yaya kange* listed above and discussed in detail in Rumsey (2007), the syntax of

---

12 I have felt gratified to find that, working totally independently of me on a translation of the *tom yaya kange* by Peter Kerua that is discussed by Don Niles in chapter 12, Melpa/Ku Waru speaker Gomb Minimbi has translated Kerua's very similar line *kanaba taka nyiba e mudupa* as 'let me silently see what's happening'.
13 For details of this and other related aspects of Ku Waru grammar, see Merlan and Rumsey 1991 (appendix B).
14 This is a form of the verb *abul-* 'to grasp in one's hand(s)' in which the root is followed by the third person singular "switch reference" marker *-ka*, indicating that its subject (the woman Rosa) is different from the subject of the next verb (Koka's hat). For details of this and other related aspects of Ku Waru grammar, see Merlan and Rumsey 1991 (appendix B).

tom yaya kange is much simpler than in spoken Ku Waru, thereby increasing the salience of the isometric poetic line and the scope for poetic parallelism across lines. Accordingly in my translations I have chosen to use "everyday" English whenever possible, with short words and simple syntax.

Having made this choice and experimented with English lines of different lengths, I have settled on a three-beat line as the optimal length for translating *tom yaya kange* lines with five or six beats (including the line-final vocable). Note that this finding is conditioned in part by my having chosen to use a "plain" English style with shorter words over a "high" style with longer ones. This can be seen by contrasting the length of my three-beat lines in text 1 with that of the lines from Ketan's translation above

Besides the fact of its being metrical, another way in which the form of my English line matches that of *tom yaya kange* is in its great flexibility regarding the number of syllables that can be included within a foot—anywhere from one to three, with, in the case of my English line, one strong syllable in each foot that is preceded and/or followed by two, one, or no weak beats. So in total my quasi-*tom-yaya* line can consist of anywhere between three and eleven syllables, in the following pattern (where "**S**" = "strong syllable" and "W" = "weak syllable"):

(W) (W) **S** (W) (W) **S** (W) (W) **S** (W) (W)

Similarly, if we exclude the final vocable, the *tom yaya kange* line in its five-beat variant in principle can consist of anywhere between four and twelve syllables, and the six-beat line of between five and fifteen. If we ignore the vocables that are occasionally used within the *tom yaya kange* line to fill out the requisite number of feet (e.g., the *a* after *kanab* in line 7 of text 1) the average number of syllables used within my three-beat line, for example in text 1 (7.16) is quite comparable to the average number used within both Konts's five-beat line (7.36). Similarly with respect to the six-beat line used by another performer, Noma, a count of syllables in the first twenty-five lines of his text on pp. 205–6 of Rumsey (2001) shows an average of 9.52 syllables per line, and 8.32 in my English translation.

In sum, by not imposing any particular structure on my English foot, I have not only allowed it (in terms of syllable count) to match closely that of the Ku Waru original, but have also allowed for a similar degree of variability in the number of syllables that may occupy it, while nonetheless maintaining a line which is of quite constant overall duration. This is possible both in Ku Waru and in English because they happen to be similar in one key respect, namely in the great variability of syllable length which is permitted in each.[15]

---

15 In this respect both Ku Waru and English differ from what are known as "syllable timed languages," in which syllables are purportedly of more even duration (Pike 1972). French is often cited as a language of this kind. It is unclear whether it actually is, or whether languages of this type actually exist (Pamies Bertrán 1999), but if they do, Ku Waru is not one of them, at least in the way it is used in *tom yaya kange*. For instrumental-phonetic evidence to the contrary, see Rumsey (2010).

Turning now from the realm of sound to that of sense, note that this topic has already been broached by my discussion of diction above and my sense of the greater appropriateness of a "plain" style than of a "high" one for translating *tom yaya kange*. Both at that gross level of distinction and at that of particular choices to be made on a word-by-word and expression-by-expression basis, there are important questions of cross-cultural disparity and/or analogy to be faced. These concern not only individual words, but the range of senses or connotations that can be expressed by them.

For example, a frequently-used word in many *tom yaya kange* performances is *kang*, which in its literal sense means 'boy'. This same word can in certain contexts be used in reference to young men and, indeed, to men of almost any age as an alternative to the word *yi* 'man'. When used in the latter way it entails a connotation of high-spirited male camaraderie. Casting about for a word to translate it, I have settled on the word 'lad' as one which is appropriate on two counts. First, it is appropriately colloquial (by contrast with, for example 'youth' or 'juvenile'). Second, like *kang,* 'lad' is used primarily in reference to boys, but also to men, also with connotations of high-spirited male camaraderie.

A case of a Ku Waru word that is used in an even more extended sense is *kis*, the ordinary sense of which is 'bad' or 'ugly'. Especially in *tom yaya kange* it is often used in exactly the opposite sense 'very good'—not in the moral sense, but in the sense of 'fine', 'marvellous', or 'good looking'. This range of senses is quite comparable to uses of the word 'bad' or 'bad-ass' in US Black Vernacular English. So I have translated it in both of those ways.

In some cases the problem of how to translate particular words and expressions is tied up with the issue of how to convey the force of a larger metaphor in which they figure (metaphor being a frequent and highly valued feature of *tom yaya kange*). An example occurs in the last two lines of the following passage from the story of Kubu Suwakl, as performed by Peter Kerua (online item 18 is a short excerpt on video of another performance by Kerua of the same tale from which these lines are taken; an image from this recording has been used on the cover of this volume):

abu waipi mele kaniyl-e	That woman whose name was Wapi
ukulu-kilye manya mele purum-e	Went down to the banks of the Ukuglu.
abolurum abolurum kana	And washed herself over and over
poin sukusingi kanarumu	Till she shone like the wood of a *poin* tree
nal sukusingi kanarumu	Till she shone like the wood of a *nakl* tree.
kanab taka nyiba mudupa	In my mind's eye the story rolls on.
lapisa abolupa aji mudurum-o	She carefully groomed her hair
bras paku mela tirim-e	And put on a black-bead necklace
kanab taka nyiba mudupa	In my mind's eye the story rolls on.
kurali gel mel kanital-e	The flowers adorning her loin cover
napilya mulyi no okupa pijirim-e	Were sluice gates in the River Nebilyer.

The metaphor in the last two lines likens the front middle part of Wapi's flowered loin cover—the part over her vagina—to the middle part of a weir that has been built across the Nebilyer River to channel its flow in order to catch fish. The Nebilyer is the biggest, most powerful river in the region. In the interpretation offered by my translation assistants (John Onga, Thomas Pai, and the composer/performer Peter Kerua), this metaphor in effect likens Wapi's erotic energy to the powerful, turbulent flow of the Nebilyer, which has been channelled and concentrated by a sluice gate just as hers has been channeled and concentrated on the male hero of this story, Kubu Suwakl. Other possible translations of the last line would be 'were like a fish trap in the Nebilyer River' or 'made the water overflow in the middle of the Nebilyer'. My translation 'were sluice gates in the River Nebilyer' is based on my understanding of the overall force of the metaphor, for which the relevant fact about the apparatus that it is being compared to is not that it used to catch fish or to make water overflow, but that it has the effect of channelling and intensifying the flow, as does a sluice gate. I have chosen the wording 'were sluice gates in the River Nebilyer' also because it meets my requirement that each line have three strong beats ('were slúice gates in the Ríver Nébilyer), because of the abundance of sibilants in the phrase 'sluice gates' and the sibilant-liquid cluster at the beginning of it, all of which aurally reinforce the idea of flow and sexual energy that the image is about.

The plots of *tom yaya kange* and *kang rom*

In previous publications I have emphasized the similarities among the plots of *tom yaya kange* relative to the wider range of them that is found among *kange* tales more generally (i.e., including those that are spoken as well the ones that are sung). I have said that many of them

> [cluster] around a prototypical plot in which a young man sets out from his home to court a young woman he has heard about in a far-away place, undertakes a long and arduous journey to her home, wins her hand, but then encounters various obstacles in his attempt to bring her back to his home and marry her, sometimes succeeding and sometimes not. (Rumsey 2006b:322; cf. Rumsey 2001:201)

But in light of more recent experience, especially at the 2006 Goroka Chanted Tales Workshop, I have become more mindful of the differences in this respect between the Melpa and Ku Waru regions, and, within the Ku Waru region, between the eastern and western reaches of it. Plots that conform to the above description are most prevalent among sung stories by performers within the Melpa region (*kang rom*), especially within the past generation or two. At the 2006 workshop we were told by a knowledgeable senior Melpa man, Ru Kundil,[16] that there are

---

16 For a biography of Ru, see Strathern (1993) and Strathern and Stewart (2000).

currently only two *kang rom* stories that are ever performed: the story of Kwint Wöp and Morokla Rakop, and the story of Miti Krai and Ambra Rangmba. Both are prototypical tales of courtship.[17] The predominance of these two tales in recent times is no doubt due in part to the huge impact of performances of them by Melpa bard Paul Pepa which were recorded and broadcast on Radio Western Highlands during the 1980s, and widely disseminated through cassette copies that were made of the broadcasts by interested listeners, as discussed by Niles in chapter 12.[18] Other recordings of the Miti Krai–Ambra Rangmba *kang rom* tale by other performers were recorded by archaeologist Ole Christensen in 1974, by Radio Western Highlands in 1981,[19] and by Andrew Strathern in 1982 (Strathern and Stewart 2005b:224).

Besides the two tales named by Ru (Kwint Wöp–Morokla Rakop and Miti Krai–Ambra Rangmba), there is evidence for a somewhat wider range of tales having been performed in the Melpa region both in the fifteen years before Pepa's first broadcast (1965–80) and during the following eighteen years (1981–98). Recordings were made during that time by Andrew Strathern of at least two other tales by other performers. Both are tales of courtship. One is about a man named Kuma Pököt, who courts a woman named Kopon Morok (or, in some variants, Rangmba). This tale starts out with the usual sequence in which the male protagonist sees a smoke signal from the young woman's distant home, travels there after elaborate preparations, wins her hand and her father's blessing, and brings her back to his home. But Morok finds that the rival suitors from her village have followed them to Pököt's. They take her back, but she leaves a lock of her hair for Pököt, moistened with her tears and wrapped in a leaf. When Pököt finds it, he goes insane with grief and hangs himself.[20]

The other tale recorded by Strathern (in 1965) is that of Mukl Miti Weipa and Kundila Rangmba (Rangkopa). That tale is a variant of the above, which unfolds in the same way up to the point when Weipa leaves with his new bride to return to his home village. Then as they are travelling home they notice smoke rising from Rangmba's village. Weipa goes back to check up and finds that Rangmba's other jealous suitors have set fire to her parents' house and killed them. Weipa attacks them in retaliation, but they succeed in killing him. He then sends his spirit to Rangmba to guide her back to his village. Not realizing that her guide is

---

17   For a plot summary and discussion of the latter, see Strathern and Stewart (1997:6–7) and Stewart and Strathern (2002:124–25).

18   For further details concerning Pepa and those performances, see Rumsey (2006b) and Niles (2007).

19   Transcriptions and translations of the Christensen recording (by a performer named Michael) and the Radio Western Highlands one (by a performer name Karaip of Gumants) have been made by Gomb Minimbi and are held by the Institute of Papua New Guinea Studies in Port Moresby.

20   For a fuller summary of the plot of this tale and discussion of it, see Strathern and Stewart (1997:4–5; 2002:50–51) and Stewart and Strathern (2002:123–24).

a ghost, when she arrives there she sees Weipa's body being carried in for burial. Mortified, she chops off several of her fingers with an axe. She mourns Weipa's death for three days, then stays with his kinsfolk for the rest of her life.[21]

In short, there are eight or nine Melpa *kang rom* performances, by six or seven different performers,[22] that have been recorded since 1965 for which we have transcripts or other information about their plots. Among them there are four different tales as identified by main characters and plot. All of them are tales of courtship with variants of the "prototypical plot" as summarized in the quote from Rumsey (2001) above.

By contrast, in the Ku Waru region, of the performances of twenty-five *tom yaya kange* that I recorded and transcribed between 1982 and 2006, ten are tales of courtship which conform to the prototype. The plots of three more include courtship as one of the elements, and twelve do not include events of courtship at all. In other publications I have included a plot summary of one of the *tom yaya* tales involving courtship (Rumsey 2005:60–61), a full free translation of another (Rumsey 2005:54–59), and a full line-by-line transcription+translation and free translation of another tale that does not include courtship at all (Rumsey 2001:228–39; 2006b:341–42). For present purposes, in order to the exemplify the wide range of plots found in *tom yaya kange*, in what follows I present briefer synopses of the latter two tales (texts 2 and 6), and of three others:[23]

Text 2. "Kupi Tagla and Kalkala Tanga," by Engal Kep. Recorded 15 February 1997.

> There was a woman at Kalkagla called Tanga and a man up at Kupi called Tagla. Tagla went up to Mount Kaylkenga and saw a fire burning in the distance. He came home, told his mother and father about it, and said he wanted to go and see the place. They told him not to, but finally gave in. They helped him roast a pig to provide him with pork for the journey. He adorned himself and set off to court the lass at Kulkagla that he had heard of named Tanga. He walked and walked, until he came to Kulkagla where he found Tanga living with her sisters. They all wanted to marry him but she and Tagla only had eyes for each other. The women loaded up Tanga's netbag with roast pork and said, "You two can go, but when you get home this woman will not go into your house. Let her

21 For a fuller summary of the plot of this tale and discussion of it, see Strathern and Stewart (1997:5–6) and Stewart and Strathern (2002:124 (cf. 113–18)).
22 The reason for the uncertainty as between eight or nine performances and six or seven performers is that it is unclear whether the two performances recorded by Christensen—both of the Miti Krai–Ambra Rangmba tale or portions of it—were by the same performer or different ones.
23 For plot summaries and discussion of two other *tom yaya kange* that differ from all the ones presented here in being set in contemporary Papua New Guinea, see Rumsey (2005:60–66); compare also the discussion of them in chapter 1 of this volume.

sleep in the middle of the road." When Tanga and Tagla got back to Kupi, she refused to go into the settlement and stayed out in a nearby meadow. Tagla rejoined his parents, who thought he had come back empty-handed. Next morning when Tagla returned to the meadow, he found that Tanga had magically transformed it into a beautiful hamlet with a long display ground, abundant gardens, countless tubes of precious tree oil, and rows of tethered cassowaries and fattened pigs. They settled down to a prosperous life together. With Tanga's support, Tagla became a leading big-man. Then he started thinking about what he had been told by Tanga from the start: "We will not do as husband and wife. You and I can't even think of that." He became angry and stopped eating. Tanga asked him, "What are you thinking about? Are you thinking of doing as man and wife?" This made Tagla feel better. They slept together in the bedroom. In the middle of the night the woman left. When the man awoke, he found himself out in a bog, covered with mud from head to foot. "My wife!" he said. "My cassowaries! My fat pigs! My tree oil! Where have all my things gone? Where has my wife gone?" He grew hungry, but had nothing to eat. He became shabby and dishevelled. His face became covered with snot. He wandered in and out of the forest, until one day he died in the middle of the bush.

Text 3. "Forest Man Nikindi (Uj Punya Nikidi) and Randam," by Konga. Recorded 15 February 1997.

There once was a beautiful lass named Randam. She was courted by men from all over, but she only wanted to marry Nikindi, the man from the forest. His parents agreed to it and the two of them set out to Nikindi's place together. As they went up Mount Bombo and looked back, they could see that Randam's parents' house was on fire. Nikindi told her to wait there while he ran back to check what had happened. When he got there the other jealous suitors threw him into the fire. His ghost came back to Randam and continued on the homeward journey with her. They stopped for the night in a broken down house on the way. When Randam tried to turn Nikindi towards her, he looked like a mouldering log. She realized he was a ghost. Next morning she went on to his home where she was greeted by his parents. She told them of his death. They invited her to live with them. She gave birth to a baby boy. One day as they were stopping in a bamboo grove, a big wind blew it over and killed both of them.

Text 4. "Kalya Dom and Rangamb," by Michael Moda. Recorded 15 February 1997.

A man named Kalya Dom courted a woman named Rangamb. She wanted to marry him, but then he disappeared. He took off his good skin and wore his ugly one instead. He had done this with several of his wives before. One day there was a celebration. Dom put on his good skin for it. He joined the line of dancers with his drum. When the dance was over, he put down his drum while he was taking off his feathers and face paint. An old man stole the drum and ran off with it. Dom chased him but couldn't catch him. Then the old man, who turned out to be a cannibal, grabbed him and threw him down into a ravine where he was holding others captive. After several weeks down there, Dom found some feathers, put them on his sides, and flew away. Then he came back and showed the others how to do the same thing. They then went to the place from where the cannibal had thrown them into the ravine and waited for him in hiding. They saw him return, take a rope out of his bag, tie it to a tree, and start to climb down into the ravine on it. They cut the rope and he fell down the ravine and died. Then Dom told everyone to fly back to their own places, which they did, himself included. When he got there he saw that his mother was crying and had cut her fingers off. "Don't cry Mother," he said. "I'm coming." She and his father were living in a cave where Dom had hidden them. Saying a magic spell, he joined his mother's fingers back to her hand. Next morning he went to the wives he had abandoned and found that they had cut off their fingers too. He magically healed them too and then disappeared again. Rangamb secretly followed him. On the way he transformed himself into a bird, then a snake, and then a pig, but Rangamb still kept up with him. He became a bird again and flew into the cave where he had put his parents. Still following him, Rangamb then revealed herself and said, "Why have you left all us wives and come here?" She then went back and rounded up all the wives, brought them to the cave, and led an attack on Dom and his parents. The parents disappeared and the cave then closed up around the wives, crushing them and killing them. Several days later it opened up again. Their parents came and took their bones back home and held funerals for them. The parents lived and died in due course.

Text 5. "Telima Tiyl and His Dog Peant," by Philip Win. Recorded 16 February 1997.

A boy named Telima Tiyl from Winjaka went out with some other boys to the sweet-potato gardens to hunt rats. After clubbing quite a few of them, they said, "Let's make a fire to cook them." They pretended they couldn't get their fire starters to work. Tiyl said, "Look, there's a fire burning

down there at Pikiyl Plain; I'll go get some embers to light our fire with."
As he was doing so, they made a fire, cooked and ate all the rats, and
left. When Tiyl came back with the embers and saw what they had done,
he cried and cried. Deciding to run away, he gathered some cuttings of
cane grass, sugarcane, and greens, and set out for Mount Giluwe with his
pet dog Peant. When they got there they slept out in the cold. Next day
they cleared some land with their machetes and planted the shoots they'd
brought. Peant hunted down some possum for them, which they lived on
till the gardens grew. Down at Kondumanda, Peant found a tethered sow,
untied her, and let her back to their camp. She bore sixteen piglets for
them. Then Peant set off to find a wife for Tiyl to tend the gardens and
pigs for them. He came across some young women bathing in the river.
He lay down on the netbag that one of them had left by the river bank.
She could see that he was a special dog. She let him spend the night in
her house, then lead her back to Telima Tiyl. They killed a pig and feasted
her. She and Tiyl were smitten with each other. He gave bridewealth
to her family and they were married. She bore Tiyl two sons. At first
she and the dog Peant got on well, but then she got tired of having him
around. One day when she came into the house, overburdened with a big
bag of sweet potatoes on her back, and saw him lounging by the fireside,
she got angry and kicked him away. Peant was devastated and decided
to run away. When Tiyl returned, he heard Peant howling in the distance
and realized what had happened. He was mortified and cut off his fingers.
Peant went back to Mount Giluwe and never returned. The pigs that Tiyl
and Peant had raised remained, but only in empty half-sections; the other
half of each of them was up at Mount Giluwe with Peant.

Text 6. "A Small Boy," by Kopia Noma. Recorded 2 February 1997.

A small boy goes out and single-handedly vanquishes the enemy tribes.
He returns home to his adoptive mother, who is unimpressed. She tells
him to stay home and work on planting gardens, tending pigs, and
building a house so he can find a wife. They quarrel. She tells him a story
of a child like himself who killed people, including a pregnant woman.
She told him how the boy in the story cut the baby boy from the pregnant
woman's belly, took it home, and gave it to his mother. She looked after
the baby until it became a young man—a disobedient one. He wandered
and did not look after the pigs he would need to pay brideprice. One day
he overheard a conversation in which the father figure complained about
the boy and told the adoptive mother about how he had gotten him from
the slain woman's belly. When the young man heard this he cried and
cried. Then he took the father's axe and ran away. He came to a clearing
where there was a man who welcomed him and invited him to spend the

night. There was a woman there roasting food and, when she saw the young man, she threw her arms around him and cried, saying "Where have you been?" When the couple heard the boy's story, they invited him to live with them, and offered to build a house for him. He gave them the axe he had brought with him. There were many men there and they passed the axe around amongst them and inspected it. The young man took the couple as his true father and mother. They took him to the river bank and showed him the trees he could cut down the next day to make his house. But when he got there the next morning, he saw that the trees had already been felled and the posts all prepared for building the house. With the others' help, he took the posts to where they were going to build the house. Next morning he came and saw that they had already erected the frame. Then next morning he came and saw that they had finished building the house and pig stall, and that it was full of pigs. He looked at them closely and found that they were the same pigs that he had been raising back at the other place. The couple said to him, "You think you are somebody else, but you are our own true son. Now you have come back to us. Here are your fattened pigs, and there is a whole bag of kina shells for you. Now you can find a wife or do whatever you like. We are overjoyed that you've come back." They got him a wife and did everything they said they would.

With respect to role played in their plots by courtship, these texts provide a roughly representative sample of *tom yaya kange* that I have recorded, as can be seen by comparing them with the overall ratio I have reported above of ten stories in which courtship is central, three in which it plays a part but is not central, and twelve stories in which courtship plays no part. Likewise, courtship plays a central role in two of the above texts, but not in the other three (although the importance of finding a spouse does figure as a theme in them). Only one of the texts, text 2, includes the opening sequence which is present in most or all of the eight or nine recorded Melpa *kang rom*, in which the young man learns of the desired young lady through the sight of distant smoke from a fire that she has lit, decides to go court her, adorns himself for the journey, and kills and roasts a pig to take with him.

But while the story in text 2 is similar to the *kang rom* in that respect, as pointed out by Strathern and Stewart (2005a:16), it differs from any *kang rom* they have ever come across in casting the courted woman as one with magical powers who endows the man with great wealth and prosperity on condition that he not betray his oath to her. They observe that, while not found in *kang rom*, this is a theme that is well attested "in many of the other mythological genre materials that we have analysed, as well as in other materials from the Melpa area" (ibid.).[24] They

---

24   See also chapter 10 for a similar story told among the Angal (Mendi) people.

identify the courted woman Tanga in text 2 as a version of the Female Spirit, who, as discussed in chapter 1, figures in myths and in rituals that were formerly practised across much of the sung-tales region.

Likewise, the plots of all the other *tom yaya kange* summarized above draw upon motifs which are common in myths of the region (cf. Lepi and Bowers 1983, Vicedom and Tischner 1977, LeRoy 1985), including the themes of the "second skin" and the cannibal ogre in text 4, the exile and return of the long lost son in text 6, and the human-like pet dog as guardian in text 5, which indeed has a family resemblance to the Female Spirit, as does the overall plot of text 5 to that of text 2.[25] These are just a few of the wide range of motifs and plots found in the full set of twenty-five *tom yaya kange*. The point here is that even the sample of five texts above displays a much wider range of plots than do the eight recorded *kang rom*.

But there is evidence that the exclusive association in the Melpa region between *kang rom* performance style and plots of courtship is a fairly recent development, dating back no more than fifty years or so. This was suggested by Ru at the 2006 workshop. After saying there are only two *kang rom* that are performed any more, he went on to contrast this with an earlier period when quite a few more than that had been performed. He cited four examples, only one of which, as far as I know, may include courtship as one of its main elements: the story of Ndepana Nikints.[26]

There is further evidence from another quarter for the now-standard *kang rom* plot of courtship not having been so central in the Melpa region within the relatively recent past. This comes from a collection of *Myths and Legends from Mount Hagen* which was recorded by the Lutheran missionary Georg Vicedom beginning in 1934 (just one year after the first arrival of Europeans in the area). The collection—originally published in German as Vicedom and Tischner (1943, vol. 3) and translated in a somewhat abbreviated version by Andrew Strathern (as Vicedom and Tischner 1977)—contains ninety-two texts. Vicedom says that while it is not exhaustive, the collection "does include all the myths which are general knowledge in the society." Given this claim, and Stewart and Strathern's (2002:135) observation that Hagen *kang rom* "are based on stories that are also told as spoken folk tales," it is striking that none of the ninety-two texts shows anything like the canonical *kang rom* plot of courtship—

25 For mention of a Duna (Yuna) *pikono* tale on the theme of dog as guardian with magical powers, see the discussion of *pikono* plots by Kendoli in chapter 2. For an example from the Melpa region, see Stewart and Strathern (2002:104–6).
26 I say *may* include courtship because the Melpa name Ndepana Nikints is cognate to the name of the leading character Uj Punya Nikidi in text 3 above, which is centrally concerned with courtship. But the Melpa story of Ndepana Nikints that Andrew Strathern recorded in 1964, as presented and discussed in Stewart and Strathern (2002:109–13), does not include an element courtship at all, and is instead a story about the relationship between Ndepana Nikints and his sister.

even in the section entitled "Love Stories." The one that comes closest to it is tale no. 85, "Waipa from Pundupukl,"[27] which has a family resemblance to the tale of "Miti Weipa and Kundila Rangopa" as summarized above and presented in Stewart and Strathern (2002:123–24). In both tales there is a main male character named Weipa (Waipa) who successfully courts a young woman named Rangapa (Rangkopa). But in the *kang rom* version that Andrew Strathern recorded in 1965, the courtship scenario—including a fatally interrupted journey by Rangapa and Weipa back to his home—comprises the entire plot. By contrast, in the version that Vicedom recorded in the 1930s (Vicedom and Tischner 1977:120–23), the courtship scenario comprises just the opening episode of the story, which is followed by another thematically unrelated one in which Rangkopa is killed, then another in which Waipa tries unsuccessfully to avenge her death, and finally by another in which he successfully does so with the help of another man.

We do not know whether the tale of Waipa from Pundupukl was ever performed in a sung *kang rom* version during the period in the 1930s when Vicedom recorded it. No mention of *kang rom* is made by him or, as far as I know, by any other ethnographer of the region prior to Andrew Strathern's first recording of one in 1965. What does seem clear is that the plot of the *kang rom* version of the Weipa tale he recorded at that time, by Oke Korpa at Kelua (near Ogelbeng, where Vicedom had worked) was adopted by drawing selectively on a pre-existing tale in such a way as to highlight the element of courtship, thereby contributing to the development of an association between *kang rom* performance style and plots which were structured entirely around that element.

Why courtship?

Commenting on the appearance of the Female Spirit theme within the *tom yaya* performance summarized in text 2 above (and translated in its entirety in Rumsey 2005:54–59), Strathern and Stewart (2005a:16) remark that by combining this theme with the "classic balladic themes"—that is, the general model of courtship that they have the called the "romance of exogamy"—the performer has "brought two separate aspects of 'cultural tradition' together." In light of the evidence discussed above we can see that the model of courtship as the central one for *kang rom* narratives may well be a fairly recent "cultural tradition."

Whether or not that is the case, how are we to account for the current exclusive association in the Melpa region between *kang rom* performance style and plots of courtship, and the significant tendency in that direction as regards *tom yaya* performance style in the Ku Waru region? As discussed above, one factor that

---

27 As discussed by Niles in chapter 12, this same tale is included in Vicedom (1937).

has certainly played a part since 1980 has been the performances by Paul Pepa that were broadcast over Radio Western Highlands, both having been tales of courtship.[28]

Another possible factor—not unrelated to the above—concerns the nature of the relationship between the performer and the protagonists in the story. As for the performer, there is, as I have discussed elsewhere (Rumsey 2001:218), "a strong sense of personal charisma associated with command of the *tom yaya* genre." Good performers are admired for the power they exert over their audience by overwhelming them with "a ceaseless flow of sound that keeps their attention focused on the story and makes them see and hear it in their own minds as the performer does in his or hers" (ibid; cf. Kendoli, this volume, regarding Duna performers). In other publications (Rumsey 2005, 2006b), I have shown how *tom yaya* performers tend to present the tales as if they themselves are stepping into the narrated world and taking the part of the protagonists or interacting with them. This is a two-way process, in that by doing so the performers also bring aspects of the narrated world into the here-and-now, identifying themselves with the protagonists, implicitly, or even explicitly in the case of Paulus Konts, who regularly casts himself as the central male character (Rumsey 2005:60–66; 2006a:58, 62).

In the case of the narratives of courtship, there is an especially close fit between the ideal persona of the *tom yaya* performer as a charismatic agent within the world of the performance event and the ideal persona of the central characters in the narratives of courtship, who are, as Stewart and Strathern (2002:132) have aptly put it, "magical character[s], supremely full of vitality and a sense of [themselves]." I suggest that one of the reasons for the association of *tom yaya* / *kang rom* performance style with the plots of courtship, at least in the modern context,[29] is the close affinity between these two personae. Within the performance event, the figure of the bard in relation to his audience is metaphorically aligned

---

28   This influence was apparently greater in the central Melpa, Meam, and eastern Ku Waru regions than it was in the northern Melpa region. Andrew Strathern (pers. comm., July 2010) reports that "in Northern Melpa most people at this time did not listen to the radio and were probably not aware of Paul Pepa." By contrast I can report that Radio Western Highlands was widely listened to at Kailge, in the eastern Ku Waru region (western Nebilyer Valley) by the time Francesca Merlan and I did our first fieldwork there in 1981, that copies of Paul Pepa's performances were made on the radio-cassette recorders that had become popular by then, and that these were often played back to highly attentive audiences. The fact that Pepa's performances were in Melpa, rather than Ku Waru, presented little or no obstacle to their intelligibility, as most Ku Waru and Meam speakers in that region can also understand Melpa.

29   I include this qualification in view of a comment that Andrew Strathern (pers. comm., July 2010) has made to me that "the identification you suggest between the performer and the protagonist is intriguing but may belong more to recent commodified and dramatized contexts than to older ones. Oke [Korpa, whom Strathern recorded in 1965] never gave any semblance of an indication of such an identification, though in general both the protagonist and the performer (the former created by the latter) are certainly to be seen as special characters, in quite different ways."

with that of the suitor in relation to his beloved. The extraordinary powers of each of these two figures are amplified by their identification with those of the other.

Acknowledgments

I wish to thank: Francesca Merlan, Don Niles, Pamela Stewart, and Andrew Strathern for their helpful comments on earlier versions of this chapter; Don Niles also for the inspiring interdisciplinary collaboration that has made the Chanted Tales Project and this volume possible; Paulus Konts and Peter Kerua for their wonderful *tom yaya* performances, and for permission to record and reproduce the ones discussed in this chapter; other Ku Waru friends who have assisted with the recording and study of *tom yaya kange* over the years, especially John Onga, Andrew Noma, and Thomas Noma; the Australian Research Council for funding the Chanted Tales Project during 2003–6; Australian National University (Research School of Pacific Studies, now the ANU College of Asia and the Pacific) for providing an ideal home for the project, and support for my research in Papua New Guinea since 1996.

References

Babcock, Barbara. 1977. "The Story in the Story: Metanarration in Folk Narrative." In *Verbal Art as Performance*, edited by Richard Baumann, 61–79. Prospect Heights, IL: Waveland Press.

Fabb, Nigel. 1997. *Linguistics and Literature: Language in the Verbal Arts of the World.* Cambridge, MA: Blackwell.

Fox, James J. 1977. "Roman Jakobson and the Comparative Study of Parallelism." In *Roman Jakobson: Echoes of His Scholarship*, edited by Cornelis H. van Schooneveld and Daniel Armstrong, 59–90. Lisse: Peter de Ridder Press.

Jakobson, Roman. 1960. "Closing Statement: Linguistics and Poetics." In *Style in Language*, edited by Thomas A. Sebeok, 350–77. Cambridge, MA: Massachusetts Institute of Technology Press.

Lepi, Pundia, and Nancy Bowers. 1983. "Kaugel Stories: *Temane* and *Kangi*." *Oral History* 11 (4): 1–145.

LeRoy, John. 1985. *Kewa Tales*. Vancouver: University of British Columbia Press.

Merlan, Francesca. 1995. "Narrative Genres in the Western Highlands of Papua New Guinea." In *SALSA II: Proceedings of the Second Annual Symposium about Language and Society, Austin*, edited by Pamela Silberman and Jonathan Loftin, 87–98. Texas Linguistic Forum, 34. Austin: University of Texas.

Merlan, Francesca, and Alan Rumsey. 1991. *Ku Waru: Language and Segmentary Politics in the Western Nebilyer Valley, Papua New Guinea*. Studies in the Social and Cultural Foundations of Language, 10. Cambridge: Cambridge University Press.

Niles, Don. 2007. "Sonic Structure in *Tom Yaya Kange*: Ku Waru Sung narratives from Papua New Guinea." In *Oceanic Music Encounters—the Print Resource and the Human Resource: Essays in Honour of Mervyn McLean*, edited by Richard Moyle, 109–22. Research in Anthropology and Linguistics Monograph, 7. Auckland: University of Auckland.

Pamies Bertrán, Antonio. 1999. "Prosodic Typology: On the Dichotomy between Stress-timed and Syllable-timed Languages." *Language Design* 2: 103–30.

Pike, Kenneth L. 1972. "The Intonation of American English." In *Intonation*, edited by Dwight Bolinger, 53–83. Harmondsworth: Penguin. (Orig. pub. 1945.)

Rumsey, Alan. 2001. "*Tom Yaya Kange*: A Metrical Narrative Genre from the New Guinea Highlands." *Journal of Linguistic Anthropology* 11 (2): 193–239.

———. 2005. "Chanted Tales in the New Guinea Highlands of Today: A Comparative Study." In *Expressive Genres and Historical Change: Indonesia, Papua New Guinea, and Taiwan*, edited by Pamela J. Stewart and Andrew Strathern, 41–81. Anthropology and Cultural History in Asia and the Indo-Pacific. Hants: Ashgate Publishing.

———. 2006a. "The Articulation of Indigenous and Exogenous Orders in Highland New Guinea and Beyond." *The Australian Journal of Anthropology* 17 (1): 47–69.

———. 2006b. "Verbal Art, Politics and Personal Style in the New Guinea Highlands and Beyond." In *Language, Culture, and the Individual: A Tribute to Paul Friedrich*, edited by Catherine O'Neil, Mary Scoggin, and Kevin Tuite, 319–46. Munich: Lincom.

———. 2007. "Musical, Poetic, and Linguistic Form in *Tom Yaya* Sung Narratives from Papua New Guinea." *Anthropological Linguistics* 49: 237–82.

———. 2010. "A Metrical System that Defies Description by Ordinary Means." In *A Journey through Austronesian and Papuan Linguistic and Cultural Space*: *Papers in Honour of Andrew K. Pawley*, edited by John Bowden and Nikolaus Himmelmann, 39–56. Pacific Linguistics, 615. Canberra: Pacific Linguistics.

Stewart, Pamela J., and Andrew Strathern. 2002. *Gender, Song and Sensibility: Folksongs and Folktales in the Highlands of New Guinea*. Westport, CT: Praeger.

———. 2005. "The Death of Moka in Post-colonial Mount Hagen, Highlands, Papua New Guinea." In *The Making of Global and Local Modernities in Melanesia: Humiliation, Transformation and the Nature of Cultural Change*, edited by Joel Robbins and Holly Wardlow, 125–34. Anthropology and Cultural History in Asia and the Indo-Pacific Series. London: Ashgate Publishing.

Strathern, Andrew. 1971. *The Rope of Moka: Big-men and Ceremonial Exchange in Mount Hagen, New Guinea*. Cambridge Studies in Social Anthropology, 4. Cambridge: Cambridge University Press. (re-issued with corrections and new preface, 2007.)

———. 1974. *Melpa Amb Kenan: Courting Songs of the Melpa People*. Boroko: Institute of Papua New Guinea Studies.

———. 1993. *Ru: Biography of a Western Highlander*. Boroko: National Research Institute.

Strathern Andrew, and Pamela J. Stewart. 1997. *Ballads as Popular Performance Art in Papua New Guinea and Scotland*. Centre for Pacific Studies Discussion Papers Series, 2. Townsville: James Cook University of North Queensland.

———. 2000. *Stories, Strength and Self-Narration*. Adelaide: Crawford House Publications.

———. 2005a. "Introduction." In *Expressive Genres and Historical Change: Indonesia, Papua New Guinea and Taiwan*, edited by Pamela J. Stewart and Andrew Strathern, 1–39. Anthropology and Cultural History in Asia and the Indo-Pacific. Hants: Ashgate Publishing.

———. 2005b. "Melpa Songs and Ballads: Junctures of Sympathy and Desire in Mount Hagen, Papua New Guinea." In *Expressive Genres and Historical Change: Indonesia, Papua New Guinea and Taiwan*, edited by Pamela J. Stewart and Andrew Strathern, 201–33. Anthropology and Cultural History in Asia and the Indo-Pacific. Hants: Ashgate Publishing.

Tedlock, Dennis. 1983. *The Spoken Word and the Work of Interpretation*. Philadelphia: University of Pennsylvania Press.

Vicedom, Georg F. 1937. "Ein neuentdecktes Volk in Neuguinea: Völkerkundliche Beobachtungen an der Bevölkerung des Hagen-Berges im ehemals deutschen Teil von Neuguinea." *Archiv für Anthropologie* 24: 11–44, 190–213.

Vicedom, Georg F., and Herbert Tischner. 1943. *Die Mbowamb: Die Kultur der Hagenberg Stämme im östlichen Zentral-Neu Guinea. Dritter Band: Mythen und Erzählungen*. Hamburg: Friedrichsen, de Gruyter.

———. 1977. *Myths and Legends from Mount Hagen*. Translated by Andrew Strathern. Boroko: Institute of Papua New Guinea Studies.

12. Metric Melodies and the Performance of Sung Tales in the Hagen Area

Don Niles

Introduction

The purpose of this chapter is to convey some sense of the melodic and metric nature of Hagen sung tales through the examination of two related, but distinct, styles. Hagen (Melpa and Ku Waru) performances appear to stand as a subgroup separate from other regions particularly because of the metric binary melodies that provide a framework for the telling of the story (e.g., cf. Duna *pikono* as described by Gillespie and San Roque in chapter 3, this volume).[1] I begin with what can be considered the most canonical of all Hagen performances, that by Paul Pepa from 1980. Aside from being recognized by Hageners as a superb performance, its status has been greatly enhanced by its repeated radio broadcast. It is also a particularly valuable example because Pepa's tale is preceded by a song, allowing me to identify some important elements of melodic style in this genre that are germane to the subsequent discussion of sung tales. I then consider other performers who have a very similar, if not identical, style of presentation to Pepa's.

In contrast, I then examine a related performance style found in the Ku Waru area of Western Highlands. While these are still definitely part of a Hagen subgroup of sung tales, there are also considerable differences in their melodic and metric realization.

Paul Pepa's *kang rom* performance (Melpa)

Manda rop pora ndond. Nanga mbi Paul ni ka.

I've finished my tale. I'm the one named Paul.

With these spoken lines, Paul Pepa (c. 1959[2]–2005; figures 1 and 4) concluded a sixteen-minute recording he had just made at Radio Western Highlands in Mount

---

1 I dedicate this contribution to the memory of Paul Pepa (d. c. April 2005) and Richard Alo (d. 28 January 2007). Both of them contributed in different, yet vital, ways to our project. I greatly valued their friendship, knowledge, and skills. They are very sorely missed, yet remain an inspiration to my work.

2 Information from Alan Rumsey (email, 20 March 2007) notes that when Rumsey first met him in 2003, Pepa said he was born in 1959. Pepa also told me the same date in 2004. Apparently born at the time of a major census in his area, he was given the name Pepa, the Tok Pisin word for 'paper', referring to the census forms used for recording information.

Hagen.[3] While the story Pepa told had ended, in many ways this recording and its subsequent broadcasts were pivotal events for the genre he had just presented in a masterful performance. Hence, his story also begins here.

Figure 1. Paul Pepa, decorated as if for courting, before performing *kang rom* in Goroka, February 2004 (photo by author).

Pepa made this recording of a Melpa *kang rom* on Monday, 17 November 1980, when he would have been about twenty-one years old. While no recordist is listed on the box of the five-inch reel of tape,[4] the typed label gives a short title, identifies Pepa as from Nengil in the Mul area, the duration of the recording, cataloguing number, and two lines suggesting that the recording was even felt at the time to be of some lasting importance: "tumbuna [Tok Pisin: traditional/ancestral] stories to be kept … please don't erase."

Shortwave radio broadcast began from Mount Hagen in 1966 at 250 watts, one year after the first Highlands station opened in Goroka, with both stations

---

3   For information about Pepa's recordings, I greatly appreciate the assistance of the station manager of Radio Western Highlands, Anna Pundia, who kindly had her staff locate the original tapes and cataloguing information for me in August 2006. In 2004, Pepa told me that he made his recordings in 1973, when he would have been about fourteen years old. However, 1973 is almost certainly incorrect, particularly since there are dates written on the tape boxes of the recordings held at the radio station.

4   In 2004, Pepa said that Kindi Lawi had recorded him at the radio station, but I have been unable to verify this, and Lawi's name is not written on the tape boxes of Pepa's recordings. During 1982–87, Lawi was the provincial Member of Parliament for Western Highlands.

increasing power to 2 kilowatts in 1971 (Mackay 1976:173–74). The present building housing Radio Western Highlands or Nek bilong Tarangau (Tok Pisin: 'voice of the eagle') was opened on 15 January 1973. In common with all Papua New Guinea radio stations at the time, considerable effort was made to record music and stories from groups in the area. This would frequently involve radio-station officers attending traditional local events to do on-location recordings. Performers would also occasionally go directly to the studio to be recorded, as in Pepa's case. Such recordings were broadcast in special time slots devoted to traditional expressions.

As noted by Strathern and Stewart (2005a:29, n. 3) and Rumsey (2006b:330), Pepa's performances[5] were broadcast frequently during the 1980s, and these broadcasts were often recorded onto cassette for further listening. These significant "transplacements" of the traditional performance context (Strathern and Stewart 2005a:23) meant new relations between performer and audience, a much larger audience, and encouraged an identification of such a performance as standing for the Melpa, if not Western Highlands in general. Repeated broadcasts also meant that the traditional variations inherent to repeated performances of such an oral tradition were absent; instead, exactly the same performance could be heard repeatedly by a much larger audience than could ever traditionally gather in a house around the fire at night. Furthermore, the intimate traditional setting was replaced by one in which the performer and audience were invisible to each other. That this performance was frequently broadcast has not lessened its impact. Instead, it is still regarded very highly, setting a standard against which other performers continue to be compared. As such it is a perfect example to begin discussion of metric melodies in this region.

Pepa's recorded performance displays three examples of his abilities in oral expression: speech, song, and sung tale. A brief spoken introduction is followed by a song, all of which precede the *kang rom*. A very short spoken ending concludes the performance; it is transcribed and translated at the beginning of this section. The timings of the different sections and their relation to the whole performance are as follows:

---

5 On 31 March 1981 Pepa again went to Radio Western Highlands to record a *kang rom*. This, however, concerns the story of Kwint Wöp and Morokla Rakop (cf. Strathern and Stewart 2005b:224, n. 1, no. 5), and is in a different melodic and metric style, again using five-beat lines, but with twelve lines to a melody (see notation in Rumsey 2006b:331, fig. 3). Pepa's performance here lasts almost twenty-six minutes and was recorded by Bo George Kelly Kagl Wingti. Pepa's final *kang rom* were commissioned by candidates in national elections, most recently in the successful 2002 campaign by Paias Wingti where Pepa's *kang rom* was played over a public address system on a truck touring the province (Rumsey 2006a:58–59). For this composition concerning Wingti, Pepa used the melody requiring twelve lines of text, but it does not seem to be as widespread among other *kang rom* performers as the melody discussed in this paper.

	min:sec	percentage
spoken introduction	00:22.7	2.4%
song	01:11.6	7.5%
kang rom	14:21.2	90.0%
spoken ending	00:01.6	0.2%
Total	***15:57.1***	***100.0%***

Spoken introduction

In summary, Pepa's spoken Melpa prelude notes that he is about to tell a story from the past concerning a man named Krai from Miti and a woman named Rangmba from Ambra.[6] Pepa further identifies himself and remarks that he is very good at telling such stories. Finally, he says that he will first sing a song, followed by the story itself. This introduction is characterized by relatively short bursts of very fast speech (lasting from 2.2 to 6.7 sec), separated by short breaths of less than a second.

Pepa never refers to the story he's about to tell as a *kang rom*. Instead, he consistently says *kang teman* or *kanga teman,* a generic term for 'narratives' combining *kang(a),* stories which are primarily seen as imaginative creations, and *(ik) teman,* which are generally felt to be more based on personal experience or historical events (Stewart and Strathern 2002:91–92).

Song (*amb kenan*)

A very brief breath follows the spoken introduction and precedes a song. While Pepa only refers to the song as a *kenan*—a generic term for a variety of songs that differ in performance context, choreography, decorations, and the gender of performers—everyone I have asked has readily identified it as an *amb kenan* courting song. Such songs are usually sung by a group of males who sit opposite couples of young men and women performing a seated dance known in Tok Pisin as *tanim het*.[7] As will be described below, *amb kenan* structurally resemble many other types of dance songs. The text sung to the first statement of the melody is as follows:[8]

---

6   Miti hill is on a range separating part of the Central Wahgi plain from the Sepik–Wahgi Divide occupied by the Minembi tribe; Ambra, to the southeast of Miti, is a hill surrounded by swampy plains. Krai means 'love magic', Rangmba 'she/he will pluck/harvest'. See further discussion of these significant features in Stewart and Strathern (2002:115–16) and Strathern and Stewart (2005b:218).

7   For more detailed descriptions of such courting, see, for example, Stewart and Strathern (2002:47–48), Strathern and Stewart (2005b:202–3), and Niles (2007:110–13).

8   The Melpa text and English translation of Paul Pepa's performance derive from the excellent and tireless work done by Gomb Minimbi. Except for minor changes, I have followed her spelling of Melpa words and her translation of their meaning. I am unable to standardize these in accordance with other contributions here concerning Melpa performances, but since my focus is on musical features, I hope this is not too distracting. Nonetheless, I remain responsible for any misinterpretations of her work.

1a. *pa wai yo lde ro*

moklken wi tömb ouil *e* okla pön *o lde ro*

met kera kaimb ouil *e* mana wöin *o lde ro*

ku lde ro lde ro pa e ya

1b. *pa wai yo lde ro*

pren mong keng amb *a* kap kot *o lde ro*

ou po pakla mune *a* ruimpka nön *a lde ro*

ku lde ro lde ro pa e ya

translation:

1a. *pa wai yo lde ro*

you stay and go up the hills of Tömb *o lde ro*

come down the hills of Kaimb *o lde ro*

ku lde ro lde ro pa e ya

1b. *pa wai yo lde ro*

my well-built, flirtatious girlfriend *o lde ro*[9]

you'll drink from the very tip of the pakla sugarcane *a lde ro*

ku lde ro lde ro pa e ya

Words in roman type are the meaningful or lexical text; italicized words are vocables, that is, without a lexical or grammatical meaning in normal discourse. However, within the context of song (and sung tales, as will be seen below), vocables have essential functions.

In the example here, lengthier series of vocables precede or follow the lexical text (e.g., *pa wai yo lde ro; ku lde ro lde ro pa e ya*), while only a few syllables of vocables follow one phrase of text (e.g., *o lde ro*) and a single vocable (*e, a*) appears between lines of text, e.g., "moklken wi tömb ouil *e* okla pön." Consistently in this example, the textual section of the melody consists of two beats of text plus one of vocables, followed by one beat of text and two beats of vocables. Hence, vocables initially establish a melody, then may fill it out when the text is insufficient. In the present *amb kenan,* 70% of the beats of the melody are sung to vocables, leaving the remaining 30% to lexical text. Indeed some performers speak of the ease of composing a new lexical text, in contrast

---

9   Strathern and Stewart (pers. comm.. Oct. 2010) note that *mong keng* 'eye cheek' in the Melpa text refers "both to a girl who looks sideways in a flirtatious way and to the basic act in turning head, in which eyes and cheeks meet in a rolling action." I appreciate their fine-tuning of the translation of this line.

to the difficulty of finding vocables for a melody. Although some songs consist entirely of vocables, most are a combination of vocables plus text. In the corpus examined to date, however, no song lacks vocables.

While the text of this song and the particular vocables used probably contribute to its identification as an *amb kenan* by listeners, its juxtaposition to the following *kang rom* concerning Miti Krai and Ambra Rangmba is also significant. Performances of *amb kenan* and *kang rom* usually belong to very different social occasions, so the combination of the two here is highly notable. Stewart and Strathern (2002:115) identify this *kang rom* story as "perhaps the most well known ... in Hagen. The two chief personae are the prototypes of couples who marry out of their own personal preferences, against the odds, and pay a price for doing so." Stewart and Strathern (2002:124–25, no. 3) also present a synopsis of the *kang rom,* fitting well with what Rumsey (2005:45) describes as the prototypical plot of Hagen sung tales:

> a young man sets out from his home to court a young woman he has heard about in a far-away place, encounters obstacles, overcomes them, wins her hand, returns home with her, sometimes living happily and prospering with her help, and sometimes not.

Yet, this story is not restricted to *kang rom* performance, and may also be told simply as a *kang* narrative, that is, without employing the metric and melodic framework to be described below. Stewart and Strathern (2002:113–18) present a translation of and commentary on such a narration from 1964. However, even earlier published versions are found. Vicedom and Tischner (1943–48, vol. 3:157–59; English translation in 1977:120–23) present a story concerning Waipa from Pundepukl and Raŋkopa from Koklŋe.[10] In such stories, Waipa or Weipa are common substitutions for Krai, as is Raŋkopa or Rangkopa for Rangmba (Stewart and Strathern 2002:115; cf. 2002:124, no. 2, 125–35; Strathern and Stewart 2005b: 214–22). An even earlier version of a fragment of this story is given by Vicedom (1937:191–92),[11] where the names of the protagonists are spelled using his earlier Melpa orthography as Bundibukc Waiba and Kokcnge Ranggoba.[12] Here, Vicedom cites the story as the origin of the *amb kenan* courting dance. While it does not appear that the story can necessarily be described as presenting the origins of *amb*

---

10   While Strathern and Stewart (pers. comm., Oct. 2010) acknowledge a resemblance of themes between *kang rom* and the story presented by Vicedom and Tischner, they note that the "denouement ... is unlike *kang rom,* because Waipa's kin simply pay brideprice to Rangkopa's kin, and the two then live together at his place." This and other versions of the story (e.g., Stewart and Strathern 2002:113–18), leave "no doubt that spoken versions circulated and could have fed into the sung performances ... The initial kernel of the story does appear [in Vicedom and Tischner], but without the tragic portrayals of other versions, either sung or spoken."

11   I can find no mention of *kang rom* in any of the publications by the early missionary anthropologists in the Hagen area—Georg Vicedom, Hermann Strauss, or William Ross—however, it is possible that some of the stories they relate were told in this style.

12   Here and elsewhere in Vicedom's 1937 article, the digraphs *gc* and *kc* are used for velarized lateral sounds, which in Vicedom's later orthography (as found in Vicedom and Tischner 1943–48) are written as *gl* and *kl,* respectively.

kenan courting, all versions do describe the courting activities of the two characters. Hence, the identification of the song as a courting song and its placement before this particular story seem particularly apposite (also see Rumsey's discussion of the courting theme in sung tales in chapter 11, this volume).

The melody to which this text is sung can be divided into two halves (figure 2).[13] The first half of the melody is partially tonally transposed a step lower in the second part. I have attempted to graphically show this and the structural use of vocables and text in the transcription. Note that although the two staves are joined together, they are *not* to be performed simultaneously—this obviously contrasts with the normal way of reading such notation. Rather, the top half-melody is sung until the repeat sign and is then followed by the half-melody in the lower staff. This is indicated in the numbering of the verses: 1a, followed by 1b; 2a, followed by 2b, etc. I have elsewhere called such melodies "binary melodies" to emphasize that the whole is made up of a particular type of pair; indeed the whole requires both parts for completion (Niles 2007:108).[14]

Figure 2. *Amb kenan* preceding Pepa's *kang rom*. An audio file of this example can be found in online item 19.

Barlines are rather arbitrarily drawn in figure 2, but have been included to show

<hr>

13 The musical transcriptions in figures 2 and 3 are transposed up by a minor third to avoid the use of ledger lines and an overabundance of accidentals in the key signature, thereby resulting in the lower tonal centre to be on G. Hence, the opening G–D in the transcription is actually sung as E–B. Figure 6 is transposed downwards by a minor second for similar reasons. Note also that I use dashed barlines in transcriptions to indicate subdivisions of half-melodies.

14 The general importance of paired structures in Melpa thought is considered in Niles (2007:117).

major structural divisions. And, while the tempo is rather rubato, a definite pulse can be detected. Both half-melodies contain the same number of beats, but the sustained pitches often differ by a step. For example, both half-melodies initially ascend to D using vocables; however, when the lexical text is sung, the sustained pitches of the first half-melody (i.e., the third of every three pitches) move D–A–A–B♭ before the final measure of vocables, while the corresponding pitches of the second half-melody proceed C–G–G–A. The final 5/4 measure of vocables is tonally transposed down a step in the second half-melody. In broad outline then, the first half-melody begins by jumping G–D and gradually descends to conclude on A as tonal centre; the second half-melody beings on this same A and jumps to D, then gradually descends to G as tonal centre, the starting point again for the first half-melody.

Repetition of the entire two-part melody here involves an almost exact repetition of the vocables and lexical text as well. The only variation from that presented above is in the first line of lexical text. As noted above, initially it is: "moklken wi tömb ouil *e* okla pön *o lde ro.*" This is changed in the second repetition of the melody to "moklken kera tömb ouil *e* okla pön *o lde ro,*" and in the third to "wi kera tömb ouil *e* okla pön *o lde ro.*" While the meaning of the first two versions is about the same—'you stay and go up the hills of Tömb *o lde ro*'—the final version is 'you go up the hills of Tömb *o lde ro*'.

In order to simplify the musical transcription here and elsewhere, only the rhythmic divisions of the beat relevant for the first lines of text are shown. Subsequent lines sung to the same melodic fragment will subdivide the beat differently in order to accommodate a greater or lesser number of syllables.

Here the entire melody is repeated three times to conclude the *amb kenan* section. This is also fairly typical of *amb kenan* performances I have examined. However, while in this case one complete melody accommodates one complete statement of the text, in other songs this ratio varies: one statement of the text may require just one half-melody, or one-and-a-half, or even two statements of the full melody.

In figure 2, Pepa's breaths are marked with commas in the Melpa text. These breaths have also helped me decide where to draw barlines. His sung phrases (i.e., the sung lines of text, prefaced and terminated by breaths) are much longer than in his spoken introduction, averaging 11 sec, while his breaths take just less than a second. In this example, Pepa always takes a breath during vocables, never in the midst of lexical text. Occasionally, he drops a vocable to take his breath, omitting the final *ya* at the end of a half-melody.

I have discussed elsewhere in more detail how Melpa speakers distinguish between the words of a song (*kenan mong* 'song seed') and its melody (*nuim kan* 'throat') (Niles 2007:115). Furthermore, the meaningful text is *ik mong* 'word seed', while vocables may be termed *we ik, ik we* (both meaning 'empty word'), or *öi wöi* (meaning unclear).

In summary then, the particular points I want to emphasize concerning this *amb kenan* are:

1. the text consists of a combination of vocables plus lexical text, with vocables used to fill out lines of melody when lexical text is insufficient;

2. the text is set syllabically to the melody;

3. the melody consists of two halves of equal length, with one half a partial, tonal transposition of the other at the interval of a step;

4. in each half-melody, vocables appear in the same position, but the text is varied;

5. sung phrases between breaths tend to be long, compared with spoken text;

6. the same two-part melody is repeated until the conclusion of the song, hence often involving complete, multiple repetitions of both the text and the melody;

7. the total duration of vocables in a melody often exceeds the total duration of lexical text;

8. while there is a definite, relatively slow, pulse to the melody, it is treated rubato, that is, with temporal variations;

9. although sung here solo, songs of all types are usually performed by a group who sing the text and melody in unison.

Most of these observations are true not just of this particular song, but of all Melpa songs, regardless of the genre concerned. Although the song occupies just over a minute of the entire performance considered here, this understanding of the typical sonic structure of Melpa song will help in appreciating what happens next, in the *kang rom* itself.

Kang rom

Following the conclusion of the third repetition of the two-part melody of the *amb kenan,* Pepa takes a slightly longer breath than he has up to this point (1.1 sec) and then melodically, metrically, and textually starts a fourth repetition of the same song with the vocables *pa wai yo lde ro* (see bottom of figure 2). Immediately thereafter, the *kang rom* begins and will continue for over fourteen minutes.

Undoubtedly the most striking indicator of this change from *amb kenan* to *kang rom,* even for non-Melpa listeners, is the change in tempo. While the song has a pulse of about 109 beats per minute (bpm), the *kang rom* pulse begins at about 268 bpm—that is, about two-and-a-half times faster—and will vary from c. 262 to 287 bpm throughout the duration of the *kang rom.* And, in contrast to the rubato of the *amb kenan* performance, the *kang rom* appears to be quite regular, in spite of the very fast tempo. Indeed, the speed of the *kang rom* performance seems more similar to the pace of Pepa's introductory speech than to his courting song. Yet, like the latter, the text of the *kang rom* fits into a repeating melody of two equal halves.

Figure 3 outlines the structure of the *kang rom* melody and the beginning text. The text here is clearly divisible into "lines" of five beats. Each line is terminated by a vocable or, occasionally, a syllable ending in a vowel. But, in contrast to the preceding *amb kenan,* a vocable *only* appears at the end of a line. Eight such isometric lines are set to a binary melody. Hence, in contrast to the 70% of beats being devoted to vocables in Pepa's *amb kenan*, in the *kang rom* only a maximum of 20% of the beats is vocables: the sound of *kang rom* is heavily dominated by fast, meaningful text, structured into lines with terminal vocables sung to a repeating binary melody.

Figure 3. Melody of Pepa's *kang rom*. An audio file of this example can be found in online item 20.

Interestingly, Pepa begins his *kang rom* on the last beat of the first measure of the melody—the beat usually devoted a vocable—with the word *mukl* 'mountain/ hill'. For this reason the first four beats of this measure are put in brackets in figure 3: their melodic and rhythmic values only become apparent in subsequent repetitions of the melody. The melody transcribed in figure 3 should be read as in figure 2, that is, the top staff is read until the repeat sign and then the bottom staff is read until the repeat sign, where the melody begins from the top staff again. However, while the *amb kenan* melody is repeated with only very minor melodic deviations from what is transcribed, there are more considerable melodic variations to be found in the repetition of the *kang rom* melody. The melody in figure 3, therefore, serves to provide the general shape of the melody, highlighting important pitches, but is not reproduced in exactly that form upon each repetition. In spite of this caveat, the melodic shape of this melody is strikingly similar to that of the preceding *amb kenan*.

The text and translation of the lines presented in figure 3 are as follows:

1a. mukl
miti wö krai mel ni
mukl miti rona murum *a*
kopanda tömbön pint ngurum *a*

1b. el nöngön gu purum *a*
pilin kumb pa nitim *o*
könin kumb pa nitim *a*
kae wamb kae namen *a*

2a. nimba kumb kelipa purum *a*
moklopa rang köndöröm mel *o*
ambra okupuna kuta pint ka
ndip to nonom kant *o,*

2b. en mel nant nitim *a*
könimb ama mbi nitim *o*
tepam nga kang ni nto
i kapulka wuu nitim *o*

3a. pilin kumb pa nitim *a*
na mam nga ambokla ni nto
nam mba köndöröm konil *o*
pein piliken en nitim *o*

3b. nimba kumb kelipa purum *o*
tepam nga kang ni nto,
i kapulka uis nitim *a*
kuntin nga wakl nökl *o*

translation:

1a. the man named Krai from Miti mountain
lived on top of Miti mountain

like a *tömbön* spear moving forward

1b. like a *nöngön* arrow with blunt barbs

"let's hear about it and

see," they said

"who are these nice people?"

2a. he said and finished his talk

on top of the mountain he looked to the east

to the sweet potato plantation of Ambra valley

"I see a fire is coming up"

2b. "what's happening there?

I must go and see"

his father said "it's fine with me"

3a. "let's hear about it," he said

his mother said

"none of us ever go to that place

where do you want to go?"

3b. she said and finished her talk

but his father said

"it's fine with me"

his *kuntin* stone axe[15]

Vocables are again italicized in the vernacular text, but are here omitted from the translation. Because of their regularity in delimiting a line of text, these vocables perhaps also allow the performer a brief rest and chance to mentally compose his or her thoughts for the next line. As has been demonstrated by Rumsey (2007) for the similar Ku Waru sung tales, each beat tends to be associated with a single word or bound morpheme, and each line terminated by a vocable tends to comprise a single syntactic unit.

---

15 This line belongs textually with what follows, rather than with the preceding lines shown here, i.e., 'his *kuntin* stone axe he pulled towards himself and went outside the house'. This illustrates the fact that a complete statement of a melody or half-melody in performance does not necessarily coincide with an integral unit in textual or thematic terms (as is generally the case in Western notions of "verse" or "stanza"). In this short textual example, notice how a particular theme extends over statements of half-melodies: 1a–1b, 1b–2a, 3c–3b. The freedom for a composer/performer to focus on the creation of a poetic text is probably greatly assisted by the unceasing repetition of melodic and metrical features. Rumsey (2007:249) has found that there is a tendency, but not a rule, for correspondences between melodic units and textual ones in some of the Ku Waru performances he has examined. I certainly agree with him that this question needs be explored in greater detail.

Occasionally, an additional syllable occurs in the text of figure 3 where none appears in the text translated above. For example, the second line of 1b is written above as "pilin kumb pa nitim *o*," while the music example has "pilin kumb a pa nitim *o*." While the additional "a" could be considered a vocable, such additions are only used sparingly and never with any regularity within lines of text—that is, they do not occur at the same metric position in repetitions of the melody. They appear to be added to pad out a line of text that otherwise would not have a sufficient number of syllables to meet the metric requirements for a line. Frequently, but not consistently, this occurs between a word ending in a consonant and a following word beginning with one. These additions may be somewhat akin to epenthetic vowels.

The perfect fifth leap (G–D) concluding the *amb kenan* and prefacing the *kang rom* is precisely the melodic distance covered in the first measure of the *kang rom*. Pepa's transition from *amb kenan* to *kang rom* is melodically seamless. Yet, as noted above, Pepa only begins this measure on the last beat. While the melodic movement is of a perfect fifth, the beginning part of the measure is filled with vocables, the last beat with lexical text: a reversal of the common structure of Pepa's *kang rom* lines in this performance. The first half-melody then moves A–C–A on the final beats of each measure (measures 2–4).

The second half-melody begins with a jump from A to D (measure 5), then the finals of each measure are G–B♭–G (measures 6–8). As in the *amb kenan,* much of the second half-melody is a tonal transposition of the first half-melody downwards by a step.

The length of Pepa's sung phrases is even greater than in the preceding song. Here they average 13 sec in length, with the longest phrase over 16.5 sec. These phrases are separated by breaths averaging about a half of a second. Such long phrases are kept up throughout the duration of the performance and are certainly one of the outstanding features of Pepa's style, in contrast to most other performers examined to date.

In Pepa's performance, 63 such phrases contain 780 lines of text, involving over 97 repetitions of the eight-bar melody. Pepa only breathes at the end of bars, perhaps dropping the final vocable or even part of the preceding beat, when that text could easily be filled in by the listener. He also appears to have definite preferences about where in the melody to breathe. His breaths occur in positions such that when he resumes, he tends to begin on the third measure (16 times or 25.4% of the whole) or on the first, fifth, or seventh measures (each 11 times or 17.5%)—note that the first and fifth measures, and the third and seventh measures are corresponding measures in each half-melody. In contrast, the other bars much less often begin a sung phrase: the second and sixth measures at 7.9% (5 times) and 9.5% (6 times), respectively, while the fourth and eighth measures at 3.2% (twice) and 1.6% (only once), respectively, are very rarely used in this way.

In general then, Pepa continually repeats the eight-bar melody until he finishes his story. When he breathes, he begins again at the appropriate place in the melody. His performance is characterized by a very fast tempo, with long phrases between breaths. Yet, even though the melody is repeated over and over, deviations do occasionally occur, even with such a master storyteller. It can be particularly enlightening to look at these exceptions to the generalizations, for they make further revelations about the performer and his performance.

Beginning his twentieth sung phrase of the *kang rom* (at 5:47.1 in the performance; see online item 21), Pepa only sings two lines of text (to measures 2–3 of the melody), by far the fewest number of lines per breath phrase in his entire performance. After a slightly longer than average breath, he exactly repeats these two lines of text and the two measures of melody, and then continues on with another seven new lines of text to the appropriate measures of the melody.

Something similar happens at the second deviation from the norm, just a few phrases after the one described above. Pepa's twenty-fourth sung phrase (at 6:37.5 in the performance; see online item 22) is again shorter than normal— only seven lines of text—and the tempo here drops to c. 262 bpm. The last line is sung as *i kapulka wuu is,* instead of its expected form *i kapulka wuu nitim a.* Pepa has apparently run out of breath. This text is followed by what is by far the longest breath pause in the whole performance (2.4 sec), Pepa then repeats the text and melody of the final two lines of the previous phrase (here, using the expected form of the line *i kapulka wuu nitim a*), consequently beginning the phrase on measure 8 of the melody—the only phrase in the entire performance to do so. He then adds another eleven lines to this phrase before pausing again for breath. However, this twenty-fifth phrase shifts the entire melody a minor third higher and begins at a faster tempo (c. 278 bpm). For the five minutes since the beginning of the *kang rom*, Pepa has been very consistent in maintaining the pitch levels of his melody, with only a gradual slight lowering of pitches over this period of time. The newly established tempo and pitch level will remain until the end of the performance, that is, for about nine minutes. This transposition of the melody is extraordinary, considering the many faithful repetitions Pepa had done up until this point. And why is there such a long pause before this transposition? One wonders if the tape recorder may have been turned off while Pepa caught his breath or organized his thoughts. Then, when it was turned on again, Pepa repeated two lines of the previous phrase, but at a higher pitch level. Since there is no audible noise on the recording at this point, this must remain only conjecture.

The final deviation can probably be termed a real error on Pepa's part, in contrast to the two previous examples that might be better considered corrections than mistakes. Pepa's fifty-first sung phrase (at 13:12.3 in the performance; see online item 23) concludes on the first measure of the melody, but in the jump of the melodic perfect fifth, his voice breaks on the higher note. After his breath, Pepa should begin with the second bar of the melody. Instead, he repeats the last textual line of the previous phrase, but uses the melody of bar seven. If this deviation would have been comparable to the two described above, Pepa would have repeated the textual line using the first measure of the melody. Here, however, he either backs up or jumps forward too far melodically. Seemingly unfazed by this error, Pepa sings another eleven phrases, all properly aligned to the repeating melody, to conclude his performance. His last phrase of the *kang rom* breaks into speech in the final line. And, after a final short breath, Pepa concludes: "I've finished my tale. I'm the one named Paul."

In considering what has been discussed here about Pepa's *kang rom* with the particular features listed above concerning his *amb kenan* performance, features nos. 1–5 are also true for his *kang rom*. However, note that in relation to no. 1, there is only one vocable per line. Nevertheless, it is of tremendous structural importance in delimiting the line metrically, melodically, and syntactically. Feature no. 6, concerning the repetition of the melody until the end of the performance, is also found in *kang rom*, but there is never a complete repetition of the entire text for the latter, although there are many repetitions of lines and much parallelism involved. While a song text may consist of a few lines of text sung to the same melody lasting a few minutes, a typical *kang rom* involves many hundreds of such lines. Thus, performers can "overwhelm the audience with a ceaseless flow of sound that keeps their attention focused upon the story and makes them see and hear it happening in their own minds as the performer does in his or hers" (Rumsey 2005:53). Indeed, I would suggest that such repeating metric melodies provide an ideal framework for such presentations: neither the audience nor the performer is distracted by unexpected metric or melodic sequences, encouraging a total focus on the story. Furthermore, such melodies are the expected framework for other sung performances. Feature nos. 7–9, however, are not found in Pepa's *kang rom*. Here the vocable is only one beat in a five-beat line, and the pulse is very fast. While there are certainly temporal variations, the pulse and pace of the performance is so fast that they are much more difficult to discern. Finally, *kang rom* is always a solo performance. Aside from many other factors, the very nature of sung tales as being composed in performance, regardless of various repeated elements, would make them impossible for group performance.

The canonical status of Pepa's performance

The frequent broadcast of Pepa's *kang rom* over Radio Western Highlands in the 1980s brought a performance that would traditionally have been heard by only a small group of people in a house at night to a much larger audience. As the size of the audience increased, so did its diversity, bringing the performance not only to people who had never heard of Pepa, but also to people who spoke different languages or dialects than the Melpa used in his performance. While Melpa is spoken by the largest group in Western Highlands Province and has some prestige attached to it because of its use around Mount Hagen town, Pepa's masterful, oft repeated performances encouraged at least some Ku Waru speakers to prefer to perform their sung tales in Melpa, "due in no small measure to the popularity of one performer in particular, a Melpa man called Paul Pepa, who for many years has been esteemed throughout the western highlands as the greatest living practitioner of this genre" (Rumsey 2001:220, n. 9).

One Ku Waru performer, Paulus Konts, learned to perform sung tales from listening to Pepa's performance described above, but never met him until 2004 when both were featured performers at a workshop in Goroka (Rumsey 2006b:330; figure 4). Initially, Konts had only performed sung tales in Melpa (in which he was fluent, like many Ku Waru speakers), but following Rumsey's request, Konts began composing in Ku Waru, after just one day's practice (ibid.:330, n. 26). Today, Konts has composed many stories in Ku Waru as sung tales, using the same eight-bar melody (as learned from Pepa's performance) for all of them (ibid.:327). As noted above, Pepa only breathes at the end of lines in his performance and has definite preferences over where in the melody he does so. In one performance recorded and analysed by Rumsey, Konts's breathing is even more predictable than Pepa's, always occurring at the end of the fourth and eighth lines (Rumsey 2001:212).[16] Another Ku Waru performer, Peter Kerua, also learned Pepa's melody and an early attempt of his in this style was recorded in 2004. Since his youth, however, Kerua has been performing in a different style, to be considered below.

Other performers have also been highly influenced by Pepa's recordings; some have even learned to perform *kang rom* from them. Andrew Strathern notes a young Melpa man named Ketepa Rongnda "learning to master the difficult art of performing song epics (*kang rom*) by listening to cassettes of a performer who has become well known through broadcasts on Radio Hagen" (Strathern 1983:80). The unnamed performer is certainly Paul Pepa. Paul Palam (or Palyim), a Melpa man, performed a *kang rom* of the same story to the same melody as Pepa's during the 2006 Kefamo workshop concerning sung tales. He also claims

---

16 Owing to an obvious typo in a later paper, it is incorrectly stated that Konts breathes at the end of the fifth [*sic*] and eighth lines (Rumsey 2005:52–53).

to have learned this style from Pepa's recording. The same melody and story were also used in a performance by a young man named Miti in Kiltkayake in 1982, recorded by Andrew Strathern and me. In this case, however, it is not clear whether his use of story or melody was influenced by Pepa's broadcasts.

Figure 4. Paulus Konts (left) with Paul Pepa, both decorated as if for courting, at the Chanted Tales Workshop in Goroka, February 2004 (photo by author).

These examples should not be taken to suggest that either the story or the melody belongs to Pepa alone. Quite to the contrary, as noted above and as discussed by Rumsey in chapter 11, the story of Miti Krai and Ambra Rangmba and similar ones with differently named protagonists (Weipa or Waipa and Rangkopa, Ranggoba, or in the Ku Waru area, Tangapa)[17] form part of a widespread oral tradition in the Hagen area, and have been recorded in various forms (as narrated *kang* and as *kang rom* sung tales) for over seventy years. Hence, Pepa's choice of story has wide-ranging relevance in the greater Hagen area as well.

Other melodies are also employed by Hagen performers (as is the case for Pepa himself), but most can definitely be considered binary melodies in the sense discussed above, and also contain lines ending in vocables. A varied form of Pepa's five-beat, eight-bar binary melody is found in performances by Oke-Korpa of Kelua (Central Melpa) and Engal Ok Puluyl (Ku Waru area). Korpa's

---

17 In a version by Konts, analysed by Rumsey (2001:213–14; 2005:60–64), the male protagonist is only identified about halfway through the story as the performer himself.

performance of the story of Miti Weipa and Kundila Rangkopa was recorded in 1965 by Andrew Strathern, apparently the first audio recording made of a *kang rom*. Considerable analysis of the poetry of this performance has been published (e.g., Stewart and Strathern 2002:125–35; Strathern and Stewart 2005b:214–22; chapter 13, this volume). Rumsey recorded Ok Puluyl's performance in 1997 as part of a series of recordings from the Kaugel area. Ok Puluyl tells of the life and death of Jesus (Rumsey 2001:201; 2005:46). In both Korpa's and Ok Puluyl's performances, the melodies used are quite similar to Pepa's, but distinctively the final pitch of each bar (that which usually sustains a vocable) is held for two beats instead of one, thus resulting in a six-beat line for the eight-bar melody. According to different performers and the different melodic styles employed, line length appears to vary from five to eight beats per line. And the number of lines per melody varies between eight, ten, and twelve. There are also possible examples of four or sixteen line melodies, but analysis is still preliminary at this stage.

The story of Miti Krai and Ambra Rangmba can also be told using a completely different melody. In a recording again made at Radio Western Highlands, Kraip of Gumants (Dei Council), presents his story in a very fast monotone with only occasional (and, apparently, unpredictable) pitch deviations above or below. While Kraip's lines appear to contain five beats with a terminating vocable, initial analysis has not revealed a binary melody or any other type of repeating melodic structure—presently a unique sonic structure in the Hagen area.

Hence, Pepa's use of a well-known story told to a melody apparently with some currency in Melpa *kang rom* performances, the brilliance and clarity of his rendition poetically and musically, and its repeated transmission via radio and cassette all combined to produce a classic performance, which continues to transfix listeners and challenge performers today.

At the 14 February 2004 opening of the Goroka workshop concerning sung tales, Paul Pepa (then c. 45 years old) performed a short extract of this same *kang rom*, lasting just over three minutes. He still performed at a very fast tempo (c. 282 bpm) and with very short breaths between phrases. However, the lengths of his sung phrases averaged eight-and-a-half seconds, and some were as short as five seconds. Nevertheless, he still managed to extend some phrases over thirteen seconds. Twenty-four years had passed since his canonical recording at Radio Western Highlands, but his amazing abilities were still very much in evidence.

Peter Kerua's *tom yaya kange* performance (Ku Waru)

Generalizing about melodic variability in the corpus of sung tales he has recorded in the Ku Waru area, Rumsey observes that some

> performers use a four-line melody more-or-less like the first half of Koj's [Konts's], but mainly or entirely in glissando (i.e., with pitch movements that are continuous rather than alternating among discrete pitch levels). (Rumsey 2001:214; 2005:53)

Rumsey has also examined a sung tale performance by Kopia Noma. Noma's performance is characterized by lines of six beats (with a vocable on the final beat), sung to a binary melody requiring ten lines, and with melodic ascents corresponding to melodic descents at various points. Melodic transcriptions of this performance appear in Rumsey (2006b:340, fig. 4) and Niles (2007:109, ex. 1).[18] An earlier recorded version of this story, told in Melpa by Noma and using the same melodic and metric structure is also analysed by Rumsey (1995:111–13).

Furthermore, Rumsey identifies vocable placement as a crucial component in the setting of a text to a melody in sung Ku Waru tales:

> The added line-final vowel is one thing that *all* performers in my sample make use of. Many ... also use a second added vowel at a regular position within the line, usually after the third foot [or beat] if the line is rhythmically regular. This added vowel often has a pitch rise on it matched by a corresponding fall on the final added vowel. (Rumsey 2001:214–15; 2005:53; italics in original)

My discussion now focuses on a melodic type containing many of the characteristics noted by Rumsey, that is, pitch movements are more "continuous," pitch levels are less discrete, lines have a rise-fall alternation in pitch at a number of different structural levels, and recurring midline vocables are used in addition to line-final ones.

In the Ku Waru area, sung tales are called *tom yaya kange* (see chapter 11). As noted earlier, while some performers have adopted a melodic and metric style based on Pepa's performance, other styles are more prevalent, particularly in places less in contact with Melpa speakers.

---

18   The complete Ku Waru text and English translation of Kopia Noma's performance are given by Rumsey (2001:228–38), who also analyses it in considerable detail (ibid.:205–11).

Figure 5. Peter Kerua performing *tom yaya kange* in Kefamo, June 2006 (photo by author).

Peter Kerua (figure 5), from Kailge in the Ku Waru area, is adept at two different melodic styles for *tom yaya kange*. While having learned Pepa's metric melodic style, the original style mastered by Kerua is quite different. He considers this the traditional style of the Kailge area. The following transcription is from a performance that Kerua gave at the Kefamo workshop on chanted tales in 2006 and was recorded by Chris Haskett. It concerns the tribal fighting in his area (figure 6).

Figure 6. Melody and sustained pitches of Kerua's *tom yaya kange*. An audio file of this example can be found in online item 24.

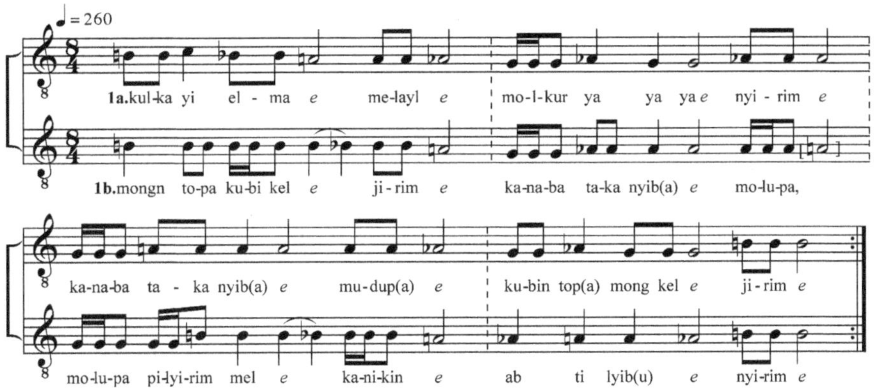

Midline and final sustanined pitches:

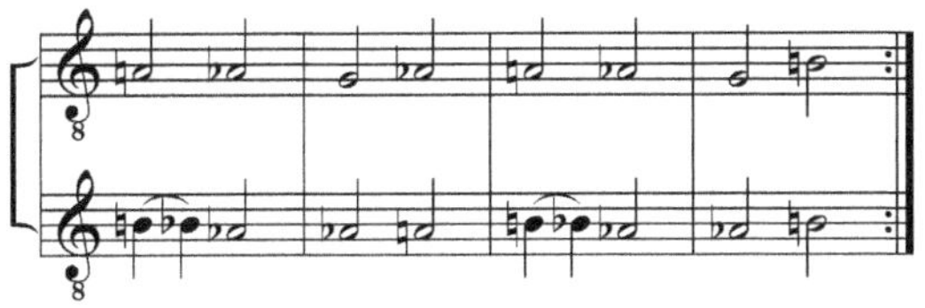

Kerua's opening lines of text, corresponding to one statement of the melody, are as follows:[19]

1a. kulka yi elma *e* melayl *e*
molkur ya ya ya *e* nyirim *e*
kanaba taka nyiba *e* mudupa *e*
kubi-n topa mong kel *e* jirim *e*

1b. mong-n topa kubi kel *e* jirim *e*
kanaba taka nyiba *e* molupa,
molupa pilyirim mel *e* kanikin *e*
ab ti lyibu *e* nyirim *e*

19 The transcription and translation of this text are again based on work done by Gomb Minimbi. In this case, however, Rumsey has standardized the orthography—according to that which he and Merlan devised for Ku Waru (Merlan and Rumsey 1991:323–24)—and slightly revised the translation.

translation:

1a. a Kulka fighting man

"they all know I'm here," he said

let me silently see what's happening

his nose made his eyes look small

1b. his eyes made his nose look small

let me silently see what's happening

he stayed there and quietly listened

he wanted to marry a woman

Vocables are italicized in the Ku Waru text, but omitted from the translation. In the text in figure 6, a number of word-final vowels are written in parentheses: for example, *nyib(a)* and *mudup(a)* (measures 2 and 3). While in spoken text, these vowels would be pronounced, here they are partially or fully omitted. Such apocope often precedes a vocable, apparently to accommodate the latter. Note also the use of *ya ya ya* in the second line. These syllables are fairly frequent in Ku Waru sung tales (in contrast to Melpa *kang rom,* where they have not been noted) and probably have contributed to the naming of the genre as *tom yaya kange.*[20]

Kerua's performance lasts just over fifteen minutes. Clearly this is in a very different melodic style, much more chromatic, and also harder to notate easily in Western staff notation since intervals are smaller and less discrete than in the Pepa example. In spite of the limitations of my transcription, it is clear that there are textual lines of eight beats, each characterized by a final vocable sustained through beats seven and eight, and also a midline vocable, held on beats four and five—midline vocables have not been found in the corpus of Melpa *kang rom* examined to date, but do appear in songs, as in Pepa's *amb kenan* discussed above. Eight lines of text are set to a binary melody. Hence, vocables account for approximately 50% of the total length of Kerua's melody. To reflect this structure, I have constructed the time signature as 5+3, that is, 5 beats accommodate the first part of the text plus vocable, and 3 beats the final text and vocable. Note also the bracket on the final pitch of measure 6. This is because Kerua takes a breath at this point in the textual fragment given; the pitch here is determined from subsequent repetitions.

As in Pepa's performance, the setting is basically syllabic. In the first half-melody, both midline and final vocables are each sustained on the same pitch for

20 Melpa *kang* and Ku Waru *kange* 'story' are cognates, as are Melpa *rom* and Ku Waru *tom,* which seem to be associated with ideas of 'praise, loud, singling out' (Niles 2007:107–8, 115–17).

two beats (notated as a minim in the transcription). However, in measures 5 and 7 of the second half-melody, the midline vocable is sung to two pitches descending by a step (two crotchets in the transcription). This is a good illustration of the fact that while binary melodies involve the transposition of most pitches, such transpositions are seldom exact, that is, there are often slight, but significant, alterations to the melody.

Hence, while the binary melodic structure of this example is clear, the process of creating such a melody is not simply a straightforward mechanical one of transposition. Personal preference often seems to play a role in the final realization of the melody. This is true of songs in general and it is even more pronounced in the performance of sung tales, where the numerous repetitions almost seem to encourage playing with the melody. The general melodic shape and structure are never varied (except through corrections or "errors," as in the case of Pepa discussed above), but the performer does have some latitude in exactly how he or she sonically realizes these features. Such melodic variation in repetition will be the subject of future research.

To illustrate the structure of Kerua's melody more clearly, the pitches of the vocables (i.e., on beats 4–5 and 6–7) are extracted in the measures at the bottom of the example. Such an extraction has sonic logic too, since these are the pitches sustained the longest amount of time in each measure: the other beats are filled with lexical text, often of much shorter durations. Hence, we can see how the melody of the first bar generally descends, the second ascends, the third descends, and the fourth ascends to a larger interval. In the second half-melody, the general progressions are the same, but transposed a minor second higher and with the slight melismatic movements on beats 4–5 in measures 5 and 7, as described above.[21]

Figure 6 is very similar to a musical transcription presented elsewhere of a performance in 1997 by a woman named Wilya, at Webuyl in the Upper Kaugel area near Tambul (Niles 2007:111, ex. 2). The melodic movement is nearly identical, midline and final vocables occur at the same positions and for the same durations in each line, and the slight melismas on two midline vocables are also duplicated. The recordist, Rumsey, notes that Wilya recounted how she learned the tradition from her mother who would perform such *tom yaya kange* to her children at night, when they went to sleep with her. She has continued the tradition and her recorded performance was a "dazzling display that was evaluated by [Rumsey's] highly critical male assistants from across the range as the best one we recorded in the Kaugel Valley" (Rumsey 2001:203).

---

21   The type of melody described here is used in Kerua's performance of the story of Kubu Suwakl, as discussed by Rumsey in chapter 11.

Other Ku Waru performers recorded by Rumsey use the same or a similar binary melody of eight beats per line, with sustained vocables on beats 4–5 and 7–8, and eight lines per melody. This is evident in earlier recordings of Kerua (1997, 2004), as well as in performances by Gabriel Bakari (1997) and Karma (1983). A slight variation on this metric melody is found in performances from 1997 by Engal Kep (Rumsey 2007), Konga, and Philip Win. Each of these performers uses a similar eight-line binary melody, but there are only seven beats per line. Here, while the midline vocable is sustained for beats 4–5, the terminal vocable only lasts one beat. Thus, this variation in the duration of the final vocable is comparable to that described above for melodies more similar to Pepa's, as performed by Oke-Korpa and Ok Puluyl.

Hagen metric melodies

Interestingly, Ku Waru people distinguish two types of *ab kunana* courting songs.[22] *Pala keripa kunana* 'fence-post sharp-point songs' are associated with the cultivated grasslands of the Nebilyer River valley floor to the east and the Melpa region further to the northeast. Musically, this form appears to be identical to Melpa courting songs, such as the one performed by Pepa as a preface to his *kang rom*: binary melodies involving discrete intervals, "diatonic" melodic movement, and the distinctive leap of a perfect fourth or fifth (as in the first measure of figure 2). Hence, *pala keripa kunana* are very similar to the melodic style used in Pepa's *kang rom*.

Additionally, however, there is another type of Ku Waru courting song called *uj ka kunana* 'tree vine song'. While not found in the Melpa area, it is shared with the Tambul region to the west and is felt by some Ku Waru speakers to be their more traditional form in comparison with *pala keripa kunana*. While *uj ka kunana* do not always employ binary melodies, when they do, they involve much smaller intervals than *pala keripa* and more "chromatic" movement. Hence, they are more akin to Kerua's melodic style as described here.

While much more needs to be done on musically distinguishing these Ku Waru genres from one another, and on their relation to Melpa *amb kenan,* the evidence does suggest that the metric melodic style described for the sung tale of Pepa (Konts, et al.) can be considered to have originally been associated with the Melpa area, while that described for Kerua (Wilya, et al.) is more linked to the Ku Waru–Tambul areas.

In spite of the melodic and metric differences highlighted, the Hagen region stands apart from other areas in which sung tales are performed through the use

---

22   Fuller descriptions with musical examples can be found in Niles (2007).

of textual lines of fixed metric length, terminated by a vocable, and the setting of these lines to a binary melody that is repeated continuously until the completion of the story. Details, such as the presence or absence of a midline vocable, the duration of vocables, the number of beats per line of text, and the "diatonic" or "chromatic" nature of the melodic movement contribute to the establishment of subgroupings within the Hagen area as a whole. All of these general and more specific features are also present in songs, but with different emphases. Hence, Hagen musical characteristics are very much evident in the metric melodic framework used for the presentation of Hagen sung tales.

Acknowledgments

I appreciate the assistance of the Australian Research Council, CulturaSenzaFrontiere (Milan), and the Institute of Papua New Guinea Studies which have supported my participation in this project in many ways. In particular, my involvement in the 2004 Goroka and 2006 Kefamo workshops stimulated my attempts to understand sung tales over the whole region and enabled me to discuss the genres with both performers and researchers—truly wonderful experiences.

Memafu Kapera, Acting Managing Director of the National Broadcasting Corporation of Papua New Guinea, kindly gave permission for excerpts of Pepa's performance to be available for download.

Much of the analysis for this paper was done while I was recovering from emergency eye surgery in Brisbane, where I was wonderfully cared for by Gordon and Robina Spearritt. I can never begin to repay their abundant hospitality, generosity, and kindness. They provided an exquisite environment for recovery and my analytical focus.

Andrew Strathern and Pamela Stewart have constantly been supportive of my studies, and their works and comments continue to encourage me. I appreciate their thoughtful comments on an earlier version of this paper. My indebtedness to the translation work of Gomb Minimbi is apparent throughout this paper. Without such assistance, this paper would have taken quite a different form.

Alan Rumsey's enthusiasm for this project has been infectious from the very beginning. Although initially I envisioned my involvement to be quite minimal, Alan's questions, encouragement, and excitement totally drew me into the world of chanted tales. His continued willingness to explore, learn, challenge, and exchange materials and ideas has inspired everyone involved in the project. While many things await further research, I hope our contributions here have begun to demonstrate the great richness of these Highlands traditions. Thank you, Alan, for involving me.

References

Mackay, Ian K. 1976. *Broadcasting in Papua New Guinea.* Melbourne: Melbourne University Press.

Merlan, Francesca, and Alan Rumsey. 1991. *Ku Waru: Language and Segmentary Politics in the Western Nebilyer Valley, Papua New Guinea.* Studies in the Social and Cultural Foundations of Language, 10. Cambridge: Cambridge University Press.

Niles, Don. 2007. "Sonic Structure in *Tom Yaya Kange*: Ku Waru Sung narratives from Papua New Guinea." In *Oceanic Music Encounters—the Print Resource and the Human Resource: Essays in Honour of Mervyn McLean*, edited by Richard Moyle, 109–22. Research in Anthropology and Linguistics Monograph, 7. Auckland: University of Auckland.

Rumsey, Alan. 1995. "Pairing and Parallelism in the New Guinea Highlands." In *SALSA II: Proceedings of the Second Annual Symposium about Language and Society, Austin*, edited by Pamela Silberman and Jonathan Loftin, 108–18. Texas Linguistic Forum, 34. Austin: University of Texas.

———. 2001. "*Tom Yaya Kange:* A Metrical Narrative Genre from the New Guinea Highlands." *Journal of Linguistic Anthropology* 11 (2): 193–239.

———. 2005. "Chanted Tales in the New Guinea Highlands of Today: A Comparative Study." In *Expressive Genres and Historical Change: Indonesia, Papua New Guinea and Taiwan*, edited by Pamela J. Stewart and Andrew Strathern, 41–81. Anthropology and Cultural History in Asia and the Indo-Pacific. Hants: Ashgate Publishing.

———. 2006a. "The Articulation of Indigenous and Exogenous Orders in Highland New Guinea and Beyond." *The Australian Journal of Anthropology* 17 (1): 47–69.

———. 2006b. "Verbal Art, Politics, and Personal Style in Highland New Guinea and Beyond." In *Language, Culture and the Individual: A Tribute to Paul Friedrich*, edited by Catherine O'Neil, Mary Scoggin, and Kevin Tuite, 319–46. Munich: Lincom.

———. 2007. "Musical, Poetic and Linguistic Form in *Tom Yaya* Sung Narratives from Papua New Guinea." *Anthropological Linguistics* 49: 237–82.

Stewart, Pamela J., and Andrew Strathern. 2002. *Gender, Song, and Sensibility: Folktales and Folksongs in the Highlands of New Guinea.* Westport, CT: Praeger.

Strathern, Andrew. 1983. Review of *Oral and Traditional Literatures* by Norman Simms. *Bikmaus* 4 (2; June): 79–80.

Strathern, Andrew, and Pamela J. Stewart. 2005a. "Introduction. In *Expressive Genres and Historical Change: Indonesia, Papua New Guinea and Taiwan*, edited by Pamela J. Stewart and Andrew Strathern, 1–39. Anthropology and Cultural History in Asia and the Indo-Pacific. Hants: Ashgate Publishing.

———. 2005b. "Melpa Songs and Ballads: Junctures of Sympathy and Desire in Mount Hagen, Papua New Guinea." In *Expressive Genres and Historical Change: Indonesia, Papua New Guinea and Taiwan*, edited by Pamela J. Stewart and Andrew Strathern, 201–33. Anthropology and Cultural History in Asia and the Indo-Pacific. Hants: Ashgate Publishing.

Vicedom, Georg F. 1937. "Ein neuentdecktes Volk in Neuguinea: Völkerkundliche Beobachtungen an der Bevölkerung des Hagen-Berges im ehemals deutschen Teil von Neuguinea." *Archiv für Anthropologie* 24: 11–44, 190–213.

Vicedom, Georg F., and Herbert Tischner. 1943–48. *Die Mbowamb: Die Kultur der Hagenberg-Stämme im östlichen Zentral-Neuguinea.* 3 vols. Monographien zur Völkerkunde, 1. Vol. 1: Hamburg: Cram, de Gruyter, 1943–48; vol. 2–3: Hamburg: Friederichsen, de Gruyter, 1943.

———. 1977. *Myths and Legends from Mount Hagen.* Translated by Andrew Strathern. Boroko: Institute of Papua New Guinea Studies. [abridged translation of Vicedom and Tischner 1943–48, vol. 3]

13. Bamboo Knives, Bows, and Waterfalls: The Presentation of "Traditional Knowledge" in Melpa *Kang Rom*, Duna *Pikono*, and the Works of Hesiod and Virgil

Andrew Strathern and Pamela J. Stewart

Introduction

Poetry and prose are often conventionally contrasted. Poetry is seen as an elevated form of language, conveying feelings and insights in rhythmic forms. Prose is often seen as the vehicle for conveying "rational thought," and also as mundane, ordinary use of language. Of course, these stereotypes are quite inaccurate. There are many different genres and uses of both prose and poetry. Prose can express complex emotions and use metaphors and similes; poetry can read like a quiet conversation, imparting local information. The rigid division between prose and poetry may perhaps be peculiar to literate cultures. In oral cultures clear distinctions are made between different ways of speaking: ordinary conversation, rhetorical speeches, genres of songs or songs to accompany particular occasions, for example (Strathern and Stewart 2000, 2005a; Stewart and Strathern 2000, 2002a, 2005a). Songs, nevertheless, may convey much practical and social information, as well as expressing and evoking emotions. And in cultural contexts where songs are important and are transmitted over time, these songs may continue to convey such information beyond the historical times in which the information or knowledge was originally created. This process becomes particularly important when rapid social and cultural changes entail alterations of knowledge or a risk of such alterations.

It is not only practical knowledge that may be preserved in this way. We have previously argued for the *pikono* ballad form among the Duna of the Southern Highlands Province in Papua New Guinea that "*Pikono* ballads keep alive and creatively rework cultural themes of the Duna past" (Stewart and Strathern 2005b:86). In particular, we noted that, although initiation rituals were abandoned as a result of early colonial influence during the 1960s in the Duna area, "the themes of maturation, of romance and the favorable influence of the female spirit who presided over the *palena* [initiation houses built in the bush areas] are all retained and expressed in the *pikono*" (ibid.:94). Here we apply this insight further to the extended transmission of forms of practical knowledge—forms which themselves are also imbued with social meanings.

Recently, an anthropologist working with findings from cognitive science and commenting on Bronislaw Malinowski's work on the language usages in Trobriand magical spells (Sørensen 2007) has raised the question of "why ritual forms of language should be deployed to convey practical kinds of knowledge that could, he suggests, be conveyed with greater facility outside of such ritual contexts" (Strathern and Stewart 2007a:xii). Answering Sørensen's question briefly from his own exposition, we noted how "one Trobriand magician's spell encapsulates in itself a whole imagined narrative of agricultural activity in which both the dangers and the counteractions against these dangers are vitally delineated" (ibid.). That is, the spell is actually a vitally condensed *recipe* or "model for all the practical actions needed to succeed in the agricultural cycle" (ibid.). The spell is an imaginative projection, a representation, and a performative act, an enactment of power.

We went on, in this passage to extend the basic argument to balladic forms from the Papua New Guinea Highlands. These are not magical utterances in any direct sense, but they are composed in standard formulaic ways (as many oral epics are) and are delivered in an elevated and ritualistic style. Their style is comparable to the classic features of magical language delineated by Stanley J. Tambiah, who also drew his inspiration from Malinowski's Trobriands corpus (Tambiah 1968). These features include: redundancy (repetition), analogical predication (metaphor), and the building up of wholes from parts (metonymy). For the Papua New Guinea ballad forms we noted that in these also "representations of practical knowledge … appear in highly condensed and imagistic forms which parallel in their characteristics the features that Tambiah … identified" (Strathern and Stewart 2007a:xii). Finally, we suggested that "such presentations of knowledge undoubtedly gain a greater salience in people's consciousness because of their aesthetic appeal … This process is underpinned by the systematic use of iteration, framing, and condensation which the poetic form itself generates" (ibid.:xiii). To reinforce our point, we argued further that similar reasons underlie the "poetic forms adopted by ancient Greek and Latin authors to convey practical forms of knowledge … Hesiod's *Works and Days* and Virgil's *Georgics* would belong to this genre" (ibid.:xiii).

In the present paper we elaborate on these points with relevant examples, returning also at times to Tambiah's formulations.

Melpa ballads: Bamboo knives

Melpa ballads (*kang rom*) are long narrative expositions of the actions of heroic figures belonging to the mythical past. The use of language in them is highly rhythmic and balanced. Only a few people have the skill to perform *kang rom*, and their artistic form is highly appreciated (Strathern and Stewart 2005a).

In earlier publications (Stewart and Strathern 2002a; Strathern and Stewart 2005b) we have given textual excerpts from these balladic forms. We draw on these here in order to illustrate our present argument.

In the ballad of the youth Miti Weipa, Weipa plans to go on a journey and he kills a pig and cooks it, ready to take it with him. The ballad gives a description of his actions, as well as of the notable size of the pig he is about to sacrifice:

> *okl na klimba nitim e*
>
> *mok na purpur nitim e*

> Its belly hung down to the ground
>
> Its feet shook with its own weight.

Weipa kills the pig by striking its forehead with a special club made from *milik*, a hardwood. He singes its hair off next, as is done customarily over a charcoal fire used to heat stones for the earth oven:

> *kng ndi kökli mon e*
>
> *pona pokl raka rurum e*

> It was not like singeing its hair
>
> More like clearing a field of weeds

so abundant and tangled was the hair on the surface of the pig's skin.

Then comes a characteristically fanciful section, a motif that is recurrent from one performance to another, which also contains a vital technical message. Weipa hears a noise coming from a thicket of *nöngin* plants nearby:

> *mel rakl kum rakl a*
>
> *tekekl nggewa nggawa nilingila*
>
> *mel rakl mel nambamel e*
>
> *Temboka Mot elim nuimb e*
>
> *Melpa Wat elim nuimb e*

Two things like two fists

Banging away at each other

Mot of Temboka said he would eat

Wat of Melpa said he would eat

The image here portrays two kinds of bamboo knives, one from the Nebilyer Valley area (Temboka refers to this area and Mot is the name given to the knife) and one from the Central Hagen area (Melpa area, also used for the language of this area; Wat is the knife's name). Mot wins the struggle, and the ballad continues with a straight-out technical description of how to butcher a pig:

woint ndurum e ndoklnga ndoklnga

pendik mint e köng nitim a

ment a ndurum ndoklnga e

te mong e pokla rurum e

He cut the pig from tail to head

Laid bare the shoulder blade meat

He cut the pig from head to tail

And pierced the opening of its anus

Then follows another imaginative touch:

kng mint e nui mon e

nde katil möka murum e

It was not like meat for eating

It was like layers of pebbles on a river bank

These few passages, which are paralleled in many other parts of the ballad, indicate how technical information is ensconced inside metaphorical comparisons. The Melpa text in fact says, for example, "It was not meat for eating, It was pebbles on a bank," challenging the listener to make the leap from one image to another along with the performer. The background to this operation is that the sharpness of the bamboo knife is very important for making a clean cut. And the desire of the cutter to eat is projected onto the knife itself, which is given its own agency. The bamboo knife cuts better than steel, and gains its glory in doing so. After that it may be discarded because it is easily replaceable. Not everyone can wield it. Cutting pork is a special skill, requiring knife and human hand together to do their magic. The ballad catches this essential embodied truth, then embellishes it. In this, the balladic language follows the paths of magical language.

Duna ballads: Bows and waterfalls

Duna *pikono*, like Melpa *kang rom*, are often centred on a young male protagonist and his search for maturation in life. We have given some specimens of *pikono* text in an earlier publication (Stewart and Strathern 2005b:90–93). The text sets up a scenario in which a youth and his sister are together. It explains that the youth was quite young and small, the wig he wore was not large but small, and his face was not yet painted with the stripes of yellow earth applied when boys used to emerge from the growth-houses in bush seclusion areas and dance before spectators, including unmarried girls. He decorated himself, therefore, as an uninitiated youth, and his father bought him a bow, a mark of hunting and manhood, to carry on his journey (the Duna language materials are given in Stewart and Strathern 2005b:90):

> His father brought him something there
>
> Brought him a bow and arrows he had made for the boy and gave it to him
>
> He brought him a bow from Uru Saiya and gave it to that boy
>
> He brought him a bow from Rukupa Rarope and gave it to that boy
>
> And from Kewa Kikayea and gave it to that boy

The ballad goes on with a recitation of the names of places from which the bamboo fibres for the bowstring were gathered and given to the boy. All of the places named belong to the local landscape. Such names appear also in other sung performances, notably funeral laments sung by women. Each name contains condensed meanings as a focus of a type of resource in an environment where emplaced knowledge is significant (see Strathern and Stewart 2007b). The repetitions therefore enclose a memory bank of information, and the place names are ones that young men looking for materials to make a bow and bowstrings would find very useful. This example is also a plain list, without metaphor or metonymy, although in some ways the whole landscape is represented metonymically in its named parts; and the overall image of the bow is a metaphor or marker of the boy's journey into adulthood.

This same *pikono* sequence has a piece in which waterfalls appear:

> Down below there a waterfall was splashing
>
> Splashing on the wig of the boy

And eleven waterfall places are then enumerated, appearing mostly in pairs, sometimes with alliterative names:

> Waterfalls from the rivers Yeati and Yease
>
> Of Nali and Ukunali, waterfall noise splashing down.

Waterfalls were places where boys secluded in the growth-houses could go to cleanse their faces and eyes (compare Meggitt 1964:211–13 on Enga practices of washing the eyes in spring-water pools within seclusion areas for bachelors undergoing maturation rituals). Behind waterfalls, on ledges, special magical plants used in the sacred practices of growth (*palena*) were sometimes found. Again, the images are a metaphor for, or are indicative of, the context of initiation, an evocation of the enchantment of initiation.

Another *pikono* (Stewart and Strathern 2002a:136–37) begins with a similar set of images of waterfalls or rushing water:

> I sing of the man Yerepi Rangerakini
>
> As we sit here and I tell you the story
>
> Yerepi stayed at the place Kali
>
> Where the water rushes and makes a noise
>
> He stayed at the place Atili,
>
> Where the water rushes and makes a noise
>
> At the place Mali, where the water rushes
>
> There he stayed, he was an orphan

Here the rushing of the water might be taken as indicative of the lonely existence of the boy. In the Duna area many rivers run underground in limestone caves, rushing out from these in places. The rushing water both evokes the isolation of the places where the boy stays, and the sense of his own movements from place to place as he sets out on his journey of exploration (on which he discovers a cannibal giant, an *auwape*, who teaches him how to eat human flesh: Yerepi Rangerakini's lack of a human family of parents seems to lead him in this direction) (see Stewart and Strathern 2002b; Strathern and Stewart 2004). The names of the places here, in the mise en scène of this narrative, appear in triplicates (Kali, Atili, Mali, and later—not quoted here—Apima, Ateli, Akepi).

These examples, like the example of the bows, appear as rhythmic and repetitive lists, lending themselves to a mnemonic function. Since they represent a journey, they also function as a partial map of the landscape, assuming knowledge on the part of the listeners, but also teaching and preserving it in the *pikono* form.

In *pikono* we find very strongly the function of preserving knowledge through repetition. *Pikono* also include many archaic and poetic words not used in everyday conversation, and these too may appear in lists, of different names for kinds of plants in the environment at large.

Kang rom seem to build interest in startling metaphors of actions; *pikono* in intense metonymic representations of landscapes. Poetic traditions may specialize differently in their appropriations from the magical potentialities of language, as Tambiah's work indicates (Tambiah 1968). We compare our Melpa and Duna examples now with Hesiod and Virgil.

Hesiod: Didactic images and mythopoetic narrative

The poet Hesiod is thought to have lived during the eighth and seventh centuries BCE (Athanassakis 2004:xi). He composed his works in the same hexameter form as used in the Homeric epics. According to his own account, he was looking after his sheep near Mt. Helikon in rural Boeotia when the Muses met him and bestowed on him "the gift of song" (ibid.:xi). His brother Perses, Hesiod claimed, tried to cheat him out of his portion of their father's land. Hesiod composed his *Works and Days* (*Erga kai Hemerai*) in order to teach his brother the proper ways of both farming and morality.

Athanassakis viewed Hesiod as a poet in the great traditions of oral composition, in which "creative performance, and powerful memory help the singer compose in a style that is largely formulaic … Meter helps him fuse formulaic and non-formulaic language … Each performance is unique" (ibid.:xiv). But Athanassakis thinks that the Greek alphabet and, with it, writing practices had reached Boeotia by Hesiod's time, and so "the question of mixed composition, oral for some themes, not so oral for other themes, must claim the attention it deserves" (p. xvi). Athanassakis further points out that Hesiod mixes practical advice with cosmological expositions and flights of fancy (p. xvii).

Kang rom and *pikono* are narrative poetic forms. They encapsulate much practical and cultural information within the integuments of their narratives, as we have seen above. With Hesiod's *Works and Days* (and with Virgil's *Georgics*), we find a different combinatory pattern, although the basic combination of poetic song and factual information is at the core of all four of our cases. Unlike the two examples from Papua New Guinea, Hesiod's work is explicitly didactic, and he foregrounds himself as the speaker and narrator. In *kang rom* and *pikono*, the singer, as performer and creator, is there and is addressing the listeners from time to time, but is not foregrounded. Hesiod's own sententious voice, by contrast, is heard throughout.

> He that wrongs another man wrongs, above all, himself,
>
> and evil schemes bring more harm on those who plot them.
>
> (*Works and Days*, lines 265–66; Athanassakis 2004:71)

So, beware Perses!

On the practical side, Hesiod is full of advice, from ploughing time till harvest:

early risers harvest fields laden with grain.

Plow in the spring. Fallowed land plowed in the summer will produce.

Sow fallow land when the soil is still loose;

such land will spare you curses and the clamor of hungry children.

(*Works and Days*, lines 461–64; Athanassakis 2004:76)

This is all straightforward, unvarnished, specification. But often Hesiod gives dramatic descriptions of harsh weather, for example:

when Thracian gusts whip thick clouds to frenzy

(*Works and Days*, line 553; Athanassakis 2004:79)

Or of summer, when:

the thistle blooms and the chirping cicada

sits on trees and pours down shrill song.

(*Works and Days*, lines 582–83; Athanassakis 2004:79)

Taboos must be observed:

Let those who drink never place the serving cup

over the mixing bowl; bad luck comes with this, too.

(*Works and Days*, lines 744–45; Athanassakis 2004:83)

Finally:

The same day can be a mother now, a stepmother later.

Happy and blessed is the man who knows all this

and does his work without offending the immortals,

ever watching birds of omen, ever shunning transgression.

(*Works and Days*, lines 825–28; Athanassakis 2004:85)

Hesiod mixes mythological references, practical advice and knowledge, and moralistic warnings and admonishments, all together in his rolling hexameters. Tucked into his poem is a farmer's seasonal manual. Narrative as such is secondary to didactics. In the New Guinea ballads, didactics are secondary to narrative entertainment, although moral points are certainly made.

Virgil: The life of the bees

Virgil (Publius Vergilius Maro) was born in 70 BCE near Mantua in Italy. He was dispossessed of his family farm after the assassination of Julius Caesar in 43 BCE and the defeat of Brutus and Cassius at the battle of Philippi (Fairclough 1956:ix). Later, with the help of the Emperor Octavius, he "either recovered his farm or received in compensation an estate in Campania" (ibid.:x); hence, Virgil's interest in rural farming.

Virgil adorns his descriptions of farming practices with numerous observations of a more philosophical sort. Hesiod is didactic in the narrower sense of giving technical formulae for times to plough, sow, and reap, and also in terms of his overall linkage of hard work with proper morality. Virgil, less concerned with moralistic homily, but equally immersed in the world of mythology inherited from the Greeks, has much to say on how, for instance, to handle hives of bees. He describes the famed division of labour among the hive's inhabitants, for example the bees that act as "sentries":

Sunt quibus ad portas cecidit custodia sorti,

Inque vicam speculantur aquas et nubila caeli,

Aut onera accipiunt venientum aut agmine facto

Ignavum fucos pecus a praesepibus arcent,

Fervet opus redolentque thymo fragrantia mella

There are those to whom falls the lot of guarding the gates,

In turn they watch for rains and clouds in the sky

Or take the loads of arrivals, or in military line

Drive out from the precincts the idle crew of drones

The place bustles with work and the fragrant honeycombs smell of thyme.

(*Georgics* IV, lines 165–69; translation, Andrew Strathern)

The commitment of the bees to their communal enterprises is lauded by Virgil in the famous aphorism where he explains that individual bees do not live beyond their seventh summer, but as a result of their combined efforts:

At genus immortale manet, multosque per annos

Stat fortuna domus, et avi numerantur avorum.

Their line remains immortal, and through many a year

The fortunes of their house stand firm and genealogies grow long.

(*Georgics* IV, lines 208–9; translation, Andrew Strathern)

Finally, Virgil appends a further cosmological statement, to effect that the bees have in them an element of the divine:

> deum namque ire per omnia,
>
> terrasque tractusque maris caelumque profundum;
>
> Hinc pecudes, armenta, viros, genus omne ferarum
>
> Quemque sibi tenuis nascentem arcessere vitas

> for divinity is said to go through all things
>
> Lands and the expanses of the sea and the deep sky
>
> From it the flocks and herds and the wild beasts and men themselves
>
> Draw the source of their slender life-breath.

> (*Georgics* IV, lines 221–24; translation, Andrew Strathern)

And in the end, through this divine power, all things return to their place among the stars, Virgil proclaims (ibid., lines 225–27).

Like the ballad singers of Papua New Guinea, Virgil uses his poetic skills to blend together much practical information with flights of narrative fancy; and, as we have seen, he weaves elements of a cosmology into this.

Conclusion: Magical language

The language of these master singers is certainly "magical," in the sense that it has the power to evoke scenes and draw from these both narrative pathos and a wider sensibility about life in general. Stanley J. Tambiah, in his examination of magical language in the more specific sense of spells used for instrumental purposes, formulated things very well:

> It is clear that the spells and myths contain information, which is not the remains of archaic beliefs, but a living knowledge related to technological and social activities. (Tambiah 1968:193)

And, on magical language:

> It ingeniously conjoins the expressive and metaphorical properties of language with the operational and empirical properties of technical activity. (Tambiah 1968:202)

What Tambiah wrote here about magical language, in the more specific sense, applies equally to the poetic language of the artistic creators or creations that we have discussed here. And to this we have added that, just as the words of

Hesiod and Virgil encode worlds that are lost to us in the contemporary world, so the balladic records of the Western and Southern Highlands encapsulate a dynamic series of life patterns which, if the genre survives, will similarly turn into heritage over time. And with the sense of heritage will come the technical and practical knowledge that composes it.[1]

Peter Fallon, an Irish writer, has made a creative and vigorous translation of the *Georgics*, and he comments on the question of "local knowledge":

> The more closely I read the poem, the more I grew amazed at all that Virgil … knew. (Fallon 2004:125)

Virgil and his companions studied emplaced knowledge:

> How attentive and responsive they were to their environment. The sureness of their knowledge was the fruit of observation … still, beside their faiths, they preserved room for mystery. (Fallon 2004:125)

What Fallon wrote here of Virgil applies well to the singers of the *kang rom* and *pikono*.[2]

Acknowledgements

We would like to thank Liz and Ralph Sheppard for their stimulating conversations over the years and especially while we were staying with them in County Donegal, Ireland, in 2007 during the "wet" phase of June while we were writing sections of this essay. We thank them also for their concern for the environment and their healthy "humanistic" perspectives. We would like especially to thank all our interlocutors, helpers, and assistants in Papua New Guinea, who have been part of our research projects and programmes over many years and have worked with us on balladic materials in the Melpa and Duna areas.

---

1   Our interest and work on "heritage" issues extends across our regional interests, see, for example Strathern and Stewart 1998, 2005c. We were also the co-organizers of an international conference entitled "Landscape, Heritage, and Conservation" held in March of 2008 at the University of Pittsburgh under the auspices of the European Union Center of Excellence in the University Center of International Studies. The publication from this conference is entitled *Landscape, Heritage, and Conservation: Farming Issues in the European Union* (Stewart and Strathern 2010). Also, in general, *wuö amb rakl noman tenda pilik mangkona pek nggi ningk morombil e kin, e ukl kai we na ama rondokl ti orandorombil.*

2   The same must be said for the untold numbers of singers and creators of epics and ballads in largely oral contexts across the world. One stream of tradition, composition, and skilful oral performance that we have recently begun to study is found in the Korean genre of *p'ansori* sung epics, which may have partly been rooted in shamanic ritual performances, but developed as an art of entertainment, exemplifying the same magical potentialities of language that we identify in *kang rom* and *pikono* (see Park 2000; Pihl 1994; Walrave 1994). We participated in a performance of *p'ansori* in Taitung, Taiwan, in 2003 and another in Seoul, South Korea, in May 2005, observing and recording the events. A fuller account of this research is forthcoming.

We also thank Prof. Huang Shu-min, director of the Institute of Ethnology, Academia Sinica, Taipei, Taiwan, for his assistance and support of our research during our stay as visiting research fellows from 21 December 2006 through 8 March 2007. Parts of this essay were worked on while conducting research in Taiwan during 2007. We also thank our colleagues at the Institute of Ethnology and those at the Dong-hua University in Hualien for their intellectual engagements with us during this period of time and in earlier years.

References

Athanassakis, Apostolos N., trans. 2004. *Hesiod: Theogony, Works and Days, Shield*. Baltimore and London: John Hopkins University Press.

Fairclough, H. Rushton, trans. 1956. *Virgil: Eclogues, Georgics, Aeneid I–VI*. Loeb Classical Library. London: William Heinemann Ltd. (Orig. pub. 1916)

Fallon, Peter. 2004. *The Georgics of Virgil*. Translated by Peter Fallon. Loughcrew, Ireland: Gallery Press.

Meggitt, Mervyn J. 1964. "Male–female Relationships in the Highlands of Australian New Guinea." *American Anthropologist*, n.s., 66 (4), pt. 2: 204–24.

Park, Chan. 2000. "'Authentic Audience' in P'ansori, a Korean Story-telling Tradition." *Journal of American Folklore* 113 (449): 270–86.

Pihl, Marshall R. 1994. *The Korean Singer of Tales*. Cambridge, MA: Council of East Asian Studies, Harvard University.

Sørensen, Jesper. 2007. "Malinowski and Magical Ritual." In *Religion, Anthropology, and Cognitive Science*, edited by Harvey Whitehouse and James Laidlaw, 81–104. Ritual Studies Monograph Series. Durham, NC: Carolina Academic Press.

Stewart, Pamela J., and Andrew Strathern. 2000. *Speaking for Life and Death: Warfare and Compensation among the Duna of Papua New Guinea*. Senri Ethnological Reports, 13. Osaka: National Museum of Ethnology.

———. 2002a. *Gender, Song and Sensibility: Folksongs and Folktales in the Highlands of New Guinea*. Westport, CT: Praeger.

———. 2002b. *Remaking the World: Myth, Mining and Ritual Change among the Duna of Papua New Guinea*. Smithsonian Series in Ethnographic Inquiry. Washington, DC: Smithsonian Institution Press.

———, eds. 2005a. *Expressive Genres and Historical Change: Indonesia, Papua New Guinea and Taiwan*. Anthropology and Cultural History in Asia and the Indo-Pacific Series. Hants: Ashgate.

———. 2005b. "Duna *Pikono*: A Popular Contemporary Genre in the Papua New Guinea Highlands." In *Expressive Genres and Historical Change: Indonesia, Papua New Guinea and Taiwan*, edited by Pamela J. Stewart and Andrew Strathern, 83–107. Anthropology and Cultural History in Asia and the Indo-Pacific Series. Hants: Ashgate.

———, eds. 2010. *Landscape, Heritage, and Conservation: Farming Issues in the European Union*. European Anthropology Series. Durham, NC: Carolina Academic Press.

Strathern, Andrew, and Pamela J. Stewart, eds. 1998. *Kuk Heritage: Issues and Debates in Papua New Guinea*. Department of Anthropology, University of Pittsburgh.

———. 2000. *Arrow Talk: Transaction, Transition, and Contradiction in New Guinea Highlands History*. Kent, OH, and London: Kent State University Press.

———. 2004. *Empowering the Past, Confronting the Future: The Duna People of Papua New Guinea*. Contemporary Anthropology of Religion Series. New York: Palgrave Macmillan.

———. 2005a. "Introduction." In *Expressive Genres and Historical Change: Indonesia, Papua New Guinea and Taiwan*, edited by Pamela J. Stewart and Andrew Strathern, 1–39. Anthropology and Cultural History in Asia and the Indo-Pacific. Hants: Ashgate Publishing.

———. 2005b. "Melpa Songs and Ballads: Junctures of Sympathy and Desire in Mount Hagen, Papua New Guinea." In *Expressive Genres and Historical Change: Indonesia, Papua New Guinea and Taiwan*, edited by Pamela J. Stewart and Andrew Strathern, 201–33. Anthropology and Cultural History in Asia and the Indo-Pacific. Hants: Ashgate Publishing.

———. 2005c. "'The Ulster-Scots': A Cross-border and Transnational Concept and Its Ritual Performance." *Journal of Ritual Studies* 19 (2): 1–16.

———. 2007a. "Ritual Studies and Cognitive Science: Anthropology's Shifting Boundaries." Preface in *Religion, Anthropology, and Cognitive Science*, edited by Harvey Whitehouse and James Laidlaw, ix–xxi. Ritual Studies Monograph Series. Durham, NC: Carolina Academic Press.

———. 2007b. "Songs, Places, and Pathways of Change: Themes from the Highlands of Papua New Guinea." In "Anthropo-aesthetic Domains: Song, Dance, and Landscape," special issue, *Taiwan Dance Research Journal* 3: 1–26.

Tambiah, Stanley J. 1968. "The Magical Power of Words." *Man*, n.s., 3 (2): 175–208.

Walrave, Boudewijn. 1994. *Songs of the Shaman: The Ritual Chants of the Korean Mudang*. London and New York: Kegan Paul International.

Index

cosmopolitanism, of New Guinea
Highlanders, 4
courting songs, 49
Huli (*dàwanda ū*), 113
Ku Waru, 298
Melpa (*amb kenan*), 278
courtship, 10, 60, 224
as theme in Hagen tales, 280
as theme in Ku Waru sung tales, 260–70
in Hagen region, 280–81
in Ku Waru region, 249
Crittenden, Robert, 212, 213
crops, grown by Ipili people, 168
CulturaSenzaFrontiere, ix, 299

D
David, Jeny, 151
de Vries, Lourens, 56
deception, in Angal sung tales, 231
Denham, T. P., 2
descent, in melodic contour of Duna sung
tales, 51–58, 60–61, 67
Diabe, 111
dialect continuum, Hagen languages as, 247
didactics, in Hesiod vs. New Guinea sung
tales, 310
disguise, in Angal sung tales, 231
distinctive features of Highlands sung tales, 5
distribution, of sung-tales genres and
languages, 22
dogs, as human-like characters in Ku Waru
sung tales, 267
Dong-hua University, 314
Draper, Norm, 29
Draper, Sheila, 29
drumming, among the Huli, 114
Dugaba (language/people), 75
Duna (language/people), 4, 5, 11, 13, 26, 49,
75, 76, 166, 214, 218, 221, 224, 225, 267,
269, 303, 307, 308. *See also* Yuna
Duna courting genre (*laingwa*), 60
Duna courting genre (*yekia*), 60
Duna lament (*khene ipakana*), 54

Duna praise name. *See* praise names, Duna
(*kẽiyaka*)
Duna stories (*hapia po*), 40, 41, 221
Duna sung tales (*pikono*), 6, 7, 11, 12, 13, 16,
21, 24, 26, 27, 39–46, 49–63, 65–73,
267, 303, 307–9
as performed by women, 49
Duna-Pogaia (language group), 23, 24, 25

E
East Kewa narrative (*lidi*), 25
East Kewa narrative (*lindi*), 25
East Kutubu (language group), 24
East Sepik Province, 13
East Strickland (language group), 24
Eastern Highlands Province, 17
el ik. See Melpa oratory (*el ik*)
el ung. See Ku Waru oratory (*el ung*)
Enga (language/people), 2, 5, 7, 10, 13, 23,
167, 213, 214, 224
Enga genre (*sangai titi pingi nemongo*), 18
Enga narative genre (*atome pii*), 7, 29, 152
Enga oral traditions, 27
Enga Province, 10, 22, 25, 151
Enga sung tales (*tindi pii*), 6, 7, 8, 12, 15, 16,
24, 25, 27, 29, 151–63
Enga sung tales (*tundu*), 24, 27
Engal Kep, 262
Engan languages, 15, 23, 24, 25, 26, 166
entertainment, as aim of sung-tale
performance, 5
entertainment value of sung tales, among the
Angal, 240
epics, 20, 21, 22
Homeric, 3
Erave (language/people), 7, 24
Erave narrative genre (*lidi*), 7
Erave narrative genre (*ora piei*), 7
Erave narrative genre (*ramani*), 7, 29
Errington, Fred, ix
Ethnologue, 208
European Union Center of Excellence, 313
evidentiality, 57

in Huli sung tale, 103

Landtman, Gunnar, 13, 17

Lang, Adrianne, 25

language varieties used in sung tales, 6

languages, 4

    of sung-tale region, 2

Lawi, Kindi, 276

Layapo (Enga Province), 18, 27, 151, 153

le yiya. See Hewa sung tales (*le yiya*)

Leben, William R., 69

Lederman, Rena, 210, 211, 212, 215, 230, 241

Lembena (language/people), 26

Lembena sung tales (*tendi pii*), 14, 24, 25, 26, 29

length, of sung tales, 26

Lepi, Pundia, 28, 267

LeRoy, John, ix, 25, 267

Lewis, Neryl, 2

lidi. See East Kewa narrative (*lidi*), Erave narrative genre (*lidi*)

lindi. See East Kewa narrative (*lindi*)

lines, 12, 13, 155

    in Karinj sung tales, 231

    in Ipili sung tales, 199

    in Ku Waru sung tales, 252

local content, in early Papua New Guinea radio programming, 277

Lockwood, Anna, ix, 16, 29

Loewecke, Eunice, 19

Lomas, Gabe C. J., 2, 8, 10, 27, 60, 75, 76, 80, 83, 84, 85, 86, 102, 103, 104, 111, 115, 170

Love, J. W., 20

Lower Nembi, 209

Lowth, Robert, 170

Lungu, Maku, 151

Lutheran Church Missouri Synod, 206

M

MacDonald, Mary, ix

Mackay, Ian K., 277

Madang (language group), 24

Mae (Enga Province), 151

Mae-Ambumu (Enga Province), 153

Mae-Tarua (Enga Province), 153

Magaja, Maga, 102, 103, 104

magical language, 312

Malamuni. *See* Maramuni

male puberty rites

    Enga, 220

    Ipili, 220

Malinowski, Bronislaw, 304

Manambu (language/people), 13

mano ho-ra. See Fasu narrative genre (*mano ho-ra*)

Maramuni (Enga Province), 15

marriage, in the Ku Waru region, 249

Maso, Philip, 151

Mawe, Theodore, ix, 209, 212, 217, 219

May, Jean, 19

Mbakali Raka, 46

Mbara (Southern Highlands Province), 49

McGuinness, Dominic, 103

Meam (language/people), 247

Meam sung tale (*kang tom*), 24

medial verbs forms, Ipili, 179–83

Meggitt, Mervyn, 152, 223

Mel, Anna, ix

Mel, Michael, ix, 28

melodic

    cell, 113

    contour, 50, 60

    form, 26

    presentation of sung tales, 6

    variation, in Hagen sung-tale performances, 297

melodies, 20, 26, 42

    descending, 67

    in Bogaya sung tales, 16

    in Enga sung tales, 15

    in Hagen sung tales, 291–95

    in Hewa sung tales, 16

    in Huli sung tales, 116

    in Ipili sung tales, 15, 201–4

    in Karinj sung tales, 16, 231, 232

    in Ku Waru sung tales, 253–54